THE GENTLEMAN AND THE TIGER

THE GENTLEMAN

AND

THE TIGER

The Autobiography of George B. McClellan, Jr.

Edited from the original manuscript in the
possession of The New-York Historical Society by

HAROLD C. SYRETT

Philadelphia and New York
J. B. LIPPINCOTT COMPANY

CONTENTS

ILLUSTRATIONS

Photographs following page 192

Introduction

I

George B. McClellan, Jr., is known today, if he is known at all, as the son of a famous father and as a politician. His relative obscurity, however, is more a reflection of our lack of interest in the past than an indication of the paucity of his accomplishments. He had not one, but many careers, for in addition to being a leading member of Tammany Hall, a congressman from New York, and mayor of the nation's largest city, he was a newspaper reporter, lawyer, student of art and history, professor of economics, lieutenant colonel in the United States Army, and author of four books. But while his interests were diverse, his opinions and prejudices remained remarkably consistent throughout his life. Born a nineteenth-century aristocrat, he retained until his death in the fifth decade of the twentieth century the views and values of a class and era that had all but vanished with his youth.

In most countries with an hereditary aristocracy, members of the upper classes have been assured of a role in public life as well as in society. Hereditary aristocrats were taught at an early age that they were both uniquely obligated and eminently qualified to assume responsibility for the management of the affairs of their fellow citizens. Knowing from childhood that they were destined for a career in the government, church, army or navy, they seldom doubted their ability to perform the tasks assigned them. If they possessed no other qualifications for office, they were endowed with ample self-assurance. They were, in substance, in a situation in which it was relatively easy for them to become natural as well as hereditary aristocrats.

Lacking an hereditary aristocracy, McClellan's America also

lacked some of its traditions. Nevertheless, there was an American aristocracy, and if its members did not always possess the self-assurance of their European counterparts, they were confident that as a class they were innately superior to those in the lower orders. When McClellan was born in 1865, the nation's industrial capitalists had not yet attained positions of power or influence in American society and government, for the economic basis of the American aristocracy was still either landed or mercantile wealth. Enormous fortunes, however, had not yet become the prerequisite for entrée into the aristocracy, and a recently acquired fortune still constituted an obstacle that could only be removed by the passage of time. If a great amount of money was not always necessary, enough money to "live comfortably" was essential. But there were other—and, perhaps, more important—hallmarks of the American aristocrat. He had something that he and his fellow aristocrats called "good breeding" and "taste"; very often some of his immediate ancestors had had outstanding careers in the public service or professions; he had gone to one of the "good" colleges, and it was likely that after graduation he had made "the grand tour"; and if he lived in a city, he belonged to the "best clubs" and spent his summers in one of the few socially acceptable resorts. In deference, no doubt, to the demands of American democracy, he was not called an aristocrat. He was a gentleman.

McClellan's career and personality can only be understood in the light of his conviction that he was a member of the American aristocracy. Nor was this conviction unfounded. In his youth he absorbed the values and prejudices of his class not only from his family and friends, but also from nurses, tutors, and boarding-school masters. Four years at Princeton with young gentlemen from the South and Northeast were followed by two years on a grand tour of Europe. When he returned to New York in 1888 to become a newspaper reporter, he was a finished product. He still had much to learn, but his standards were fixed, and for the remainder of his life he used them to judge—and usually to find wanting—a world that bore little resemblance to that in which he had spent his formative years.

Unlike European aristocrats, McClellan had to make his way in a democratic society in which membership in the upper classes was often a handicap rather than a prerequisite for a career as a public servant. Henry Adams faced the same problem, for while fully aware of his class' tradition of service, he also knew that the world was no longer the one for which he had been trained. He was too much of an aristocrat to abandon his past for the sake of his future; but he was never happy in his choice, and he lived out his days with a sense of alienation that was only partially concealed by a pose of cynical aloofness. If the role of the aristocrat in America presented a problem that Adams could not solve, there were other American aristocrats who never recognized the problem's existence. Neither Theodore Roosevelt nor Franklin Roosevelt, for example, ever permitted the considerations that restrained Adams to prevent them from seeking and accepting positions in government. If on occasion they were forced to compromise with an unpleasant reality (which might be named Platt or Hague), this took second place to their ambition and their conviction that they were living up to the obligation of the "better classes" to go into public life. Lacking the contemplative mind of Henry Adams, they apparently found it comparatively easy to convince themselves that in seeking to raise the standards of American politics they were not lowering their own.

McClellan fell somewhere in between the positions occupied by Adams and the two Roosevelts. He could be as cynical about public life as Adams, but his cynicism did not lead to withdrawal. He could be as politically ambitious as either Roosevelt, but he did not necessarily believe that he had a mission to improve the lot or morals of his fellow man. Throughout most of his political career he was a member of the most notorious city machine in the nation's history. He was not ashamed of this fact. Nor did he think it incongruous that at the same time he moved in the upper reaches of American and European society and was on intimate terms with leading artists and scholars on both sides of the Atlantic. Although he knew that Tammany Hall was corrupt, he also knew that it could not corrupt him. Smaller men, less exalted men might suffer from evil company, but a gentleman remained a gentleman regardless of his associates. McClellan did not wish to change Tammany Hall, and it never entered his thoughts that Tammany Hall could change him. He was, in the words of a contemporary, "one New York gentleman to the manner born, who has eaten of the tree of knowledge of Tammany Hall and has had no stomach ache." [1]

If an aristocrat could join Tammany Hall and remain—at least in his own mind—unsullied, he also possessed enough self-assurance to defy the majority by taking an unpopular stand at a time of heated passions. From 1914 to 1917, McClellan was one of the few men of some prominence in the United States who refused to support the Allies rather than the Central Powers. Because he repeatedly publicized his views, many of his contemporaries considered him at best a pacifist and at worst pro-German.[2] He insisted, however, that he was neither, for on the one hand he advocated preparedness and upholding "the national honor and the national interests," [3] while on the other he asserted: "I am . . . a neutral who believes in *real* neutrality. I favor with all my heart the preservation of our time honored friendships with all the nations of the earth, not the least of whom is the German Empire." [4] But he did not stop there, for during the period of American neutrality he visited Germany when other prominent Americans were visiting England,[5] met and talked with an Irish patriot in Munich who was trying to raise troops to fight Great Britain, sought to devise ways to increase trade between the United States and the Central Powers, and chaired committees for aiding the war widows and orphans of, not Belgium, but Germany. McClellan may or may not have been pro-German, but the label is relatively unimportant, for the essential point remains. His opinions were not those of most of his class, but his willingness to state them regardless of public opinion made him an exemplar of the aristocratic tradition at its best.

McClellan made no attempt to conceal his views on the First World War, for during his trip to Europe in 1915 he recorded his impressions of the belligerent nations in a series of articles

[1] New York *Evening Telegram*, May 29, 1900.

[2] McClellan to New York *Evening Post*, May 23, 1916, George B. McClellan, Jr. MSS, Library of Congress. Subsequently cited as McClellan MSS.

[3] McClellan to Woodrow Wilson, March 2, 1917, *ibid.*

[4] McClellan to T. St. John Gaffney, July 18, 1916, *ibid.*

[5] Following McClellan's visit to Berlin, James W. Gerard, the United States ambassador to Germany, wrote him: ". . . We shall be very glad to see you in Berlin again. You made a great hit with all the high cards. . . ." James W. Gerard to McClellan, June 20, 1916, *ibid.*

that first appeared in the Sunday magazine section of the New York *Times* and were then published in book form under the title of *The Heel of War*.[6] Throughout this book McClellan managed to say almost everything that his fellow Americans did not want to hear. He asserted that life in Belgium under the Germans was "not abnormal in any way," that the "accounts of serious damage to the city [of Louvain were] greatly exaggerated," that conditions in Germany were "practically normal," and that in France "there was no real hatred for Germany except among [the] American colony and a small section of unrepresentative French."[7] On the other hand, he insisted that he had only the greatest admiration for the people of the various countries that he visited. When McClellan's articles first appeared in the *Times,* he was considered "sufficiently favorable to the Germans to call forth a good many criticisms from the pro-Allies,"[8] and this opinion was repeatedly stated following the publication of the book. One critic thought *The Heel of War* "an astonishing book, callous and in exceedingly bad taste,"[9] while another wrote that its "only effect can be to supply fresh material to the discredited German propaganda."[10] In general, those who reviewed *The Heel of War* revealed a great deal about their own opinions and very little about McClellan's reliability as a reporter. It is, moreover, significant that one of the few individuals to praise *The Heel of War* was a fellow aristocrat who shared McClellan's views on the war and his conception of the aristocracy's duty. Soon after the book's appearance in 1916, Brooks Adams wrote to McClellan:

> Last night I read your book. I read it with very great interest and profit. It seems to me to be written in a fair and impartial spirit, and especially your chapters on Germany are excellent. . . . Also and chiefly I respect your courage because you have done a thing which, here, just now, is unpopular and which must have subjected you to rather unpleasant remarks.[11]

[6] George B. McClellan, *The Heel of War* (New York, 1916).
[7] *Ibid.*, v-vi.
[8] New York *Times,* February 6, 1916.
[9] *Bookman,* 43 (March 16, 1916), 4.
[10] Springfield *Republican,* March 16, 1916. For somewhat more favorable estimates, see *Review of Reviews,* 53 (March 16, 1916), 380 and *Literary Digest,* 52 (March 6, 1916), 1288. Most reviews, however, were harshly critical.
[11] Brooks Adams to McClellan, February 21, 1916, McClellan MSS.

It was characteristic of McClellan that, when war came to the United States, he was (despite the fact that he was fifty-one years old) among the first to volunteer for military service. In taking this step he was not only acting as many other Americans did and as his father before him had done, but he was also living up to an unwritten code that placed members of the upper classes under a special obligation to defend a country in which they were the natural aristocracy. McClellan's opinions both before and after the United States declaration of war were, of course, shared by others from all classes. It was not, however, his opinions that are significant, but rather his conviction that a man of his background was uniquely obliged to act on his principles.

If McClellan was a gentleman, he was also the son of one of the most controversial military and political figures in nineteenth-century America. His father had been dismissed as head of the Union Army in the midst of the Civil War, and in 1864 he had lost the presidency while attracting the support of some of the most disloyal elements in the North. Both events occurred before the son had been born, but both colored his own as well as his father's thinking. McClellan was brought up in a household in which no one was ever permitted to forget that he was in the presence of a great man who had been cruelly wronged by a government and people that lacked both gratitude and perception. There was, moreover, a genuine bond of affection between father and son. Under the circumstances, it was not surprising that McClellan made his father's grievances his own. If he ever doubted the wisdom of this attitude —and he never did—he was repeatedly re-enforced in his opinions throughout much of his later life by those who had supported his father in war and politics. The fact that he was Little Mac's son affected his own outlook on life in at least two ways. In the first place, as the son of a famous man, he had exalted standards of attainment to which he aspired in public life. Secondly, as the son of a good man wronged, he developed a protective coat of cynicism to defend himself against misfortunes similar to those that had befallen his father.

Although McClellan did not follow his father into the regular army, he always hoped that he could succeed in politics where his father had failed. William Prendergast, a prominent New

TAKING MEASUREMENTS.

—*The Brooklyn Eagle, February 27, 1904*

York Republican and associate of McClellan, has recalled that he "was very ambitious politically," and "years before his election to the mayoralty . . . his ambition in life was to be elected President and thus vindicate the memory of his father." [12] And for a time it looked as though he might realize his ambition. Following a minor political job on the board administering the Brooklyn Bridge and two years as president of the Board of Aldermen, he served for five successive terms in the House of Representatives. In 1903, when only thirty-eight, he was elected mayor of New York City, and in 1905 he was re-elected to a four-year term. Making few mistakes and many friends during his rapid rise to power, he seemed assured of a secure future in politics. In the spring of 1900, while still a member of Congress, he was mentioned as a possible vice-presidential candidate by several papers in New York and other cities.[13] Four years later he had some supporters for the Democratic presidential nomination.[14] But following his re-election as mayor in 1905, he broke with Tammany and was never nominated for another office. The abruptness with which such a promising political career had ended would probably have made any man something of a cynic, but in McClellan's case it merely served to re-enforce an attitude that he had always found congenial.

Long before he became mayor, he had grown accustomed to concealing his ambition behind a façade of world-weariness that conveyed the impression that he thought life amusing but futile. At least superficially his cynicism was like that of Henry Adams, but there was a fundamental difference between the two men. Adams, one of the most profound thinkers of his age, revealed his cynicism through his distrust of accepted institutions. McClellan personalized his skepticism. He was suspicious of men who had been able to fulfill their ambitions rather than of the type of society which had made this ful-

12 William Prendergast, "Reminiscences" (Columbia University Oral History Project), II, 207.

13 New York *Journal*, April 27, 1900; New York *Herald*, May 19, 1900; New York *Sun,* May 19, 1900; New York *World,* June 25, 1900; Brooklyn *Eagle,* May 8, 1900; St. Louis *Republic,* May 19, 1900; Washington *Star,* May 22, 1900; Washington *Times,* June 26, 1900.

14 See New York *Tribune,* May 25, 1904, and New York *Daily News,* June 28, 1904.

fillment possible. If any man attained a prominent position in public life, McClellan was able to point out all the reasons why his prominence was undeserved. The foibles of the great were his constant delight. He liked gossip, and the fact that he knew so much of it about so many well-known people undoubtedly helped him ease the pain of his own thwarted ambition.

It is, of course, impossible to attribute McClellan's cynicism to any single set of factors in his life or personality. On the other hand, it is probably correct to assume that his father's unfortunate experiences in public life and his own inability to continue a political career contributed to his jaundiced views of those who had succeeded where he and his father had failed. It is, moreover, significant that his father was the only prominent man whom he took at face value. All others were blemished by some quirk or deficiency in character that made them something less than adequate for the positions they held. The conclusion seemed obvious. The finest man he had ever known had failed in public life, while others had succeeded. The rewards, it appeared, went to the undeserving. But if this were the case, it provided all the more reason for ridiculing—if not condemning—those who had received the rewards. Brought up on the belief that the deserving failed, he had little respect for those who had succeeded and considerable consolation for what he considered his own failure.

If his father's experience helped to make McClellan a cynic, his father's name gave him a head start in life that was denied those who had displayed less wisdom in selecting a parent. While some despised and others revered the name of George B. McClellan, all knew it. Moreover, as the passions engendered in the North during the Civil War receded into history, much of the former animosity to Little Mac disappeared; but his supporters remained, and on numerous occasions they indicated their willingness to transfer the loyalty they had once given the father to the son who bore the same name.[15] At the start of McClellan's career, "the channels of the army, of government preferment, of commerce and art were wide open to the son

15 The following letter from an Alabama storekeeper was typical of many McClellan received throughout his political career. "I . . . always have been a great admirer of your father. . . . Being the son of such a man I know you are o.k. [I am] hoping to vote for you for President of the U. S." George Morris to McClellan, December 2, 1904, Mayors' Papers, New York City Municipal Archives.

of the hero of Antietam." [16] He chose "government preferment," but he never would have been given the choice if some
of his father's prestige had not rubbed off on him.

McClellan also owed his party affiliation to his father. Much
in his background might have inclined him in different circumstances to join the Republican party. But the circumstances
were not different. His father's triumphs and disappointments
were inextricably intertwined with those of the Democracy,
and for McClellan to embrace his father's political creed
seemed to him not only natural but inevitable. He did not
decide to become a Democrat; he was a Democrat. He had
strong convictions on the subject, but they were convictions
arising from environment rather than from principle. The
Democrats on occasion might be wrong, but to be a Democrat
was right. Some people love their mothers because their
mothers are lovable people; others love their mothers because
any other attitude is inconceivable. To McClellan being a
Republican was inconceivable.

No man, of course, can be explained solely by the environment of his formative years, for every individual is born with
physical, mental, and emotional traits that set him off from all
other individuals. Although this generalization applies to
McClellan as well as to every other individual, it does not
obviate the fact that his early training had a decisive effect
on his attitudes as an adult. His upper-class background and
his father's influence may not fully explain the man, but neither
can they be ignored by those wishing to understand his career
and personality.

II

When McClellan entered politics, the Democratic party's
voting strength was divided between Southern agrarians and
members of Northern city machines. Although these two
groups provided the shock troops for Democratic campaigns,
the party's leadership was usually in the hands of a relatively
small clique of Northeastern lawyer-businessmen who were

[16] New York *Evening Telegram*, May 29, 1900.

closely associated with the nation's mercantile interests. The Southern Democrats dominated the party in Congress and the Northern bosses ruled as feudal overlords in their respective duchies, but in campaign years the presidential candidates more often than not were Northeastern lawyer-businessmen. With the exception of the three Bryan campaigns, the Democrats selected standard-bearers who gave the impression that they considered James Buchanan, and not Andrew Jackson, their party's patron saint. Samuel Tilden, Grover Cleveland, and Alton V. Parker were all conservatives who came from the Northeast, were more at home in the world of merchants and financiers than of industrialists, and had little comprehension of the economic forces that were transforming America in the years between the Civil War and the First World War. They believed in low tariffs and hard money, but these were inherited prejudices rather than integral parts of a thought-out social philosophy. Like the Republican conservatives of the same period, they neither understood nor approved of the demands of the nation's farmers and workers. To them government was more or less a necessary evil, and they asked little more than that it be honest and passive. Behind the political spokesmen of the Northeastern elite were powerful financial interests whose principal representatives were August Belmont and Thomas Fortune Ryan. It was to this small, but distinguished, wing of the Democratic party that McClellan belonged.

Like other gentlemen Democrats from the Northeast, McClellan was a conservative. He considered Bryan a dangerous radical, and in 1896 he informed the leaders of Tammany that he would rather withdraw from the congressional campaign than run on a ticket endorsing the Commoner and free silver.[17] His disagreement with Bryan was basic, for he could not conceive of government as an instrument for social change and reform. He thought that "that community is best governed which is least governed" and that "good government" ended, rather than began, with "honesty, economy and efficiency." [18] Reform, then, was an individual responsibility that should under no circumstances be confused with the state's responsibility to

---

[17] McClellan to Richard Croker, September 8, 1896; McClellan to Charles F. Murphy, October 5, 1896, McClellan MSS.
[18] New York *Tribune,* October 6, 1905.

maintain law and order.[19] Because McClellan believed that in the last analysis natural laws governed men, he considered it both futile and dangerous to attempt to reform mankind by statute. In 1908, he developed this idea in a speech in which he said:

> In these days of stupendous national wealth and development, of economic change so rapid as to be bewildering, men discover new diseases in the body politic for the sake of applying ready-made remedies. Every momentary evil, every passing cloud, is viewed by a large part of our people through a microscope and exaggerated into an impending national calamity. The remedy which is always suggested, and unfortunately always at hand, is legislation. Many of us have hypnotized ourselves into the belief that Congress can accomplish anything, provided it legislates early enough and often enough.
>
> This passion for trying to cure all the political, economic, social, moral and physical ills of humanity by legislation would be as absurd as it is futile, were it not that it gives direct encouragement to the forces of lawlessness and disorder.
>
> If a majority of the American people ever is convinced that the millennium can be achieved by legislation, anarchy, under its favorite alias of socialism, will seize its opportunity.
>
> The hope of the nation is in the innate spirit of conservatism which is bred in the bone of the American people. . . .[20]

Unlike most other gentlemen Democrats in the Northeast, McClellan was a member of Tammany Hall. While Tilden and Cleveland were able to make political capital out of attacking Tammany, McClellan became both a sachem and one of the machine's most prominent public figures. He undoubtedly belonged to the organization because he saw it as one way to fulfill his ambition, but he also believed that it behooved citizens of the "better type" to assume some responsibility for Tammany rather than to let it go by default to the "lower classes." The *World* probably came as close to the truth as possible when it wrote: "He had doubtless the scholar's distrust of the political shrewdness of the ignorant. He believes the organization and boss inevitable." [21] Regardless of his motives

---

19 Copy of speech delivered at Syracuse State Fair, September 14, 1909, McClellan Notebooks, New-York Historical Society.

20 New York *Tribune,* December 3, 1908.

21 New York *World,* September 20, 1905.

for joining Tammany, he did not underestimate his indebtedness to either it or its rulers. In 1896, in discussing his nomination for Congress, he wrote to Richard Croker, the boss of Tammany Hall: "I know that I owe this to you, as I owe everything else that I have in politics. I thank you for it with all my heart." [22] At the time that McClellan wrote this letter, Croker was in Europe and New York City Democrats were split over Bryan's candidacy and the silver issue. McClellan, urging the boss to stay in Europe so as not to become involved —and thus discredited—by the party's squabbles, concluded: "Much as Tammany needs you now, much as I need you in my canvass, believe me, I am not exaggerating when I say that I would rather make my fight without your help than imperil not only your influence, but the future of the organization that you and I both love so well. . . ." [23]

McClellan had reason to be grateful to Tammany, for every public office that he held was bestowed on him by the organization. It is true that he was elected by the voters, but it is also true that he was nominated by Tammany. This arrangement had certain disadvantages for McClellan, for, as he was to learn to his distress, Tammany could break as well as make politicians. In addition, affiliation with such a notoriously corrupt organization may at times have placed him in a somewhat embarrassing position. On one occasion, the *Commercial Advertiser* thought his role as a politician and gentleman unusual enough to use headlines to proclaim that he was a "Union Clubman and Tammany Official," [24] and the *Times,* following his election to Congress in 1894, reported the following, perhaps apocryphal, story:

A very prominent literary gentleman, well known in the city, and for that matter in the whole country, who had been in Congress himself, met Colonel McClellan soon after he was elected. "How are you, McClellan? By the way, have you seen Cochran lately?" McClellan had not seen Mr. Cochran, and told his friend that he had sailed for Europe the day before. "Um— ah! Too bad; fine man. Great pity to lose him from public life. By the way, who was elected down in his district? Some Tam-

22 McClellan to Richard Croker, September 8, 1896, McClellan MSS.
23 *Ibid.*
24 New York *Commercial Advertiser,* March 19, 1894.

many tough, I suppose. Too bad." Colonel McClellan shook hands with the literary man and went his way, not venturing to suggest that he was the "Tammany tough" who had succeeded the admirable Cochran.[25]

If McClellan was placed in an awkward position because of his affiliation with Tammany Hall, he displayed remarkable skill in concealing the fact. During his years in Congress he was a relatively free agent, for Tammany's principal interest was the city rather than the nation. As a consequence, on major issues he followed his conscience rather than Tammany's dictates, and as a representative he won the respect and friendship of members of both parties, established something of a reputation as an orator, became an authority on the tariff and military affairs, and secured—with Croker's help [26]—a coveted place on the Ways and Means Committee. Nor did his connection with Tammany have an adverse effect on his life outside of Congress. As befitted a member of the upper classes in the nation's capital, he went "into society" (as his contemporaries put it) and played the role of the gentleman scholar by doing research in Italian history. The Washington *Star,* while noting that he was a "protégé of Richard Croker's," added that he was "bright, handsome, and ambitious; a fluent talker, and . . . an all-round good fellow." [27] The Washington *Post's* impression was much the same, for it wrote: "He is good looking, short of stature, and smooth of face, but with something of a thoroughbred air about him, good clothes . . . and an attractive smile, which seems to be Irish. He is very youthful looking . . . , and he still seems such a boy." [28]

In Congress McClellan added to the luster but not the power of Tammany Hall. The organization, however, required more of its members than the measure of prestige supplied by Mc-

25 New York *Times,* December 29, 1895. The reference is to Bourke Cochran, who was not always "admirable" and who, most of the time, was as willing as McClellan to receive the support of Tammany Hall.

26 McClellan to Richard Croker, January 9, 1897, McClellan MSS.

27 Washington *Star,* December 7, 1895. On another occasion, the *Star* wrote: "In appearance Mr. McClellan might be taken for a member of a football team, who had discarded the business, cut and brushed his hair, and left in the enjoyment of the vigorous health that comes from athletic training." (Washington *Star,* November 21, 1895.)

28 Washington *Post,* March 15, 1896.

Clellan's name and record, and in 1903 the high command ordered him home to report for active duty. His years in Congress, as he frequently said, may have been the pleasantest in his life, but he was a good soldier, and he returned to New York to accept the Democratic party's nomination for mayor. In any event, he had little choice, for if he had refused to obey, he would have been forced to abandon his political career. While the mayor of New York City enjoyed more prestige than a mere congressman, McClellan's nomination was not necessarily a promotion. As he knew, the mayoralty in the past had proved to be a political graveyard in which officials lost rather than made their reputations. Acceptance of the nomination, moreover, exposed him to the not altogether unjustified accusation that he was willing to serve as a front man for Charles F. Murphy, the boss of Tammany. The *Herald* stated that he was the machine's choice because he "will take orders and he doesn't look it," [29] while the London *Times* correspondent in New York considered him "a mere tool" of the Tammany boss.[30] For the first time in his political career McClellan had to give more to Tammany than it gave to him.

McClellan's name, Murphy's skill as a party leader, and factionalism within the Republican ranks all combined to secure a Tammany victory in 1903. No one, however, quite knew the meaning of the victory, for if Tammany had won, so had McClellan. While one contemporary, long after the event, remembered that there was "satisfaction in the fact that Mr. McClellan was a man of high character and would not tolerate dishonesty in his administration," [31] another recalled that on election night "boys and girls [went] running up and down the streets . . . crying—between prodigious blasts on their tin horns: 'The lid is off! The lid is off!' " [32] McClellan, too, may have wondered about the significance of his election. At the height of his victory celebration, he is reported to have turned to Murphy and said: "Charley, I wonder if they'll be cheering me two years hence." To which the boss is alleged to have replied: "If they're not, it won't be my fault, George. It'll be

29 New York *Herald,* May 3, 1903.
30 London *Times,* November 5, 1903.
31 Prendergast, "Reminiscences," II, 107.
32 Benjamin R. C. Low, *Seth Low* (New York, 1925) , 70-71.

yours." [33] As it developed, neither the mayor nor the boss could claim sole responsibility for the record of the first McClellan administration.

Although McClellan in his autobiography quite naturally attempts to place his first administration as mayor of New York City in the most favorable light possible, his account is in general accurate and his estimates of his own accomplishments are seldom exaggerated. While he was not unbossed in the sense that Abram S. Hewitt and Seth Low before him had been, he did display far more independence than the run of Tammany mayors. Nor was his administration ever disgraced by the scandals that the public had come to associate with Tammany rule. Despite the predictions of the Republicans, prostitution and gambling did not flourish while he was in office. At the same time, the police force, generally considered one of the most reliable tests of the integrity of any municipal administration, was at least as efficient and honest as it had been under Low and the Republicans. The *Herald* thought that "the 'lid' . . . [had been] kept on . . . as effectively as at any time since Theodore Roosevelt was Commissioner of Police" and that "in a score of ways Mayor McClellan has sought to conciliate the 'better element' in which are included the natural foes of Tammany." [34] Even the Reverend Charles H. Parkhurst, the city's most spectacular crusader against vice and the scourge of former Tammany mayors, conceded that

> McClellan has given the city a clean administration as far as it was possible. He has been handicapped by the organization back of him, and yet he has shown by his actions in many respects that he did not sell himself body and soul to Tammany Hall. It should not be lost sight of that McClellan, no matter what some of those associated with him may be, is a gentleman, and has the instincts of a gentleman. [35]

Murphy's influence on McClellan's first administration was revealed most clearly by the character of the mayor's appointments. Although McClellan placed his own, rather than Tammany's, men in charge of the Police, Health, and Street

[33] John Heffernan, "Reminiscences" (Columbia University Oral History Project), 39-40.

[34] New York *Herald,* October 1, 1905.

[35] New York *Evening Post,* September 27, 1905.

"HE'S GOOD ENOUGH FOR ME."

—The New York Herald, December 5, 1904

Cleaning departments, for the rest the machine got most of the appointments that it wanted. District leaders were named to some of the more important commissions, and Murphy's followers occupied most of the lesser posts. But if Murphy was responsible for many appointments, he was still far from being the ruler of New York. McClellan dismissed some of the more obviously incompetent officials foisted on the city by Murphy and kept a fairly close check on most of the others.[36] No one

36 Lawson Purdy, president of the Department of Taxes and Assessments of New York from 1906 to 1917, thought McClellan "a good man . . . [who] was too pliant to requests," and that during his administration "conditions got pretty bad." Purdy recalled that on one occasion Lawrence Veiller, who had served under Low as deputy commissioner of the Tenement House Department, "went to McClellan and said, 'Will you give me two hours of your time and I will show you things that I think you should know.' McClellan went with him and saw the

ever accused him of being a reformer, but he satisfied most non-Tammany Democrats without alienating the machine.[37] Jacob Riis was probably right when he stated that McClellan was "the best organization Mayor" New York had ever had.[38]

McClellan's victory over William Randolph Hearst in the disputed mayoralty election of 1905 [39] proved to be a turning point in his political career. His re-election led directly to a break with Murphy, and his fight with the boss, in turn, ended whatever chances he might otherwise have had for political preferment. The origins of the dispute between the mayor and the machine are shadowy, and the autobiography does not furnish the details that are lacking in contemporary accounts. The background of the conflict, nevertheless, can be stated with some accuracy. Murphy's position in Tammany Hall was far more secure after McClellan's re-election than it had been in the preceding two years. He was, therefore, prepared to move in on the mayor in a fashion which had seemed impolitic in the first term. McClellan, for his part, was apparently impressed by the strength of anti-machine sentiment evinced by the large vote given Hearst. He may, moreover, have felt that while Tammany had given him his start, it could no longer provide him with assistance in national politics and that the time had come for him to establish a reputation as an independent. Personal considerations may also have been a factor. While liking and even admiring Croker, McClellan had little use for Murphy.

---

terrible conditions of the New York tenements and as a result McClellan eased out the man in charge of the department and replaced him with a straight-laced gentleman named Butler, who rigidly enforced the law." (Lawson Purdy, "Reminiscences" [Columbia University Oral History Project], 36.)

37 For a somewhat similar estimate of McClellan's relations with Tammany during his first administration, see New York *Mail*, December 30, 1909; New York *Times*, October 6, 1905; New York *Herald*, October 1, 1905. The view that McClellan was extremely subservient to Tammany in his first administration can be found in the New York *Tribune*, October 6, 1905 and Albert Fein, "New York City Politics, 1897-1902" (Master's Essay, Columbia University), 151.

38 New York *World*, September 20, 1905.

39 The election was for a new four-year term, and McClellan's plurality was only 3,500 in a total vote of almost 600,000. Hearst, claiming that he had been defrauded, demanded a recount, and the issue was not finally settled until 1909, the last year of McClellan's term. Although McClellan's victory was upheld at every turn in the protracted dispute, it is still impossible to ascertain whether or not Hearst was counted out of the mayoralty.

If it is impossible to ascertain the causes of the break between Murphy and McClellan, there is relatively little doubt concerning the incident that precipitated the conflict. The boss demanded that all the jobs in the new administration go to Tammany; McClellan refused. When McClellan announced his appointments on December 30, 1905, there were only two Tammany leaders on the new list of officeholders, and both had publicly sworn fealty to the mayor rather than the boss. Although the *World* told its readers that "the death-blow to Murphyism" had been struck and that "Murphy is done for," [40] news of the boss's death proved premature. The mayor could eliminate Murphy's influence in City Hall, but he could not dethrone him in Tammany. For the remainder of his term McClellan dismissed anyone displaying the slightest signs of sympathy or loyalty to Murphy, made frequent pronouncements against Tammany and its overlord,[41] and had John Purroy Mitchel, the special counsel for the commissioners of accounts, investigate those areas of the city government in which Tammany corruption seemed almost certain to exist. But these were mere skirmishes, for the decisive battles were waged in the primary contests for the control of the party; and Murphy, fighting on home ground with a disciplined army, was invincible.[42] By the end of McClellan's second term, he not only had failed to build up a rival organization, but Murphy's control over the Democratic party in New York City was more absolute than at any time in the past.

In many ways McClellan proved to be admirably suited for the numerous and varied duties imposed on the mayor of the largest city in the United States. His intellect was clearly

[40] New York *World*, January 6, 1906.

[41] For example, on January 1, 1907, he said: "I cannot recognize the existing control in Tammany Hall, or tolerate any relations with its present leader. . . . I should like to have the support of the Democratic organization, because I have always been a believer in party responsibility in administration, but if I cannot have that support under conditions which favor clean and efficient government, then I am content to do without it." (New York *Evening World*, January 2, 1907; Memorandum dated January 2, 1907, in Mayors' Papers, New York City Municipal Archives. Also see Bingham to McClellan, September 28, 1906, McClellan MSS.)

[42] For the outcome of the various primary contests, see New York *Herald*, September 9, 1906; New York *Tribune*, September 10, 19, 1906; New York *Telegram*, September 17, 1906; New York *Times*, September 16, 19, 1906; New York *World*, September 19, 1906.

superior to that of most of his predecessors and successors in City Hall; he was an excellent public speaker; and many of those who met him in an official capacity agreed with the *Herald* reporter that he was "modest and unassuming in his manner, democratic and affable in his intercourse with others, cautiously tactful and considerate." [43] Most of his contemporaries who were in a position to judge considered him a good administrator. He acted with decision after making up his mind, was remarkably well informed on city affairs, possessed a high sense of integrity, and did not hesitate to delegate both authority and responsibility to his subordinates. Finally, and perhaps most important, he always had a sense of perspective. This is another way of saying—and the point is repeatedly illustrated in his autobiography—that he never lost his sense of humor.

Despite his more than creditable record as mayor, McClellan's last day in City Hall was his last day in public office. Although he would on occasion help to elect others,[44] he would never again be given the chance to campaign for his own election. Nor was this for want of trying. On the same day in 1917 that the newspapers announced the death of Michael F. Conry, a Democratic congressman from New York, McClellan sought to secure the vacant seat by appealing to Murphy through Thomas Fortune Ryan.[45] Similar requests for assistance were subsequently sent to Colonel Edward House and Frank L. Polk, counselor of the State Department.[46] But Murphy would neither forgive nor forget, and the only pleasure McClellan could have derived from the situation was the chance it gave him to refuse Murphy's request that he serve as vice chairman of the Democratic Finance Committee in the mayoralty campaign of 1917.[47]

McClellan's two terms as mayor reveal both his assets and defects as a politician and public official. Cautious and conservative by nature, he had no taste for experiment in public

---

[43] New York *Herald*, October 1, 1905.

[44] See, for example, Homer S. Cummings to McClellan, July 12, 1916, McClellan MSS.

[45] McClellan to Thomas Fortune Ryan, March 3, 1917, *ibid.*

[46] E. M. House to McClellan, March 16, 1917; Frank L. Polk to McClellan, March 24, 1917, *ibid.*

[47] McClellan to Charles F. Murphy, July 7, 1917, *ibid.*

administration or policy. He wished to make the existing system as efficient as possible, but he had little interest in changing the system. Despite his clash with Murphy, he was not a fighter, for, although he could stick to his principles regardless of opposition, he was as temperamentally unsuited for offensive warfare as his father before him had been. While many politicians were able to further their ambitions by attacking Tammany Hall, it is significant that McClellan's break with the machine marked the end rather than the beginning of his career in politics.

III

McClellan left City Hall with little besides his reputation as a gentleman. Throughout his six years as mayor he had been accused of every variety of political sin, but even his critics conceded that he possessed certain qualities that had set him off from most of his predecessors and all of his ertswhile associates in Tammany Hall. On his last day in office, the *Post,* which had seldom endorsed his policies, wrote approvingly of "his unquestioned standing as a gentleman . . . , his breeding and instincts, . . . [and] his taste and civic pride." To the *Post,* his administration, despite its shortcomings, had "shown the advantage of having an educated man for mayor." [48] The *Times* considered him "a man of cultivated mind" who deserved to be compared with Hewitt and Low,[49] and the Brooklyn *Eagle* stated that he was "a gentleman," who was distinguished by "his culture and knowledge" and "his refinement of character." [50] Even the *Tribune,* the city's leading Republican paper and McClellan's most consistent critic, thought that he had "many attractive personal qualities." [51]

McClellan may have been gratified by the news that he was, after all, a man of culture and refinement, but he was enough of a realist to know that an unemployed gentleman had to have

[48] New York *Evening Post,* December 31, 1909.
[49] New York *Times,* December 31, 1909.
[50] Brooklyn *Eagle,* December 31, 1909.
[51] New York *Tribune,* October 6, 1905.

more than his press clippings to obtain a job. And he needed a job, for he was still a comparatively young man who had long since grown accustomed to both power and success. A professional politician who had been debarred by his associates from the practice of the only trade that he had ever learned, he was confronted by the formidable task of finding a new vocation around which to build his life. His choices were limited, but he did have a law degree, and in 1910 he gratefully accepted a partnership in a New York law firm. He soon realized that he had made a mistake, for he found the work uncongenial and his lack of experience a serious handicap.

At the end of one of the unhappiest years of his life, he was rescued from what he had come to consider an intolerable situation by an offer to join the Princeton faculty, first as a lecturer on public affairs and then as a professor of economic history. He taught his first class in 1911 and remained a member of the faculty—with a leave of absence during the First World War— until 1931 when he retired. He spent the remaining years of his life in a Washington that had little in common with the city that he had enjoyed so much as a young congressman. From the second Cleveland administration to the New Deal was a long step, and like so many others of his generation and background, McClellan never took it.

Although he had to forgo his political ambitions, McClellan found his life as a professor congenial. He had many friends in the town as well as on the faculty; he enjoyed the students; and he had ample opportunity for travel. Equally important from his standpoint, his role as a part-time teacher permitted him to continue the studies of art and history that he had begun as a young man. Early in life he had come to consider Italy his second home, and it was that country's artistic treasures that first aroused his interest in painting, sculpture, and architecture. In similar fashion, it was the Italian, rather than the American, past to which he devoted his historical researches.

McClellan's interest in art was always that of an amateur student with eclectic tastes. Although it was in Italy that he first learned to appreciate the fine arts, he had no desire to become an authority on the art of that or any other country. Art, like good food, was to be enjoyed wherever one could find it, and his admiration of Europe's old masters in no way lessened his enthusiasm for contemporary American art and artists. In many small, but significant, ways he sought to promote the interest of his countrymen in the fine arts and to narrow the gap between the artist and his public. As a young congressman he sponsored a bill for the abolition of duties on foreign works of art, and in later years he became an incorporator, trustee, and vice president of the American Academy of Rome. He was, moreover, the first mayor of New York to display more than a perfunctory interest in the design of the city's buildings. The Municipal Art Commission, which he always considered among the more important branches of the city government, stated that no other mayor had "ever stood more firmly than he for sound principles in the construction of public buildings and in the outer adornment of the city." [52] Numerous architects shared this opinion.[53] He was made an honorary member of the American Institute of Architects, and in 1909 he was awarded the medal of the Beaux Arts Society of Architects.

McClellan enjoyed artists as much as art, and he knew most of the country's leading painters and sculptors. On more than one occasion he used his official position to draw public attention to the work of an artist he admired. Many artists, in turn, considered him a friend who understood their problems as well as their art. Some indication of the respect in which he was held by artists is afforded by the invitation he received in 1908 to address the memorial meeting for Augustus Saint-Gaudens. If it was unusual for a professional politician to be chosen for such a task, it was even more unusual that he had no difficulty in filling the assignment. After hearing the former Tammany sachem discuss the subtleties of his father's art and character, Homer Saint-Gaudens wrote that he "had found a friend" to whom he "owed a sincere debt of gratitude." [54] At the same time, F. D. Millet, one of America's leading painters and one of the sculptor's closest friends, wrote to McClellan:

[52] New York *Evening Post,* December 31, 1909.

[53] For example, see C. Grant La Farge to McClellan, April 6, 1909, Mayors' Papers, New York City Municipal Archives.

[54] Homer Saint-Gaudens to McClellan, May 9, 1908, Mayors' Papers, New York City Municipal Archives.

Your address at the Saint-Gaudens memorial meeting . . . was so appreciative, so fair, so finished, in fact so perfectly satisfactory in every respect that I came away feeling that the right thing had been said at last, the right thing in the right way. . What you said about the Rock Creek figure expressed my opinion to a dot and I have never heard this opinion stated before. And your brief analysis of Saint-Gaudens' character was perfect. I was probably the oldest friend of Saint-Gaudens in the audience and having been on terms of the closest intimacy with him for years, I claim, justly, I believe, to have known him well. Therefore I feel a strong sense of personal gratitude to you for what you said and I must add that I have the greatest admiration for the manner in which you said it.[55]

If McClellan's attitude toward the fine arts was essentially that of a dilettante, his approach to history was in many respects that of the specialist. The author of three books on Italian history, he was one of the few Americans who deserved at that time to be ranked as an authority on the history of Venice. He began his researches in Venetian history before entering Congress, and in 1904, the first year of his mayoralty, he published *The Oligarchy of Venice*. After a long interlude, *The Oligarchy of Venice* was followed by *Venice and Bonaparte* in 1931 and *Modern Italy* in 1933. In each of these three books McClellan was somewhat handicapped by his lack of formal academic training in historical research, and the reviews of the volumes in the *American Historical Review* were in varying degrees critical of his scholarship.[56] In part such criticism may have been the reaction of professional historians to the amateur seeking to enter their field, but at some points it was fully justified. On the other hand, McClellan's historical studies, like everything else that he wrote, are distinguished by the clarity and conciseness with which he presents his ideas and factual material. Even when his views are of dubious validity, they are refreshingly blunt. The result at times may be poor history, but it is often good reading.

When McClellan began his study of Venetian history, few Americans had done any work in the field. *The Oligarchy of*

    55 F. D. Millet to McClellan, March 2, 1908, Mayors' Papers, New York City Municipal Archives.
    56 *American Historical Review*, 9 (July, 1904), 784-785; 38 (October, 1932), 153-154; 39 (January, 1934), 369-370.

Venice, which was subtitled "an essay," made no pretense of breaking new ground, for its material was obtained almost exclusively from the published works of European scholars. Dealing with the history of a political machine composed entirely of aristocrats, *The Oligarchy of Venice* throws almost as much light on McClellan as on Venice. One of its most penetrating chapters is entitled "The Machine," and the book's conclusion is that after centuries of successful rule the oligarchy collapsed when its members put the interests of their class over those of their state. Although McClellan emphasized the role of foreign developments in causing Venice's decline, he considered these less important than the ultimate failure of the aristocrats to maintain the aristocratic tradition of service to the community at large. McClellan chose to write about Venice because he had so thoroughly enjoyed the city on his visits to Italy,[57] but he also found much in its past that reminded him of his own experiences in American politics.

Contemporary newspapers accorded *The Oligarchy of Venice* far more attention than that given to comparable books by less illustrious authors. If most reviewers were surprised that a Tammany politician was literate, this fact was obscured by their genuine astonishment over a Tammany mayor who was also an authority on such a recondite subject as Venetian history. The comments, in general, were favorable, if platitudinous, for few critics were equipped to deal with the book as a work of scholarship, and many implied that it would be unsporting to find fault with any volume emanating from such an unexpected source. On the other hand, some of the reviews coincided with, if they did not reflect, the political views of the editorial pages in the papers in which they appeared. Thus, while the anti-McClellan *Post* stated that *The Oligarchy of Venice* "seldom rises above the commonplace,"[58] the pro-Tammany *Daily News* considered it "an admirable short history of the birth, growth, decay and death of a nation."[59] Occupying a cautious middle ground between these extremes were the *Mail and Express* ("a creditable historical survey")[60] and the

[57] See Dedication in *Venice and Bonaparte* (Princeton, 1931), v.
[58] New York *Evening Post*, February 11, 1904.
[59] New York *Daily News*, February 10, 1904.
[60] New York *Mail and Express*, February 10, 1904.

Sun ("a very interesting little book").[61] Regardless of their estimate of the book, the reviewers seemed more impressed by its author's occupation than its contents.

Venice and Bonaparte, in contrast to *The Oligarchy of Venice,* is a monograph based on the Venetian archives. The first book in English to appear on the subject, *Venice and Bonaparte* is easily the most rewarding of McClellan's historical studies. An introductory section providing information on Venetian life at the end of the nineteenth century is followed by "the story" of Napoleon's relations with Venice during the final years of the Republic. Throughout the volume McClellan sought to correct what he considered mistaken notions concerning Venice's past. He depicts Venetian society as drab and dull, condemned the oligarchy for its cowardice, praised the short-lived democracy, and concluded that Napoleon's policy toward the city was justified.[62] Although some reviewers criticized McClellan for ignoring the material in the French and Austrian archives, the book was in general well received by those most competent to judge it.[63] As in *The Oligarchy of Venice,* the author saw many similarities between Venetian and American politics, but he did not labor the point or permit it to overshadow either his narrative or analysis.[64]

Modern Italy is in every respect the least successful of McClellan's books. Although he stated in his Preface that the "book makes no claim to scholarship," [65] this disclaimer does not excuse his overlooking some of the most important secondary sources on the subject. Covering the period from the Congress of Vienna through the rise of fascism, *Modern Italy* lacks both a central thesis and all but the most banal conclusions. Because history is viewed as a series of wars and political

[61] New York *Sun,* February 13, 1904. For the views of other newspapers of *The Oligarchy of Venice,* see New York *Tribune,* February 10, 1904; New York *Times,* February 20, 1904; Boston *Transcript,* February 10, 1904; Chicago *Tribune,* February 27, 1904.

[62] *Venice and Bonaparte,* 124, 129, 168, 208, 240.

[63] *American Historical Review,* 38 (October, 1932), 153; *Review of Reviews,* 84 (November, 1931), 6; *Saturday Review of Literature,* 8 (February 20, 1932), 546.

[64] The critic in the *Times Literary Supplement* wrote: "The account of the Venetian oligarchy and its 'managers' translated into terms of modern American politics is both refreshing and illuminating; for the parallel is often remarkably close." (*Times Literary Supplement,* 30 [November 26, 1931], 936.)

[65] *Modern Italy,* vii.

maneuvers, the reader finishes the volume without having been told anything of Italian intellectual, cultural, economic, and social life. *Modern Italy*'s most distressing feature, however, is its unqualified endorsement of Mussolini and fascism. Insisting that the Italians, as "Latins," had neither the desire nor aptitude for democracy and that before the advent of fascism Italy had never been genuinely democratic,[66] McClellan concluded that Mussolini's dictatorship was an "honest and efficient actuality" that was "welcomed as a great improvement" by all Italians other than those "who had lost their means of political livelihood and those dreamers who honestly believed that the former government had really been democratic." [67] In the book's final chapters, he emphasized the regime's "accomplishments," discounted criticisms of fascism, and ended with the following panegyric of Italy's strong man:

> He has evolved a new theory of government and made a new state, both peculiarly adapted to the genius of the Italian people. He has ruled that state with an eye single to its best interests. He found it suffering from the loss of its self-esteem due to the settlement of the World War, and has made it one of the great powers of Europe. He found it distracted with internal disorder, with ill feeling against its former allies, and with almost ruined finances. He has restored peace at home and goodwill abroad, and the finances of his country.
>
> With infinite patience, a patience seldom met anywhere, but most rarely in Italy, he has taught his people the habit of fascismo and by so doing has broken down regionalism. For the first time there is a united country of men and women who, forgetting that they come from this or that province, under the inspiration of the duce remember only that they are the children of one great nation.
>
> He has taught his people to think nationally and has after many years fulfilled the hope of d'Azeglio, for as Cavour made Italy, Mussolini has made Italians.[68]

Following the publication of *Modern Italy* McClellan began work on an autobiography which he completed before his death in 1942 and turned over to the New-York Historical Society with the stipulation that it could not be published until after

---

66 *Ibid.*, 137, 224-225, 228, 279.
67 *Ibid.*, 232.
68 *Ibid.*, 281.

his wife's death. Entitled "The Grand Tour," the manuscript of McClellan's autobiography totals 709 typed pages which are divided into thirty-five chapters. Mrs. McClellan died in 1952, and the autobiography is now published under the title *The Gentleman and the Tiger*. The present volume is approximately two-thirds the size of McClellan's manuscript, and the original thirty-seven chapters have been reduced to seventeen. The portions of the manuscript that have been omitted from *The Gentleman and the Tiger* in general consist of either McClellan's descriptions of those events in which he did not himself participate or those parts of the narrative that the editor has arbitrarily decided would be of little interest to either the general reader or the more specialized student of American history.[69]

McClellan's defects as a historian proved to be assets when he turned to autobiography. With an intensely personal outlook and strong prejudices, he was much better equipped to deal with the present than the past. His view of the present may have been no more accurate than his view of the past, but his value as an observer lies not in his accuracy but in his opinions. Writing in his old age, he at times confused the facts of his earlier life. His impressions, however, were never confused, for he saw everyone and everything in primary colors, and he never knew what it meant to have mixed feelings. The result may at times tend toward over-simplification, but this is more than balanced in the reader's mind by the knowledge that he is face to face with a forthright man. McClellan is never indifferent and he never equivocates.

McClellan's account of his life and times provides present-day Americans with an unusual yardstick with which to measure a period of rapid change and innovation. His own political career began in the age of the robber barons and ended in the middle of the Progressive era, but he was neither overawed by the wealth of the new plutocracy nor dazzled by the reformers' dreams of unlimited progress. His standards were those of a nineteenth-century aristocrat, and by adhering to them he was able to avoid the intellectual fashions of the day and to achieve a kind of perspective that was denied to those

---

[69] For a more detailed account of the method used in editing this volume, see the Editor's Preface, p. 41.

Americans who prided themselves on their ability to keep up with the times. In his autobiography he does not so much reflect the times in which he lived; rather he offers us a series of judgments which rest on values that he assumes we share.

The autobiography is more than a record of one man's life, for it also contains a series of perceptive interpretations of the newspaper business, congressional and municipal politics, university life, and the United States Army. Much of McClellan's information will be new to many readers, but it is his point of view rather than his material that raises his account above the level of mere reporting. Because he was both an active participant and a somewhat aloof observer of the events that he describes—and, of course, because he was McClellan—he is particularly concerned with the contrast between form and content, appearance and reality. Thus, he rejects the reformer's view of the evils of the political machine for an analysis that in many respects is similar to that of most modern political scientists. In similar fashion, his description of the typical Southern congressman's opinion of the Negro in 1900 makes that opinion not only unjust but essentially ludicrous. Again, his discussion of his experiences at Princeton gains its effectiveness from his ability to follow a particular thread of university intrigue from its origins to its culmination in an official pronouncement whose euphemistic pomposity was designed to conceal the fact that any intrigue had existed. The line separating the cynic from the realist is at best a thin one, and in McClellan's case it often disappears entirely.

Although McClellan deals with events, his principal concern is with personalities. He judges individuals not by their ideas on politics and economics but by their failure or success—and it is usually failure—to live up to his code of personal behavior. He does not ask that they accept his views on, say, the tariff, but he does ask that they be honest, straightforward, intelligent, free from cant, and aware of their own limitations. These are almost ridiculously simple standards, but we realize as we read McClellan's autobiography how rarely they have been used to judge the personages of an historical period.

Because McClellan in a sense stood apart from his contemporaries, he was able to view them in a way which—paradoxically enough—makes him closer to our age than his own.

His description of Woodrow Wilson's experiences as president of Princeton, for example, is perhaps more similar in emphasis and approach to that of recent scholarship than anything written on that subject by Wilson's other contemporaries. The very fact that McClellan had a bias that was not shared by many others in this instance converts his bias into a kind of objectivity. To most Americans at the turn of the century, engrossed by the issues raised by the Progressive movement, Wilson was an idealist seeking to reform an unregenerate and reactionary Princeton; to McClellan he was an ambitious and sanctimonious man who failed to keep his word. In similar vein, he looked on J. P. Morgan not as a plutocrat whose wealth made him a likely object of suspicion but as an honorable man who also happened to be wealthy. On the other hand, in reviewing his experiences with Andrew Carnegie, he neither condemns the steel executive's practices as a businessman nor praises his philanthropies, but concludes that he was a selfish man who would resort to almost any device to attract attention.

The range of McClellan's autobiography is enormous, for he was in a position to know most of the leading figures of his age. He is, therefore, able to present intimate and often revealing details about every President from Cleveland to Wilson, the leading members of Congress at the turn of the century, newspaper publishers, Tammany bosses, painters and sculptors, millionaires, university presidents, New York mayors, and Democratic politicians who attained prominence in either the city or nation. William Jennings Bryan, Theodore Roosevelt, Bosses Murphy and Croker, Joseph Pulitzer, Henry George, Augustus Saint-Gaudens, Russell Sage, and Seth Low are just a few of the prominent Americans whose characters and behavior are described by McClellan. His autobiography is, however, more than a summary of his experiences with the giants of his day, for some of the book's most rewarding pages deal with the machinations of New York ward heelers, the oddities of obscure congressmen, the vagaries of the academic mind, and the lack of romance in the lives of the broken-down newspaper reporters who helped to create the romances of yellow journalism.

Although McClellan finds many reasons to criticize most of his contemporaries, he is especially scornful of the numerous stuffed shirts with whom he was forced to associate. He can think of nothing more damning about an individual than to say that he lacks a sense of humor, and one often has the impression that McClellan believes that there should be a special and particularly awful part of Hell reserved for the humorless. He is not content, however, merely to observe that someone is deluded by his own importance; he insists on picturing such an individual at either a ludicrous or grotesque point in his life. Thus, we see Mayor William J. Gaynor displaying the bullet in his throat to a startled bank clerk, Seth Low not permitting his father's death to interrupt his breakfast of buckwheat cakes, Theodore Roosevelt writing to Mrs. Grover Cleveland that he hopes her husband's funeral will not conflict with the Harvard-Yale boat race, and President James McCosh of Princeton urging McClellan to pray with extra vigor for the soul of a roommate who had the misfortune of being an Episcopalian. In addition to presenting a number of worthies with their defenses down, he has assembled a collection of portraits of minor figures that includes John Scannell, a Tammany district leader, who was equally adept at reciting whole volumes of Shakespeare and re-enacting a murder which he had committed; J. Sergeant Cram, the Harvard graduate, who taught Boss Murphy to eat peas with a fork; and the city editor who was ordered by the younger Bennett to wear evening clothes when he sent the paper to press only to be fired by Bennett on the ground that no serious newspaperman would wear evening clothes on the job.

McClellan's prose accurately reflects his attitude toward life. His writing is precise, his method of presentation is direct, and his sentence structure is relatively simple and straightforward. The reader never feels that the author is seeking to create an effect for its own sake or that he is attempting to pad his narrative. The scarcity of adjectives and adverbs in his prose is in part a measure of his honesty with himself and his readers. He seems constitutionally incapable of overwriting, for to do so is not only poor taste but also a distortion of the truth. In both style and content McClellan's autobiography stands as a fitting monument to a man who above all prided himself on his integrity.

HAROLD C. SYRETT.

Editor's Preface

The Gentleman and the Tiger is a condensation of a 709-page typewritten manuscript. The present volume is approximately two-thirds the size of the original. Omissions in the text are indicated by the customary three dots. In a few instances the editor has changed the order of the material. In such cases the sentences or paragraphs that have been shifted from their original position in the manuscript are both preceded and followed by three dots. Incorrect spelling, typographical errors, and blatant mistakes in punctuation have been corrected by the editor, and some small paragraphs have been combined. On the few occasions when the editor has added words or sentences to the original text, this material is enclosed in brackets. Because the manuscript's thirty-five chapters have been reduced to seventeen, it has not been possible to use McClellan's chapter titles. The chapter titles in the present volume are quotations, each of which is taken from the particular chapter for which the quotation serves as a title.

Footnotes have been used to identify individuals inadequately identified in the text, to correct errors of fact in the text, and to explain certain points that are mentioned but not explained in the text. If individuals have been sufficiently identified in the text for the purposes of the author's narrative, footnotes have not been used to furnish further information on such individuals.

HAROLD C. SYRETT.

THE GENTLEMAN AND THE TIGER

Chapter I

MY DEAREST FRIEND WAS MY FATHER

THE McCLELLANS, who came originally from the Isle of Man, were a family of considerable importance in and around Kirkcudbright in Galloway on the Scottish border. One of them served under William Wallace and was with that valiant hero when he was hanged. In the fifteenth century there were eleven of the name who had won knighthood. When Mary Stuart fled from Scotland to England and her death, according to tradition she took ship near Furness Abbey under the auspices of one of the McClellans. In 1630, the head of the house was raised to the peerage by Charles I as Baron Kirkcudbright in the peerage of Scotland, again according to tradition, in reward for the somewhat tenuous service of having presented to the Crown a certain bronze gun called "Mons Meg" which may be seen to this day by the curious on the ramparts of Edinburgh Castle.

Lord Kirkcudbright's glory was, however, short-lived. Being a very earnest and emphatic Presbyterian he refused to accept the Church of England rector, who had been imposed upon the parish, and cast the unfortunate clergyman into the dungeons of the castle to die, it was charged, of starvation. Punishment was swift and merciless. Lord Kirkcudbright's estates were seized, and he himself was imprisoned in Edinburgh Castle, where he soon died. The peerage lay dormant for half a century to be revived in the person of the last peer's grandson who was keeping a glove shop in Edinburgh and was known ever after as the "glove-selling peer." The peerage again became dormant in 1832 when Camden Grey, sixteenth Baron

Kirkcudbright and sometime a captain in the Scots Greys, died and was buried at Bruges, Belgium.

Meanwhile, the "glove-selling peer's" younger brother William, who had been "out in the Fifteen," [1] had been pardoned, and had become a Presbyterian minister. [He] was called to a parish in Northern Ireland. Some years later, with a number of his parishioners, he came to this country only to return home the next year. Finally in 1724 the expedition started once more, this time on the ship *Eagle's Wing*, and settled at Worcester, Massachusetts. William's son, Samuel, who was born in 1730, moved to Woodstock, Connecticut, was a member of the Connecticut legislature . . . and a brigadier general commanding the 5th Brigade of the Connecticut Militia during the Revolutionary War. Samuel's grandson, George, after graduating from Yale, moved to Philadelphia, where he married Elizabeth Brinton and became a very famous surgeon. [2]

George's second son, George Brinton, . . . was the great soldier, and I have the honor to be his son. . . . My mother was Mary Ellen Marcy, daughter of Major General Randolph B. Marcy, my father's chief of staff [from 1861 to 1863] and later [1878 to 1881] inspector general of the United States Army. In 1864, after his defeat for the presidency by Abraham Lincoln, my father, who had resigned from the army on election day, bestirred himself to find employment. He had had a prosperous career as a railroad man before the war, but what money he had saved went in maintaining the dignity of his position as commanding general. During the war some of his admirers had given my mother the house at 22 West Thirty-first Street in New York. As it was beyond their means to live in it, it was always rented, and it was this rent that was their principal source of income when my father retired into private life.

Everywhere he went seeking work he found the door closed through fear of the resentment of the national administra-

---

1 This is a reference to the Jacobite uprising of 1715 and means that William McClellan participated in the armed attempt of that year to restore the Stuarts to the throne.

2 His fame was due to his founding of the Jefferson Medical College in 1825, his establishment of a clinic in the college, his boldness and skill as a surgeon, and the joy with which he fought all who opposed his plans.

tion.[3]. . . Finally, he and his friends concluded that he must disappear for long enough to permit the political bitterness against him to die down. Accordingly, he went abroad for four years in the spring of 1865. The first winter was spent at Dresden, Saxony, in a modest apartment near the railway station, No. 2 (now No. 4) Wiener Strasse, where at ten minutes past one in the afternoon of November 23rd, 1865, I was born. . . . While I was named George Brinton after my father, in order to avoid the confusion of having two Georges in the family, I was always known as Max, being presumably a Teutonic version of the name of "Little Mac," by which my father's men called him. . . .

When we . . . [returned to] New York [in 1868] Mr. Edwin A. Stevens,[4] a very rich man, one of several who claimed to have invented the screw propeller and a great admirer of my father, . . . [gave] him the first real work that he had . . . since his resignation from the army. Mr. Stevens had certain ideas on the subject of a gunboat which was to revolutionize naval warfare and asked him to take charge of the construction of the *Stevens Battery,* as the new vessel was called. We accordingly settled in that most dismal of all places, Hoboken, and my father began the hopeless task of trying to carry out Mr. Stevens's ideas.

Soon . . . we moved to New York. The *Stevens Battery* had been abandoned, but, fortunately for my father, more work was offered him than he could possibly attend to. During the next four years he not only built his home on Orange Mountain in New Jersey, but he was able to invest enough to give him an income which in those days meant moderate wealth.

I was a very lonely little boy, for I had no playmates. I

---

3 McClellan's father was the unsuccessful candidate for President of the United States on the Democratic ticket in 1864. Although it was an exceedingly bitter campaign in which General McClellan was unjustly accused of disloyalty, it is not accurate to assert, as McClellan does, that his father could not get work because of the "fear of the resentment of the national administration." Actually General McClellan's letters in November, 1864, reveal that he first decided to go abroad right after the election, or long before he was allegedly persecuted by the Lincoln administration. See William Starr Myers, *General George Brinton McClellan* (New York, 1934), 468-469.

4 Stevens was the son of John Stevens, and, like his father, was an engineer, financier, inventor, and promoter. His bequest made possible the establishment of Stevens Institute of Technology in Hoboken, New Jersey.

suffered greatly from bronchial asthma, and between attacks I invented games and daydreamed. . . . My dearest friend was my father. Despite all that he had been through, despite all that he had suffered, despite all the injustice of which he had been the victim, his heart remained young and his spirit unwarped. There was no bitterness in his soul, no envy, hatred, malice or uncharitableness. He always understood me and was able to see my point of view and always talked with me as with an equal, so that I never feared to take to him my small troubles. . . .

In the spring of 1872 we moved into the house that my father had built on the so-called Orange Mountain, in New Jersey, which he had named Maywood after my sister.[5] He had been born at Philadelphia, had lived at Chicago and Cincinnati before the war and had been nominated for the presidency from New Jersey, and considered himself a Jerseyman.

We had only lived in our new home one summer when in 1873 my father's health broke down from overwork and the doctor ordered him complete rest for two years if he wished to recover. On October eighth of that year we sailed for Europe on the Cunard flagship *Russia*. . . . We went to Palermo for the winter, . . . to St. Moritz for the summer . . . , and the next winter . . . to Egypt. . . . We returned to the United States in the autumn of 1875 and spent the next two winters at Baltimore, where my parents were received with open arms, despite the fact that at the beginning of the Civil War my father had placed the entire legislature of Maryland under arrest, thus keeping the state in the Union.[6]

As I was now able to read, . . . I was sent to a day school. . . .

---

[5] May Marcy McClellan was McClellan's only sister and was five years older than he. Following her father's death in 1885, she and her mother lived in England and France. In 1893, she married Paul Desprez, counselor of the French legation in Washington, and became a permanent resident of France. Her home in Nice was named Villa Antietam, and it was there that she died in 1945.

[6] On September 10, 1861, Secretary of War Simon Cameron instructed Generals John A. Dix and Nathaniel P. Banks (but not General McClellan) to arrest as many members of the Maryland legislature as was necessary to prevent that body from adopting an ordinance of secession. Ten legislators (not the entire legislature) were arrested. It is, of course, impossible to demonstrate that these arrests were responsible for "keeping the state in the Union." (*The War of the Rebellion: . . . Official Records . . .* [Washington, 1880-1901], Series I, Vol. V, pp. 193-197.)

Here I learned for the first time the joys of political martyrdom. As soon as my schoolmates found out whose son I was, they, less courteous than their parents, proceeded to demonstrate their love of "the lost cause" by kicking, thumping and cursing me as "a damned little Yankee." When later I went to boarding school in the North I received much the same treatment, on the ground that I was "a damned little Copperhead." Truly in those days it required courage to be a Northern Democrat. . . .

To the great disappointment of my parents I had asthma more seriously on Orange Mountain than anywhere else. It was not until I was thirty that I finally got rid of it. My mother was extremely catholic in her medical beliefs, and I was dosed by practitioners of every school and description, but nothing did me any good as long as I was at Orange. When my asthma became so bad that I grew black in the face I was shipped to New York, . . . [where I] stayed at either the house of Mr. and Mrs. Joseph W. Alsop [7] of the old New York family of that name, at 32 Washington Square, or at that of Mr. William C. Prime,[8] my father's closest friend, at 38 East Twenty-third Street. . . .

On September 17th, 1877, the fifteenth anniversary of the battle of Antietam, my father delivered the dedicatory address of the war monument on Boston Common. His reception was very enthusiastic and I think that he was happier than he had been for many a long day. On reaching New York on our return he received a telegram announcing his entirely unexpected nomination for the governorship of New Jersey.

At that time the Democratic party in New Jersey was divided into two factions, one controlled by Leon Abbett, afterwards governor, United States Senator John R. McPherson, and their friends, the other controlled by Stafford Little, clerk of the Supreme Court of the state, Henry C. Kelsey, secretary of state

[7] Alsop was a merchant and a member of a family which had supplied New York with merchants since the American Revolution. In 1883, five years after Alsop had died, the house on Washington Square in which he had lived was purchased by General McClellan, and it remained his town house until his death in 1885.

[8] Prime was editor of the New York *Journal of Commerce* (1861-69) and president of the New York Associated Press (1861-69). For several years after 1869 he had a financial interest in the *Journal of Commerce*. He also wrote several books on art and was a member of the Princeton Art Department.

of New Jersey and their crowd. The Abbett faction controlled the state organization and most of the patronage, while the Little-Kelsey faction was in opposition.

The state convention was "stampeded" for my father over the heads and against the protests of the organization. It was a well-managed and well-carried-out plan, which could not have succeeded but for the great popularity of the candidate with the rank and file of the party.

In politics my father was very trusting. Believing that Abbett and his friends were corrupt, as they undoubtedly were, he reasoned that the opposition [leaders] were spotlessly pure, as they undoubtedly were not. Accordingly, he gave himself unreservedly in political matters into Mr. Kelsey's hands, who forthwith, using the governor's patronage, began to gain control of the Democratic organization in the state and to maneuver the governor himself into a definite break with Abbett and McPherson.

After his election my father took a house at Trenton and settled down for his term of office. I was sent to the Trenton Model School where, as the governor's son, I was treated with deference, but learned little. After a few weeks a Jesuit Father was engaged to make up the defects of the Model School. I went to school in the morning and had Father Miller [9] in the afternoon. He was a good-looking German and a born teacher. His great ambition was to be sent up country in China and there to find martyrdom, an ambition which was soon after gratified, for he died very nobly for his faith.

The next year I went to boarding school, to St. John's School at Sing Sing, now Ossining, New York. It was by no means a cheap school, but it was by no means a good one. . . . We were taught the manual of arms, the collects, epistles and gospels, "penmanship," spelling, a little elementary Latin, and a smattering of German, French and dancing, as extras, and that was about all. In my time no boy entered college from St. John's without conditions, and in those days college entrance examinations were notoriously easy.

---

9 McClellan was apparently confused, for no Father Miller appears in the Jesuit records for this period. I am indebted to Mr. Maurice L. Ahern, archivist at Fordham University, for undertaking for me what proved to be a vain search for Father Miller's name and record.

During my first year at school, I had almost literally to fight for life, for I was kicked, cuffed, and beaten unmercifully, until like a cornered rat I learned to defend myself as a fairly efficient little rough-and-tumble fighter, for the rules of the ring and fair play were quite unknown at St. John's.

I was anxious to go to West Point, but my father wouldn't hear of it on the ground that the army had ceased to be a career, and that in my time there would be no more wars. As he had graduated from the Military Academy before he was twenty-one, he was ambitious for me to graduate from Princeton, for which college I was destined, at the same age. After my first year [at St. John's] I was quite regularly head of the school, which only meant that I was a one-eyed boy in the country of the blind. My father, however, built high hope on my standing and determined that if possible I should enter Princeton a year ahead of my class. . . . During the Easter vacation of my third year at school I developed inflammatory rheumatism, and on my recovery it was determined that I should not return to St. John's, but should be coached for my college examinations at home.

On the advice of Professor William M. Sloane,[10] then of Princeton, the services were obtained of Paul van Dyke,[11] Princeton '81, who was a student at the Princeton Theological Seminary. . . . When we went to Orange Mountain for the summer, Paul van Dyke went with us, and my schoolmate Jim Harriman[12] joined us later. I don't know how van Dyke did it, but, thanks to him, Harriman and I entered Princeton with one condition each, which we passed without difficulty in the autumn.

September, 1882, found me a full-fledged freshman in the class of '86 in the College of New Jersey, now Princeton University.

[10] Sloane was a leading historian who specialized in French and American history. He was a member of the Princeton faculty from 1877 until 1896, when he became Seth Low professor of history at Columbia University. He remained at Columbia until his retirement in 1916.

[11] Van Dyke was ordained a Presbyterian minister in 1887. For the next ten years he devoted his life to religious work. From 1898 to 1928 he was professor of modern history at Princeton University.

[12] After graduating from Princeton in 1886, James Arden Harriman became a member of the firm of H. B. Hollins & Company in New York City. He retired in 1898 and died eleven years later in Paris.

Physically Princeton was very different from what it is today. It was a small college, measured by present standards, of less than six hundred students, including undergraduates, postgraduates, "scientifs," and "specials." The endowment was very small and the buildings few. Nassau Hall, or "Old North" as we called it, the Green wing of the library, the present office building, Reunion, West, Witherspoon and Dodd are the only survivors of my time. Witherspoon, which today shares with Alexander and the library the distinction of being the greatest eyesore on the campus, was the newest building and was considered a work of great majesty and beauty.

Rooms in the dormitories were in theory drawn for, but in practice transferred by purchase, the purchase price including the furniture, the seller agreeing to persuade all who had entered the drawing to withdraw in favor of the purchaser.

Jim Harriman and I bought 4 West Middle Witherspoon . . . and moved in at the beginning of third term freshman year. We paid $700 for the transfer of a study and two bedrooms, some worn-out furniture, some battered hangings and ornaments, and an iron spittoon made in the similitude of a top hat, which forty years later I found still adorning the room.

The chimney smoked so badly that on windy days it was impossible to light a fire and, as there was no other heat, in cold weather we were often obliged to sit in our overcoats. In each entry there was a single tap of cold water, the only washing facilities in college being a tin bathtub and two tin showers in the basement of the gymnasium. I had a tin hat-bath in my room and by taking a cold tub every morning earned a reputation for mingled eccentricity and courage. The sanitary arrangements were deplorable and consisted of a privy, colloquially known as "Ord Hall," standing between Whig and Clio, wooden barns on the sites of their present marble successors.

The college year consisted of three terms, the first from September until the Christmas vacation, the second from January until the spring vacation, which was fixed with stern Presbyterian disregard of Easter, and the third only half as long as the other two from spring vacation until commencement at the end of June.

Five days a week we had three recitations or lectures, two in the morning and one in the afternoon, while on Saturdays we had religious instruction in the mornings and the afternoons free. Morning chapel was compulsory as were morning and afternoon chapel on Sunday, when the library and gym were closed, all outdoor sports forbidden and even the riding of a bicycle was unlawful.

I entered college at least a year too young, for I was two months short of seventeen, very badly prepared, very immature, and physically sadly underdeveloped. My preparation had been so bad that during my first two years it was as much as I could do to keep in college. In junior year things went better, and in senior I really enjoyed my college work. During senior year I made much progress but my first three years pulled me down, and I graduated below the middle of the class. With better preparation and with better teaching at college I think that I could have done fairly well. . . .

In my time the preceptorial system, as well as the honor system, was unknown, and the elective system had only recently been inaugurated. During freshman and sophomore years every subject was required, while in junior year we were allowed to elect one quarter of the subjects and in senior year one half. We were given a smattering of many subjects and a thorough knowledge of none. Most of our classes were merely recitations, questions and answers on a textbook, and I only attended six courses in which lectures had a part. . . .

Dr. McCosh,[13] or "Jimmy" as he was generally called, was president of the college and had already begun to break. By our senior year when we had him in philosophy he had failed very much and had great difficulty in delivering his lectures and in keeping his temper. On pleasant days, when the great outdoors called, someone in the back of the room would make a disturbance, the doctor would lose his temper, denounce us in unmeasured terms, and drive us out of his presence to our unqualified delight.

In my junior year my roommate Harriman had diphtheria.

[13] James McCosh was a Scottish divine and philosopher, who served as president of Princeton from 1868 to 1888. He was one of the first ministers in America to defend Darwinism, and he was responsible for broadening Princeton's curriculum and enlarging its physical plant. McClellan's unsympathetic view of McCosh is in marked contrast to that of many others who were students at Princeton during the seventies and eighties. For example, see Henry Fairfield Osborn, *Fifty Years of Princeton '77* (Princeton, 1927), 40.

As there was neither hospital, infirmary, nor trained nurse in Princeton, nor apparently knowledge that diphtheria was a communicable disease, he was left in our room in Witherspoon, with me as nurse, risking the lives of every boy in college. One day Jimmy called to see him, and I entertained the doctor in the study. Presently he asked me, "This James Harriman, is he a Christian?" With great solemnity I replied, "Doctor, I am sorry to say that he is an Episcopalian." Without a moment's hesitation the doctor shouted, "Down on your knees, young man, down on your knees while we pray for his soul."

Of the professors under whom I sat William M. Sloane, Alexander Johnston, Cyrus Brackett and Henry C. Cameron were well worth while. Sloane gave us a course in senior year in which he covered the history of the world from the earliest times to our own. It was a brilliant stunt and we enjoyed it and did get something from it. Johnston, who by himself constituted the Department of Economics, gave us a course in political economy which was admirable and awoke in me a desire to continue the subject. Brackett was a born teacher and made of physics a delight, while Professor Henry C. Cameron, with his great learning and his dry Scottish humor, made Homer live for us. . . . With these four exceptions there was no professor who, to put it politely, was interesting. . . .

The moral tone of the undergraduates in the early eighties was very much as it is now. Our average age was at least a year younger. We were the same healthy, enthusiastic, essentially clean, decent boys as are our successors fifty years later. There was a good deal of drinking and a good deal of poker playing, mostly on Sunday, when there was nothing else to do. I doubt, however, if there was more drunkenness then than there is now.

Discipline was enforced at meetings of the faculty attended by the president and dean and such professors as were sadistically inclined. The delinquent was brought before the faculty and subjected to a third degree worthy of the most approved police methods.

In freshman year Jim Harriman and I gave a dinner in our rooms at the University Hotel to a friend who had come from Harvard to spend the weekend with us. As the dinner became lively, and it became very lively, it came to the notice of the dean, and Harriman and I were summoned before the faculty.

On entering the faculty room I faced an inquisition of eight Presbyterian clergymen of the narrowest and most orthodox type. The charge against me was "having wine in room." To this I promptly pleaded guilty. I was then asked to give a list of our guests, which I declined to do. I was then put through the third degree by my eight inquisitors for over two hours. Dr. McCosh said to me, "Do you mean to say that your father, a Christian gentleman, as I suppose, has wine on his table?" "Yes, Doctor," I replied, "he has. For that matter when I lunched at your house the day you had the President of the United States, unless I am much mistaken, you had sherry on your table." "Um, um," replied Jimmy, "that is a matter that we will not discuss." The verdict against us was expulsion, with permission to apply for reinstatement at the end of a fortnight.

My father was very angry at the way I had been treated, and wrote Dr. McCosh a frank expression of his opinion. As the result of the letter I was allowed to return promptly at the end of a fortnight. . . .

When in 1884 Cleveland was nominated for the presidency, what few Democrats there were at Princeton organized a "Cleveland and Hendricks Legion and Drum Corps." As I had been at a military school, I was elected adjutant and [Henry Kirkland] Jones '85, whose father was an army officer, was elected commandant. Headed by the Drum Corps, we made night hideous by marching around the campus in the cause of Democracy. Before election we were invited to join a Democratic procession in Trenton and paraded thirty-five strong. After election we paraded again. This time, such is the heartening effect of victory, the whole college turned out and we paraded Trenton nearly four hundred strong. The state committee furnished us oilcloth caps and capes and torches, and after the parade gave us a "feed" of ham sandwiches and beer. We had a glorious time.

My father took a tremendous interest in the campaign and at once offered his services to the National Committee, which kept him very busy all summer speaking all over the United States. He saw Governor Cleveland from time to time and received what he considered positive assurance that in the event of Democratic success he would be appointed Secretary of War.

This immensely pleased him, for he thought that such an appointment would be a final answer to all his critics.

It is a safe rule in politics never to count one's chickens until they are hatched. Had my father followed this rule, he would have been saved a great disappointment. My mother assuming that my father was as good as appointed announced to all and sundry that she was going to the inauguration and did not deny her expectation that my father would be the next Secretary of War. She made up a party and rooms were engaged at the Arlington long in advance and we were irrevocably committed to being in Washington on the fourth of March.

Immediately after election my father received a letter from Governor Cleveland in which he said, "I can never be grateful enough to you for all that you have done for me. I can never repay all that I owe you." My father took the letter *au grand serieux* and thought the matter of his appointment settled. After the letter nothing—no invitation to call, no asking of advice, no communication of any kind. Apparently as far as Grover Cleveland was concerned George B. McClellan, having served his purpose in rallying the soldier vote to the Democratic ticket, had ceased to exist.

When we reached Washington for the inauguration, the city was full of rumors. Various people assured my father that he was to be appointed, but from the appointing power there came never a word. It was not until the cabinet list was announced that my father finally gave up hope, after which he was obliged to stand behind the cabinet at the inauguration and look as though he were enjoying himself. . . .

Some weeks after the inauguration on returning from a walk, my father found a telegram which, having read, he handed to me. It was as follows: "Russia is a first class mission. Will you accept it? [Secretary of State] Thomas F. Bayard." "I am so sorry," said my father, "that there had been any delay in answering this," and at once sent the following reply: "No thanks," and with a twinkle in his eye said to me, "They can take my answer as they please." We learned later that my father was the sixth to whom the Russian mission was offered, and when General [George Van Ness] Lothrop [a Michigan lawyer of considerable means] accepted, it already had been offered to eleven others.

Years afterwards Professor William M. Sloane and Paul van Dyke told me that Mr. Cleveland had told them that he (Mr. Cleveland) had intended to offer the War Department to my father but that Senator John R. McPherson of New Jersey had come to him and said, "New Jersey has nothing to ask in the way of patronage, but serves notice that if McClellan's name is sent to the Senate, I shall use senatorial courtesy to defeat his nomination." "There was nothing for me to do under the circumstances," added Mr. Cleveland, "but to drop McClellan from consideration."

It is a pity that Mr. Cleveland did not have the tact to send for my father and explain the matter to him. Had he done so my father of course would have understood. The chickens of the old fight between Henry C. Kelsey and Mr. McPherson in which Governor McClellan had backed the former, had come home to roost with a vengeance. My mother, who was somewhat emphatic in her expressions, ever after referred to President Cleveland as "That fiend," so that when later I came in contact with him officially I had to live down his idea that I shared my mother's opinion.

Mr. Abram S. Hewitt, who had a very distinguished career as representative in Congress and mayor of New York, told me of an experience that he had had with Governor Cleveland which illustrated the latter's lack of tact. During the height of the presidential campaign of 1884, Mr. Hewitt received a telegram from Governor Cleveland summoning him and his brother-in-law and business partner, Edward Cooper, to Albany. On their arrival, Cleveland said to them, "Dan Manning" (the chairman of the Democratic National Committee) "tells me that he must have $50,000 by next Monday. This is Saturday, can you two men raise it for him? I authorize you to make any promises that may be necessary, but get that money by Monday as it is absolutely essential." Mr. Hewitt replied, "Governor, we shall do our best." Hewitt and Cooper decided to give the required amount as their personal contributions to the campaign and returned to Albany the following Monday, taking with them their checks for the desired $50,000. On being received by the governor, Mr. Hewitt gave him the two checks. Whereupon the governor asked, "What promises did you have to make to get the money?" "None whatever," replied Mr.

Hewitt, "it is our personal contribution." "Thank God," said the governor and dismissed them. "It was rather nice of Cleveland to thank God," said Mr. Hewitt in concluding the story, "for he certainly never thanked either Cooper or myself." It is interesting to note that both Hewitt and Cooper were among those subsequently offered the mission to Russia. . . .

During the early part of October [1885], on going to Orange from college for a weekend, I found a number of my sister's friends. My father was in unusually good spirits and made himself as agreeable to us young people as he always did. On Monday morning we went to New York. He took the downtown, and I the uptown ferry. His boat was just getting under way. He ran, jumped, made it, and waved his hat to me. I never saw him again, but my last impression was of a man full of life and vigor, of good spirits and of youth.

On the morning of October 30, as I was going to chapel at Princeton, a messenger stopped me and gave me a telegram from my sister which read: "Papa very ill, come home at once." I knew immediately what had happened. On the train I heard two men with G.A.R. buttons in their coats talking behind me. "Well," said one, "the old general has gone." "Yes," answered the other, "he was a man, that feller, God rest his soul." My father would have asked no better tribute.

On reaching Maywood I found that my father had died the previous night of angina pectoris. He had had an attack some days before in the ferry boat going to New York. . . . His death was a frightful shock to all of us, for we had never associated him with illness or weakness. He suffered much before he died, for my mother was at that time going through a period of homeopathy and the homeopathic doctor who was called in did not believe in narcotics. We held the funeral in New York, at the Madison Square Presbyterian Church. My father had often told me that he wanted his funeral to be as simple as possible with no speeches or military parades. I had great difficulty in dissuading Dr. Parkhurst from delivering a funeral oration. He did not care particularly for my father, but it was a good opportunity for the limelight.[14]

14 Charles Henry Parkhurst managed to remain in the limelight throughout much of his adult life. As minister of the Madison Square Presbyterian Church in New York City from 1880 to 1918, he delivered innumerable sermons attack-

We buried him in Trenton, and the only military display was the sounding of taps by two trumpeters of the engineers battalion in which he had seen his first service. The national administration was unrepresented at the funeral, President Cleveland entirely ignoring it. General [Philip H.] Sheridan, as commanding general of the army, came, as did many of my father's old comrades. The press treated his memory very fairly. The only exception . . . [was] the *Evening Post,* in which its editor, E. Lawrence Godkin, outdid himself in the indecency of his attack.[15]

It is almost impossible for me to write impartially of my father. I cared so much for him and I revere his memory so profoundly that I have great difficulty in speaking of him except in superlatives. My father came into the world with the advantages of a distinguished ancestry, birth, and breeding. In accordance with the good old Scots tradition he was taught by his parents that "birth" imposes upon its fortunate possessor obligations and duties that must never for a moment be ignored, that there are certain things that a gentleman simply cannot do. He cannot stoop to meanness, pettiness, untruth or to financial, mental or moral dishonesty. The doctrine of *noblesse oblige* makes him almost unconsciously do the right thing at the right moment and in the right way.

If you like, my father was an aristocrat, but an aristocrat in the best sense of the word. He was simple, unpretentious and unaffected almost to the point of shyness. He thought himself no better than his fellows and readily overlooked in others

---

ing Tammany Hall and organized vice. His most notorious exploits were his tours of the underworld's dives in search of materials for his sermons.

15 The editorial in the *Post* reads in part as follows: "The death of General McClellan . . . at the early age of fifty-nine removes one more of the striking figures of the Civil War. Probably no soldier who did so little fighting has ever had his qualities as a commander so minutely, and we may add, so fiercely discussed. In command of an organized and regular force against a foreign enemy, he probably would have played a very creditable part among generals of the second order. With an improvised force, seething with political passion, he was clearly unfit to face the storms of civil strife. . . . But he was a man of high character, of pure motives, and had in an eminent degree the art of attaching to him and securing the confidence of those who served under him. His military fame was dimmed by his allowing himself to be taken up as a political candidate by a party engaged in the commission of the worst and least forgettable of all mistakes, that of discouraging a fight for national existence." (New York *Evening Post,* October 30, 1885.)

shortcomings for which he could not forgive himself. He was
the beau ideal of a grand seigneur, the greatest gentleman I
have ever known.

He was a devout Christian, and never had the slightest
hesitation or doubt in his faith. . . . He was a very handsome
man with regular features, grey eyes and bronzed skin. He wore
a moustache and short imperial after the manner of French
officers of his time. In youth his hair was dark brown, almost
black, his beard was sandy. His height was 5 feet 8½ inches
and his chest measurement 42 inches. His body was long and
his legs short so that on a horse he looked much taller than he
was. He had the reputation in his day of being the best rider
and fencer in the army. He was very strong, especially in the
hands. I have seen him tear a pack of cards in two, and still
have two quarter dollar pieces that he bent double for me with
the fingers of his right hand. His army nickname of "Little
Mac" was a term of affection and not of description, and
strangely enough his father had also been called "Little Mac"
before him.

He was a good but not brilliant public speaker, and yet such
was the charm of his personality that when he went before an
audience it invariably went wild with enthusiasm.

Like his forebears he was a Democrat. Daniel Webster was
his father's patient and intimate friend, in fact the celebrated
daguerreotype of "Webster in the beaver hat" was taken in
my grandfather's company. Nevertheless Dr. McClellan never
swerved from the political faith of his fathers, and handed that
faith on to his children.

All my father's early associations were with Democrats.
Jefferson Davis as Secretary of War sent him as an observer to
the Crimean War and later put him in charge of the expedition
that surveyed the route of what became afterwards the Northern
Pacific Railroad.[16] Stephen A. Douglas was his intimate friend
and promised to make him Secretary of War in the event of
Democratic success in 1860.

When the Civil War came he found it impossible to change
his politics as a matter of policy, as did so many Democrats of

[16] McClellan has the order of these two events reversed, for his father headed
the expedition to survey the proposed railroad route in 1852 and was sent to the
Crimea in 1855.

the period. The Democratic party meant so much to him that he lived and died a Democrat even though he disagreed with many of the policies of the party. He by no means believed in slavery and in fact by his order making slaves contraband of war anticipated the Emancipation Proclamation.[17]

It was deplorable that Lincoln and he could not get on, but it is difficult to think of two men more different. They had nothing whatever in common except love of country and a determination to save the Union at all cost. . . .

There have lately been a number of writers of fiction, mostly non-Americans like Buchan, Drinkwater and Emil Ludwig,[18] the latter posing as a historian, who have made of Lincoln the perfect hero and of my father the perfect villain. The story that Ludwig tells with infinite gusto as an historical fact, that my father kept Lincoln, who had called on him, waiting for an hour and then refused to see him, sending word that he was too tired, is, of course, apocryphal and originated according to my father in this way.

My father returning from an all-night inspection had gone to bed. The London *Times* correspondent "Bull Run" Russell [19] called to see him and was refused admission by the orderly . . . , [who] to make his refusal final said, "No one can see him. I've turned a dozen people away including the President." This was not true, of course, but Russell, a solemn and literal person, believed that he had got hold of a good "story" and promptly put on the wire the surprising news that the President had called on the commanding general and that the latter had refused to see him. . . .[20]

17 There is no record of an order by General McClellan making slaves contraband of war.

18 McClellan is referring to John Buchan, *Two Ordeals of Democracy* (Boston, 1925); John Drinkwater, *Abraham Lincoln: A Play* (London, 1919); and Emil Ludwig, *Lincoln* (Boston, 1930).

19 William Howard Russell was born in Ireland and worked most of his adult life for the London *Times*. He achieved world-wide fame for his work as a correspondent in the Crimean War, and he also reported the early stages of the Civil War. His account of the Union retreat at the first Battle of Bull Run (July 21, 1861) was a vivid and, on the whole, accurate account that has been reprinted in many anthologies and was, of course, responsible for his nickname in this country.

20 There is no evidence to support McClellan's version of this affair. The source used by Lincoln scholars for this incident is the diary of John Hay, whose entry for November 13, 1861, reads in part as follows: "The President, Governor

Next to his country and his wife my father loved the Army of the Potomac. He had created it out of nothing, had organized it into a marvelously efficient fighting machine, and with it had won victory after victory, despite the treasonable activities of those in Washington, who, rather than see a Democratic general win the war, had put every possible obstacle in his way. He inspired the love and adoration of his men as has no other general since Napoleon.

When he was finally relieved of his command there can be no question but that had he said the word the army would have followed him to Washington and supported him in taking over the government. That he refused to listen to the suggestion and preferred to go into retirement and obscurity rather than violate his oath as an officer show the quality of the man.

Seward, and I, went over to McClellan's house tonight. The servant at the door said the General was at the wedding of Col. Wheaton at General Buell's, and would soon return. We went in, and after we had waited about an hour, McC. came in and without paying any particular attention to the porter, who told him the President was waiting to see him, went up stairs, passing the door of the room where the President and Secretary of State were seated. They waited about half-an-hour, and sent once more a servant to tell the General they were there, and the answer coolly came that the General had gone to bed." (Tyler Dennett, ed., *Lincoln and the Civil War in the Diaries and Letters of John Hay* [New York, 1939], 34.)

Chapter II

Bright Newspapermen Leave the Work

AFTER MY father's funeral I returned to Princeton to receive my degree. . . . At commencement I took but little part in the festivities, being in deep mourning, although I was on the class day committee, as I had been on the sophomore reception committee two years before. The only friends who came to see me graduate were General [William H.] Sterling and Colonel [Edward H.] Wright, who had been my father's aides, the first when he was governor, the second when he was in command of the army.[1] Neither my mother nor sister came because of their mourning, and I was very grateful to the two old soldiers for their kindness. . . .

My mother, my sister, and I sailed for Antwerp on the S. S. *Westernland* at the end of June [1886]. I had wanted to go to work immediately on graduation, for my father's estate, thanks to a copper company in which he had invested,[2] had turned out by no means as well as we had expected, and I realized that the sooner I was able to earn my own living the better it would be.

My mother was so insistent that I should go with her to Europe and Mr. Prime urged it so strongly that I went, very much against my inclination.

I had gathered the impression that Mr. Prime intended to take me on the *Journal of Commerce,* which he still owned.[3]

[1] McClellan is mistaken, for Wright served as General McClellan's aide not only during the war, but also when the general was governor of New Jersey. Both Wright and Sterling were colonels in the New Jersey National Guard.

[2] This was the Grand Belt Copper Company, of which General McClellan was president when he died.

[3] McClellan is mistaken, for Prime had sold his interest in the *Journal of Commerce* in 1884.

He had repeatedly advised me to become a newspaperman, frequently told me of the delights of working on the *Journal of Commerce,* urged me to spend at least a year, or better, two, abroad in preparation, told me that he regarded me as his son, and convinced me, without saying so, that the *Journal of Commerce* was to be my life's work. Firmly persuaded that I should return from Europe with a job awaiting me I sailed happily away. . . .

By the beginning of 1888 [after approximately a year and one half in Europe], I reached the conclusion that I had played long enough and that it was high time for me to go to work. Leaving my mother and sister in Rome, on February 19, 1888, I sailed from Southampton on the Hamburg-American S. S. *Lahn,* and, after a very rough crossing, in due time reached New York. I had come home convinced that Mr. Prime had a place waiting for me on the *Journal of Commerce,* but I was to be bitterly disappointed.

When I went to see him, he . . . [was] very glad to see me. He asked me what I thought of doing, and I told him that I wanted to go into newspaper work as he had advised me two years before. He applauded my ambition and gave me a card of introduction to his managing editor, Mr. Stone,[4] with whom he said he had talked about me. I was delighted, for I thought my future settled and lost no time in going to the *Journal of Commerce* office treading on air as I went.

Mr. Stone received me courteously, said I was wise to take up newspaper work, but advised me first to obtain some good post in an insurance office, which would give me leisure in which to begin writing editorials. "Eventually," he added, "when and if your editorials are accepted you may be able to work your way on to the editorial staff of some newspaper." He then gave me a card of introduction to Mr. [Joseph W.] Harper, [Jr.,] the head of Harper Brothers, the publishers, and politely dismissed me. I called on Mr. Harper but I was no longer walking on air, in fact I had considerable difficulty in dragging one weary foot after another.

4 Prime and David Marvin Stone became associated with the *Journal of Commerce* in 1861 when it was suppressed because of charges of disloyal conduct and forbidden to resume publication until a new and responsible editor had been appointed. Prime and Stone purchased controlling interest in the paper, and Prime served as editor of the paper until 1869, when he was succeeded by Stone.

Mr. Harper was glad, very glad to see me, he had had a great admiration and affection for my father, he was so sorry that he was over-manned and did not have a single vacancy. "I know," he concluded after giving me about five minutes of his time, "that you would like to see our plant," and ringing for an office boy, he directed the latter to show me around and bowed me out. I made my escape as soon as I could, and walked the streets for hours trying to face the situation. . . . I really did not know where to turn or what to do. Work I had to have, for I could not continue living indefinitely on my mother and I did not know how to go about getting it.

When things looked their bluest, I met Tony [Antonio de] Navarro [a lawyer,] whom I had not seen since I had left him the year before in Paris. He asked me what I was doing, and I told him the position in which I found myself. He said that he was a small stockholder in the New York *Morning Journal*, then owned and managed by Albert Pulitzer, the brother of Joseph, to whom he gave me a letter. Mr. Pulitzer was very polite and gladdened my heart by saying that he would take me on at ten dollars a week and directed me to report to the managing editor, J. I. C. Clark. In those days the *Journal* was a four-page, one-cent paper, run on much the same lines as the present-time tabloids. Albert Pulitzer had founded it and had made it a great financial success. Mr. Pulitzer being thrifty, the expenses were kept at the lowest possible figure. The entire editorial page and the Sunday supplement were got out by five of us. Mr. Clark, who was a very brilliant newspaperman and earned every cent of his two hundred dollars a week, not only managed the paper and sent it to press every morning but also wrote the leading editorials and the weekly cable letter from "our special correspondent in London," which he compiled from a file of the London *Times* and *Truth*. Under Mr. Clark and his assistant was Mr. [Thomas] Chrystal, a rather dyspeptic but kindly gentleman, under whom I worked. He drew sixty dollars a week, wrote what editorials Clark turned over to him, compiled the funny column, by rewriting jokes clipped from other papers, and of which he had an enormous number, classified alphabetically under proper headings, as, for example, "Mother-in-law," "Piazza squeezers," "Good children," "Bad children," etc., and furnished such other features as were necessary to fill the editorial page. He also "got out" the rather thin Sunday supplement.

Then there was a mysterious man who did his work outside of the office and popped in and out from time to time leaving behind him "stories" of New York society, always of a scandalous and often of a libelous nature. He was known as "Captain John," was supposed to be an ex-British Army officer who had the entrée of the most exclusive circles. As he was a terrible cad, thoroughly disreputable in appearance and usually the worse for liquor, I imagine that his information was gathered below rather than above stairs.

Just before my arrival the "Art Department" had been in the hands of what Tom Chrystal used to call "a real-to-goodness artist." One day Mr. Pulitzer discovered that George, the office boy, possessed artistic ambitions, and Mr. Pulitzer believed in talent, whereupon the "real-to-goodness artist" was discharged. George's salary was raised from five dollars to twelve dollars a week and in addition to his duties as office boy was charged with the duties and responsibilities of art editor. George's proud soul revolted at the ignominy of combining art and office boying, but Mr. Pulitzer was obdurate and no other paper was willing to employ George as an artist at any price.

Last of all and the junior was I.

I reached the office every morning at nine and left at seven or eight with half an hour off for lunch. I wrote some of the editorials, understudied Tom Chrystal on his days off with the funny column, conducted "The Pulse of the People" column, which consisted of letters from readers asking questions, and the *Journal's* replies thereto (both questions and answers being written by me) wrote little stories called "Things Seen and Heard," and after Mr. Pulitzer found that I could read French wrote the weekly Paris letter for the Sunday edition "from our special correspondent" which I produced by rewriting scandalous stories obtained from two or three Boulevard newspapers to which we subscribed. I earned every penny of my ten dollars a week, for I have never in my life worked harder. . . .

After I had been on the *Journal* about six weeks, I met [E.] Ballard Smith one day in the street. Ballard Smith, who was news editor of the New York *World,* was a very brilliant newspaperman who had been a friend of my family. He stopped me and said: "I hear that you are working on the *Journal*. Why didn't you come to me for a job? Come to see me and I will see if I can place you." I called on him the next day and was promptly appointed second assistant city editor at a salary of twenty-five dollars a week.

When I told Albert Pulitzer that I was leaving the *Journal*, he said, "You are making a great mistake. If you will stay, I will raise your salary to twenty-five dollars. I might even make you my private secretary and perhaps take you to Karlsbad with me." Had I needed anything to strengthen my desire to go, it would have been that awful possibility.

I now found myself a real, though humble, newspaperman.

The city editor was a very disagreeable, ill-mannered little man named [Edwin A.] Grozier, who took an immediate dislike to me, as he resented Ballard Smith's having put me to work without consulting him. My immediate boss was Freddy Shipman, the assistant city editor, who was very kind and helped me to make good. My work consisted in understudying Shipman, in reading, distributing, and rewriting, when necessary, the Scripps-McRae local news "flimsy" [5] as it came in, in reading and distributing the city desk mail, and most important of all in reading the other New York newspapers for "beats." . . .

Much of my day was spent in receiving the hundreds of people who called on the city editor. The *World* posed as the friend of the plain people and the defender of the oppressed. Many simple souls believed that the *World* meant what it said and came to the office with their troubles. It was my duty to pass on to Shipman or Grozier those who were worth while or who had the makings of a "story," and to get rid of cranks and time-wasters as quickly and as courteously as possible. . . .

I enjoyed my work on the *World* and made many interesting friends. Of the proprietor, Joseph Pulitzer, we never saw anything. I never once set eyes on him while I was on the *World*. But we heard him frequently. When anything went wrong,

---

[5] McClellan is mistaken, for the Scripps-McRae Press Association was not organized until 1897. On the other hand, he may have meant either the Associated Press or the old United Press (which is not to be confused with the present press association of the same name).

and things seemed to go wrong with him very often, there would come from his office, which adjoined the "city room," a stream of profanity and filth that almost overwhelmed even that expert blasphemist, our managing editor, Colonel John A. Cockerill.

Much of the success of the *World* under Pulitzer was unquestionably due to John Cockerill, who had already helped his employer in booming the St. Louis *Post-Dispatch*. The colonel had killed in self-defense a certain Slayback who had drawn a "six gun" on him and in consequence was said by office gossip to have been greatly saddened and embittered.[6] I never, however, found him either sad or bitter but uniformly cheerful and with a dry humor which he emphasized with the most marvellous vocabulary of profanity I have ever known. His second in command, the news editor, was E. Ballard Smith, who was as brilliant as his chief and probably for that reason did not get on with him.

The foreign editor, Fritz Cunliffe-Owen, and I used the same cubicle; I during the day, he from seven P.M. until the paper went to press. As we met every evening, I saw a good deal of him. He was the son of the keeper of the Victoria and Albert Museum at South Kensington and was the godson and namesake of the Emperor Frederick. He had been in the British diplomatic service and claimed to have served in almost every capital of Europe and to have an intimate acquaintance with every living statesman which he proved by wearing innumerable decorations of somewhat vaguely described orders of chivalry.

Morrill Goddard was the Sunday editor and George Harvey, afterwards ambassador to London, had charge of the New Jersey edition. In the city room besides the city editor, Grozier, his assistant Freddy Shipman and myself, there were about a score of reporters on general work, young fellows of from twenty to forty years of age. There were some of them on space at five dollars a column, most of them on salaries from twenty-five to forty dollars a week, for Pulitzer rightly believed the latter method of compensation to be the cheapest. It was be-

---

6 In 1882, Cockerill wrote an editorial in the St. Louis *Post-Dispatch* criticizing the law firm of Broadhead, Slayback & Haeussler. On October 5, 1882, Slayback started a fist fight with Cockerill in an effort to force a retraction, and Cockerill shot and killed his assailant.

fore the days of signed stories, and all the stories, except a few in the Sunday supplement, were anonymous.

Of course with the great of the earth my relations were entirely official, for I was far too lowly a newspaper cub to associate with the editors. My friends were in the city room, and all were reporters. Our star reporter was Harold Raymond, the brilliant nephew of the equally brilliant Henry G. Raymond, who had been managing editor of the New York *Times* and died lieutenant governor of New York. Harold Raymond, during a good week, could earn as much as one hundred dollars, which was what the city editor received and far more than what was earned by any other *World* reporter. He was very versatile, with great power of description, and in these days would doubtless have been one of our leading news commentators. When I knew him he had already begun to show signs of what was then called "consumption," of which he died not long afterwards. . . .

Towards the end of the summer Ballard Smith was sent to London as *World* correspondent, and almost immediately thereafter, Grozier fired me from my job and put me on general work.

Late one afternoon Grozier, just before leaving the office, assigned me to interview Henry George. He warned me not to fail to produce the interview and suggested that my job depended on my making good. It was a mean trick to play on me, for he knew perfectly well that George never under any circumstances gave interviews, a fact . . . of which I was unaware. During my senior year at Princeton I had read everything that Henry George had written, and with the enthusiasm of youth had conceived a great admiration for the man and his work. . . .

When I sent up my card to him at his hotel, he received me and dashed my hopes by telling me that under no circumstances would he give an interview. He then proceeded to talk to me as to an intellectual equal and completely fascinated me. At the end of an hour he had skillfully pumped me dry and had learned everything about me that there was to learn, my hopes, my ambitions, why I had gone into newspaper work, and even the precariousness of my hold on my New York *World* job.

Finally he rose and said, "I make it a rule never to give interviews, but I am going to make an exception in your case. Come back at half past eleven this evening, and I will have a statement ready for you, on condition that you agree to print it without altering or adding a word." The statement proved to be a typical Georgian discussion of political conditions nearly a column long. I never saw him again, . . . [but] I shall always remember with sincere pleasure the courtesy, kindliness, and charm of that sincere and very near great man.

Grozier seemed disappointed with my success with Henry George and did not hesitate to tell the office that sooner or later he intended to "get me," and I think that he would have done so but for my good luck.

After covering a Chinese funeral and the state fair at Trenton I was ordered to report to Hugh Hastings, the *World*'s Albany correspondent and principal political writer. Hugh Hastings' uncle of the same name had been the owner of the *Commercial Advertiser* and brought his nephew up with the idea that he was to inherit it, only later to disinherit him. The younger Hastings went on the *World* as a political reporter, and very soon became one of the best of Albany correspondents. A pleasant manner, a marvellous memory, especially for names and faces, and absolute trustworthiness and honesty, made him innumerable friends among politicians, and gave him a knowledge and grasp of politics second to that of none in his time.

Hastings had taken a fancy to me and had applied for me as his assistant. The presidential campaign of 1888 was under way, and very soon after I had joined Hastings he was sent west to look over the ground, and I found myself in charge of Democratic politics in New York for the *World* with just ten days' training. The *Sun* man covering politics was Eddy Riggs, the *Herald* man was Mike Blake, afterwards a Municipal Court judge, and the *Times* man was Henry Oviatt. The *Tribune* man was required by his office to work alone. We four morning-paper men worked together in an offensive and defensive alliance against the evening papers, always trying to hold back the news until after the evening papers had gone to press. We divided up the routine, my assignment being Democratic national headquarters. The national secretary was a pleasant man named [William] McClelland from . . . Wisconsin. He claimed a distant relationship with my father and was very kind to me. The national chairman was Calvin S. Brice, afterwards United States senator from Ohio, who was also then and afterwards my friend. Both Brice and McClelland would see me and give me news when they would not see the others. Hence, my assignment to "cover" them.

Cleveland and [Allen G.] Thurman were the Democratic candidates for President and Vice-President, [Benjamin] Harrison and [Levi P.] Morton the Republican. David B. Hill was running for re-election as governor.

Besides our routine and unofficial assignments, we morning-paper men always made the rounds of the various headquarters, together in the late afternoon and evening and together interviewed any prominent politician who might be in New York. . . .

I was talking one day with McClelland, the secretary of the Democratic National Committee, when he said to me, "I think that Mr. Brice has a good story that he may give you if you ask him." I promptly went to Brice who gave me a copy of a letter marked "Confidential," from Colonel [William W.] Dudley, Republican national committeeman from Indiana, urging his correspondent, evidently a county chairman, to divide the Republican workers into "blocks of five" for purposes of control and corruption, the idea being that one of the five was to be bought and held responsible for the other four. The letter, known to fame as The Blocks of Five Letter, made a tremendous sensation, and poor Colonel Dudley was made the scapegoat although he had undoubtedly written the letter or letters under the direction of superior authority.[7]

7 Dudley was the Republican party treasurer and one of the most indiscreet men in American politics. He was not, however, punished for either his indiscretion or corruption, for the case growing out of the Blocks of Five letter was tried before a Republican judge and dismissed on a technicality. The famous letter, which was written under the Republican National Committee letterhead and addressed to Republican campaign workers in Indiana, reads in part as follows: "I hope you have kept copies of the lists [of floating voters]. . . . Such information is very valuable and . . . has enabled me to demonstrate to friends . . . that with proper assistance Indiana is surely Republican for Governor and President, and has resulted as I hoped it would in securing for Indiana the aid necessary. Your committee will certainly receive . . . the assistance necessary to hold floaters and doubtful voters, and gain enough of the other side to give Harrison and Morton 10,000 plurality. . . . Divide the floaters into blocks of five and put a trusted man with the necessary funds in charge of these five and make

The Democratic campaign was closed in New York by Allen G. Thurman, candidate for Vice-President, formerly senator from Ohio. Mr. Thurman was in the habit of using a large red bandanna handkerchief, which became a sort of party emblem during the campaign. When nominated, he was seventy-five years old and not overactive for his age. When the time came to take Mr. Thurman to Madison Square Garden, it was found that he had been dining so well that he was incapable of uttering a coherent sentence, much less of making a speech. Strangely enough his mind was fairly clear. Mr. Brice wanted him to go to bed and have the public informed that he had been taken suddenly ill, but the old gentleman insisted on going to the Garden, which was directly across Madison Square from the Hoffman House where he was stopping. Accordingly, escorted by Mr. Brice and two or three discreet newspapermen, myself included, he went to the meeting. On arriving on the platform, the chairman of the meeting announced that Mr. Thurman, because of a bad cold, had lost his voice and had wrenched his knee on the train, whereupon he was assisted to his feet and leaning against the chairman's table solemnly drew out his red bandanna which he waved for upwards of five minutes amid the delirious cheers of the multitude, after which he was assisted to his hotel and bed. . . .

When election day came I cast my first vote for Hill. In those days there were separate ballots for the various candidates and separate boxes for the various offices to be filled. It was, therefore, a simple matter to drop the red ballot carrying the name of David B. Hill into the box marked governor, before voting for anyone else.

It was the first New York election I had ever seen, and I went to perhaps a dozen polling places to satisfy my curiosity and to write a "story" for the *World*. In the so-called "silk stocking" districts the voting was generally orderly and apparently fair. In the slum districts on the West and East Sides of town the voting was by no means orderly and obviously far from fair.

Every little while the election district captain, either Democrat or Republican, would usher into the polling place a procession of voters, sometimes two or three, sometimes a dozen or

them responsible that none get away and that all vote our ticket." (New York *World*, November 1, 1888.)

more, walking in single file and holding their left hands raised above their heads, the hands grasping a bunch of ballots which were voted in the order of their arrangement. These were voters who had been bought but not yet paid. They were rounded up at some distance from the polls, handed their ballots, which in those days were printed by and at the expense of the political parties, and holding them aloft to prevent a possibility of substitution, were convoyed to the polls where they were watched in the process of voting. As the ballots were always printed on highly colored paper, differing for the parties and candidates, it was difficult for a voter to "double-cross" his district captain. When the purchased voter had satisfied his captain, he returned to district headquarters where he received his pay. This open and quite shameless corruption went on unchecked until the adoption of the Australian ballot.

When the votes were counted Cleveland had lost and Harrison had won. Cleveland had failed to carry New York, and Hill had been re-elected. There were cries of fraud, and it was charged that Hill had sold out Cleveland. Years later I asked Hill what truth there was in the charge and he replied, "No, I never sold out Cleveland. When our fellows came to me and asked, 'What do you want us to do?' I answered, 'Don't kill yourselves working for Cleveland.' That's all there was to the charge." This same policy of not killing themselves for Cleveland kept the Democratic vote down in New York, and undoubtedly accounted for the state going for Harrison. . . .

Hugh Hastings had saved me for the moment but as soon as [the] election was over I realized that Grozier still was trying to "get" me and sooner or later would do so. I made up my mind that the sooner I found another job the better it would be for me. Mrs. John G. Heckscher, my future mother-in-law, who was a friend of James Gordon Bennett, asked the latter to give me a trial. Accordingly I called on the great man who having looked me over put me in charge of the *Herald*'s railroad news at thirty dollars a week.

The old *Herald* was probably in many respects the most extraordinary newspaper that ever existed. It had been created by the elder James Gordon Bennett, and when inherited by his son was undoubtedly the most profitable property of its kind in the United States, with the largest circulation. With the best will in the world the younger Bennett failed to destroy it, and when after his death it was absorbed by the *Tribune* it was still profitable.

Bennett or, as he liked to be called, "The Commodore" (he had been commodore of the New York Yacht Club) edited the *Herald* from Paris. He refused to have a managing editor on the theory that he held that office himself. He had a news editor and a city editor, the latter being really in charge of the paper. He constantly assured his staff of the truth of his father's statement that "the cheapest commercial commodity is brains" and lived up to his theory. He paid low salaries and gave presents from time to time to those who pleased him. He believed that anyone was good enough to do any work on a newspaper.

When I was on the *Herald* he sent a cable ordering the news editor and the latter's secretary to exchange places. One day he read . . . an account [by an Englishman] of a prize fight that pleased him. He sent for the author, hired him to go to New York and report to the news editor for instructions. The prize-fight expert on reporting for duty was told that he was to be music critic. As he knew nothing of music and was very deaf he found his assignment rather difficult. However, being a clever and plucky fellow he threw himself on the mercy of the other music critics, who with great good nature, helped him out with so much success that shortly afterwards the commodore made him his private secretary.

While I was on the *World,* a pleasant and good-looking young Englishman named Byron Stevenson joined the city staff, having lately been fired by the commodore from the management of the Paris *Herald.* The story of his firing was very characteristic of the *Herald* office. One night Stevenson was busily engaged in sending the paper to press. He was in the clothes he had worn all day and in his shirt sleeves. About midnight in dropped the commodore, and on seeing Stevenson walked up to him in great indignation and said, "Mr. Stevenson, I expect my employees to be gentlemen, to behave like gentlemen, and to be dressed like gentlemen. If I ever again find you here after six o'clock in the evening in your shirt sleeves or dressed otherwise than in evening clothes, I shall at once discharge you." The next night and the next Stevenson donned his dress coat (it was before the days of dinner jackets) and white tie and did his best to keep clean while handling forms and printer's ink. On the third night the commodore appeared. When he saw Stevenson, he almost exploded with wrath. "Mr. Stevenson," he said, "do I pay you a salary to dress like a popinjay, to make my paper a joke by spending your time at cabarets and theatres, and then when it pleases you coming in here and graciously sending the paper to press? You are discharged." The only satisfaction that Stevenson derived from his explanation was to be called "an impudent prevaricator."

Harry Melzer, the music critic, told me that the commodore had ordered him by cable to leave the music desk and to go at once to St. Petersburg where he would find money awaiting him, upon the receipt of which he was to make a tour of Russia writing his impressions of any revolutionary sentiment he might find. Surely a difficult assignment for a musician who had never been in Russia and spoke no word of the language. On reaching St. Petersburg Melzer who was "broke" called on the commodore's agent who informed him that he had no money for him but only a telegram. Melzer tore open the envelope and read, "You are hereby discharged." Imagine his sensations, penniless in Russia, without knowledge of Russian or a single acquaintance in the city. As he was a British subject, he went to the British Consulate and finally persuaded the consul general to ship him on a freighter to London. He never found out why the commodore had ordered him to Russia, nor why he had been discharged.

Bennett's hotel on the Champs Elysées had two doors each with a different number. Letters for his personal reading went to one number, all other mail to the other number. During my second term as mayor the commodore reached the conclusion that I was, as he expressed it, "on the level" and supported me vigorously. He sent his secretary, the deaf Englishman, who had been music critic, to see me with the message that if I ever wanted to reach him personally and quickly I might do so by addressing him at his personal number. It was a very friendly gesture, but I never had occasion to take advantage of it.

Another Englishman arrived one day at the *Herald* office in New York under the impression that he was to review books, only to find that he was to be news editor. Strangely enough he made good.

Maurice M. Minton was made city editor without previous experience, presumably because his father had been the brilliant financial editor of the paper and a friend of the commodore. Just as the paper was going to press one night there arrived a telegram to the effect that the Jesuits had murdered President Diaz of Mexico and that civil war was raging south of the Rio Grande. Without waiting to check up on the story Minton spread it on the front page. The next day, when the story proved to be a fake, the commodore relieved Minton from the city editorship, and ordered him to occupy a room on the top floor, there "to think up original ideas" at the same salary, one hundred dollars a week. Minton refused to move upstairs and resigned and was succeeded by William C. Rieck, who had been Bennett's private secretary and was a first-rate all-round newspaperman.

My work was not very hard. I reported at the office about noon, got what flimsy there was, and received orders from the news editor, who was my chief. I then went downtown where all the newspapermen covering railroads met in a soda water shop in the basement at the corner of Wall and Nassau streets. If there were people to be interviewed, we divided up the work. Otherwise, we called at a certain number of brokers' offices and at the railroad executive offices and picked up what items of news there might be. When the market closed, I returned to the *Herald* office and wrote my "stuff." I shared a room with Tom Hamilton, the financial editor, the yachting editor, the sporting editor, and his assistant. . . .

One of the hardest things I had to do was to carry out an order of the commodore that for a month every member of the staff should write his own headlines which in each case should be a verse or couplet from a poem appropriate to the subject of the story. I was at my wit's end to find a poem dealing with railways, when Eddy Riggs told me that Saxe [8] had written something beginning "Bless me, this is pleasant riding on the rail." I rushed back to the office, took Saxe's poems from the library, found the poem describing the joys of railway travel and for a month used it, couplet by couplet, as headlines for my daily railway column. Fortunately the poem lasted out the

8 John G. Saxe was the owner and editor of the Burlington, Vermont, *Sentinel* until his death in 1887. He was the author of several volumes of humorous verse.

month. Had it not, I don't know what I should have done for material.

One of the rules of the *Herald* was that no man should leave until after the paper had gone to press. So that, although my work was over by seven o'clock, I had to cool my heels in the office until two A.M.

The drama critic used very often to give me one of the less important first nights. I always received my instructions from him in advance as to what my criticism should be, as for example, "The author is a friend of the commodore so boost the show for all you are worth" or "The commodore had a row with the manager, so soak hell out of the play." This system simplified matters very much. It was possible to write the criticism before seeing the play, and thus enjoy it without the thought of writing it up afterwards. I wonder if dramatic criticisms are still written in this way. . . .

The editorial page was a dreary joke. The editorial writers did not dare to take a positive position on any subject without direct orders from the commodore who had a most disheartening habit of cabling editorials marked "must," which usually arrived just in time to catch the last edition of the paper. His most remarkable effort was an editorial on the death of the Comte de Paris, the Orleanist and Bourbon pretender to the throne of France, whom he called the head of the house of Bonaparte "closely resembling his great uncle Napoleon." . . .

My first experience with Mr. J. P. Morgan . . . [occurred] when I was working on the New York *Herald*. My boss, the news editor, was a harmless and inexperienced man named [George H.] Nicholas. One morning before going down to Wall Street, he sent for me, and said, "I want you to get a nice, bright, chatty interview with J. P. Morgan on financial conditions in general. Let it run for about a column or a column and a half." I objected that Mr. Morgan never gave interviews, to which Nicholas replied, "That's nonsense, of course he will give an interview to the *Herald*." Taking my courage in both hands, I entered the Morgan building and for some reason or other made my way unopposed to Mr. Morgan's office. He was sitting at his desk facing the open door, and there was no one else in the room. As I stood in the doorway with my hat in my hand, he looked up and saw me. "Well, what do you want?" he

asked. "I am a reporter from the *Herald*," I answered, whereupon he shouted, "Get the hell out of here, and do it damned
quick," and I "got," as the office boys, clerks and doormen came
rushing in at the sound of their master's voice. And that was
that.

I soon realized that there was no future for me in newspaper
work. It is a curious fact that an old newspaperman is as rare
as, according to Charles Dickens, are old post boys. There are
always a few among the higher-ups, but among the hard-working subordinates they are practically non-existent. I think the
explanation is that bright newspapermen leave the work at
the first opportunity, [and] the others are sooner or later merci-
lessly scrapped. . . . [It was because of these considerations that
I was happy to be able to shift from reporting to politics in
1889.]

[My last year in newspaper work was a memorable one for
another reason, for] on October 30, 1889, Georgiana Louise
Heckscher and I were married by Bishop Henry C. Potter, of
New York, at the Chapel of All Saints at Newport, Rhode
Island.[9] James A. Harriman, who had been my schoolmate and
roommate at college, was my best man, and my sister-in-law
and my sister were bridesmaids. Upon our return to New York
we rented a small apartment at 23 West Eleventh Street which
was so new and damp that I constantly had asthma, and it became evident that I could not stay there. Our landlord took
the apartment off our hands, and we moved to a little house
we rented for $1,000 a year at 215 East Seventeenth Street.

----

[9] McClellan's wedding was attended by representatives of some of the wealthi-
est families in the United States, and a reporter in 1905 recalled the wedding as
"one of the social events of that season." (New York *Herald*, October 1, 1905).
Mrs. McClellan, who died in 1952, remained well in the background throughout
her husband's public career. The New York *Evening Telegram* (December 20,
1895) described her as "very attractive . . . with quiet manners and a bright face,"
while the Washington *Post* (March 15, 1896) referred to her as "a very pretty,
trim little figure." The McClellans had no children.

Chapter III

SACRIFICES TO GET ON

[MY POLITICAL career began in 1889 with an appointment to the board administering the Brooklyn Bridge.] When the New York and Brooklyn Bridge was built, it was placed in the hands of an unsalaried board of trustees, ten from New York and ten from Brooklyn, the president being paid $10,000 a year. The latter office had become the almost private property of ex-Mayor James Howell of Brooklyn. The other members of the board were inconspicuous and respectable gentlemen whom the two city bosses, Croker [1] and McLaughlin,[2] wanted to honor as cheaply as possible. . . . While Brooklyn had the president and secretary and all the engineering and administrative positions, New York had no patronage whatever. President Howell finally agreed to the creation of the office of treasurer at the salary of $4,000, the job to go to New York. . . . [As soon as I learned of the existence of this position,] I began to pull wires for the appointment. Mr. Heckscher [3] enlisted the support of nearly

[1] Richard Croker was the leader of Tammany Hall from 1886 to 1901, although he voluntarily relinquished the leadership from 1894 to 1897. He entered the machine under Tweed and served as "Honest John" Kelly's first lieutenant. He gave McClellan his start in politics, and in return McClellan always gave Croker his loyalty. Croker was a typical Tammany boss, who made a fortune out of corrupt practices and was once accused, but not convicted, of murder. McClellan, however, always insisted that Croker was a superior machine leader.

[2] Hugh McLaughlin bossed Brooklyn's Democrats from the mid-sixties until 1903, when he was succeeded by Patrick McCarren. The first machine leader to be called "boss," he successfully opposed all Tammany efforts to invade his domain and was a man of considerable influence in the state and national councils of his party.

[3] John Gerard Heckscher, McClellan's father-in-law, served in the Union Army and after the Civil War "engaged in business pursuits." The New York *Evening Telegram* (May 29, 1900) referred to him as "one of the best known

every member of the Union Club who had the slightest political influence, and I appealed to every friend of my father's whom I could reach and to every political and financial friend or acquaintance whom I had made as a newspaperman. There were two candidates . . . , but my backing was so strong and my father's name so potent that I won easily. . . .

On my appointment as treasurer of the Brooklyn Bridge, I . . . joined the Tammany organization in the Eleventh Assembly District in which I then lived. . . . The Eleventh Assembly District was then known as "the silk stocking district" because of the number of clubs, millionaires, and generally smart people within its boundaries, and was overwhelmingly Republican. . . . Our leader was John J. Scannell, a man of about fifty who had made a fortune as the keeper of a gambling hall. Ten years previously he had murdered,[4] in cold blood in a barroom, another gambler who had the night before murdered Scannell's brother. Scannell pleaded emotional insanity, was acquitted, sent to Bloomingdale Asylum, whence a fortnight later he was discharged cured. He always claimed that he had killed his victim as "the avenger of me brother's murder" and insisted that the people of New York owed him a "vindication" in the form of an election to some office, preferably the House of Representatives. Richard Croker, who had been his boyhood friend, stood loyally behind Scannell to the extent of making him district leader.[5]

Scannell's method of leading the district was peculiar. He never tried to increase the Democratic vote and never made the slightest effort to carry the district. About half the members of his general committee were decent young fellows who being Democrats and living in the district had nowhere else to go if they were interested in politics, and gamblers and thugs who

---

and most popular of old New Yorkers," and added that he was a member of "one of the most exclusive families of the city." In 1907, Heckscher wrote that his life "for years past [had been] chiefly devoted to gentlemanly sport." (*Who's Who in New York* . . . [New York, 1907], III, 651.)

4 Actually, the murder had occurred in 1874.

5 The friendship between Croker and Scannell was not only a product of their youth, but was also the result of an experience which they shared and which is denied to most men. In 1874, they were at the same time inmates of the Tombs prison waiting for their respective trials as alleged murderers. Croker was charged with murdering a member of a rival political gang in a street fight, and, like Scannell, he escaped conviction.

came from what the notorious police Captain Alec Williams called "the tenderloin." [6] The latter class paid cheerfully for such protection as Scannell could give them, through his influence as district leader, while we, the aspiring youths, were separated from what money we could afford to give, encouraged by the hope of receiving, sooner or later, a nomination for either alderman or assemblyman, with no possibility of election, but with the certainty of considerable amusement.

Our leader's step-brother George, who held a $5,000 sinecure in the surrogate's office, acted as collector for his brother. We used to have monthly meetings of the general committee of the district, when after we had paid our dues, John Scannell would recite Shakespeare to us by the hour. He was an ignorant thug and yet he had committed to memory the whole of *Hamlet,* most of *Romeo and Juliet, Macbeth,* and parts of a dozen other plays.

During the summer of 1889 Croker and Scannell went to Europe. Before their return George Scannell announced that it would be very agreeable to "our honored leader" if the general committee of the district were to welcome him with a brass band at Quarantine, and that the assessment for the reception would be twenty-five dollars for each member of the committee. After we had paid up the reception was called off. At the next meeting of the committee Albert Gallup, . . . park commissioner [from 1889 to 1892] and at that time a new member, moved that as there had been no reception the assessment be returned. Whereupon George Scannell informed him that the invariable custom under such circumstances was that any balance remaining after such a reception was given to "our honored leader" as a slight mark of esteem, that as there had been no reception, the entire fund was balance and as such had already been given to brother John. Scannell must have made a large income from his leadership, what with membership dues, campaign contributions, and protection money. Why Croker tolerated him was always a mystery.

[6] "It was Captain [Alexander] Williams who gave the Tenderloin District its famous name. This district extended from Fourteenth Street to Forty-second Street and from Fourth Avenue to Seventh Avenue. When Captain Williams was transferred from a precinct far uptown to the precinct which took in this district, he remarked to his friends that he was leaving the rump to feed on the tenderloin." (M. R. Werner, *Tammany Hall* [New York, 1928], 361.)

He had at Saratoga a large house which he called the Villa Ophelia in memory of his dead wife, and also, he told me, in honor of his favorite character in Shakespeare. One room was a sort of chamber of horrors, for in it hung, what he called "them old masters," a collection of grisly and awful pictures that he had bought while abroad. Here in the villa, after his return from Europe, he installed a French lady of uncertain origin, but of obvious profession, who posed as a Polish countess, and who, with a gigolo whom she called her son, lived at the expense of the Eleventh Assembly District for nearly a year.

In 1890, Scannell concluded that the time had arrived for his vindication and demanded from Croker the nomination for Congress in the Twelfth District which included a part of the Eleventh Assembly District. Croker's friendship, however, had its limits, and he refused to imperil the entire ticket to gratify Scannell. On Scannell's insistence he finally consented to allow the delegation from the Eleventh to cast its vote for Scannell, the other delegates to vote for Bourke Cockran.[7] I was not a delegate but went to district headquarters before the convention, for the entire general committee was summoned. Scannell told us that he had been refused his vindication and, thereupon, acted out for us the murder of his brother's murderer. It was one of the most ghastly performances I have ever seen.

As soon as we moved into the Eleventh Street apartment, I transferred from Scannell's leadership to that of Barney Martin,[8] and when we moved to Seventeenth Street, I again transferred to the Twelfth Assembly District, whose leader was Edward J. Hagan.[9] I was extremely glad to leave the Eleventh District and to see the last of Scannell as leader. Take him all in all, I think that he was the toughest district leader whom I have ever known and one of the toughest men.

[7] (William) Bourke Cockran, Tammany Hall's most illustrious orator, served several terms (1887-89, 1891-95, 1904-09, 1921-23) in Congress, but his reputation as a public figure rested in large part on his skill and persistence as a talker.

[8] Bernard F. Martin was not much of an improvement over Scannell. He was indicted for accepting bribes while serving as a deputy sheriff and only escaped conviction when the indictment was dismissed on a technicality. See *Testimony Taken before the Senate Committee on Cities . . . 1890* (Albany, 1890), I, 282-287.

[9] Hagan was a relatively superior type of Tammany politician. Although in politics "for a living," he made a better than average record in the state Senate and Assembly. See New York *World*, February 21, 1893.

On July 4th, 1890, I made my "first appearance on any stage," when I read the Declaration of Independence at the annual celebration at Tammany Hall. Judge [A. B.] Tappen, the grand sachem, who was a very kindly old man, asked me if I did not want to try the acoustics of the hall, which was a polite way of giving me an opportunity of rehearsing. I accepted his offer and was locked up inside the hall by the . . . janitor, whereupon I read the Declaration over and over again until I had nearly committed it to memory.

Needless to say, I was very nervous when I faced my first audience but got through my talk, all things considered, fairly well. The next day the newspapers were very kind. The *Times* said that I read well,[10] the *Herald,* that I was introduced "amidst applause and read the grand old document with great impressiveness," and the *Star,* "Colonel [11] George B. McClellan was greeted with a storm of applause as he took the stand to read the Declaration of Independence, which service he performed gracefully and earnestly and with a round full voice which penetrated to the furthest limits of the big hall."

The following autumn I made my first political speech. There was a mass meeting at Tammany Hall on October 23, 1890, and I had gone to hear Senator [Charles J.] Faulkner of West Virginia and Bill [William McK.] Springer of Illinois and of the House of Representatives. Croker saw me in the lobby and invited me to the platform where I took a seat behind him. During Faulkner's speech Croker turned to me and said, "You're next." "Next to what?" I asked in all innocence. "You speak next," he replied. "But," I said, "I have never made a speech in my life." "It doesn't matter," he concluded, "you speak next."

When Faulkner finished, I got up and faced my audience. To this day I have no idea what I said, for I have never suffered such acute agony in my life. All that I remember is facing a thick fog in which I was utterly unable to distinguish any face in front of me. As I sat down Springer closed his watch, and

10 "Mr. Tappen arose . . . under his mighty silk hat and introduced Col. George B. McClellan, who read the Declaration of Independence. The Declaration is always read at Tammany's Fourth of July celebration. It was well read yesterday. To be sure, there were people in the audience who had never heard it before. . . ." (New York *Times,* July 5, 1890.)

11 McClellan was a colonel on the staff of the governor of New York.

said to me, "You spoke 4-3/4 minutes." The crowd cheered enthusiastically for the son of "Little Mac," and I was most thankful to have it over. Again the newspapers were kind, the *Journal* said, "The next speaker was Colonel George B. Mc-Clellan, Little Mac's son, and at that name Tammany let itself loose. The Colonel confined himself to the municipal campaign. He claimed that there was only one Democratic ticket in the field, 'and we are going to bury its opponents with their faces down,' said the Colonel concluding, 'so that every time they scratch they'll get nearer home.' "

The next week I asked a speaking assignment of the state committee, and I was sent to South Mount Vernon in Westchester County. I wrote my speech, committed it to memory, and rehearsed it carefully, with my wife for an audience, and we were very much pleased with it. On the day of the meeting I journeyed to South Mount Vernon, which proved to be a village in the back of beyond of Woodlawn Cemetery. The meeting was over the fire engine house and the crowd numbered perhaps a hundred. I made my speech with considerable self-satisfaction. The local chairman escorted me to the door and as he bade me good night patted me on the shoulder and said, "Don't feel too badly about it, son, for I know you can do better than you done tonight." I made no further speeches during the campaign of 1890. . . .

[My political education was also furthered during this period through my contacts with Governor David B. Hill,[12] who in 1889] made me an aide on his staff with the rank of colonel. . . .[13] Hill always took one or two of his aides with him when he travelled officially. I was thrown a great deal with him, and he became my first and, I am afraid, my last political hero.

Take him all in all, he was in many ways the strangest man I have ever known. He had absolutely no vices, had never smoked, gambled or touched alcohol. . . . Hill was a thinking machine with neither likes nor dislikes that he could not easily overcome when necessary. He was absolutely cold-blooded and would sacrifice a supporter or favor an opponent with equal

12 Hill was a Democratic politician, who served as state legislator, mayor of Elmira, lieutenant governor during the governorship of Grover Cleveland (1883-1884), governor (1885-1891), and United States senator (1892-1897).

13 In 1905, McClellan stated that his appointment by Hill was his "first step toward a public career." (New York *Herald*, October 1, 1905.)

facility if it was to his interest to do so. He was unscrupulous
in politics and absolutely money honest. Money meant nothing
to him, except as a lubricant to the political machine. He had
devoted supporters, but no real friends. The only human being
I ever heard him speak of with affection was his mother. He
often regretted that she did not live to see him rise, for as he
said: "It would have greatly pleased her." . . .

He was not a college man but was an omnivorous reader in
certain lines. In American history he was one of the best
informed men I have ever met, as he was in political science.
Of Europe he knew little and cared less; he had never left the
United States and had no interest outside our country. He
knew the writings of Jefferson almost by heart and cared less
than nothing for fiction. His only recreations were the theatre
and baseball. He was about 5 feet 10 inches high, almost completely bald. He wore a moustache and short side whiskers
which served partially to conceal the scar of a razor wound given
him by a murderer whom he had convicted when an assistant
district attorney of Chemung County.

He always dressed in black, and wore a frock coat, open waistcoat, narrow black tie, and turndown collar. He always had
three frock coats, the best he wore on state occasions, the second
best he wore ordinarily, and the third best he used as a dressing
gown, with carpet slippers, in his home. When the third best
coat grew threadbare it disappeared, the second took its place,
and a new one was bought to head the list. When not wearing
a rather battered top hat, which he usually did out of doors,
he wore a funny little grey soft hat that could be rolled up and
put in his pocket. . . .

He believed that everyone intending to enter politics should
be admitted to the bar, and said to me: "As you hope to go
into politics, take my advice and be admitted. If you hold
office, you will probably not be able to practice or keep up
with decisions. You may not be able to advise yourself on
questions of law that come before you, but being grounded
in the principles of law, you will know when and if your legal
adviser is advising you correctly." I took his advice . . .[and
after studying at Columbia and the New York Law School and
clerking in a law office, I was admitted to the bar in 1892.]

[My first opportunity to judge Hill's effectiveness as a

politician was in 1891 at the Democratic state convention at Saratoga.] The convention of 1891 was so well in hand that it functioned like clockwork. The program was all arranged in advance, the candidates to be nominated chosen before, as well as the officers of the convention and those who were to make the nominating and seconding speeches. Hill used to say that it was only fair that the candidate for governor should be given sufficient time to raise the money with which to pay his assessment for the nomination. The convention always lasted for at least two days in order to give the hotel, restaurant, and bar-keepers of the favored city an opportunity to make a sufficient profit to put them in a good humor so as to count upon their financial help for the campaign.

The place of holding national conventions goes frankly to the highest bidder, a citizens' committee receiving the money from local businessmen, who try to get back their contributions during the days that the convention lasts. Saratoga is an ideal convention town. There is ample hotel accommodation, [and] the hotels are near together so that the delegates can be "rounded up" easily. Besides racing, there used to be quite open gambling, plenty to drink, and many ways of killing the great amount of time that the ordinary delegate has upon his hands.

The Tammany delegation, with their friends and admirers, came up on special trains the night before the meeting of the convention, most of the "boys" wearing the silk hat (called colloquially "plug" or "high one") so dear to the heart of the New York politician of those days. The hotel lobbies were crowded until all hours, while delegates tried to find out what the ticket was going to be. . . .

Although the convention was called for ten o'clock, it did not meet until nearly noon. We sat around listening to a brass band and killing time as we could. About eleven-thirty arrived Charlie de Freest, secretary of the state committee and perpetual secretary of state conventions. When the Democrats had the Assembly, de Freest was always elected clerk; when the Republicans had the Assembly, de Freest retired to his farm.

At a little before noon the delegates at the back of the hall began to cheer, down the middle aisle came Governor Hill in his frock coat and top hat, accompanied by George Raines,[14] of Rochester, Edward Murphy, mayor of Troy and chairman of the state committee and Judge Muller,[15] one of Hill's closest henchmen. Murphy mounted the platform, and called the convention to order, after which he stated that he had been instructed by the state committee to nominate George Raines as temporary chairman and Charles R. de Freest as temporary secretary, whereupon Raines was escorted to the chair and made his "keynote speech." . . .

My first convention nominated Roswell P. Flower, a New York banker, who always referred to himself as "a plain bithnethman," for he lisped painfully. He was a worthy soul who delighted the politicians by a willingness to pay top prices for political recognition.[16] He served one term inconspicuously in the House of Representatives [17] after having defeated W. W. Astor in what was said to have been the most expensive election ever fought in New York City. On Flower's election as governor he dropped me from his staff and closed my career as a toy soldier. . . .

[Although I learned a great deal about practical politics from my various experiences with the city and state Democratic organizations, I found] life on the Brooklyn Bridge [Board] . . . difficult and very unpleasant, for everyone's hand was against the New Yorker who had been forced into the Brooklyn family party. . . . [I was, therefore, delighted when Croker in 1892 called me to Tammany Hall and] said: . . . "We are going to nominate Tom Gilroy [18] (then commissioner of public works) for mayor, Theodore Myers [19] for comptroller, and you for

14 Raines was an upstate Democratic politician who with his brother John controlled politics in Monroe County. George was the county's leading Democrat and John its leading Republican.

15 William J. Muller was a Chemung County Democratic politician and Hill's law partner.

16 The New York *World* (September 17, 1891) wrote that "Flower had a barrel and would take out the bung."

17 Actually, Flower served more than one term in Congress. He defeated William Waldorf Astor in 1881, and was re-elected in 1888 and 1890.

18 Thomas F. Gilroy, a Tammany politician, served as county clerk (1885-88), under-sheriff (1888), commissioner of public works (1889-92), and mayor (1893-94).

19 Myers, a New York City banker, was city comptroller for two terms (1888-92). Although first elected on the Democratic ticket, he was so successful in

president of the Board of Aldermen. Your assessment will be $300. I've put it low because I know you haven't much money, and the salary of the president of the Board of Aldermen is only $3,000, $1,000 less than you are getting now." The news came to me as an absolute surprise and a very welcome one. . . . Needless to say, my wife was delighted. The reduction of $1,000 in our income was a rather serious matter, but both of us have always been good political gamblers and willing to make sacrifices to get on.

The city convention was duly held, and the Croker program went through without a hitch. . . .[20] Being my first campaign for elective office, I threw myself into it with all the enthusiasm of my twenty-seven years, speaking several times a night and personally canvassing my own assembly district. . . . We candidates, under Gilroy's influence, decided to make as cheap a campaign as possible, relying on the national ticket and the Democratic drift to carry us through. We agreed to issue no lithographs or circulars and to confine ourselves to speaking for the national ticket. . . .

Long before election day it became evident that Cleveland, as well as the entire local ticket, would be elected. When the ballots were counted, it was found that I had run well ahead of all other candidates in New York City, including Cleveland, with a plurality of 78,210, the largest plurality ever given up to that time, to any candidate on any ticket. My father's name, and I suppose my youth, appealed to the voters.

The possession of a distinquished name is a tremendous advantage at the beginning of a political career. When the career has been well started it becomes a handicap. At first "the son of his father" is pushed by the leaders and accepted by the voters for his father's sake. When, however, "the son of his father" is able to stand on his own feet and seeks higher office, there is a tendency to attack him on the ground that he is exploiting his father's name. We forget so quickly that it is

---

lowering the city's taxes that he was elected for a second term on both the Democratic and Republican tickets.

20 Following McClellan's nomination for the presidency of the Board of Aldermen, the New York *Times* (October 20, 1892) wrote: "He is a young man of high character, with many points of resemblance to his father, and has evidently a distinguished career before him."

THE CITY KNIGHTS OF THE ROUND TABLE.

—*The New York Evening Telegram, January 23, 1905*

not long before the father's name is forgotten, and then at last the son is judged on his own merits. . . .

On January 1st, 1893, I became president of the Board of Aldermen. As I look back across the years, I marvel at the valor of my ignorance. I was an honest, right-thinking boy of twenty-seven [21] with no experience of public life and very little of politics, believing that others were as honest and as right thinking as I was, called upon to preside over the deliberations of thirty aldermen nearly all of whom were as typical ward heelers as could be got together. The board was unanimously Tammany, not a single Republican having been elected. Its average of intelligence was extremely low, about that of the ordinary twelve-year-old child.

The vice-president of the board was Andrew A. Noonan, known as "Handy Andy"; the chairman of the Finance Committee was [Nicholas T. Brown] known from his occupation as "Shoemaker Brown." The only members of the board who were professional men were Samuel Wesley Smith, who was a physician, and Rollin M. Morgan, who was a lawyer. The rest were shopkeepers in a very small way, clerks, janitors, and liquor dealers. At its first meeting the board elected, under orders from Croker, not only its vice-president, but also its clerk and sergeant-at-arms.

The clerk was Michael F. Blake, formerly City Hall reporter on the *Herald* and afterwards a Municipal Court judge. Mike Blake was always intensely loyal to the head of Tammany Hall. When the organization and I parted company, Mike not only abused me to all who would listen to him, but cut me dead when he met me, making very unpleasant remarks as he cut me. He used to demonstrate his loyalty by naming his sons, and there were very many of them, as they came into the world,

---

[21] Many papers commented on McClellan's youthfulness while he was president of the Board of Aldermen. For example, in 1893, when Mayor Gilroy was out of the city and McClellan was acting mayor, the New York *World* (July 26, 1893) wrote: "George Brinton McClellan, not yet twenty-eight years of age . . . is perhaps the youngest man that ever sat in the Mayor's chair, . . . and he looks even younger than he is. As he sat at the Mayor's broad, carved oak table yesterday, smooth faced, blue eyed, with clustering brown hair he looked almost boyish. . . . The face was square, full of character, expressive and showing dimples in the cheeks when he laughed, which he frequently did. . . . Altogether he had the appearance of a well-groomed young man, the clean, wholesome look of a man who takes a bath every morning."

after the distinguished lights of Tammany. Thus there was a Richard Croker Blake, a Roswell Pettibone Flower Blake, a Thomas F. Gilroy Blake, a W. Bourke Cockran Blake, and a John C. Sheehan Blake. When Cockran and Sheehan were cast by Croker into outer darkness, Mike Blake was much disturbed, but only for a moment, for little Cockran and Sheehan Blake, promptly became plain William and John.

The sergeant-at-arms was a venerable gentleman named John Maguire, who never succeeded in finding out what it was all about. As his duties were limited to sleeping in an armchair in a corner of the chamber and drawing his salary, his worthlessness did not matter.

The board, besides appointing commissioners of deeds, had power over public improvements and franchises, as well as to reduce but not increase the budget. I found that my predecessors in office had been in the habit of never appearing at City Hall except for the meetings of the board and the Board of Estimate and Sinking Fund Commission. I had a desk put in a corner of the so-called committee room of the aldermen, which was really their loafing room, and sat at it every morning. This the aldermen resented very much.[22] They had been in the habit of holding their conferences there, and they objected to an outsider being present.

To my surprise and horror I soon reached the conclusion that nothing of importance passed the board without the use of money. There was nothing that I could actually prove, it was merely the suspicion that came from hearing the aldermen talk. Of the lot I had complete confidence in only three, Jacob C. Wund, a Third Avenue grocer, William H. Murphy, a liquor dealer representing my own Assembly District, the Twelfth, and Rollin M. Morgan.

Murphy was one of three brothers, his elder was Charles

---

22 A reporter wrote the following, concerning the Board of Aldermen during McClellan's presidency: "Michael F. Blake, the clerk of the council, winds up the machine once a week, and it runs along very nicely. . . . All that is left for the City Fathers to do is to look wise and say 'aye' when President McClellan says 'aye.' As the President's name is called first, there is small chance of their making mistakes. . . . President McClellan is sharp and quick; he has the parliamentary rules at his finger ends; he rarely makes a mistake; when he does . . . , he turns his decision around the other way with a dignity that awes the Aldermen." (New York *Commercial Advertiser*, March 18, 1893.)

Francis, afterwards boss of Tammany Hall, his younger was John, afterwards a councilman. Billy Murphy was not only honest, but intelligent and able. During my second year as president he discovered that he had cancer of the throat. He told no one of his discovery, went to the hospital by himself, was operated on and died under the knife. A simple, straightforward, modest hero.

Whenever Wund or Murphy found out that any particularly rotten work was under way they would let me know, and I would do my best to kill it, which I was usually able to do. Under my rules I had great power which could only be checked by a direct and open vote of the board. They were unwilling to resort to this extremity because of a wholesome fear of the press.

One day Jake Wund came to me and said, "The boys are all set to put that franchise through that's coming up tomorrow. They are to get $5,000 apiece and Shoemaker Brown, who is handling the stuff, is to get $10,000." "Can we stop it?" I asked. "I doubt it," he answered, "it's the biggest graft in years, and you have ridden them so hard that they haven't made much since you have been here. If you try your usual strong-arm work they will throw you down and take the consequences, for the money is so big that they don't care." All that morning I thought the matter over. After lunch I went to Tammany Hall and told the story to Croker. He listened to me in silence, and when I had finished asked, "What time does the board meet tomorrow?" I told him one o'clock. He said nothing more, and I left him thoroughly discouraged.

The next morning when I reached City Hall Mr. Croker telephoned me to go to Tammany Hall at once. On my arrival there I found him in his little back room walking up and down, smoking. In a corner sat Shoemaker Brown, looking very unhappy and twiddling his hat in his hands. When I went in, Croker stopped in front of his table and without even saying good morning said to me, "Tell him what you told me yesterday." Dreadfully embarrassed, I demurred. "Go ahead and tell him," grunted Croker, and I repeated what I had said the day before. "Is that true?" asked Croker turning to the Shoemaker, who nodded his head and said, "Yes." Croker then said, "Shoemaker, I'm going to do you the greatest kindness

that was ever done you; I am going to keep you out of Sing
Sing. Go down to City Hall and withdraw that franchise. If
you don't, I give you my word I'll send you up the river." It
was all said in Croker's quiet, low voice without emphasis, and
with scarcely any expression. When the board met, the franchise was withdrawn by unanimous consent. At the end of his
term the Shoemaker was retired to private life, to emerge seven
years later as a successful candidate for coroner on the so-called
"reform" ticket headed by Seth Low.[23]

Needless to say I was by no means popular with the aldermen.
The effect of the lesson Croker had taught them was so great
that I had no difficulty in stopping further large-scale graft. I
don't doubt that in small matters the "boys" got their bit, but
I believe that it was a very small bit indeed. . . .

[It was also during my presidency of the Board of Aldermen
that I] began my friendship with [Charles F.] Murphy [24] that
lasted until I became mayor. . . . In February, 1893, state
Senator Eddy Hagan, the leader of my Assembly district, the
Twelfth, died. Alderman Billy Murphy came to me and said
that his brother Charley was a candidate for the succession. I
asked the alderman why he was not a candidate himself, and
he replied that he would be but for his health, that Charley
was really a better man, and . . . [that he needed my] help.
I answered that, while I thought the alderman was better qualified, that if he could not make the race I would gladly back his
brother, whom I knew as a very decent, capable citizen.

I first headed a delegation of district captains to Croker
in Charley Murphy's behalf, and on February twenty-seventh
I had a confidential talk with Croker and Gilroy. There was a
good deal of opposition to Murphy, and Croker was in doubt

23 Low, a Republican, was mayor of Brooklyn (1882-86), president of Columbia University (1889-1901), and mayor of New York City (1902-03). In 1903, he
was defeated for re-election as mayor by McClellan.

24 Murphy was the boss of Tammany Hall from 1902 until his death in 1924.
The only official position he ever held was that of dock commissioner during the
mayoralty of Robert A. Van Wyck. He and McClellan quarreled in 1905-06, and
in subsequent years McClellan repeatedly made derogatory remarks about his
character. Murphy was, however, a far more enlightened boss than his predecessors. He created what was called the "New Tammany," which was distinguished
by the statesmanship of men like Alfred E. Smith and Robert Wagner in the
state government and by the nomination and election of such men as McClellan
and William Gaynor as mayors of New York City.

about the advisability of choosing him. I saw the boss again the next day and finally convinced him that Murphy was the best man for the place. I think that I may fairly claim that it was due to me that Murphy was chosen district leader, and Murphy for a time at least recognized the obligation. . . .

[The only other close contact that I had with Murphy before I ran for mayor was in 1898 when] I saved . . . [him] from being deposed from the leadership of his assembly district. He was very anxious that his friend Frank O'Donnel [25] should be sent to the state Senate in place of Thomas F. Grady.[26] Croker very properly refused Murphy's request on the ground that Grady, who was one of the best mob orators in public life, was needed in Albany, and that O'Donnel could not make a speech to save his soul. Murphy sulked and refused to take his delegation to the senatorial convention.

The convention was held, and Grady was renominated in the absence of Murphy delegates. I heard of the row after the convention had adjourned, and hurried down to the Gas House District, and found Murphy standing as usual outside his district club, which was over one of his barrooms at the corner of Twentieth Street and Second Avenue. Murphy was very angry and very sullen. I told him that he was facing serious trouble, but he insisted that he did not care. I asked his authority to see Croker on his behalf, and he refused to give it. I told him that, nevertheless, I should see Croker and forthwith went to the Murray Hill Hotel where Croker lived. I found the boss in bed and asleep. I woke him up, and sitting beside his bed I asked him what he intended to do with Murphy. He answered, "Reorganize his district and kick him out." I pleaded with him for an hour, and finally he said, "If Murphy comes here before nine tomorrow morning and eats

[25] When McClellan was mayor, O'Donnel served as his commissioner of taxes and assessments from 1904 to 1906.

[26] Grady, who spent most of his mature years in the state Senate, won more than local notoriety when Governor Grover Cleveland found him so objectionable that he asked John Kelly, boss of Tammany, not to send him back to Albany. On his death the New York *Evening Post* (February 3, 1912) wrote: "He engineered many vicious bills, perhaps more than any other in his generation." A contemporary has stated that Grady "had no more mental capacity than a monkey," but that he "was the best orator in Tammany Hall . . . with the exception of . . . Bourke Cockran." (John T. Hettrick, "Reminiscences" [Columbia University Oral History Project], 194.)

humble pie, I'll let up on him. If you can persuade him to come, all right. If you can't, out he goes before tomorrow night."

I hurried back to the Gas House and found Murphy where I had left him an hour and a half before. He was just as angry, just as sullen, and just as stubborn. For two hours I talked with him, and reasoned with him, and argued with him. Finally at one-thirty, when I had almost given up, he said, "All right, I'll go."

Bright and early the next morning I met Murphy and convoyed him to Croker's room. Half an hour later he came out and said, "It's all right." What passed between the two men I never knew, but of this I am sure, that neither ever again had the slightest use for the other.

At that time Murphy was an honest and able man, a good politician and a strong leader. It was not until he acquired a desire for money and a taste for alcohol that he began morally to disintegrate. He was a silent man of only very limited education. I had great difficulty in inducing him to refer to himself in writing as "I" and not as "i." I doubt if he ever read anything but an occasional newspaper. It was impossible to carry on a conversation with him on any subject but local politics, for local politics was his intellectual limit. While his successors have been in every way smaller men than he, his predecessor, Croker, was infinitely his superior. Murphy stood by me loyally until our paths diverged, but on the other hand he received as much as he gave. Whatever may have been our differences in later years until then the score was even.

Chapter IV

THE DUTY OF REGULARITY

THE BOARD of strategy that controlled the general policies of the city government and of Tammany Hall [in 1893-94 when Thomas Gilroy was mayor] consisted of the mayor, [Police Commissioner James J.] Martin and Bourke Cockran. . . . While Croker was recognized as the boss of the organization, he had by no means acquired absolute power. . . . Gilroy was too much of a personage to take orders from anyone. With a few good men around him, with great executive ability, long experience in the public service, and honesty, he succeeded in giving New York the best administration in years. . . . [Nevertheless, by 1894] it had become evident that Gilroy could not be re-elected,[1] and he announced that he would not run again, but suggested that I should be renominated, a suggestion that was promptly squelched by Croker, who was always my friend.[2]

I went to see Governor Hill and asked him if it would be

[1] Although McClellan does not explain why it had become "evident" that Gilroy could not be re-elected, the facts are relatively simple. For some years the Reverend Charles H. Parkhurst had been conducting a campaign to demonstrate the alliance between the city's police and organized vice. In 1894, a campaign year, Thomas C. Platt, the state's Republican boss, decided to capitalize on Parkhurst's crusade. He, accordingly, had the Republican legislature create a committee to investigate New York City's police. The result was the Lexow investigation, which more than fulfilled Platt's expectations. Croker was so disturbed by the revelations of police corruption that he resigned his leadership and went to Europe. Moreover, developments in national politics and affairs strongly favored the Republicans. Under the circumstances Gilroy did not have a chance of re-election. For the Lexow investigation, see *Report and Proceedings of the Senate Committee Appointed to Investigate the Police Department of the City of New York* (Albany, 1895).

[2] McClellan realized that he had no more chance than Gilroy of being elected mayor in a year in which all the signs pointed to a Republican victory.

possible for me to get a congressional nomination. He replied that General Sickles [3] could not make up his mind whether or not to go back to Washington, that it was probable that he would not go, and that in that event I could have the nomination in the Tenth District. I then went to Gilroy with the same result. Both Hill and Gilroy expressed themselves as being very anxious to see me in the House.

Meanwhile Croker had retired from the boss-ship of Tammany Hall and been succeeded by John C. Sheehan, leader of one of the West Side districts, a carpetbagger from Buffalo. Croker had been abroad but had returned to New York and was living in retirement. The Tammany organization was being managed by a triumvirate of Sheehan, Gilroy and Bourke Cockran, who were gradually getting rid of Croker's old friends in favor of their own men. Realizing that Tammany was destined for defeat at the mayoralty election, Croker determined to keep hands off and let Sheehan and his friends shoulder the responsibility,[4] with the intention of resuming the leadership later on.

Every time I saw Gilroy he patted me on the back and assured me that my congressional hopes would undoubtedly be gratified. One afternoon, at the beginning of October, a few days before the congressional convention, Gilroy asked me to go with him to call on the captain of a visiting French warship, as I spoke French. We went uptown in the elevated. With us were the corporation counsel, [William H.] Clarke, and

[3] Daniel Sickles had a turbulent career in which a few of the high and low spots were his assassination of his wife's lover, his acquittal by pleading (for the first time in American history) temporary aberration of the mind, the amputation of his leg at the Battle of Gettysburg, the endless debate concerning the disposition of the troops under his command at Gettysburg, the enthusiasm with which he sought to carry out the Radical Reconstruction program as military governor of the Carolinas, his spectacular inability to settle the *Virginius* affair when he was minister to Spain, his removal as chairman of the New York State Monuments Commission in 1912 because of mishandling of funds, and his deathbed reconciliation with his second wife after three decades of separation. Of a somewhat more prosaic nature were his three terms as a Democrat in the House of Representatives and his successful campaign in 1852 for the establishment of Central Park in New York City.

[4] During most of the time that Sheehan and his associates ran the organization (1894-97) Croker remained in Europe and made only occasional visits to New York. Croker preferred to remain in the background, for the Republicans were in the ascendancy, and he was more than willing to have others accept the responsibility for Democratic setbacks.

[James J.] Martin, the president of the Police Commission, who were going home. We discussed a matter that was coming up in the Board of Estimate, and Gilroy said to Clarke, "Have you got that memorandum that I gave you? Show it to George." Clarke put his hand in his pocket, pulled out a paper, and handed it to me. It was an envelope on the back of which was written "Congress" and then followed what was evidently the congressional slate. I had just time to read opposite the number 10 the name of Sulzer,[5] and not that of either Sickles or McClellan, when Clarke grabbed the envelope from me and almost shouted, "I have made a mistake and given you the wrong paper."

Later in the day I said to Gilroy, "Is there anything new in the congressional situation?" "No," he answered. "But if Sickles don't make up his mind pretty soon, he will be dropped and you will get his seat." Then I knew that Gilroy had been lying to me and had been lying from the beginning. It was a great shock, for Gilroy had been very kind to me and I was very fond of him. But worse was yet to come.

The next morning Hill's messenger came to my house at seven o'clock and told me that the governor wanted to see me at once, for this was in the early days of the telephone and we had none. Hill had been nominated for governor much against his will and was making a desperate fight for election against terrible odds. It was a Republican year in nation, state, and city, and the Democratic party was faced with almost certain defeat. Pulitzer and the *World* had been opposing Hill because of the latter's supposed friendship for a certain Borckway, warden of the Elmira Reformatory, against whom Pulitzer was crusading because of Brockway's alleged brutality.[6]

5 William Sulzer, a Tammany politician, was a member of the state Assembly (1889-94) and the House of Representatives (1895-1912). After being elected governor as Tammany's candidate in 1912, he displayed a remarkable amount of either courage or indiscretion by refusing to accept Boss Murphy's slate of appointees. At Murphy's instigation, impeachment proceedings were instituted, and Sulzer was tried, convicted, and removed from office.

6 On March 19, 1894, a State Board of Charities report to the governor stated that Z. R. Brockway, general superintendent of the state reformatory at Elmira, was guilty of "cruel, brutal, excessive, degrading and unusual punishment of inmates." The *World*, referring to Brockway as "The Paddler," began a campaign for his removal. Although Governor Roswell P. Flower had no direct authority over Brockway, he appointed a commission to conduct hearings on

On reaching Hill's sitting room at the Normandy Hotel, I found the governor in conference with George Harvey,[7] whom I had known when we were both on the *World*. Harvey had become a sort of jackal for William C. Whitney [8] and the latter's political liaison man with politicians. When I entered the room Hill said to me, "George, I want you to take the first train to Bar Harbor. When you get there, see Pulitzer and tell him that if he will agree to support me, I will agree to remove Brockway as soon as I am inaugurated, . . . [and] if I am beaten, I promise that Governor Flower will remove Brockway nevertheless." . . .

I hurried home, packed a portmanteau and caught my train. I reached Bar Harbor the following afternoon. The next morning I drove out to Pulitzer's house and sent in my name, and was received by Pulitzer's private secretary, a young Englishman named [Claude] Ponsonby, very smart but very impecunious. Pulitzer always had as his private secretary some poverty-stricken gentleman whom he always treated abominably. He paid one hundred dollars a week, a large salary in those days, in return for which the secretary was required to take smiling the lashings of Pulitzer's very active tongue.

Ponsonby asked me my business, and when I told him that I had come with a message from Senator Hill, he said that he would tell his chief. He left the room and presently the door opened and Pulitzer came in, leaning on Ponsonby's arm. It was the first and only time that I ever saw Pulitzer. He was very tall and almost blind. In appearance he was very like the newspaper caricatures of him. He spoke with a pronounced

---

charges of misconduct and incompetence of the managers of the reformatory. Following the hearings, the commission wrote a report exonerating the managers, and on December 10, 1894, the governor announced that the charges had been dismissed. (*Public Papers of Roswell P. Flower . . . 1894* [Albany, 1895], 422-446; New York *World*, October 31, November 1, 5, 1894.)

7 Harvey through his business association with William C. Whitney had made a fortune. In 1889, he bought the *North American Review*, and in 1901 with J. P. Morgan's backing he obtained control of *Harper's Weekly*. His full name was George Brinton McClellan Harvey.

8 Whitney, a Democratic politician and corporation lawyer, helped overthrow Boss Tweed, served as corporation counsel of New York City (1875-82), and was Secretary of the Navy during Cleveland's first administration. A major figure in Democratic affairs at the city, state, and national levels, he was a man of considerable wealth and a member of his party's conservative wing.

German accent and emphasized his conversation with "cuss words."

He began proceedings by telling Ponsonby to bring cigars, and on the latter bringing the wrong cigars cursed him up hill and down dale. When Ponsonby had left, he asked me what I wanted, and I delivered Hill's message, that he agreed to remove Brockway or have him removed in return for the support of the New York *World*. "I am surprised that Hill should make me such a proposition," said Pulitzer. "He knows that I am not for sale, nor is the *World* for sale." I hastened to assure him that nothing was further from the senator's thought than the proposal to buy the *World*, he was only suggesting a friendly little arrangement. We discussed the matter for some time and finally Pulitzer said, "I feel that Brockway must be got rid of at all costs, and I have always liked Hill. You can tell him that I never make a political bargain. At the same time if he agrees that Brockway shall go, I agree to support the Democratic ticket. Understand, this is not a bargain," and he grinned horribly, "just a friendly little arrangement."

I caught the day train to Boston and the night train to Albany. I drove directly to . . . Hill's home, and found the governor eating his breakfast, clad in carpet slippers and his oldest frock coat. When I had made my report, Hill put his arm around me and said, "George, my boy, you have done me a great service, one that I can never forget. I am very grateful to you," and really seemed to mean it. For him, he showed considerable feeling.

I reached New York early in the afternoon and went directly home, where my wife told me that ever since I had left Mr. Croker had been incessantly trying to reach me and wanted to see me immediately on my return. I went at once to his home and found him almost ruffled out of his usual calm. "You're a nice fellow," he said, "going away when the congressional conventions are to be held tonight. Why did you go away, anyway?" I told him that I had been to Bar Harbor, sent by Senator Hill, and what the object of my trip had been.

"Hill sent you, eh?" he said. "Now listen to me. I am arranging to take the convention away from Bourke Cockran in the Twelfth District [9] and have you nominated in his place. Hill

---

[9] The Twelfth District, from which McClellan was to be elected to Congress

sends you out of town, far away, so that you can't be here to help your own fight and while you are away tries to beat you."

"Oh, that's impossible," I said with much warmth.

"Impossible nothing," answered Croker. "Hill wrote to Scannell" (the leader of the Eleventh Assembly District) "and asked him to vote his delegation in the convention against you and for Cockran. Scannell showed me the letter, and I saw Hill's mean little signature at the bottom. What do you think of your friend Hill now? I think that I can turn the trick and have you nominated tonight, but in return you must give me your word of honor that you will accept the nomination and under no circumstances withdraw after accepting."

I cheerfully gave my word and thanked my good friend.

The Twelfth Congress District included the Eleventh, Twelfth, and Fourteenth Assembly districts entire with a little of the Tenth and Sixteenth. The leaders were Scannell of the Eleventh, Murphy of the Twelfth, my own district, and [James J.] Keating of the Fourteenth. Murphy's and Keating's delegations voted for me, and I was nominated on the first ballot.

The next morning, on reaching City Hall, I found a letter from a certain George Walton Green, a lawyer with political ambitions that were never gratified, informing me that he had been nominated by the "State Democracy" of the Twelfth District for Congress, offering to withdraw in favor of Bourke Cockran, if I would also withdraw and assuring me that if I did not agree to his proposal he would run and the Republican candidate would be elected. I at once wrote him as follows:

New York, October 23, 1894

George Walton Green, Esq.,

Dear Sir:

I beg to acknowledge receipt of your letter of October 22, 1894, which purports to be a personal request from you for my consideration, but which for some reason best known to you, you appear to have sent to the newspapers before sending to me. The only possible answer to it you must certainly have foreseen. Under no circumstances can I recognize the thor-

---

in 1894, was bounded by West Fortieth Street, Lexington Avenue, East Forty-second Street, East River, East Fourteenth Street, Third Avenue, East and West Twenty-third Street, Sixth Avenue, West Twenty-fifth Street, and Seventh Avenue.

oughly undemocratic principle you suggest, that two candidates, after having been nominated can withdraw, and by mutual consent nominate a third.

Neither you nor I have the right to determine who shall or who shall not be a candidate for public office. That right belongs to those who have nominated these candidates in regular convention and to whom their nominees, having once accepted, are responsible.

I should have been glad had Mr. Cockran been selected as the candidate for congress in the Twelfth District, to have supported him most heartily. But having been nominated myself and having accepted the nomination, I recognize among the highest personal obligations that which I owe to the party which has placed me before the voters of the district.

As the regular Democratic candidate for Congress in the Twelfth Congress District, I must decline to entertain your proposition.

I am

> Yours truly,
> GEO. B. McCLELLAN

I had hardly sent my answer to Green when Hill's messenger arrived and told me that "the Major" wanted to see me, the Major being Major [James M.] Hinckley [of Poughkeepsie], Hill's chairman of the Democratic state committee.

I found Hinckley sitting at his desk at state headquarters. There were three doors to the room, that through which I had entered, a closed door to the left, and a door opposite which was open and through which I saw Hill sitting at a desk apparently occupied in chewing a toothpick.

The major began very sorrowfully, "George, the governor and I are greatly distressed by what happened last night. How could you have done it?" "Done what?" I asked in innocent surprise. "Gone against his wish. You should have known that he wanted Cockran nominated, and stayed out of the convention." "On the other hand," I answered, "the governor knew perfectly well that I wanted a nomination for Congress and he had promised to back me for the Tenth District if General Sickles did not run. Sickles did not run and Sulzer was nominated in the Tenth. Until yesterday I had no idea that the governor was interested in Cockran's candidacy, for I was at Bar Harbor on a mission of the governor's. When I found out that Sulzer was slated for the Tenth, I glady accepted support for the Twelfth. A fight and a bitter one was made against me in the convention inspired as you suggest by the governor." All of this Hill heard, for I could see him through the door listening attentively and apparently not enjoying what I said.

"Come," said the major, "withdraw in favor of Cockran. I don't know that Cockran would accept the nomination. He is in Florida and we can't get in touch with him, but I think that the governor can persuade him. Now get out of the race, and please the governor." "From what you say," I answered, "I assume that not only did the governor try to prevent my nomination but that he put Green in the race as an independent candidate in the hope of beating the regularly nominated candidate of the party."

"Now, George," said the major, "please don't get angry. Calm yourself and say that you will relieve the governor's distress and retire."

I rose to go and said, "Major, there is no use wasting your time or mine. Tell the governor for me that he always taught me the duty of regularity. The Democratic convention nominated me, and I propose to abide by its decision. If he is the good and regular Democrat that he claims to be, let him abide by it also."

I clapped my hat on my head and bowing in the direction of Hill who was still listening, I stalked from the room. As I was rather excited, instead of opening the door by which I had come in, I opened the door on the left, and before Hinckley could stop me walked almost into the arms of Bourke Cockran, who was sitting in the room beyond. I apologized and withdrew and as I passed Hinckley's desk smiled sweetly at him. I am sorry to say that instead of returning my smile the major scowled and muttered quite audibly, "The damned impudent puppy," and I am afraid that he referred to me.

When I told Mr. Croker of my interview with Major Hinckley, I thought that he would never stop laughing. "And Hill heard it all," he shouted. "Oh, great! Oh, great!" He highly approved of my letter to Green and took general charge of the direction of my campaign.

The Republicans nominated a very rich man named [Robert

A.] Chesebrough, who was the owner of . . . [a company which manufactured vaseline products]. Chesebrough spent money right and left and, I suspected, corrupted my former leader, John Scannell. I had practically no money, the whole campaign including assessments paid to the district leaders at ten dollars an election district, printing and everything else cost[ing] only $1,800. I had to make up by my activity what I lacked in cash. I spoke at every local meeting in the congressional district and spent my days canvassing voters.

Toward the close of the campaign a newspaperman told me that he remembered that Chesebrough had signed a petition against a bill allowing bicycles the use of Central Park. I sent to Albany to the secretary of state's office, dug up the petition and there was Robert A. Chesebrough's name. I had it photoed and sent a copy to the League of American Wheelmen, with a photo of myself on a bike. The *Journal* of the L. A. W. published both and came out enthusiastically in favor of "that distinguished wheelman" McClellan and against "the wheelman's enemy Chesebrough."

Unfortunately for Chesebrough he had dipped into poetry. He had had an "affinity" and to her he had written a book full of somewhat erotic, and very idiotic, verse and had been so pleased with it that he had published it "for private circulation." The New York *Sun* got hold of a copy, and it was submitted to Charles A. Dana. Dana had no love for me, for he had transferred to me his hatred of my father. But Dana had one redeeming quality, an acute sense of humor. When he read the Chesebrough poems he was so delighted with them that he felt he must share them with the world. Accordingly, the *Sun* fed them out, day by day, to an eager public, and Chesebrough found himself famous for the only time in his life.[10]

Between being made ridiculous by the *Sun,* and odious to the wheelmen by their journal, Chesebrough found himself on the defensive. The power of the League of American Wheelmen was very great, for almost everyone rode a wheel and all who rode paid one dollar a year to the League, which, at the height of the cycling craze, numbered one and a half million members.

[10] Although the *Sun* ridiculed Chesebrough's efforts as a poet, it supported Chesebrough rather than McClellan for Congress.

Nathan Straus, of R. H. Macy and Company, had been nominated on the Tammany ticket for mayor, but as soon as the anti-Tammany newspapers began to attack him, he lost his nerve and to the horror of his friends withdrew from the race. Hugh Grant [11] had been largely responsible for his nomination, and had worked night and day to bring it about. The day of his withdrawal Croker sent for me and said, "Nathan Straus has turned yellow and quit. Grant was responsible for his nomination, and therefore ought to run in his place. As Straus has welshed, Grant refuses to run and so you must take the nomination."

I was absolutely stunned. "Don't ask me to run," I said, "I have the one thing of all others I want, a nomination for Congress. Besides I don't want to be mayor, and moreover there is no chance of election."

"No," Croker replied, "there is no chance of election, but if I can't persuade Grant to run, you must take it for the purpose of keeping the party together."

I regretfully agreed to make the sacrifice and waited anxiously during the next twenty-four hours until Grant was finally persuaded to run.

When election day arrived it brought with it the expected Republican landslide in nation, state, and city. Hill was beaten for governor by Morton and Grant for mayor by [William L.] Strong. Both Senate and House of Representatives went Republican by large majorities, . . . [but] I won with a plurality of 1,341 over Chesebrough, Green polling 2,042 votes.

And so I began my five terms of service in the House, which were destined to be by far the happiest period of my wife's and my lives. I had won, however, at the cost of much of my faith in human nature. Gilroy had gone back on me and so had Hill. I was young, enthusiastic, and impressionable. Hill was the first prominent politician with whom I had been intimately associated, and I had felt for him an admiration little short of adoration. Had he sent for me and said, "I don't want you to

11 Grant, a Tammany politician, was sheriff (1886-88) and mayor (1889-92). Matthew Breen summed up the opinion of all responsible observers when he wrote that Grant "was far from being a man of mental or moral strength," and that "Croker ruled him with a rod of iron." (Matthew P. Breen, *Thirty Years of New York Politics Up-To-Date* [New York, 1899], 770-771.)

run for Congress," I should have cheerfully forgone my ambition. Instead of that he promised to help me, got me out of the way, and tried to knife me in the back. It was a terrible shock to me to have my idol crumble. Hill was my first hero, and I am sorry to say he was my last. . . .

As soon as election was over we moved down to Washington to get ready for the opening of Congress. While under our law a voter who is absent from the state in the service of the United States neither "gains nor loses" a residence, I thought it more tactful to hire a room in a rooming house on East Eighteenth Street, which I used as my legal voting residence while I was in Congress. Although my home was actually in Washington I was able to claim legal residence in my own Congress district. . . .

The Fifty-fourth Congress met, as provided by the Constitution, on the first Monday of December, which in 1895 came on the second. Thomas B. Reed of Maine, who had been speaker of the Fifty-first Congress, was elected speaker, and Charles F. Crisp of Georgia, who had been speaker of the last two Democratic houses, was the Democratic candidate and thereby became the leader of the party. . . . When the committees were announced, I fared extremely well for a new member, receiving [places on the] Military Affairs and Pensions [committees]. . . .

I made up my mind that if I was to make good in the House I must, so to speak, "go to school" and work hard at my job. Accordingly, I was always in my seat at prayers, never missed a day's attendance or a roll call, and followed the proceedings with the greatest care. . . .[12]

I have always liked soldiering and wanted to go to West Point when a boy, so the work of the Military Committee was very agreeable. I studied army organizations, and regulations, and past budgets as though for an examination and read and reread . . . [military authorities like] Clauswitz until I almost knew them by heart. I soon found that I knew more of our

[12] "During this session there has always been one member in his seat in and out of season, promptly in the morning, and whenever there is a night session, late at night, and if for nothing else he ever wins popular laurels he deserves public commendation for being a living rebuke to the tardy and absentee member. . . . He is George B. McClellan." (Washington *Post,* March 15, 1896.)

subject than any other member of the committee and could always get an audience when I spoke on military matters.

The work of Invalid Pensions was very unpleasant. The rule of the committee was that no private pension bill would be considered unless the beneficiary's claim had been finally rejected by the Pension Bureau. The presumption, therefore, was that the beneficiary had no pensionable status whatever and was not entitled legally to relief.

We met twice a week, the roll of the committee would be called and as each member's name was called he would call up by number the bill he wanted reported, which, without even being read and with no reasons being given, would thereupon be ordered reported favorably and would be placed upon the calendar. I think that it is a fair estimate to say that of the bills reported ninety per cent had no merit whatever and were purely Treasury steals, nine per cent had some slight merit but not enough to warrant their passage, and probably, to be liberal one per cent ought to have been passed. When the bills had been ordered reported, the three committee clerks had the task of drawing the reports, which were purely perfunctory, and in the face of the previous adverse action of the Pension Bureau, necessarily of no great weight. Every alternate Monday was private pension day, when from 150 to 200 bills were usually passed.

Under the very able leadership of Judge [Constantine] Erdman, [a Democrat,] who was a "Pennsylvania Dutchman" from Reading [and] a courageous and independent man who cared not the slightest for the ill will of his fellow members, an opposition was organized consisting of the Judge [Joshua W.] Miles [a Democrat from Maryland], and myself. In committee we took turns in demanding the reading of the Pension Bureau reports, and a roll call on each bill. We never prevented the reporting of a bill, but we slowed down the work of the committee so much that before the second session had ended it was obliged to meet every day to comply with the demands of the G. A. R.

On Mondays we took turns in opposing each bill as it came up. We had already divided up the calendar among us and familiarized ourselves with the infamies of the bills. It was hot and heavy work, very ungrateful and disagreeable, for we

earned the ill will of every member who had a bill on the
calendar. On the other hand, it was of tremendous benefit to
me, for I learned perforce, to be a fair rough-and-ready debater
and a very fair parliamentarian.

We never succeeded in beating a bill, no matter how bad it
was, but we did succeed in delaying the work of the Treasury
looters, for we cut down the average from around 200 to 25 a
Monday. "The brethern," as Reed called our fellow members,
became very angry and alarmed and appealed to the speaker
for help. The latter, because of his presidential ambitions, was
quite as anxious to please the G. A. R. as anyone else. Accordingly, he directed the Committee on Rules to report a rule
providing for a night session every Friday instead of the bi-
weekly day session. . . . The Friday night sessions lasted from
eight o'clock until nearly midnight. By delaying business as
much as possible, insisting on the presence of a quorum, and
fighting each bill as it came up, we managed to keep the average
fairly low, but not so low as on the Monday session which had
been very much shorter. It was some satisfaction to force one
hundred Republicans, who were interested in pensions, to spend
their Friday evenings sitting around the Capitol.

The Democrats took no interest in our fight, and it was almost impossible to get them to help us in our efforts for the
yeas and nays on the floor of the House. The truth was that in
pension matters most of the Democrats were as bad offenders
as the Republicans. When the bills reached President Cleveland, he vetoed almost all, and they were promptly passed over
his veto. The last pension bill he sent back to the House was
passed over his veto by an almost unanimous vote. I was one
of a handful of Democrats voting to maintain the veto. The
other Democrats who voted to over-ride the veto were largely
influenced by their dislike of the President, who, in their eyes
could do no right.

Very soon after the opening of the session the Republican
members of the Committee on Invalid Pensions began the
drafting of a General Pension Bill designed to liberalize existing pension laws in the interest of those who had no possible
moral right to draw pensions. The real author was the notorious "Corporal" Tanner, a one-legged pension attorney and a

rather unsavory individual.[13] The bill was finally reported out on February eleventh and placed on the calendar.

Shortly afterwards the Secretary of the Interior, Hoke Smith, sent for me, and told me that the President was anxious to have a defense of his pension record made in Congress. He had been industriously vetoing rotten bills and had been getting much undeserved abuse from the G. A. R. as an alleged enemy of the old soldier. Cleveland's war record left something to be desired, for he had hired a substitute at the time of the draft, which gave his opponents an argument, specious it is true, but none the less effective, in favor of the charge that he was opposed to the interests of those who had gone to the front. Actually he had been extremely liberal in his position in regard to those who had really and honestly served. The liberality and fairness of his attitude, and of that of the Secretary of the Interior and the Pension Bureau, had been either lost sight of or ignored.

The secretary asked me if I would make a speech against the pending General Pension Bill by way of a defense of the administration. I had made some reputation because of my attitude on private pension legislation, besides which, as the son of my father, I would get an audience among the veterans, probably larger than that of any other Democratic member. He, therefore, hoped that I would fall in with his wishes. On my prompt acceptance he turned me over to the Assistant Secretary, John M. Reynolds, in charge of pensions and the Commissioner of Pensions, Dominic J. Murphy, who gave me a vast amount of material. Out of this I constructed my speech and submitted it to the secretary, who handed it to Reynolds, and after it had been largely revised, I committed it to memory, and it was an awful job.

On April 23, 1896, the bill was called up under a rule, and I made my maiden speech. It took over an hour to deliver, for I was constantly interrupted. When I concluded, I received a very good "hand" on the Democratic side, and the newspapers were exceedingly kind. It established my position in the House

[13] Actually James Tanner had two wooden legs, for wounds he had received as a Union soldier at Bull Run necessitated the amputation of both legs four inches below the knees. A professional veteran and an inveterate lobbyist, he enjoyed a certain notoriety as a flamboyant and irresponsible spokesman for the veterans' wing of the Republican party.

as a coming man, but made me many enemies on the Republican side. It took me years to live down the antagonism created by my defense of Grover Cleveland.

The next morning my mail contained a number of very kindly letters of congratulation. The Secretary of the Interior, Reynolds, and the pension commissioner sent me their thanks, while [Richard] Olney, Secretary of State, [Daniel S.] Lamont, Secretary of War, and [Judson] Harmon, Attorney General, all wrote telling me that I had done well and that the administration was very grateful. I was so pleased with myself that I said to my wife, "I think that I will call on the President and find out what he has to say." I went to the White House and being a representative walked upstairs and into the room of the President's secretary, a man named Henry T. Thurber, between whom and members of Congress no love was lost, for he possessed the gentle art of making enemies to an even higher degree than did his chief. I found Thurber sitting on the edge of his desk, swinging his legs and recounting to a friend an adventure of the previous evening. As Thurber paid no attention to me, I said, "I am Representative McClellan, and I want to see the President." "I know perfectly well who you are," replied Thurber and went on with his story. After a while the President rang, and Thurber disappeared. He came back, and without looking at me said, "You can go in," and I went in.

After the General Pension Bill had passed the day before, we had passed a number of private bills, including one which seemed harmless and for which I had voted. This bill, however, one of the few private bills for which I had ever voted, happened to be one of Cleveland's pet horrors and had been vetoed by him in the Fifty-third Congress, a fact of which I was unaware. This will explain what happened when I entered the presidential office.

The President was writing as I walked across the room, and at first paid no attention to me. I reached his desk and stood waiting for him to look up. When he had finished writing, he carefully blotted the page and then turned and looked at me and said, "Damn you Mac, why did you vote for that damned bill yesterday?" I was to say the least somewhat surprised and answered, "I thought it a pretty good bill, Mr. President." "You know it wasn't a pretty good, or any other kind of a bill except a damned bad one." By this time I was feeling anything but comfortable. I ventured to suggest that I had made a defense of the pension policy of the administration. To which the President replied, "I don't care a damn what you did, as long as you voted for that damned bill." "Under the circumstances," I said, "perhaps I had better leave." "I think damned well you better," said the great man, and I left. . . .

Politically the Fifty-fourth Congress was an interlude and extremely barren in legislative results. It was generally conceded throughout the country that in the next presidential election the Democrats were certain to lose, and the Republicans in Congress spent their time in "putting Cleveland in a hole" for the purpose of helping their cause. The Democrats were hopelessly divided on the silver question, and every effort was made on the other side of the Chamber to emphasize that division. The President was inundated with private pension bills, which he almost automatically vetoed, only to have [them] passed over his veto as soon as returned to the House. With the exception of the appropriation bills, nothing of importance was enacted.

For one brief moment, and for one only, Cleveland became popular, and that was when he sent to Congress his message on the Venezuela boundary dispute with Great Britain. . . .[14]

As the first session drew to its close it became more and more evident that the Democratic convention would be dominated by the free silver men. The convention was held at Chicago where I went as a delegate from my own district. On reaching Chicago the first acquaintance whom I met was Benton McMillin of Tennessee. His seat in the House was directly behind mine, and we were good friends. I ran into him in the lobby of the Auditorium Hotel where we walked up and down with our arms around each other's waists in true House of Repre-

---

[14] This refers to United States intervention in the long-standing dispute over the boundary line between Venezuela and British Guiana. In 1895, Secretary of State Richard Olney in a note to the British invoked the Monroe Doctrine and demanded that the dispute be settled by arbitration. When the British rejected this proposal, Cleveland asked Congress for the authority to ascertain and maintain the boundary. Like Olney, he based his stand on the Monroe Doctrine. Cleveland's message was followed by a war scare that soon ended with renewed professions of friendship on both sides of the Atlantic. In 1899, a compromise boundary line was worked out by arbitrators in accordance with the terms of a treaty signed in 1897.

sentative style. "Who is to be the candidate?" I asked him. "Mac," he answered, "I am afraid that it is going to be that little whelp, Bill Bryan of Nebraska." It was the first time that I had heard Bryan's name as that of a serious possibility and I was greatly surprised. McMillin continued, "There is something going on here that I can't get the hang of. There are a lot of men here who are going to try to slip him over, but how they are going to do it I can't find out." That Bryan came to the convention expecting to be nominated was evident from the fact that, when he had been nominated and the newspapermen rushed to his room to interview him, he distributed his photographs from a pile on his bed, and they were photographs that had been taken at Lincoln, Nebraska, and evidently brought with him in expectation of the nomination. . . .

When the roll was called for nominations, besides certain favorite sons, [Richard P.] Bland, of Missouri, and [Horace] Boies, of Iowa, were presented as serious candidates. Bland was a member of the House,[15] the author of the Bland [-Allison] Free Silver Bill [of 1878], and one of the fathers of the free silver cause. He was a nice old man, rather dull, and perfectly sincere in his love for silver. Boies had been governor of his state [from 1890 to 1893], and while a declared free silverite was by no means an extremist. It was at this point that William C. Whitney made his fatal mistake.

He had the well-deserved reputation of being a very astute politician. He had been one of the leaders of the old County Democracy in New York City and had been corporation counsel [from 1875 to 1882]. . . . Later he had been one of Dan Manning's right hand men and had charge of Cleveland's first campaign in the city. Cleveland was very fond of him and made him Secretary of the Navy in his first administration. After Cleveland's defeat, Whitney kept the Cleveland machine alive among the ex-officeholders and made Cleveland's third nomination possible. In the second Cleveland administration he received no office, either because he did not want one or because of Cleveland's spartan rule of not rewarding his friends any more than he had to. He had married Miss [Flora] Payne,

---

[15] Bland was not a member of the House at the time of the convention. Elected to Congress in 1873, he served until his death in 1899, except for the years 1895-1897.

the daughter of Payne of the Standard Oil,[16] who had an enormous fortune, to which he greatly added by successful and ruthless operations in Wall Street.

Whitney absolutely controlled our delegation through Croker and Ed Murphy of Troy. After the free silver plank in the platform had been adopted, New York and New Jersey, which followed our lead, under Whitney's orders declined to take any further part in the proceedings of the convention. When the result of the balloting was announced, Bryan had not received two-thirds of the votes of all the delegates, but Senator [Stephen M.] White, of California, who was permanent chairman, ruled that as Bryan had received two-thirds of the votes of those delegates voting, he was nominated. The convention was acting under the House rules, and Senator White's ruling was perfectly correct. Had New York and New Jersey voted for Bland, who had the greatest support next to that of Bryan, the latter could not have been nominated on the first ballot, and it is altogether probable that Bland would have been the candidate.[17] He would have made a feeble campaign and been defeated worse than was Bryan, and the silver question would have been dead beyond the hope of resurrection. . . .

After Bryan had been declared the candidate his supporters seizing the state seat designations began what was the first convention parade, which has since become a matter of mere routine. In Bryan's first convention, however, it was no routine, but unadulterated enthusiasm. The delegates scarcely knew what they were doing, and for the moment were almost insane. As James J. Martin and I stood guard over New York's standard, a very large and enormously fat man came up shouting, "Bryan, Bryan, Bryan," and tried to take it away from us. I hit him squarely on the point of his jaw and he went down in a heap

---

[16] Actually, her brother, Oliver H. Payne, rather than her father, Henry B. Payne, was a Standard Oil director and a Wall Street operator.

[17] McClellan is confused about developments at the convention. Bryan was not nominated on the first ballot. Bland led on the first three ballots without securing the necessary majority. Bryan moved into the lead on the fourth ballot and was nominated on the fifth ballot. Although it is true that Bryan, as McClellan states, was nominated by two-thirds of those voting rather than by two-thirds of all the delegates, it is not correct to assume that New Jersey's and New York's votes could have swung the nomination to Bland. In short, there was no conceivable way in which Whitney could have prevented Bryan's nomination.

still shouting, "Bryan." He picked himself up apparently
quite unaware that he had been knocked down and went on
his way shouting, "Bryan, Bryan," just as though nothing had
happened. Some years later I met him. He rejoiced in the
picturesque name of Hogg and was then governor of Texas.[18]

The nomination of Bryan and the free silver plank in the
Democratic platform left the sound money men in the House
in an extremely embarrassing situation. Some withdrew from
politics altogether to await the coming of better times, some
supported the Palmer and Buckner bolting ticket,[19] while
many went over to the free silver cause.

During the summer I made up my mind that my chances of
continuing in the House were very slight. I could not support
the free silver cause, while a nomination on the Palmer and
Buckner ticket meant certain defeat. While my prospects were
at their darkest, I received a note from Daniel S. Lamont, then
Secretary of War, asking me to call on him. Lamont had always shown me great friendliness, and I knew him better than
anyone in Cleveland's administration. He was by far the ablest
politician among Cleveland's supporters and was one of the
few of Cleveland's friends who not only was on good terms
with Congress, but who had kept the good will of the Democratic organization in New York.

When I saw the secretary, he said to me, "You want to go
back to the House, don't you?" I answered, "I most certainly
do." "All right," he said, "I think that we can manage it. I
have arranged that if you get the regular nomination for Congress in your district, you will also get the Palmer and Buckner
nomination. There is only one condition. That is that you
keep your mouth shut during the campaign. You are not to
be asked to repudiate Bryan or say anything against him. On
the other hand, you are not to say anything in support of the

18 McClellan is mistaken about his dates, for James S. Hogg at the time of
the Democratic convention of 1896 had already completed two terms as governor
of Texas, and he did not again hold public office.

19 Following Bryan's nomination, a National Democratic Party, composed of
so-called "Gold Democrats," was organized at Indianapolis on September 2-3,
1896, and nominated Senator John McA. Palmer for President and Simon B.
Buckner for Vice-President on a gold platform. The Palmer-Buckner ticket received only 134,645 votes, and the Gold Democrats did not nominate candidates
in 1900.

sound money ticket. You are simply to say nothing at all for or against either ticket or platform. Do you think that you can do that?" I answered, "I can only try. Of course, I must first see Mr. Croker and tell him of the arrangement." "Of course," said Lamont, "I wouldn't have you do anything without consulting him." I at once saw Mr. Croker, who told me to go ahead and that as far as the organization was concerned I would not be required to commit myself.

The Republican candidate was Charley Hess,[20] a very able . . . [man], who was the brother of Jake Hess,[21] one of the Republican city leaders, and who lived at Madison, New Jersey, being only a technical citizen of New York. The three Tammany district leaders in my congressional district were Charles F. Murphy, of my home district, James J. Keating, who was a close friend of Croker, and John J. Scannell. It was common rumor that Hess had offered Scannell $10,000 if he succeeded in either defeating my nomination, causing the convention to adopt a free silver resolution, or forcing me to declare myself either for or against free silver.[22] The convention was extremely disorderly and violent. Murphy and Keating stood by me manfully, my fight being made by Thomas F. Grady who was then Croker's personal representative in the state Senate. I was finally nominated by the votes of Murphy's and Keating's districts, Scannell refusing to make the nomination unanimous, but the convention adopted no resolutions of any kind.[23]

I then began the most curious campaign that I have ever

[20] The New York *Evening Post* (October 8, 1896) referred to Charles A. Hess's nomination as "a political outrage," and added that he "is not even a Republican. . . . His nearest approach to being a member of the party has been only in years of political success, and then he has been nothing but a prosaic camp-follower and a hungry grub-beggar. At all other times he has been a Democrat and a bosom friend and political relative of John J. Scannell, the notorious Tammany Hall murderer."

[21] If Jacob Hess is remembered at all today, it is as the Republican leader of the district in which Theodore Roosevelt got his start in politics.

[22] Before the nominating convention was held, McClellan cabled Croker in England: "John Scannell kicks on my nomination for Congress. Please cable him at once to support me without question." (McClellan to Richard Croker [no date], McClellan MSS.)

[23] In the course of the debate in the convention over McClellan, Scannell said: "He [McClellan] cannot win. If he is a Democrat, let him say so. If he is a renegade, put him where he belongs. If he was my brother, I would not support him. Give us any man who will stand on the platform, and I will give $2,500 to his campaign fund." (New York *Times,* October 6, 1896.)

taken part in. Charles A. Dana, hating me as he had hated my father, determined to "smoke me out." He assigned one of his cleverest political reporters, "Jersey" [Ernest O.] Chamberlain, to me, and every day Chamberlain wrote a story about "The Artful Dodger," as the *Sun* called me, and the *Sun* carried an almost daily editorial abusing me. The other New York papers, with the exception of the *Daily News,* a one-cent, evening, workman's paper, followed the *Sun*'s lead in less violent fashion.[24] I doubt if any congressional fight in New York City has ever been given so much space by the press.

It was a heartbreaking campaign. It was extremely unpleasant for me to go to the Union Club during the campaign. The fact that I was on the Bryan ticket made my fellow members regard me as a social pariah and I stayed away. There was scarcely a day that I was not run to earth by the reporters and bombarded with questions which I had to dodge as best I could. Croker took a personal interest in my fight and whenever I saw him urged me to keep up my courage and to keep my head. When election day arrived, I had kept my faith with Lamont and had "kept my mouth shut," but it had been very hard work. . . . I was re-elected by a plurality over Hess of 1,777— 436 more than I had received two years before—at a total cost of only $2,600, thanks to the decency of Murphy and Keating.

At the state convention of 1897 I was a member of the Committee on Resolutions. Major Hinckley, our chairman, produced a platform which he said had been drafted by Senator Hill who wished us to report it as drafted. When the platform was read to us, it developed that its currency plank was extremely "wobbly," leaning, in fact, in the direction of the free coinage of silver. I offered as an amendment a straight-out gold plank. To my surprise John DeWitt Warner and [Charles] Tracy of Albany, both former representatives in Congress, Edward F. Shepard, a professional reformer,[25] and several

---

24 The New York *Mail and Express* (October 7, 1896) wrote: "If George McClellan has the bravery of his father, he will step out and say whether he is for honest money or repudiation." The New York *Commercial Advertiser* (October 7, 1896) stated that McClellan was "too feeble minded to declare where he stands." A New York *Herald* (October 22, 1896) headline read: "Where's McClellan [?] Reward For The Recovery Of A Lost Candidate Whose Views Are Unidentified."

25 In addition to being a "professional reformer," Shepard was a prominent New York lawyer and an influential Democrat. He was a co-author of the state's

others, all pronounced gold men, remained silent, and I was obliged to make my fight unaided. Hinckley left the chair and the room, and on his return brought word from Hill that my amendment was "not only inopportune, but very dangerous." Nevertheless it was adopted, and I gave notice that if it was opposed on the floor of the convention I should precipitate a sound money vs. free silver fight. Hill made the best of what was from his point of view a bad situation, and the Democratic party in New York had the distinction of leading the way from the free silver heresy. . . .

---

first Civil Service Reform Bill, the independent Democratic candidate for mayor of Brooklyn in 1895, and the regular Democratic candidate for mayor of New York City in 1901.

Chapter V

McKinley Was No Cleveland

No two men could have been more absolutely different than were Cleveland and McKinley, not only in their conception of the duties of the office, but in their personalities. Cleveland told me that he was inexpressibly shocked when in driving to the Capitol on inauguration day McKinley had said that he conceived it to be the duty of the President to carry out the will of the people even if it should run counter to his own opinions.

Cleveland was dour, hard, unyielding. With no tact or ability to handle men and no experience with Congress, his break with the latter was inevitable. McKinley was one of the most tactful, kindly, courteous men I have ever known. His twenty years' service in Congress had given him a thorough knowledge of what Tom Reed used to call "the atmosphere of the House." He could say "No" more pleasantly than most men can say "Yes." Everyone liked him, and he had almost as many friends on the Democratic side in both houses as he had on the Republican.

When the body of General Grant was placed in his tomb on Riverside Drive, Speaker Reed appointed me on the House committee to attend the ceremonies, and made himself chairman. When we arrived we found that no seats had been reserved for us and only succeeded in getting on the stand through the persistence of our very efficient sergeant-at-arms. After the speeches had been concluded the invited guests were marched into the Claremont restaurant for lunch, headed by the President and Jack [John Jacob] Astor, who was chairman of the committee of arrangements. We started to join the procession, when we were politely but firmly informed that we were not expected at the lunch. We stepped to one side and as the President passed us we uncovered. He recognized us and at once saw that something was wrong. He halted the procession, and asked Astor why we were not going to lunch. On being informed that no provision had been made for us, he said, "Then I shall not go without them." Reed begged him not to disarrange the program and assured him that we would get on very well on our own. "All right," he answered, "just as you like, but it is most unfortunate that you should have been overlooked." He then delayed proceedings while he shook hands with each of us, and chatted for about a quarter of an hour. Our sergeant-at-arms produced a most excellent cold lunch which we ate on the platform to the great delight of the crowd in the street, who cheered madly every time a champagne bottle was opened. It was a graceful and considerate gesture of McKinley, a gesture of which very few Presidents would have been capable.

Joe Cannon came to me one day and said, "Mac, I want you to keep the brethren on your side quiet when I bring up an amendment to the Urgent Deficiency Bill. You know that there are two items carried in the Sundry Civil Bill for repairs to the White House, $25,000 that is accounted for and $25,000 that is not accounted for. Mrs. McKinley has blown in both items, and no one knows how she has spent them. The White House roof is leaking badly and must be repaired at once. It is most humiliating for the President, and I want you to explain to your side the circumstances and ask your people not to raise a point of order or to ask questions." I at once went among the Democrats and explained the matter. The item went through without a word of comment.

Mrs. McKinley was an epileptic and quite irresponsible. As a very young man McKinley had married above him and made a love match. He was devoted to his wife and treated her with the consideration and chivalry of a medieval knight. She should have been in a sanitorium, but the President kept her with him, and she insisted on appearing in public. She was subject to fits and to violent outbreaks of temper, when only the President could control her. When my wife called to pay her respects with a number of other ladies, she found Mrs. Mc-

Kinley sitting beside a table on which were a great number of McKinley campaign buttons. As each lady came up to be presented, Mrs. McKinley took one of the buttons and, pinning it on the lady's dress, said, "Take a picture of Precious," which was her pet name for her husband.

She wore in front of her dress a square piece of cloth which was called by the disrespectful "the McKinley bib." When she had a fit in public the bib was thrown over her face and she was carried from the room. At public dinners the President always walked out with his wife on his arm and sat beside her at table. One night when we were dining at the White House, I was sitting diagonally opposite to her. Suddenly she began to scream and kick. The President promptly threw the bib over her face, and presently she calmed down and the bib was lowered.[1]

With the exception of James G. Blaine, McKinley had the most extraordinary memory for faces of any one I have known. The last time that he ever spoke in public, before he went to Buffalo and his death, was at Antietam battlefield, where he dedicated a monument. He asked John Dalzell [a Republican congressman from Pennsylvania,] and me to go with him and to speak. He was in his usual good spirits, and as we sat in the tent beside the platform before going out to speak he joked Dalzell and me for being nervous. "The trouble about you two men," he said, "is that you have your speeches in your heads, while I have mine in my pocket." In front of the tent the crowd was kept back by a rope guarded by Maryland militia commanded by Johnston Poe, who had been at Princeton with me. McKinley got up from his chair, lighted a cigar, and walked to the flap of the tent. He looked over the crowd and his eye fell on an old fellow in Grand Army uniform. "Hullo, Comrade," he said, "I saw you in the crowd at Gettysburg, last month when I spoke there, didn't I?" "Yes," said the old man, "but how did you recognize me?"

At the close of his last session I went to say goodby to him. As I entered his office he looked up and shook his finger at me,

---

1 McClellan's stories about Mrs. McKinley are not exaggerated, for many others in Washington knew and told similar anecdotes about her. For example, see Arthur Dunn, *From Harrison to Harding . . . 1888-1922* (New York, 1922), I, 207-208.

and said, "Mac, I think I've got you. What were you doing at
the corner of New Jersey Avenue and R Street last Wednesday
at half-past four? I saw you." Naturally I was overcome, for I
had walked home that day via New Jersey Avenue. "How do
you do it, Mr. President?" I asked. "Oh, I don't know," he
answered, "it just comes naturally."

He was always very kind to me. He had been a great admirer
of my father, under whom he had served in the Army of the
Potomac when a boy of fifteen, and he seemed to like me. We
dined at the White House every winter while he was President
and were asked to most of the receptions. We never dined
there before his time, nor have we been asked to dine there
since.

When Czolgosz shot him, we were in Paris. [Senator Henry]
Cabot Lodge [of Massachusetts] who was also there came to our
hotel and said to me, "Let's go out and see if we can pick up
any information about the President's condition." We went to
the offices of the Paris *Herald,* the Associated Press and *Figaro,*
but nowhere could we get any news except that he had been
shot. We sailed for home on the same steamer. As we left
Cherbourg, we stood in the stern of the ship watching the shore.
Just as we passed the breakwater, the flag on the citadel was
lowered to half staff. We both uncovered, and Lodge said, "He
has gone." . . .

There have undoubtedly been greater and stronger Presidents than he was; but none was a more kindly nor more
courteous gentleman, and none has died more regretted by his
countrymen, nor more beloved. . . .

[McKinley undoubtedly had many attractive personal
qualties, but he also had a cabinet that was] as weak as any
that has held office, which is saying a great deal. To the key
positions, those that counted most during the next four years,
the President appointed John Sherman, senator from Ohio,
Secretary of State; Lyman J. Gage, a prominent Middle Western
banker, Secretary of the Treasury; Russell A. Alger, senator
from Michigan, Secretary of War; John D. Long, ex-governor
and ex-representative of and from Massachusetts, Secretary of
the Navy; and Joseph McKenna, ex-representative from California, Attorney General. On the surface [they were] a very
personable lot. Actually the story was very different.

John Sherman, a most agreeable and delightful old man, had begun to break mentally [even while he was in the Senate.] Of his two brothers one was the general, William Tecumseh, the other had been chief justice of Ohio, one of whose daughters had married Don Cameron, senator from Pennsylvania, the other General [Nelson A.] Miles, commanding the army. The Sherman clan was very powerful, and the people of Ohio for sentimental reasons, if for no other, would have bitterly resented any effort to remove Sherman from the Senate against his will. The Republican party was faced with a very serious problem, for Mark Hanna wanted to go to the Senate, and Sherman did not want to leave.

Hanna's political career was one of the most extraordinary in history. He was a self-made man who had amassed a very large fortune in Ohio, and while always dabbling in politics, did not turn his thoughts seriously to political leadership until he had retired from active business after he was fifty years of age. In appearance he greatly resembled Davenport's cartoons.[2] It was not necessary to caricature him, nature had done that. It was only necessary to draw him to life. He was stout, with several chins and a pair of short greying side whiskers. He dressed rather flamboyantly and wore a heavy gold watch chain across his ample waistcoat. All that Davenport had to do was to ornament his clothes with $ marks, and the caricature was complete. While somewhat crude and very cynical, he had a good sense of humor, told an amusing story, was a good mixer and made and retained friends easily. He took to politics as a duck takes to water and before very long had become the undisputed boss of the Republican party in Ohio. He early developed a very sincere and warm friendship with McKinley and the ambition somehow and sometime to make the latter President of the United States. . . . [Having secured] McKinley's nomination for the presidency, . . . Hanna . . . [became] chairman of the Republican National Committee. After McKinley's triumphal election, Hanna as titular head of the party felt that

2 Homer C. Davenport, a cartoonist for the San Francisco *Examiner*, New York *Evening Journal*, and New York *Evening Mail*, won a national reputation for his cartoons of the silver campaign of 1896, the Spanish-American War, and several prominent political figures. His drawing of Mark Hanna in a $-marked suit of clothes has been reproduced countless times and is probably his best known cartoon.

he must be in Washington at the side of the President and fixed upon the senatorship as the proper position for the gratification of his ambitions. Sherman, however, stood in the way, and to get rid of him it was necessary to kick him upstairs. He was accordingly appointed Secretary of State.

As Secretary of State John Sherman was a pathetic figure. He had been an able and forceful member of the Senate and as his mind began to go his mental shortcomings were not apparent, for he took no part in Senate business. After he became Secretary of State he stood out at the front of the stage, and his weakness could not be hidden. He lived in a fog, and the work of the department was performed by his subordinates.

We were dining one evening at his niece's, Mrs. Don Cameron's. The secretary was there, and we were very late in going in to dinner. It was a large dinner and I noticed to my surprise that two men sat together. Towards the close of the dinner the secretary turned to our hostess and asked, "My dear, am I dining here?" "No, Uncle John," she replied, "you are not." "Dear me," said the secretary, "I know that I am dining somewhere. I wonder where I am dining." The poor old gentleman had completely forgotten the name of his hostess, who was probably waiting for his arrival with great anxiety.

Gage and Long were harmless mediocrities who would have passed muster in ordinary times, but who fell far short of rising to the war emergency. Long was greatly handicapped by having as his Assistant Secretary, Theodore Roosevelt, of whom much more later.

McKenna was a very pleasant man and a fair lawyer who afterwards made a good justice of the Supreme Court. Tom Reed, who loathed McKinley with an intensity worthy of a better cause, used to say that when McKinley and McKenna were in the House together the latter would sit in front of and close to the former when he was speaking, lead the applause, and murmur from time to time in a loud stage whisper, "Marvellous, wonderful, what a man!" [and] McKinley was so touched by these evidences of admiration that he made McKenna Attorney General. But Reed was prejudiced.

Alger, like Sherman, was in his dotage, and as Secretary of War was a tragedy. He was generally thought by members of Congress to be an unmitigated liar. Actually the poor old gentleman meant well, but as his memory had almost completely gone he was unable to remember today what he had agreed to yesterday. Fortunately for the country the adjutant general, who then occupied a position not unlike that of chief of staff today, Henry C. Corbin, was a man of great ability and force. Shocking as was the mismanagement of the Spanish War, matters would have been infinitely worse but for him. . . .

With these utterly inadequate tools, but with the best of good intentions, McKinley began his administration. . . .

At the beginning of the first regular session of the Fifty-fifth Congress the administration turned its attention to the annexation of Hawaii. While perhaps not quite so blatant a scandal as the annexation of Panama by Roosevelt, it was an utterly unjust and unjustifiable proceeding. . . . When the Hawaiian Annexation Bill was introduced in the House it at once raised a storm of opposition led by the speaker himself. The favorite argument advanced in favor of annexation was that Hawaii was the only halfway point between this country and the Orient, and that as such it was essential to us as a coaling station.

Reed had a large terrestrial globe placed in the speaker's lobby of the House and would demonstrate to all who would listen to him, by means of a piece of string which he carried in his pocket, that the shortest route between the United States and Asia was not via Hawaii but to the north via the Aleutian Islands. The members, however, did not want to listen to arguments. The spirit of imperialism was abroad and had begun to influence the country. The administration wanted annexation, the sensational press wanted it, and members were carried off their feet by the glamour of an empire.

When the bill was finally reported, I was selected by my colleagues on committee to close the debate against it. William L. Wilson, author of the Wilson Tariff Bill [3] in the Fifty-third Congress and Postmaster General at the close of Cleveland's second term, had been made president of Washington and Lee University at Lexington, Virginia. He asked me to make the

---

3 In 1893, Wilson, a Democratic representative from West Virginia, introduced a bill providing for the free admission of many raw materials, the moderate reduction of duties on manufactured goods, and the substitution of *ad valorem* for specific duties. After passing the House, the Wilson Bill was drastically altered by the Senate, and the resulting Wilson-Gorman Bill (1894) was a protectionist measure.

commencement address before the university, and I accepted. The commencement was the day before the last day's debate on the Hawaiian Annexation Bill, which I was to close. By taking the night train from a town some ten miles from Lexington it was easy for me to reach Washington in ample time to make my speech.

After dining with Wilson I set off for the railway accompanied by Hilary Herbert, Cleveland's last Secretary of the Navy, who had been addressing the law school and who also had an important engagement in Washington the next morning. We had a small one-horse carriage with a native Negro driver. When still five miles from our destination the horse balked. Neither threats, violence nor persuasion would induce him to move. Finally, our driver turned to us and said, "Boss, when this here horse gets thisaway there ain't no use in trying to make him behave. We all must just have patience and wait until he gits ready to move." Herbert and I concluded that there was nothing for us to do but walk and started to do so.

After about half a mile Herbert stopped and said, "One of my heart attacks is coming on," and lay down on the bank beside the road. There was a house not far off to which I went for help only to be told to "git out and go along." Presently two men in a buggy came along, and I hailed them with no better result. Herbert, who now felt better, said to me, "You don't understand these people. Let me tackle the next who comes by." Not long afterwards another buggy appeared, and Herbert standing in the middle of the road waved it to a halt and thus addressed its occupants: "Gentlemen, we ask your assistance. I am ex-Secretary Herbert of the Navy, and this gentleman is Representative McClellan of New York." At which the driver of the buggy replied, "Why don't you all say you're God Almighty and be done with it. Go to hell," and whipping up his horse drove on. Just then our horse who had finally consented to move appeared, and as we got in the carriage we heard the whistle of our train and saw its lights three miles away.

We spent the night over the railway station and reached Washington the next day after the House had adjourned. I had the poor consolation of printing my speech in the record under leave to print. When the bill came to a vote on the day following, Reed was ill and could not be present. John Dalzell who was acting as temporary speaker announced, "I have been requested by the speaker to state that had he been present he would have voted and that he would have voted NO." [4] Reed, [Samuel W.] McCall [of Massachusetts] and [Charles A.] Boutelle of Maine were the only Republicans voting against the bill.[5]

The passage of the Hawaiian Annexation Bill was a grievous disappointment to Reed, for it proved that he had completely lost control of his party in the House. Not long afterwards he announced that he would not be a candidate for re-election. He said to me, "I can't remain in the House with self-respect. I am completely out of sympathy with my own party and the logical thing for me to do would be to join the Democrats, whom I have been fighting all my life. That, of course, I will not and can not do."

The annexation of Hawaii embarked our country on that course of imperialism which has cost us so very much, and it lost to the public service one of the strongest and ablest men who has ever been in public life. When he had left the House, Reed opened a law office in New York and did very well. He never came out openly against the McKinley administration, but in private conversation he was exceedingly bitter in his references to the President and all his works.

The Spanish War was one of the most unnecessary that has ever been fought. Its alleged purpose, the freeing of Cuba, could have been attained without firing a shot, spending a dollar or wasting a man. It was brought about by a group of able and tireless jingoes, who after long preparation and hard work succeeded in instilling the war spirit in the minds of the American people and in making them believe that the war would be nothing but a summer's holiday and that it would transform the United States into a great imperialistic power. By the time the war had actually begun, a majority of the people undoubtedly wanted it and enjoyed its sensation and

4 Dalzell's statement, as given by McClellan, is a paraphrase rather than a quotation. (*Congressional Record,* 55 Cong., 2 Sess., VII, 6019.)

5 McClellan is mistaken, for both Boutelle and McCall voted for the resolution to annex Hawaii. Reed, of course, did not actually vote against the resolution, for he was not present. (*Ibid.*)

excitement, ... [but they had] no realization of its seriousness and horror.

The Spanish War jingoes fell naturally into two fairly well defined groups: those who sincerely believed that the Cuban question could only be finally settled by war and that a successful war would reunite the North and the South and definitely obliterate the memories of the Civil War and the Reconstruction period, and those who were fishers in troubled waters. There were also a great number who, while having more or less well defined convictions as to the necessity of war, were not averse to letting their convictions serve their ambitions.

In Congress the outstanding jingo was Senator Lodge of Massachusetts. He honestly believed that war with Spain was a national necessity and in season and out of season, like the elder Cato, shouted his slogan, *"Delenda est Hispania."* His ability and influence were great, and he was the recognized leader of the war party.

The sensational papers carried every day scare headlines telling of the unspeakable atrocities of the Spaniards in Cuba. A Cuban girl named Cisneros was produced who said that she had been the victim of Spanish lust and torture.[6] Mrs. John A. Logan, the widow of the general of that name, was hired as chaperone, and the girl was sent on a lecture tour over the United States to tell the people of her wrongs. She spoke well and moved her audiences to tears. Long afterwards she confessed that her story, to say the least, was exaggerated, but at the time it served the purpose of the jingoes and helped to rouse the war spirit.

A carefully selected delegation of congressmen was sent to Havana at the expense of the proprietor of one of the jingo papers to see the Spaniards doing their worst, and Representa-

---

[6] It was William Randolph Hearst's New York *Evening Journal* that made the case of Evangelina Cisneros a *cause célèbre*. Some nine months after her imprisonment in Havana by the Spaniards on a charge of rebellion, her case was taken up by the *Journal*. Stating that her only offense had been to protect herself against the advances of a Spanish officer, the *Journal* created a journalistic sensation and an international incident. When the public began to lose interest in the matter, a *Journal* reporter smuggled her out of jail and into the United States, where she made a triumphant tour that was fully covered by *Journal* staff writers.

tive William Alden Smith of Michigan returned with a blood-curdling story of how frock-coated and top-hatted, with only his trusty umbrella as a weapon, he had singlehandedly put to rout a band of Spanish hirelings intent on murdering him. The truth of the story was proved by a snapshot, which was printed showing William Alden in action, frock coat, top hat, umbrella, and all.

A Cuban junta was organized with headquarters at Washington. . . . The junta did yeoman service, and with apparently unlimited funds at its disposal, kept the Cuban cause constantly in the limelight. Their most successful achievement was burglarizing the chancellory of the Spanish legation where they found on the desk of the Spanish minister [to the United States], Dupuy de Lôme, a letter to his chief in Madrid in which he reflected very insultingly on the President of the United States.[7] As soon as the letter was published, the minister was given his passports. Spain apologized, and the incident was declared officially closed. It was, however, by no means forgotten and greatly helped to fan the war spirit.

Conditions in Cuba were undoubtedly very bad and daily went from bad to worse. Spain temporized, and the winter passed with the war spirit constantly increasing step by step with the increase of Spanish severity to the Cubans.

Some time after the war's close I heard Senator Lodge tell the inside facts of the last incident before war became absolutely certain. We had been dining at the Lodges', and after dinner . . . Lodge without any preface told us the following story:

"The morning of February 15, 1898, Cushman Davis" (senator from Minnesota, and chairman of the Senate Committee on Foreign Relations) "and I called on McKinley whom we found in unusually good spirits. He told us that he had just received a cable from General Stewart L. Woodford, our minister at Madrid, saying that the Spanish Minister of Foreign Affairs" (the Duke of Tetuán) "had sent for him and said that if the

---

[7] The de Lôme letter, which was a private rather than an official communication, was stolen, not from the Spanish legation as McClellan states, but from the mails in Havana. It was then turned over to Hearst, who published it in the New York *Evening Journal* on February 8, 1898. In this letter de Lôme states that McKinley was "weak and a bidder for the admiration of the crowd, besides being a would-be politician who tries to leave a door open behind himself while keeping on good terms with the jingoes of his party."

United States would send an ultimatum to Spain demanding
the evacuation of Cuba by Spain, that Spain would evacuate,
provided that the ultimatum was courteously drawn.

"McKinley had the ultimatum on his desk and read it to us.
'I want you two to take it away with you,' he said. 'Think it
over, and then let me know if you approve it, so that it can
be cabled tonight. Thank God, I think that war has been
avoided.'

"Davis and I left the White House and walked to the Capitol
feeling very much depressed, for we felt that despite all our
efforts there would be no war. On reaching the Capitol we
agreed to meet later in the day to discuss the ultimatum before
returning to the President. Before we met the news reached
us that the *Maine* had been blown up with the loss of 266
American officers and men,[8] and we breathed again. The
ultimatum was never sent. Had McKinley sent it without delaying to consult Davis and me, there would probably have
been no war." . . .[9]

The destruction of the *Maine* played directly into the hands
of the war party, for it was assumed that the Spaniards had
blown her up, and the war cry was changed from one demanding justice for Cuba to one demanding "vengeance for our murdered dead." The words, "Remember the *Maine*," were carried
at the head of the editorial pages of the jingo newspapers,
posted on the billboards, and shouted as his peroration by every
jingo orator. McKinley [however] still refused to be stampeded
into war and still hoped to be able to preserve the peace.

How the *Maine* was destroyed will always remain a mystery. . . .[10] The jingoes [however] made such good use of the
destruction of the *Maine* that before long it was generally accepted as a fact that Spain had destroyed her, and anyone dis-
agreeing with the popular opinion was at once branded as a
traitor. McKinley was charged by Roosevelt with having the

---

[8] Actually, the figure was 260.

[9] Lodge's story, as reported by McClellan, may well be true, but it has not
been possible to verify it.

[10] A United States naval inquiry reported on March 21, 1898, that the *Maine*
was destroyed by a submarine mine. Although the report did not state that the
Spaniards were responsible for the explosion, Americans immediately assumed
that this was the case. On March 22, 1898, a Spanish naval inquiry reported that
the *Maine* was destroyed by an accidental explosion inside the ship.

backbone of a chocolate éclair and by Lodge with being feeble and vacillating. Actually McKinley showed much courage and hoped until the last to preserve the peace. In his place Cleveland would probably have prevented war, but McKinley was no Cleveland. He held out longer than would most men, but when he was finally convinced that the country wanted war, following his conception of the duty of the President, he surrendered and swam with the tide.

The congressional committee having solemnly decided that the *Maine* had been blown up from the outside, and Spain having refused the ultimatum . . . [sent by the United States,] the President in April sent a message to Congress declaring that a state of war existed between the United States and Spain.

From the day that the *Maine* had been blown up war had been inevitable, for the people wanted it. Our dealings with Spain became very acrimonious, so that she refused concessions that before she had been willing to grant. . . .

When the President's message reached the House, the Republican leaders had already determined on their course of procedure. There was a considerable number of members on both sides who believed that hostilities might have been prevented and were extremely loath to vote for a flat declaration of war. The President very naturally desired the unanimous backing of Congress if it could be obtained, and accordingly Spain was very skillfully maneuvered into a course that really amounted to waging at least a technical war against the United States. So that when he insisted that a state of war existed between the two countries, he was stating nothing but the actual fact. The House leaders, therefore, instead of submitting a formal declaration of war, which would have been bitterly fought, prepared a joint resolution declaring that a state of "war . . . [existed] between the United States and the Kingdom of Spain." [11] As there was no doubt whatever that a state of war did exist, it was easy for those who were opposed to the war, in the belief that it might have been avoided, to vote for the resolution. . . . The

[11] A resolution authorizing the President to use the army and navy to secure the withdrawal of Spanish troops from Cuba and to secure Cuban independence was adopted on April 20, 1898. On April 25, Congress formally declared war on Spain and made the declaration retroactive to April 20. It is the formal declaration of war rather than the resolution of April 20 to which McClellan is referring. He has confused the resolution and the declaration of war.

resolution passed . . . [both the Senate and House], and the United States was embarked in its first foreign war since 1846.

To say that we were unprepared would be understating the case. A few of us on the inside knew the facts, but those of us who tried to wake Congress from its lethargy and to induce it to prepare the country for the war that seemed inevitable were only voices crying in the wilderness. Some time before [on January 17, 1898,] I had made a speech [to the House of Representatives] in which I had shown that our seacoast was entirely undefended, that we had neither great guns nor ammunition, and that any of the first-class navies could lie outside New York and destroy the city without the guns of the city's alleged defences being able to reach them. General [Nelson A.] Miles, who then commanded the army, replied, stating that I had not told the truth.[12] Having, however, investigated the matter, he found that I was right and issued another statement in which in a very manly way he withdrew his previous statement and apologized to me. Think of it! The commanding general of the army did not know the condition of our coast defences. . . .

We had what was called the Bureau of Military Information, which did good work as far as its limited funds and personnel permitted. The real chief executive of the army, however, was the adjutant general. He was the secretary's right-hand man and through his office passed all matters of any importance. Corbin was the right man in the right place and later, as the first chief of staff, was entirely responsible for successfully putting into operation the general staff law. The department chiefs, except Corbin, were fossils who had reached high command by right of seniority and being sure of their jobs did their best to lead easy lives to the vital hurt of the army. Once appointed at the head of their departments, they had life tenures.

With a Secretary of War in his dotage, with all but one of the heads of the army departments incompetent, without reserves of arms, ammunition supplies, or trained men, with politicians openly influencing the appointment and assignment of officers, the people of the United States entered the war with Spain in the spirit of a party of children starting on a picnic.

[12] McClellan's charges and Miles's reply can be found in the New York *Evening Journal,* January 19, 1898.

The Germans have a proverb that there is a special Providence which guards drunkards, little children, and the United States of America. Certainly that special Providence did its full duty by us during the Spanish War, and we needed its guardianship as we have never needed it either before or since. Whenever it was possible to make a mistake, we made it, and had we been fighting against even a second-class power or had Spain been as strong in fact as she was on paper, we should have had great difficulty in winning, and might even have lost, the war. . . .

The Spanish [-American] War was fought very largely in and by the newspapers. Not only were correspondents present everywhere, but their dispatches went through uncensored. Generals, admirals, and even colonels had their official or unofficial press agents and their favorite correspondents, and strove unceasingly to occupy the center of the stage. News stories were printed featuring this or that man at the expense of the rest, so that it was not until long after the war was over that the actual facts were developed. . . . [Moreover,] as soon as the peace came, the newspapers were filled with criticisms by those who thought that they had not received their due.

[At the start of the war I had] . . . reached the conclusion that it was my duty to support the administration through thick and thin.[13] The great majority of the Democrats were of the contrary opinion, and under the leadership of Joe Bailey [of Texas] constantly voted against appropriation bills for the support of the army and the navy. I organized a bolt from the party which the newspaper men called "The McClellan Democracy." We started in over thirty strong, but the constant pressure of the Democratic leaders was so great that before the peace came the McClellan Democracy had been reduced to [John J.] Fitzgerald of New York and [John F.] Fitzgerald of Massachusetts and

13 On April 28, 1898, in the course of the debate on the war revenue measure, McClellan said: "This is not a time to play politics. This is not a time to draw party lines. If my ideas as to how the means for carrying on the war ought to be raised should not prove to be the ideas of this House, if the views of the minority should be voted down, then I shall feel that it is my duty to refrain from putting even the insignificant obstacle of one vote in the way of the successful prosecution of this war. Then I shall feel that it is my duty, as a man and as an American, to ignore my personal predilections, to ignore my partisanship, and, forgetting that I am a partisan, to remember only that I am a citizen of the United States who loves his country." (*Congressional Record*, 55 Cong., 2 Sess., V, 4363.)

myself. We may not have accomplished very much, but at least we preserved our patriotism and our self-respect. . . .

[My break with the Democrats during the war had no adverse effect on my political fortunes. In 1898, I was re-elected to Congress while polling almost twice the votes received by Howard Conkling, my Republican opponent. Two years later] I was re-elected to the Fifty-sixth Congress by a plurality of over 7,500, although my opponent, Herbert Parsons [a young New York lawyer] made a very vigorous fight. His father John E. Parsons [who was president of the New York City Bar Association] announced at the beginning of the campaign, "I warn McClellan that if he tries any crooked work, I shall have him sent to jail." As no one has ever been able truthfully to charge me with crookedness, Mr. Parsons' outburst hurt his son far more than it helped him. Mrs. Herbert Parsons was the daughter of Henry Clews, a Wall Street operator. She was a very bright woman, but lacked discretion. She was about to have a baby, but, nevertheless, made a personal canvass of the Gas House, my home district, going from tenement house to tenement house and violently abusing me to the inhabitants. As I had many friends among the Gas House men and women, her efforts were not taken kindly, and I was very much worried lest she should get into trouble. Accordingly, I assigned two of my "strong-armed" supporters to shadow her as a body-guard with instructions to protect her should she draw the wrath of my constituents. If anything had happened to her, I should, of course, have been blamed. Parsons went to a good friend of mine and asked her if she knew anything discreditable about me. She told him in no uncertain terms what she thought of him. Parsons did not possess a very lovely character.

Shortly before election Parsons gave a supper to his supporters in his district clubhouse. The "silk stocking" supporters were invited into an inner room where they were given chicken croquets and champagne while the collarless supporters were feasted in an outer room on beer and ham sandwiches. It only needed this error of tact to make his defeat certain. . . . [14]

14 McClellan is not altogether frank in his account of this campaign, for it was almost as difficult for him as that of 1896 had been. Once again, Bryan was running for President, and once again McClellan refused to support him. Bryan made it even more difficult for McClellan by delivering a campaign speech in McClellan's own district in which he said: "In this district you are going to

[During the remaining years that I served in Congress the most interesting work that I did was in my capacity as a member of the Committee on Ways and Means. In 1897,] at the beginning of the first regular session of the Fifty-fifth Congress, I . . . [had been] appointed to fill a vacancy on the committee, . . . [and at the time it had been] a very pleasant surprise to find how many friends I had made in both houses and on both sides, who without my asking them went to the speaker to urge my appointment. . . .[15] The Committee on Ways and Means was by far the most important and influential committee in the House. It was a sort of Treasury Front Bench, and its members were the recognized leaders in House affairs. . . . My membership on Ways and Means placed me on the inside of things, and thereafter I knew a great deal of what was going on. . . .

The second session of the Fifty-sixth Congress in the House was chiefly occupied in repealing the War Revenue Act, and I had my first experience, on the inside, of the difficulty of enacting any tariff bill. I was on the subcommittee on Internal Revenue of the Committee on Ways and Means, and had an excellent opportunity of seeing the lobbyists of conflicting interests at work. I marvel that Congress is ever able to enact any tariff legislation whatever. There is scarcely a member who has not in his district importers and exporters, manufacturers, brewers, distilleries, or tobacco houses. All of these have vital interests in tariff legislation, and many of their interests are conflicting. It is obvious that all cannot be satisfied, and members who seek re-election fear to antagonize powerful constituents.

Our subcommittee on Internal Revenue held public hearings, and it soon developed that there was not a distiller, brewer, or

---

elect McClellan, and I know that I can rely on him to help me." (New York *Sun,* October 28, 1900.) Throughout the campaign McClellan did his best to avoid discussing the issues, and the *Sun* criticized him for his evasiveness. At various times the *Sun* referred to him as "the mummy," "the clam candidate," "Croker's deaf and dumb candidate," "the political ostrich of the present campaign," "the gum shoe man," and "the third-story man . . . who hopes to sneak into Congress." (New York *Sun,* October 29, 30, 31, November 1, 1900.)

15 McClellan's friends undoubtedly helped him to secure the appointment, but he also used whatever influence he possessed to obtain the position. As soon as he learned of the vacancy, he wrote to Croker requesting him to ask Boss Platt to recommend McClellan to the speaker for the job. (McClellan to Richard Croker, January 7, 1897, McClellan MSS.)

tobacco manufacturer who did not insist that he was enormously
overtaxed. I had spent considerable time in working out the
maximum revenue-raising points in the tobacco, spirits, and
beer schedules and had found them, in each case, somewhat in
excess of the war rates. In other words, the three interests
involved were in no case overtaxed, but nevertheless each
claimed that it was terribly oppressed.

The brewers were especially vociferous, and all insisted that
with an alcoholic content of not more than five per cent in
their product they should be treated as manufacturing a quasi
non-alcoholic beverage.

I submitted to them the Bavarian law which taxes beer on
its alcoholic content, and showed them that with an alcoholic
content of only five per cent they would be better off under that
law than they would be with the rate they proposed of two
dollars a barrel. Only two firms were willing to accept an
adaptation of the Bavarian law, the rest flatly refused to consider
it. The truth of the matter was that with the exception of these
two brews every beer on the market contained nearer ten per
cent than five per cent of alcohol. The brewers got substantially
what they wanted, as did the distillers and the tobacco manufacturers. For all practical purposes the new tariff law was
drafted by the interests affected and not by the House committee, and this I am sorry to say is generally the case with tariff
legislation no matter which party is in power. When the bill
went to the Senate, it was as usual amended in many important
particulars, and as usual the Senate had its way when the bill
went to conference.

The first conference on which I ever sat was a revelation to
me. In my second session I was the Democratic conferee on
the Army Appropriation Bill, which came back from the Senate
two days before final adjournment with some sixty amendments, to many of which our committee vigorously objected.
The conference met in the committee room of the Senate Committee on Appropriations, Senator [Matthews S.] Quay [the Republican boss], of Pennsylvania being chairman of the Senate
conferees. Quay began proceedings by saying to us of the
House, "Gentlemen, the Senate is willing to yield on the following amendments," and he then read by number a list of
some twenty-five amendments of no particular importance and

continued, "The Senate refuses to yield on the rest. As my two Senate colleagues and I are going to the baseball game, I suggest that we adjourn to meet tomorrow morning. We have yielded on enough amendments to save your faces, you can think it over and let us know tomorrow if you will concur on the other amendments."

Being young, enthusiastic, and inexperienced I was outraged by the Senate's highhanded action. Governor [John A. T.] Hull, [a Republican representative from Iowa and] our chairman, tried to calm me by saying that that was the usual procedure in dealing with the Senate, that he would have no objection to my moving to non-concur, but that he had no idea that the House would risk an extra session by a deadlock. The next morning my two colleagues agreed to the Senate's proposals, I reserving the right to move on the floor to non-concur.

When Hull presented the conference report he was quite eloquent in telling the House of the tremendous victory he had won in inducing the Senate to yield on twenty-five amendments and urged the House to agree to the others. I moved to non-concur and to send the bill back to conference, but as the House did not want an extra session my motion was voted down and the Senate had its way.

It is the Senate's custom to hold back appropriation bills until the very end of the session and then send them to the House loaded down with new legislation, most of it utterly ungermane to the bills. As most senators have homes in Washington and as they only come up for re-election one third every two years, long sessions have no terrors for them. The members of the House, on the other hand, most of whom live in hotels or boardinghouses, and all of whom come up for re-election every two years, greatly dread long sessions, which keep them from going home for the mending of their political fences. Accordingly, when faced with the alternative of either accepting Senate amendments of which they do not approve or of staying indefinitely in Washington, they invariably choose the former. Their action may be deficient in public spirit, but it is very human.

When we came back to Washington for the first session of the Fifty-seventh Congress, one of Roosevelt's first official acts was to urge the two houses to keep faith with Cuba and to enact a reciprocity law which would permit her to live, by materially reducing our tariff duties on sugar. There was at once a loud outcry from the cane sugar interests of Louisiana and the beet sugar growers, and the lobbyists of these two interests were so numerous as almost to stop traffic in the streets of the capital. I doubt if there has ever been a more noisy, blatant, and unscrupulous lot of lobbyists gathered together.

The Democrats were generally opposed to any form of reciprocity that would injure the interests of the Democratic sugar-growing states, and, besides, on general principles they opposed anything the President wanted. I could not see my way clear to breaking faith with Cuba for the purpose of protecting the dividends of the cane and beet sugar companies. I announced myself in favor of enacting a reciprocity bill and with my committee colleague, Chester I. Long, a Republican from Kansas, and afterwards a senator, began to draft the necessary legislation. I soon found that it was by far the most complicated subject that I had ever handled, and literally went to school with the Treasury experts as my instructors. For the time being I acquired a very fair knowledge of the sugar question. Sam McCall once said in a speech, "I never knew but one man who really knew what the sugar differential was. That was George McClellan, and he was utterly unable to explain it to anyone else."

We finally reported a bill that, after a stormy debate, which I opened, passed the House but the Congress died before the Senate had taken action.

Chapter VI

The Very Pleasantest of Clubs

THE HAPPIEST years of my life were those we spent in Washington in the days of our youth. We had youth and good health, . . . [and] people liked us. I had what seemed to be a sure seat, with the prospect of a life service in Congress, and I enjoyed my work in the House more than any I have ever done. With great ambition, diligence, and fair ability, I had high hope for the future. Life was still before us and all the world was young.

The House is a little world by itself, in some respects the very pleasantest of clubs. Roughly the members of the House may be divided into three classes, those who are there for serious business, those who are there to have a good time, and the accidentals who are cast up by the tide of politics to disappear when the tide recedes after one inconspicuous term.

It does not take long for a man to find his place in the House, and the House very soon judges a man at his true worth. The members who are there merely because of their wealth or because they need the salary (as for example, many of those sent by the Democratic and Republican machines in the great cities) are tolerated but count for nothing in the management of public business, while the accidents are frankly ignored. It is the serious men who count and control the House.

The longer a member stays and the harder he works the more important he becomes. While the seniority rule, which promotes men on their committees automatically, gives many a committee an incompetent chairman, no satisfactory substitute has ever been devised.

The important members are by no means always those who have the best press, or whose names appear oftenest in the

Congressional Record. The men of the greatest influence are those who, with sure seats, are able and willing to devote their entire time to the work of the House, who have the ability to master its rules and procedure, are specialists in the work of their committees and have the liking as well as the respect of their fellow members. For such men the galleries, including even the press gallery, do not exist. When they speak it is on a question with which they are familiar, and they address themselves to their fellow members and not to the gallery. They are unconscious of any audience being present except that upon the floor, and applause from the gallery is resented and not welcomed.

On the other hand, the cheaper members of the House, and there are always many such, toady to the press, seek the applause of the gallery, and strive to "get into the *Record*" on every important question that comes up. It is a matter of indifference to them whether they actually address the House or only print their undelivered speeches in the Appendix under "leave to print."

It may be an old man's prejudice, but it seems to me that the quality of the House has deteriorated very much since my time. . . . One of the greatest mistakes ever made was in raising salaries [from $5,000] to $10,000. With a salary of $5,000, unless a member had private means, he was obliged to make a great sacrifice to go to Congress, which meant that he liked the work and the honor and was public spirited. As soon as the salary was increased, a seat in the House or Senate became worth while from the money point of view. Service in the House became what is called in New York a "district leader's job," and in many states the salary is the largest to which a politician may aspire, larger even than that of governor or of those of the justices of the highest state court. . . .

I lay . . . [the deterioration of the quality of the House] not only to the increase in salaries, but more especially to the direct primary. The direct primary necessitates two campaigns for the successful candidate, so that apart from the additional expense, the member seeking re-election must devote most of his time to the maintenance of his political fences. A senator need only think of the grind of local politics during the sixth and last year of his term, and between times may be as much of a statesman as he knows how, while a representative who has not a "safe district" must think of the "folks at home." In other words, [he] must think parochially and more or less as a demagogue most of the time. In the old days of nomination by conventions the actual fighting for re-election began only a few weeks before election day; now it sometimes begins a year in advance. To retain a doubtful district nowadays, the representative must spend almost as much time at home as he does in Washington.

During my service in the House I was fortunate enough to have two New York leaders, Croker and Murphy, neither of whom took any interest in what went on in Washington. Never but twice did Croker interfere with me. Once he asked me to support Sulzer for speaker, whose speakership "boom" came to nothing, and once he sent for me, [when] I was dean of the delegation, and said, "George, we are for imperialism." The Philippine Bill was coming up for discussion, and the party was solidly against it. "But, my dear Mr. Croker," I replied, "our platform has declared against imperialism as the paramount issue of the last campaign, and every Democrat in Congress has stood on that platform." "I don't care," he said, "we're for imperialism." I left him a very sorrowful man, for I could not vote for the bill and keep my self-respect, and I realized that voting against the bill meant my finish in politics. The next day he again sent for me and said, "George, I guess we're against imperialism," and a great load was taken from my mind.[1]

During the nominal boss-ship of John C. Sheehan I never received from him but one request of any importance.[2] Before the Great War it was the custom of the State Department to issue "special passports" to private citizens of more or less dis-

[1] Croker may not have understood the issues, but he had a gift for summing them up in a few colorful words. He once said: "My idea of Anti-Imperialism is opposition to the fashion of shooting everybody who doesn't speak English." On another occasion, when asked what he thought about the free-silver controversy, he replied: "What's the use of discussing what's the best kind of money? I'm in favour of all kinds of money—the more the better." Quoted in M. R. Werner, *Tammany Hall,* 441.

[2] In reply to even the minor requests made by Sheehan, McClellan refused to commit himself or make any definite promises. For example, see William F. Sheehan to McClellan, June 1, 1896, March 19, 1897; McClellan to Sheehan, June 2, 1896, March 20, 1897, McClellan MSS.

tinction on the application of a senator or representative. While these special passports conferred no special privileges, they were of undoubted service in obtaining courtesies from foreign governments. Sheehan wrote me asking for a special passport for one of his "intimate friends," which I forthwith obtained and sent to him and promptly forgot the matter. During the summer John Hay, then Secretary of State, wrote me a rather excited letter asking for information about Sheehan's friend who it appeared had organized an unsuccessful rebellion in one of the South American or Central American states, eloped with the dictator's wife, and absconded with the rebellion's treasure chest. Sheehan, when queried, calmly stated that when he had said "intimate friend" he had spoken metaphorically and that he actually knew nothing whatever about the man.[3] It took me a long time to pacify the righteous wrath of the State Department, and thereafter I was very careful for whom I asked special passports. . . .

Now . . . New York Democratic leaders, while knowing no more of what is going on in Washington than their predecessors, do not hesitate at least to try to deliver their delegations solidly for or against pending legislation. All that is now required of a New York City member is to obey orders and to be seen frequently at the district clubhouse. . . .

In my day in Congress there was undoubtedly a great deal of drinking among members, and a great deal of barroom loafing, and it was not unusual to see in the House restaurant members who were the worse for wear.

At a men's dinner at Senator Murphy's one night soon after my arrival I met Senator [George G.] Vest, [a Democrat] of Missouri, for the first time. He was a little man with a fierce white moustache and goatee, the typical Southern brigadier, who, however, had not served in the Confederate Army but in the Confederate Congress. There was plenty to drink, and Senator Vest drank industriously. Suddenly someone exclaimed, "Where is Vest?" His seat was vacant, and no one had seen him go out. Our host became very anxious, fearing that Vest

[3] The name of this colorful individual was William Grauert. His exploits are described in detail by the United States minister to Bolivia in a letter to the Assistant Secretary of State. (Thomas Moonlight to Alvey A. Adee, July 12, 1896 [copy], McClellan MSS.)

had been taken ill. A search of the house failed to discover the senator and assuming that he had gone home we resumed our dinner. Toward the close of the evening there was a commotion under the table, and Senator Vest appeared rumpled but fairly sober. He had slid down from his chair, curled up under the table, and had a pleasant hour's sleep. . . .

Every year the House was in the habit of inserting in one of the appropriations bills a proviso banning the sale of alcoholic drinks from the House restaurant. This was for home consumption of those constituencies that contained prohibitionists. When the bill reached the Senate, the Senate always obligingly struck out the proviso. Prohibitionist constituents were impressed, and no inconvenience was suffered by the House. One year Senator [Eugene] Hale, [a Maine Republican] who had a good sense of humor and hated hypocrisy, made an impassioned plea to the Senate for the maintenance of the proviso, and the Senate followed him. The proviso remained in the bill, and from that time on drink was banished from the House wing of the Capitol, and members who wanted their whiskey were obliged to go to the Senate restaurant to get it. It served the House right, but it was hard on those of us who had always voted against the proviso. . . .

When I served in the House, the sectional lines between North and South were very sharply drawn. I began my service just thirty years after Appomattox and found among my fellow members a great many who had been soldiers of the Confederacy. The horrors of Reconstruction had only ended some eighteen years before and were a vivid and bitter memory in the heart of every Southern representative. Unlike the Scots who . . . gloried in being called "rebels," the Southerners in Congress violently objected to having the Civil War referred to as "the war of the rebellion." They themselves always spoke of it as "the war between the states," and from time to time one or another of them would make a futile effort to have that expression substituted for the official designation, "the Civil War." They regarded all Republicans as possible ex-carpetbaggers and called them "radicals" or "damned Yankees."

The Democratic party in the House was then, as it always has been since the Civil War until lately, absolutely in the control of the South. Randall and Rainey, Northern men, were elected speaker [4] by the grace of the South and occasionally a Northern man has reached an important chairmanship, but in the vast majority of cases, when the Democrats have controlled the House, the speakership and all important chairmanships have been filled by Southern men. In the same way Southern policies have until lately usually dominated the Democrats in Congress.[5] The Southern prejudice against Republicans is reflected in the attitude of the average Southern congressman towards the Northern Democrats. I soon found that we were tolerated, but not loved.

The South has been glad enough to use the North in furthering Southern policies and Southern schemes. Southern men have been glad enough to migrate to New York and "carpetbag" in the most approved way [and] to organize and utilize the Southern vote for all it is worth in forcing New York leaders to give offices to Southerners. On the other hand, the South for some not very apparent reason has looked down on the North, expected Northern Democrats to do its bidding, and in Congress given them only grudging recognition.

Legislation affecting New York has always been difficult to obtain and has required for its success a great amount of "log rolling." To obtain the appropriation for the construction of the thirty-foot-deep Ambrose Channel, necessary not only for New York but for the whole country as well, we were obliged to vote for every item on a forty million dollar River and Harbor Bill, the largest passed up to that time. To induce Congress to pay the deficit of the Buffalo Exposition due to the McKinley murder, our delegation had to vote for similar legislation in behalf of state expositions in the states of Washington and North Carolina. . . .

The typical Southerner, as I knew him in Congress forty years ago, was in his outlook as parochial as was any man in the United States. For him the world was bounded by the Mason-Dixon line. South of that line were "white men," for the "nigrar" did not count. To the north of that line and beyond were nothing but barbarians. If he failed to recognize

[4] Samuel J. Randall of Pennsylvania was speaker from 1876 to 1881, and Henry T. Rainey of Illinois was speaker from 1933 to 1934.

[5] It should be kept in mind that McClellan was writing in the Franklin D. Roosevelt administration when Democratic policies more often than not were sponsored by Northern New Dealers rather than by Southern party leaders.

that great truth, he would not be re-elected. I remember Jesse Stallings of Alabama saying to me, "I wish that I could see Europe." "Why don't you go?" I queried. "If it were known," he answered, "that I had gone abroad, my district, safe as it seems, would turn me down." . . .

The average Southerner's attitude on the Negro question is to a Northerner difficult to understand. He regards the Negro as a man belonging to an inferior race, to be kindly treated but to be treated as he was in slave days. It is claimed by Southerners, at least by those from the "black belt," that the Negro can only be kept in subjection by the fear of lynching for sexual crimes. I have been often told by Southerners living on plantations that they never left their womenfolk at home without the greatest anxiety, lest on their return they might find that they had been the victims of Negro lust. . . .

In the Fifty-sixth Congress there were two Negro members, both from North Carolina, named Murray [6] and White.[7] Murray was jet black in color and of very limited intelligence. He was later put out of politics by the convenient method of a penitentiary sentence for larceny. White on the other hand was of more than average intelligence, a good speaker and a decent enough fellow. Incidently he was nearly white. White and Murray always lunched by themselves at a little table in a corner of the restaurant. There was great excitement one day among the Southerners because a white member had been seen lunching at the same table with the Negroes. The most bloodthirsty plans were discussed and it was even suggested that a Democrat should be chosen to tweak the nose of the offender. Fortunately for the peace of the House nothing ever came of it.

The occasional white Republicans who came to the House from Southern states, largely by Negro votes, were treated very much as were the Negroes themselves. Even Richmond Pearson from North Carolina, a very fine fellow and a Princeton man [who was a representative from 1895 to 1901] was sent to Coventry by his fellow Southerners.

Not long before his death, Harry [Henry St. George] Tucker

[6] George W. Murray, a schoolteacher, served as a Republican representative from South Carolina from 1893 to 1897. He was not, however, a member of the Fifty-sixth Congress, which convened after he had left the House.

[7] George H. White, who was a lawyer and banker, was a Republican member of the House of Representatives from North Carolina from 1897 to 1901.

[a Democrat representative] of Virgina said to me, "An unbelievable thing happened yesterday. Martin Madden" (chairman of Appropriations and [a Republican] from Chicago) "said on the floor that he was proud to represent a Negro district. I had rather liked him, but after that I can have no more use for him."

The Southerners insist, as they did in slave days, that the Negro question is a "peculiar institution" to be dealt with by the South in its own way without the impertinent interference of the North.

In my day the Southerners still talked loudly of "affairs of honor," and Joe Bailey once sent Speaker Reed a challenge, called a "cyartell," for some fancied slight. Reed walked up to Bailey and said, "Joe, don't be a damned fool." That ended the "affair."

I was sitting one day in the speaker's lobby with a half-dozen Southerners who were telling me of "affairs of honor" within their experience, when there strolled up a [Republican] member from Ohio, William B. Shattuc, who had made some study of dueling in the South. He listened for a while and then said, "Can any of you fellows tell me of any real honest-to-goodness duel of which you have personal knowledge?" They at once, with one accord, began to tell of "affairs of honor" with which they were familiar. Shattuc, as each story was told, asked very searching questions and said as he walked away: "I notice that in every case that you fellows have mentioned, the victim was shot in the back, or was potted from behind an ash barrel, a lamp post, or a tree. You haven't told me and you can't tell me of an actual duel in which both men stood up with equal chances and fired at each other."

There was an old fellow in the House, from Tennessee, [a Gold Democrat] named Josiah Patterson. He was beaten for re-election in 1896 by another Democrat, a brilliant newspaperman named Edward W. Carmack. Patterson contested Carmack's election, and the latter handled his case on the floor of the House himself. He closed his speech by telling the following story: When Patterson was colonel of a Confederate regiment he was leading his command in retreat before the enemy. Presently the colonel heard firing in the rear and summoned his adjutant who like all Confederate adjutants held the rank of lieutenant colonel, "Cyernal," asked Josiah, "what is that poppin' I hear at the rear?" "That, Sah," replied the adjutant, "is some of our boys a-firin' at the Yanks." "Fo' God's sake tell 'em to stop firin' at the Yanks," shouted Josiah, "it only makes 'em madder." The House burst into uproarious applause, and Carmack retained his seat. Not long afterwards [in 1908] Carmack was shot in the back and killed in broad daylight on one of the principal streets of the state capital. It was apparently considered an affair of honor, for no great effort was ever made to find the murderer. I knew Carmack well and liked him extremely. Had he lived, he would have gone far.

Joe Bailey, who succeeded Crisp as Democratic leader [in 1896], was a man of great ability and a first-rate constitutional lawyer. Unfortunately he had absolutely no sense of humor. One day he opposed a bill of no great importance on the ground of its unconstitutionality and made a very admirable argument in support of his position. James Hamilton Lewis [a Democrat from Washington] opposed him in one of his delightfully amusing speeches which made the House roar with laughter. When the House divided, most of the Democrats, as a joke, voted with Lewis, the Republicans not voting. Joe asked for the yeas and nays, but they were refused. That night Bailey resigned his leadership on the ground that he had been humiliated by his party and refused to reconsider his action.

Not long afterwards at a committee meeting Bailey leaned across the table and said to me, "McClellan, I don't think that you take me seriously enough." "No, Joe," I answered, "I don't take you seriously at all." Bailey scowled at me, "McClellan, the trouble with you is that you are an aristocrat." As his origin was by no means aristocratic, he considered this a crowning insult. He refused to speak to me again, but on my last day in the House I went over to the Senate, where he was serving with great distinction, and said to him, "Joe, why should we continue to make fools of ourselves? Shake hands." He grudgingly did so, and I never saw him again.

Once when Henry St. George Tucker of Virginia was stopping with us the weather turned cold. I took up to his room the blanket under which I have slept all my life. It had been captured from a British officer during the War of 1812 and had been given to my father when he was in command of our army.

The next morning Tucker came downstairs looking very solemn. "George," he said, "there is a serious matter I must speak to you about. Did you give me that blanket intentionally? Of course I did not, and could not, sleep under it." "My dear Harry," I answered, "what is the matter? What is wrong with the blanket?" "Have you never read the inscription in the corner?" [he asked,] and then my awful mistake nearly staggered me, for in the corner of the blanket the donor had embroidered the following words: "This blanket was captured from a British officer in the War of 1812. In this war with traitors may its owner use it with pride and pleasure." I assured Tucker that I had intended no reflection on the South in giving him the blanket and that I had quite forgotten the words embroidered in the corner, that had I remembered them he would have never seen the blanket.

The Southerners who were "born" were delightful gentlemen, well educated, of great courtesy, charming companions, and loyal friends. . . .

It must be conceded that in my time the Republicans in the House outclassed us as effective debaters and as practical men of affairs. . . . Of the Republican debaters, Charles Littlefield of Maine was by far the ablest of my time. . . . He was absolutely fearless and independent, refused to be bound by party ties, and was as much feared by the Republicans as he was by the Democrats. When Brigham H. Roberts, the Mormon elder and polygamist from Utah, was elected to the House [in 1898] in violation of the state constitution, the Women's Christian Temperance Union demanded that he be not permitted to take the oath. Littlefield, McCall, and I believed that the House had no power to prevent him taking the oath, but that after doing so he should be expelled. The House, however, bowed to the demand of the W.C.T.U. and determined to exclude him, constitution, law, and precedents to the contrary notwithstanding. Littlefield carried the whole fight on his own shoulders, and fought one of the bravest and most brilliant losing battles in which I have ever taken part. When we were beaten (we only mustered about a dozen votes), the galleries, packed with members of the W.C.T.U., rose as one woman and hissed us. We three left the floor together and found the corridor packed with hard-faced ladies. [Robert] Taylor, [a

Republican] of Ohio, who had managed the bill, preceded us. As he appeared, he was seized by a stern-faced lady, kissed and passed to the next lady in line, kissed again, and thus passed out to the entrance. When we appeared we were booed, hissed, and generally insulted; and yet our fate was certainly to be preferred to that of Taylor. . . .

Of the orators, so-called, to whom the House was always willing to listen, the most important on the Republican side were [Jonathan P.] Dolliver [of Iowa] and [David B.] Henderson [who was also from Iowa]. They were chiefly used in closing debates of importance really more for their effect on the public than for the making of votes on the floor, where members' minds are usually made up long before the debate begins. When prepared Dolliver could make an excellent speech and so could Henderson. The latter was extremely picturesque. He was a fine-looking man who had lost a leg in the Civil War, and when he spoke, he was in the habit of taking off his cork leg and placing his stump on the desk before him. This gruesome procedure always caught the gallery. His voice was vibrant and musical, and when he "pulled out the sob stop," he often moved the women in the gallery to tears.

Reed had taken a great fancy to [Robert G.] Cousins of Iowa, a youngish man with a build and voice not unlike his own. Cousins used to typewrite his speeches on small sheets of paper, which he held in his left hand and read so cleverly that he seemed to be speaking extemporaneously. Reed pushed him as much as he was able, and Cousins made his greatest success in closing the debate on the Spanish War resolution, reading at length Kipling's "Recessional," which had only lately been published. Many thought Cousins much overrated, but the galleries loved him.

On the Democratic side all the Southerners considered themselves orators. While all of them could speak indefinitely on any subject whatever, whether they knew anything about it or not, some of them were very effective. Bailey and John Sharpe Williams were our best. When they went to the Senate, their places were taken by Champ Clark [of Missouri], James D. Richardson of Tennessee, and Oscar Underwood of Alabama.

Clark had made a well deserved reputation as a humorist. When he developed ambitions for leadership, he found it very difficult to be taken seriously and to live down his former fame. It was greatly to his credit that he succeeded.

Richardson, as the Democratic leader, was obliged to close debates from time to time, but he was not a success as an orator. "The Major" or "the dear Major" as he was called to his face, "Slippery Jim" as he was called behind his back, had served in the Confederate Army, in what he called "the war between the states." He was an excellent parliamentarian and was at his best when arguing a point of order, which he usually did with complete success. As a debater on general subjects, however, and as an orator, he left much to be desired. As leader of the party, he did not shine. He was a very courteous, pleasant man to meet casually in the House, but he was so almost ingenuously selfish that he failed to win the confidence of the members.

Shortly after his election as leader he submitted to the speaker, according to custom, his recommendations for the filling of minority vacancies on the committees. Most of those whom he recommended had opposed him in the caucus, while almost all his supporters were ignored. John Maddox and Carter Tate of Georgia, who had managed his campaign, went to him to protest. Maddox said to me, "Cyarter and I went to the dear Major and told him that his supporters had got nothing out of his victory. The dear Major looked at us with that hurt look of his and said, 'Boys, what are you-all a-kickin' about? Ain't you got me?'"

The Major's greatest triumph was in passing a bill for the erection of a statue of General [Albert] Pike, a Confederate brigadier. The procedure in the erection of all statues is the same. The admirers of the person to be honored raise what money they can, sometimes only a few thousand dollars, sometimes a considerable amount. Congress then appropriates a lump sum of $50,000 for "the preparation of the site and the construction of the pedestal." The bill always contains a proviso "that any part of this sum not required for these purposes may be expended for the completion of the statue." As "these purposes" seldom require more than a few thousand dollars, the greater part of the $50,000 is available for the statue itself. General Pike was honored ostensibly as the head of the Southern wing of the Scottish Rite Masons. When the statue was unveiled, the general was found to be wearing a Confederate uniform, and the "dear Major" gloried in having flim-flammed a Republican Congress into erecting a monument to a Confederate soldier.[8]

At the end of his ninth term the Major concluded to retire from the House and to devote his time to the affairs of the Scottish Rite Masons, Southern Branch, of which he had been elected head. For some years he lived in the "Palace" of the Scottish Rite, Southern Branch, in Washington, where he died quite unexpectedly.

I could never understand the fame that Oscar Underwood subsequently acquired. When I knew him he was a nice-look-ing, well-dressed, extremely solemn, man of between forty and fifty, with a disagreeable whiney voice, with which, at every opportunity, he did his best to "subtract from the sum of human knowledge." Richardson and he were great friends, and when the former became leader he made the latter party whip and assistant leader. The Democrats bitterly resented this, for they claimed, with reason, that the major had no right whatever to create the two positions. Nevertheless, from that time on the voice of Oscar was heard in the land on every possible occasion, proclaiming with tremendous impressiveness great truths with which everyone was perfectly familiar.

When the Spanish War Revenue Act was repealed we Demo-crats were allowed one and only one amendment. As the major seemed to take no interest in the matter, the minority members of the Committee on Ways and Means authorized me to pre-pare and report the amendment. I wrote the views of the minority and submitted as our amendment the Mills Tariff Bill [9] of the Fiftieth Congress. All signed my report but Under-wood, who said to me, "George, I can't sign that report. I am a

[8] Pike at best represented a minor victory, for he left a great deal to be de-sired as both a Confederate and a soldier. A Northerner who had migrated to Arkansas, he was opposed to slavery and only a lukewarm supporter of secession. Although he commanded some Indians at the Battle of Pea Ridge, Arkansas (March 7-8, 1862), he resigned from the Confederate Army in the same year and spent the remainder of the war criticizing the Confederacy's civilian and military leaders.

[9] In 1887, Cleveland in a special message to Congress requested a reduction of the tariff. The House responded by passing the so-called "Mills Bill," which provided for a reduction in the duties of several manufactured goods and placed hemp, flax, lumber, and wool on the free list. This bill did not become law, for it was not passed by the Senate.

free trader, and as the Mills Bill contains elements of protection, I can't support it. I cannot palter with my conscience." I learned later that Oscar owned a steel mill at Birmingham which had recently been absorbed by the steel trust. Oscar was really a high protectionist,[10] which may in part account for the support he subsequently received from certain vested interests for the presidential nomination. . . .

The House invariably has on its rolls a number of men who acquire fame by making themselves unmitigated nuisances. They noisily project themselves into every important debate, ask pointless and impertinent questions of the men who have the floor, and strive to advertise themselves by every possible means in the hope of getting their names in the newspapers, and thus impressing "the folks back home."

John Wesley Gaines, [a Democrat] of Tennessee, spoke on all possible occasions with no very clear idea on any subject. He spoke at the top of his lungs, hurling denunciations at the Republicans, shouting the praises of his native state but never by any chance speaking to the question before the House. He had absolutely no sense of humor and seemed to live in a sort of intellectual fog, far removed from what was going on about him. The New York *Sun* published as an editorial paragraph a short poem in his honor which ran:

> John Wesley Gaines, John Wesley Gaines,
> Thou monumental pile of brains,
> Because of thee
> Proud Tennessee
> Still great remains,
> John Wesley Gaines, John Wesley Gaines.

Gaines took the poem quite seriously and with much pride showed it to everyone who would look at it. It is said that he called on Bob Taylor, the governor [from 1887 to 1891] of his state and found him busy writing at his desk. As Gaines was announced, the governor without looking up said, "Take a chair, Mr. Gaines." Gaines, who greatly felt his importance,

---

[10] In 1911, Underwood in a speech to the House said: "I am a stockholder in the Woodward Iron Company, located near Birmingham, Alabama. . . . My brother-in-law . . . is the vice president and general manager of that company." He then stated that these facts never influenced his views on the tariff. *Congressional Record*, 62 Cong., 1 Sess., IV, 3510-3513.

replied more in sorrow than in anger, "I fear that you don't know who I am, Governor. I am Representative John Wesley Gaines." Still without looking up the governor said: "Take two chairs, Mr. Gaines," who forever afterwards was known as "Two Chair Gaines." . . .

Two of the most picturesque representatives from New York City were "Pop" [George H.] Lindsay and [John H. G.] Vehslage, [both of whom were Democrats]. The former was a retail liquor dealer in Brooklyn, and after the committees had been announced said to me: "The speaker was mighty decent to me. He put me on alcoholic liquor traffic, for he must have known that I kept a place." He was under the impression that his committee regulated the barrooms throughout the country and saw himself as a sort of dictator of his associates in New York.

Vehslage, who ran a small delicatessen shop in Manhattan, acquired fame by means of a poster put out by his Republican opponent which read, "What is the difference between Prince Bismarck and Vehslage? One is a grosse Deutscher and the other is a Deutscher grocer."

In point of non-continuous service the senior member of our delegation was General John E. Ketcham who served off and on for sixteen terms.[11] He came from Dutchess County where he was a great power in Republican politics. What he got out of his service in the House I could never understand, for he was almost stone deaf, was quite feeble, and seldom came to the Capitol, spending most of his time at a little hotel on Seventeenth Street where he lived all by himself. He was known as "Whispering Johnny" from his habit of always, like so many deaf people, speaking in whispers A story was told of him that one day as he was walking home from the House a beggar asked him for a dime. Whispering Johnny shook his head and whispered, "I don't understand. I'm deef" (he pronounced the word as does ex-President Hoover). Charmed and emboldened by his benevolent appearance, the beggar tried again, this time asking for a quarter. The general smiled sweetly and again shook his head and said that he was "deef." The beggar at the top of his lungs shouted, "Can you spare me half a dollar?" at which Whispering Johnny turned on him and

11 Actually, Ketcham served seventeen terms.

in a very loud voice replied, "Damn you, you said a dime just now." . . .

A Populist from Nebraska, named [Omer M.] Kem, acquired fame by objecting to all requests for unanimous consent. His home papers praised him highly for protecting the Treasury, and for weeks not a private bill was passed. Finally after Kem had become the most hated man in the House, the speaker told him that unless he mended his ways he would never be recognized for any purpose whatsoever, either in the House or in Committee of the Whole. The awful prospect of being deprived of the right to talk, without which no Populist or Progressive can live, was too much for him, and the private bill mill once more began to grind.

His colleague, "Sockless Jerry" Simpson, who had achieved distinction as the crudest member of the Fifty-third Congress and literally wore no socks,[12] returned to the Fifty-fifth Congress much tamed and civilized. He not only had taken to wearing socks, those badges of the bourgeoisie, but had become a very quiet, sensible man. So much was this the case that at the next election his constituents repudiated him.

Seth Cobb [a Democrat] of Alabama,[13] who all too frequently talked about nothing in particular in a sleepy, dreamy sort of way, had his brief moment in the sun. He was making one of his usual pointless speeches when he completely lost the thread of his argument. He paused with his eyes closed for nearly a minute, and then pulling himself together with a very obvious effort turned to the chair and asked, "Mr. Speakah, whar am I at?" He had touched the heights with four words, for he had added a phrase to our language.

[12] Simpson was far from being crude and gave every evidence of being sensible. Hamlin Garland wrote: "He is a clear thinker, a remarkable speaker, and has a naturally philosophical mind which carries his reasoning down to the most fundamental facts of organic law and human rights." (Hamlin Garland, "The Alliance Wedge in Congress," *The Arena*, V [May, 1892], 451.)

The fable that Simpson wore no socks originated in the following fashion: "Simpson's Republican opponent in the race for Congress [in 1890] was a well-groomed gentleman, Colonel James R. Hallowell, whom Simpson, on the defensive because of the jibes at his own rural appearance, promptly dubbed 'Prince Hal' and accused of wearing silk stockings. Victor Murdock, then a young reporter, came back with the retort that Simpson wore no socks at all; hence the appellation, 'Sockless Jerry,' which followed Simpson the rest of his life." (John D. Hicks, *The Populist Revolt* [Minneapolis, 1931], 162.)

[13] Cobb was actually a representative from Missouri.

Among the Republicans there were not so many nuisances, for their discipline was far better than was ours. The Republican caucus has always been able to enforce its will on the Republican side of the House. The Democratic caucus was more or less of a joke, and during my five terms I never knew it to agree on anything but a motion to adjourn. In addition, Republican leadership was generally more effective than ours, and members on that side of the House stood more in awe of their leaders than did the Democrats. A hint from his leader would generally suppress a Republican who tried too far the patience of his side.

The real, effective hard work of the House is always done by a group of wheelhorses whose names seldom appear in the newspapers and of whom the public knows next to nothing, but who are sincerely appreciated by their fellow members. Most of their work is done in committee, their appearances on the floor being usually limited to the discussion of bills reported from their own committees. In my time, [among] the really important members who did the heavy spadework were, besides the speaker, Dingley, Payne, Dalzell, McCall, Cannon, Holman, . . . and Dockery. . . . [All but Holman and Dockery were Republicans.]

Nelson A. Dingley, [a Republican from Maine who was] always called "Governor" for he had been governor of Maine, was a little weazened-up old man with a hooked nose and scraggly beard. . . . He invariably wore on the floor a black broadcloth frock coat, a low-cut waistcoat, a shoestring black tie, and winter and summer a pair of arctic overshoes. He knew . . . [the tariff] inside out, and although titular floor leader, never spoke except on matters connected with the tariff. He hailed from Lewiston, and his point of view was largely that of his native town. I asked him why he had made the hundred dollar exemption clause so low, the clause in the tariff law which limits to one hundred dollars the amount of purchases made abroad that returning American tourists may bring in free. He replied that he had done so because one hundred dollars was quite enough for any woman to spend on her year's wardrobe. . . .

[Sereno E.] Payne [of New York] and Dalzell knew as much of the tariff as did Dingley. In addition to Ways and Means,

Dalzell was on Rules and was the real floor leader during my service.

[Joseph G.] Cannon was chairman of Appropriations in the Fifty-fourth, Fifty-fifth, and Fifty-sixth congresses, after which he became speaker. He had been born in South Carolina and moved to Illinois when a child. He had a district that was so sure that it continued to return him even after his mind began to fail. He was a rough diamond with a sense of humor. He was a powerful debater but seldom spoke except on matters coming from his committee. He belonged to that never beloved and rapidly disappearing race of watchdogs of the Treasury, whose one ambition in life is a balanced budget to be secured regardless of the personal feelings of the members of the House, for he was not only a strong but an absolutely ruthless man. He was a hard man but a fair fighter, he was honest, sincere, and courageous. He served his country faithfully and well and deserved well of the Republic.

Judge [William S.] Holman of Indiana had been chairman of Appropriations in the Fifty-second and Fifty-third Democratic congresses but had been beaten in the Republican tidal wave of 1894. He came back to the Fifty-fifth Congress with a great reputation as the one and only watchdog of the Treasury. His health, however, had begun to fail, and he took but little interest in the business of the House, dying at the close of the first session. He was a very suspicious man, taking nothing for granted, and invariably insisting on the most complete proof of any proposition submitted to him; in the expression of the day "he wanted to be shown." Amos Cummings, [a Democrat representative from New York,] told me that he and the judge were standing on the steps of the Metropolitan Hotel, at that time much frequented by members of Congress, when a flock of sheep passed by that had just come from the shearers. Cummings turning to the judge said, "They have just been sheared." "Yes," answered the judge, "they appear to have been, at least on this side." Years later this story was told at a Gridiron Club dinner at Senator [William B.] Allison's [of Iowa] expense, but I think there can be no doubt that Judge Holman was its original hero.

Like all watchdogs, the judge had his weaknesses, his particular weakness being his home town. Once when the River and

Harbor Appropriation Bill came before the House, the judge made an impassioned speech in favor of a large appropriation to make navigable a small stream that flowed through his district. When the judge sat down, [Alexander M.] Dockery of Missouri rose and turning to him quoted, " 'And, lo, the faithful watchdog bays deep-voiced welcome as he draws near home.' " The House was convulsed, but the judge got his appropriation.

Dockery was himself no mean watchdog, but likewise had a great regard for his constituents. He asked me to withhold objection to a private pension bill in which he was greatly interested. I told him that I would look into it and see what I could do. I found that the bill was to pension a man who had served in a sort of Confederate free-booters' organization during the Civil War, and had at the war's close joined a semi-military Union cavalry unit in which he had been injured from not being able to ride. I told Dockery that it was about as bad a bill as had ever come out of committee. To which he replied, "Well, Mac, we all have to do things sometimes that we would rather not do."

He was my deskmate in the Fifty-fourth Congress and kept urging me to break the ice and address the chair. One day when the House was debating a bill under the five minute rule, I thought I saw the possibility of making a good point. I submitted my point to Dockery, who brushed it aside saying, "There's nothing in that. Think of something better." A little later in the debate he took the floor and calmly proceeded to develop my point. When he sat down, full of righteous wrath I said to him, "Well I never!" To which he smilingly replied: "Live and learn, Mac, live and learn." . . .

[Of all the people I knew in the House,] Samuel W. McCall was in a class quite by himself. He was the best friend I had in the House, one of the best friends I have ever had. We were on Ways and Means together and also on the Committee on Library. After Charley Russell of Connecticut died [in 1902], he was my pair in committee and in the House. I saw a great deal of him and was very fond of him. He was the most morally honest and courageous man I have ever known. He was incapable of thinking a mean or an ungenerous thought. When he thought a cause right, he was for it; when he thought a cause wrong, he was against it, and no power could move him from his course. He voted against his party almost as often as with it and incurred the ill will of the Republican leaders by his independence. He represented the Cambridge district, and the constant efforts of Senator Lodge to displace him were utterly ineffectual. He was a poor speaker and very lazy, which made his influence less than it would otherwise have been. He wrote extremely well and his speeches read much better than they sounded when delivered. His reports were admirable, and that on the John Paul Jones statue is an admirable short biography. He wrote several able books, including the official life of Speaker Reed, the life of Thad Stevens, in the American Statesmen series, and a very valuable work on the procedure of the House. He was a sound money man, and yet curiously enough in the Fifty-third Congress in a set speech he coined the phrase, "You shall not crucify mankind upon a cross of gold," [14] a phrase that William J. Bryan appropriated. He won the nomination for governor in the teeth of Senator Lodge and served two distinguished terms,[15] when he retired to the practice of law. I was so fortunate as to see him occasionally when I left the House. After the war I went to see him at his office in Boston and to my sorrow found him considerably aged. Shortly afterwards [in 1923] he died. If ever a man deserved well in the hereafter, it was he. He was an honest man, a strong man, and of near greatness. But far more than that, he was a simple, kindly, Christian gentleman.

[14] None of McCall's speeches in the *Congressional Record* contains this phrase.

[15] McCall served only one term as governor, for although twice a candidate, he was defeated once.

Chapter VII

Grooming Me for the Mayoralty

THE RE-APPORTIONMENT that followed the census of 1900 gave me a district with a Democratic majority of 18,000 in normal years. With a safe district I felt that I could look forward to a life career in the House of Representatives [and] the work that I have enjoyed more than any that I have ever done. But my satisfaction and content were short-lived.

[While I was still serving in Congress,] . . . in New York City the Van Wyck administration had been elected, had lived for four years, and on January 1st, 1902, had come to an inglorious end. . . . During the Van Wyck mayoralty, Croker frankly and openly ruled New York as dictator, the mayor being nothing but a rubber stamp for the boss. Van Wyck was the most pitiable object who ever held a great public office, for he entirely surrendered himself into the hands of Croker and acted exactly as though the latter held him under a hypnotic spell.[1]

Croker was 5 feet, 6½ inches tall, the same height as Napoleon and the Duke of Wellington, as his admirers always emphasized. He had short legs, long arms, and a barrel of a chest. Until his last years when he shaved clean, he wore a closely clipped black beard and moustache with iron-grey hair. He was a boilermaker by trade, the son of a veterinary surgeon. In early life he developed great prowess as a rough-and-tumble fighter and was exceedingly strong, which fact undoubtedly

1 Robert A. Van Wyck, a Tammany politician, served as a City Court judge (1889-97) and as mayor (1898-1901). McClellan has exaggerated neither Van Wyck's subservience to Croker nor the low moral tone of his administration. The New York *Evening Post* (November 18, 1918) stated that there were more "scandals hanging about his administration than any mayor since A. Oakey Hall of Tweed times."

helped him in his early political career. As the result of his boilermaking experiences he was rather deaf and spoke in a quiet, low, and not unmusical voice. While his education was of the slightest, he was not ungrammatical.[2]

Unlike John Kelly[3] and McCarren,[4] he could not make a public speech, although when necessary he could express himself very forcibly to the Executive Committee of Tammany Hall. He had devoted friends and violent enemies, while he himself never went back on a friend (provided the friend blindly obeyed orders) nor forgave an enemy. He summarized his philosophy when he said to me, "After all, there is nothing like friendship."

He was caricatured more often than any man of his time, and hardly a week passed that his picture did not appear in the papers. Yet even so it was remarkable how he could pass through the crowd unrecognized. One night at Tammany Hall I was going upstairs with him from his office on the ground floor to the great hall on the top floor. On the way up we took the wrong turn and landed on the stage of Tony Pastor's Theatre, which was under the same roof. It was in the midst of the Van Wyck campaign during which the main issue had been Croker himself. He had been far more talked about, advertised, and pictured than had been the candidate. Tony Pastor's Theatre was packed, the curtain was up, and a variety act was in progress. Croker, a little confused, reached nearly the middle of the stage before he turned and walked off. Not a single member of the audience recognized him, and it was evidently assumed that we were either a part of the act or stagehands sent on by the manager for some esoteric purpose.

There has probably never been anyone who understood,

[2] McClellan is mistaken, for there is little doubt that Croker was ungrammatical. See Albert Fein, "New York City Politics from 1899-1903" (Columbia University Master's Essay, 1954), 6.

[3] "Honest John" Kelly became boss of Tammany Hall following Tweed's downfall. He remained in control of the organization from 1874 until his death in 1886.

[4] Patrick H. McCarren ousted Hugh McLaughlin as the leader of the Brooklyn Democratic organization in 1903. Although he overthrew McLaughlin with the aid of Charles F. Murphy and Tammany, in 1904 he broke with Murphy, and until his death in 1909 he ran the Brooklyn Democratic organization as an autonomous machine.

grasped, and controlled local politics better than did Croker in his prime.

The election of Van Wyck was the turning point in Croker's life and began his political downfall. Up to that time he had lived very modestly, had simple habits and simple ways, deprecated adulation, and always kept his head. After his triumphant success in electing the first mayor of Greater New York, he completely changed. Surrounding himself with a court of sycophants, he developed extravagant tastes, including a country place in England (and afterwards in Ireland) and a racing stable with which he subsequently won the Derby, only to be refused the customary presentation to the King.

Immediately after election day in 1897 Croker established himself at Lakewood, New Jersey, accompanied by Van Wyck, Thomas F. Grady, and a number of other intimates. Thither all other officeseekers and their friends journeyed and presented their claims for recognition. Charles F. Murphy, who was anxious to be a member of the Board of Dock Commissioners, asked me to see Croker in his behalf. Accordingly, I went to Lakewood. I arrived about lunchtime and was placed by Croker at his right, he sitting at the head of a long table in the middle of the dining room, at which I counted some twenty-four prominent members of the organization, some of whom were members of Croker's court and were more or less permanently at the hotel; the rest were birds of passage who had evidently come to Lakewood to have speech with the boss and not with Van Wyck, whom they ignored. There was besides another long table of newspapermen.

After lunch, [when] Croker rose and lighted a cigar, the twenty-four also rose and lighted cigars. Then, taking me by the arm, Croker led the way into the garden, where, followed in solemn procession by the twenty-four, marching two by two, and by an almost equal number of newspapermen, we walked for nearly an hour.[5] I told Croker why I had come and ex-

---

[5] Croker's stay at Lakewood produced countless stories, and the Tammany braves never quite recovered from their experiences there. George Washington Plunkitt, the Democratic leader of the Fifteenth Assembly District, in 1905 recalled: "There was nothing but dress-suits at dinner at Lakewood, and Croker wouldn't let any Tammany men go to dinner without them." Plunkitt then told the story of a young politician who wore his first dress suit at Lakewood and then went rapidly downhill until he was in such wretched circumstances

plained that Murphy's appointment was the only favor that I had to ask of the new administration. He told me that while he did not have too much confidence in Murphy he would give him the appointment as a favor to me. He then said that he would return to Washington with me as he wanted to see Senator Murphy.[6] "We'll fool the newspapermen and sneak away." Which we proceeded to do at great trouble to ourselves, only to be met on our arrival at Senator Murphy's house by almost every correspondent at the capital. On the train Croker suddenly asked me, "Did you speak to Bob Van Wyck about Murphy's appointment?" Knowing Van Wyck, I replied, "No, was it necessary?" To which the boss answered, "No, it was not at all necessary, but it might have flattered him if you had consulted him." And Van Wyck was the mayor-elect of New York.

Soon after Van Wyck's inauguration Croker took control of the moribund Democratic Club, issued orders that all the faithful were to join, and reconstructed and redecorated the club building in a style that closely resembled a combination of a Turkish bath and a prosperous barroom. He gave up going to Tammany Hall and used the Democratic Club as his headquarters and made it his home. Anyone who wanted to see him was obliged to go there, where he was accessible in the evening. The mayor reported there every night and sat in a corner unnoticed until Croker had finished his work, when the latter would nod to the chief executive, who would then follow his boss upstairs to receive his orders for the next day.

The prosperity of the Democratic Club was maintained by a very original method. Every month Croker inspected the house accounts of the members, and those who he thought were not spending enough were informed by the club's president that "the Chief" wished them to spend more, which if they wanted to retain their jobs, they promptly did.

There has always been a certain mystery as to how Croker

---

that the only political job he could get was enrolling voters for the Citizens' Union. (William L. Riordon, *Plunkitt of Tammany Hall* [New York, 1948 edition], 67-68.)

6 This is the same Edward Murphy that McClellan refers to in Chapter III as mayor of Troy and chairman of the state committee. Murphy was a United States senator from New York from 1893 to 1899.

made his fortune, which must have been large.[7] In the course of his testimony before a legislative investigating committee he blandly stated that as chairman of the Tammany Hall Finance Committee he had only one personal bank account through which passed, not only his own funds, but also the funds of the Democratic organization, and that he kept no books or accounts of his receipts or expenditures. He added with a smile, "I am out for my pocket all the time." [8]

The greater part of Croker's rule was before the enactment of the Corrupt Practices Act,[9] that much heralded law which, according to the professional reformers, was guaranteed to bring the political millennium. The act required candidates and campaign committees to file, with the proper official, statements of their campaign expenditures and limited these expenditures to the printing and circulating of books, papers and other documents, and the hiring of halls, speakers and bands of music. So far, no exception could be taken to the terms of the law, especially as it forbade the assessment of officeholders for political purposes and the acceptance of contributions from corporations. One sentence, however, largely nullified the avowed purpose of the act and opened the way to legalized bribery. While the number of watchers in polling places was limited to one for each party, it was permitted to hire an un-

---

[7] When Croker died in 1922 at the age of seventy-nine, his estate was estimated at more than $5,000,000. During his lifetime there was a great deal of speculation on the source of his wealth, with one contemporary even suggesting that he made it in Florida real estate. See Hettrick, "Reminiscences," I, 75.

[8] It was at the Mazet investigation in 1899 that the following exchange took place:

> *Mr. Moss:* So we have it then, that you, participating in the selection of judges before election, participate in the emolument that comes . . . at the end of their judicial proceeding, namely, judicial sales.
> *Mr. Croker:* Yes, sir.
> *Mr. Moss:* And it goes into your pocket?
> *Mr. Croker:* I get—that is a part of my profit. . . .
> *Mr. Moss:* Then you are working for your own pocket, are you not?
> *Mr. Croker:* All the time, same as you.

(*Report of the Special Committee of the Assembly Appointed to investigate the Public Offices and Departments of the City of New York and of the Counties Therein Included* [Albany, 1900], I, 442.) Hereafter referred to as *Mazet Investigation.*

[9] New York State adopted a number of corrupt practices acts, the first being passed in 1890. McClellan is referring to a measure which was adopted in 1906 and extensively amended in 1909.

limited number, provided they did not go within a hundred feet of the booths. In addition, it was permitted to pay for "the conveyance of voters to and from the polls."

Under the first provision those who needed financial encouragement on election day were decorated with badges bearing the inscription "watcher." [They] loafed in the neighborhood of the polling place while the polls were open and received their pay, quite legally, when the polls were closed. The second provision was obviously intended to meet the needs of Republican rural leaders. It was a notorious fact that scarcely a single Republican farmer ever voted unless paid at the rate of "$5 for a one horse team, $10 for a two horse team." In return for these payments, patriotic farmers were expected to bring their farmhands to the polls. This second provision met and legalized the rather awkward problem of the so-called "four o'clock voters." These were thrifty voters who, while unwilling to vote for the party to which they did not belong, would not vote at all unless paid to do so. They remained at home until sent for by their district captains. In the unregenerate days they were paid directly; after the enactment of the Corrupt Practices Act, they were "conveyed to the polls" in the hacks of drivers of correct political principles who, on being paid, "divided up" with their passengers.

The Corrupt Practices Act was drafted by professional reformers. Its workings were perfectly well known to the public, and yet for years no effort was made to strengthen its provisions. It is questionable whether conditions were very much improved by it, as originally enacted, especially as it bore the earmarks of extremely smug hypocrisy. It must, however, be said in its favor, that it was a step in the right direction and did at least make illegal some of the most glaring customs that had hitherto been permitted and had been quite openly practiced.

In Croker's time, except direct bribery, there was hardly a political act, which is now condemned, that was not legal, and practiced by both of the great parties. Candidates for elective office were openly assessed for their nominations. For example, the prevailing rates for a nomination to the state Supreme Court varied from one to three years' salary, according to the prospect of election in the Democratic or Republican departments as the case might be. All officeholders were expected to pay ten per cent of their annual salaries during the month before election, and this was true of every section of the state and of both parties. Civil servants in Washington, if they could not come home to vote, were expected to send twenty-five dollars to their respective state committees or forfeit the good will of their senators and representatives.

In New York City under Croker, conditions only differed from elsewhere in being better organized. The collections were made by Dan Donegan, who bore the picturesque title of Wiskinkie of the Tammany Society or Columbian Order, and was, needless to say, one of the most unpopular men in the city. When he was caught "holding out on the boss," his dismissal into outer darkness was not regretted.[10]

Donegan's collections were received by Croker as chairman of the Finance Committee of Tammany Hall and banked in his personal account, out of which the general expenses of the campaign were paid. These expenses were always very large, including a great amount of printing, mass meetings, speakers, parades, and the salaries of an army of clerks who carried the organization of the campaign. One of the principal expenses was the money used on election day. The day before election was known as "dough day" when the various district leaders of both parties were given bags containing cash, proportionate to the total amount available and to their actual needs. This money was used in theory at least by the Democratic and Republican leaders, more as a reward for faithful services, . . . the strengthening of the weakhearted and the encouragement of the doubtful, than in the direct purchase of votes.

The local campaigns in the various Assembly districts were paid for out of funds raised locally, the local candidates in most cases bearing the heaviest burden. A very large part of the cost of municipal campaigns came from contributions made by cor-

10 "[Daniel M.] Donegan collected millions of dollars from Tammany officeholders during the many years he was Wiskinkie of the Tammany organization. He was the most successful collector of campaign contributions Tammany ever had, and he was never accused of keeping any of the money for himself. He has been rewarded with public office, never being long without a salaried place. Two years ago he resigned the place of Wiskinkie, declaring that the work of collecting contributions for the Bryan campaign had made him unpopular with many Tammany men." (New York *Tribune,* March 10, 1899.)

porations, who, having no souls, were in the habit of contributing impartially to both parties. Since corporation contributions have been made illegal, it is to be noted that the largest campaign contributors whose names appear on the published returns are men intimately associated in the management or ownership of large corporations.

The Democratic organization in New York is no more corrupt, in intention at least, than is the Republican. That its reputation is unsavory is due primarily to the fact that its opportunities are greater than those of its opponent (just as the opportunities of the Republican machines are greater in Republican cities), and also to the unexplained fact that the press has always judged politics in New York according to two standards: strict for the Democrats and loose for the Republicans. New York, being the metropolis of the country, receives more attention than does any other city, and events that would be ignored elsewhere are featured when occurring there. Republican politicians in New York have usually been able successfully to camouflage themselves as reformers and to "get away" with policies and performances that would not be tolerated if performed by Democrats.

The Republican organization in New York, like the Democratic organization in some of the great Republician cities, instead of being an opposition party, has only too often been nothing but an adjunct of the party in power that has more or less successfully controlled its organization by the use of money and patronage. During the campaign of 1924 I spent an evening speaking in Brooklyn under the chaperonage of one of the principal local Democratic leaders. Before reaching the largest meeting of the evening I asked my chaperon the name of the Republican boss. I found that he was a man with whose very equivocal record I happened to be familiar. Accordingly, I devoted my speech to attacking him to the unbounded delight of the audience. As we were driving to the next meeting I said to my chaperon with considerable satisfaction, "Well, I seemed to have pleased my audience." To which he glumly replied, "You have pleased them too damn' well. We bought that fellow last week."

After the expenses of the campaign had been met, it is to be presumed that Croker considered that, as chairman of the

Finance Committee, any balance was his personal property. Huge as must have been the campaign contributions and large as must have been the balances remaining after elections, they could not have been large enough to explain the fortune of which he died possessed. In 1898, he had become the silent partner of Peter F. Meyer, one of the shrewdest real estate operators in the city.[11] During the Van Wyck administration an enormous number of street openings and improvements were undertaken. With advance information as to what new streets were to be opened and what old streets were to be improved, it was a simple matter for Meyer to buy options on real estate contiguous to the improvements and to sell at a great profit when the improvements were officially announced. It is altogether probable that most of Croker's fortune was made in this way. As he held no public office, what he did was, at least technically, perfectly legal. . . .

Van Wyck, on the other hand, skated on very thin ice when he and his great friend, John F. Carroll,[12] bought a large interest in the American Ice Company[13] and then excluded all rivals from the use of the city docks. The so-called "ice scandal" was the last nail in Van Wyck's political coffin, for the newspapers made the most of it, called him the "Ice Man," and charged that he was making a fortune at the expense of the tenement dwellers of the city.

[11] Some years before 1898, the firm of Meyer and Croker was organized as an auctioneering concern. Tammany judges were able to give the firm what amounted to a monopoly of judicial sales of real estate. At the Mazet investigation in 1899 Croker testified: "We will show you the books. There is Peter Meyer's there, and I want to say to you now that my half in that business has amounted anywhere from $25,000 to $30,000 for the last seven years, right along." (*Mazet Investigation*, I, 442.)

[12] Carroll, a Tammany stalwart, resigned as clerk of the Court of General Sessions following Van Wyck's election, and throughout the Van Wyck administration he was Croker's right-hand man. Shortly before the end of Croker's reign he made an unsuccessful attempt to supersede the boss.

[13] The American Ice Company, or "ice trust" as it was called by contemporaries, was created by Charles W. Morse, who subsequently went to jail for violating the banking laws. In 1899, he brought together a number of independent companies, and in return for shares of stock distributed at favorable rates to politicians of both parties he obtained control over the city piers at which ice could be landed. He then tried to double the price of ice, but because of public opposition he had to settle for a much smaller increase in price. Van Wyck and Carroll were just two of several politicians who owned stock in the American Ice Company.

By the summer of 1901 Croker at least realized that it would be almost impossible to elect a Tammany ticket in the autumn. He accordingly determined to go outside the organization for his candidate and selected Edward F. Shepard, a corporation lawyer from Brooklyn, who . . . was highly esteemed by the so-called "reformers." Hugh McLaughlin, the Brooklyn boss, wanted to nominate his favorite, Bird S. Coler,[14] who as city comptroller had won some distinction in opposing and defeating the unsavory Ramapo water scandal,[15] which had been supported by Van Wyck.

I was chairman of the city convention that nominated Shepard and managed to pull through with reasonable dignity what several times nearly degenerated into a riot. As chairman of the Notification Committee, I saw Shepard before he was notified and begged him in his speech of acceptance to repudiate the Van Wyck administration and to announce that he would not retain as police commissioner the notorious Devery,[16] who had brought more discredit to the city government than any of its members. To my great surprise I found that our candidate, whom I had supposed to be a man of courage, [was] in a blue funk. "If I do that," he said, "I shall be beaten." "But," I answered, "as an honest man you cannot possibly

[14] Coler, a banker from Brooklyn, served as comptroller from 1898 to 1901. He was the unsuccessful Democratic candidate for governor in 1902 and in 1918 was defeated for state comptroller.

[15] The Ramapo Water Company was a private corporation in which both Democratic and Republican politicians had invested. A Republican legislature had granted it the right to condemn watersheds and sell water to municipalities, and the company had more power to obtain and sell water than did New York City. In August, 1899, the people of the city learned from the newspapers that the Van Wyck administration intended to award the company a forty-year contract to provide the city with 200,000,000 gallons of water a day at $70 a million gallons. This would have cost the city approximately $5,000,000 a year. The contract was blocked in large part by the efforts of the New York *World* and (as McClellan states) Coler.

[16] William S. Devery, one of the most colorful Tammany politicians of this period, liked to boast: "I carried my father's dinner pail when he was laying the bricks of Tammany Hall." Van Wyck made Devery chief of police, and while he held office the city's saloons, gambling places, and brothels openly broke the law through a corrupt alliance with the police. When the Republican legislature abolished the office of chief of police, Croker ordered Van Wyck to make Devery deputy police commissioner, a position that carried even more power than that of police chief, and Van Wyck obeyed. In 1902, Devery broke with Murphy, and after one of the most spectacular fights in Tammany history lost the leadership of his West Side Assembly District.

support the Van Wyck administration. Besides, if you are tied
up to Van Wyck in the public mind, you have absolutely no
hope of election. If you cut loose from Van Wyck, and especially from Devery, you will have just a sporting chance of
winning. In either event, whether win or lose, you will keep
your self-respect." [17] Shepard could not see my point, and in his
speech of acceptance, while he did not endorse Van Wyck, he
made a labored argument to the effect that he could make no
promises as to what officials he would or would not retain if
elected, as such promises would be in violation of the law as
making pledges in return for votes. . . . Shepard received what
he deserved, an overwhelming defeat at the polls, and retired
permanently from politics. Van Wyck, whom Croker had nominated for the Supreme Court of the state, was beaten by a large
majority and went abroad, never to return.[18]

After Van Wyck's defeat Croker formally and finally left
politics and retired to his country seat near Dublin, where he
lived the life of a sporting country gentleman, until his death
some ten years later.[19]

Croker had appointed as his successor as leader of the organization, Lewis Nixon, a former naval officer, an able and an
honest man, but utterly unqualified for the work of leading
Tammany Hall. He soon found that the district leaders would
have none of him, and within a month resigned.[20] The Executive Committee then chose a committee of three to manage
the organization, consisting of Charles F. Murphy of the East
Side, Daniel F. McMahon of the West Side, and Lewis F. Haf-

[17] McClellan is not altogether frank at this point, or at least he failed to
practice what he preached to Shepard. In his speech to the delegates to the
Democratic convention in 1901, McClellan said: "We meet here to endorse the
Democratic administration that has been presided over so ably by that unswerv-
ing, fearless Democrat, Robert A. Van Wyck. When the Democracy assumed
control four years ago, there was a condition of absolute municipal chaos. Now
a splendidly organized government exists. We have no apologies to offer. We
have nothing for which to apologize. The Democracy of this mighty metropolis,
conscious of duty well performed, submits its case to the people upon its record
of promises fulfilled and pledges kept." (New York *Tribune,* October 4, 1901.)

[18] According to a reporter, Van Wyck got drunk on his last day in office, and
"he drew few sober breaths from that day until the day he died." (Hettrick,
"Reminiscences," I, 74.)

[19] Actually Croker died in 1922, or about twenty years after he had retired
from politics.

[20] McClellan is mistaken, for Nixon took office in January, 1902, and resigned
on May 14 of the same year.

fen of the Bronx. Devery characterized the committee as consisting of "a sport, a two spot, and a joke." Before very long Murphy absolutely dominated his colleagues and they resigned, and Murphy ruled alone.

Murphy was a man of great force and shrewd native ability. He was a born leader of men, and, until he attained great power, right thinking and honest. Unfortunately, like most of those who have been the boss, he developed the acquisitive sense. On his death the newspapers reported that his estate amounted to $2,000,000. . . .

At the state convention of 1902, at Saratoga, Murphy insisted that I march at the head of the delegation with him and thereafter began to push me to the front and to "feature" me on all possible occasions. I realized that he was grooming me for the mayoralty, and protested vigorously.[21] He would not commit himself one way or the other, and I sailed for Europe in the spring of 1903 convinced that I was secure in Congress. On my return in the autumn I found that matters had gone much further than I had any idea, and the nomination was put squarely up to me. It was argued that my service in Washington had kept me out of all factional fights in the city, that I had made a good record in Congress, and that I possessed that supreme qualification for a candidate: that of all those mentioned for the office I was the least objectionable to those who counted. Murphy made a personal appeal to me. He said that everything that I had had in politics I had received from the organization, that the leaders of the organization believed me to be the only Tammany Hall Democrat who could beat Seth Low, and that they in fact demanded that I should accept the nomination as a matter of public duty. There was nothing else for me to do but accept, and very regretfully I accepted.

Hugh McLaughlin presented as his candidate Judge Gaynor[22] of Brooklyn, and I won in the convention by the votes of Manhattan, Bronx, Queens, and Richmond. Brooklyn sup-

21 In 1896, when McClellan was mentioned as a possible candidate for mayor, he said: "I don't want the mayoralty. There's nothing about the place I would care for. It's hard work, hard knocks, a hard name, and political death. I want none of it." (New York *Journal*, March 15, 1896.)

22 William J. Gaynor first attracted attention as a civic reformer in Brooklyn. He was a justice of the New York Supreme Court from 1893 to 1909 and McClellan's successor as mayor.

ported the judge,[23] who never forgave me for taking a nomination that I did not want from him who wanted it very much
indeed.

The cleverest political coup of Murphy's career was the kid-
napping of Low's [24] running mates, Edward N. Grout and
Francis V. Fornes, who had been renominated by the Republicans (or, as they always like to call themselves in New York
City, the Fusionists) for comptroller and president of the Board
of Aldermen respectively.[25] They were approached by Murphy
and offered nominations on the Democratic ticket. They were
both of the brand which is known as "independent Democrats,"
a euphemism for opportunist. Murphy was perfectly justified
in offering them nominations. Whether they were justified in
accepting is an entirely different matter. They had served for
two years as members of Low's administration, and at his request had been renominated with him and had accepted. Low
claimed with considerable justice that in accepting Democratic
nominations they had betrayed him. Whether or not they
expected to run on both tickets and be unanimously re-elected,
I do not know. If they had any such expectation they were
disappointed, for as soon as we had nominated them the Fusion
caucus was reconvened, and they were put off the ticket. They
both protested loudly, but in vain, and were obliged to throw
themselves wholeheartedly into the fight with me. Their nominations undoubtedly helped our ticket very much, for it served
notice on the public that the Democratic organization was not
trying to "grab everything in sight."

I opened headquarters at the Bartoldi Hotel, at the corner
of Broadway and Twenty-third Street, with John A. Delany

[23] McLaughlin opposed McClellan's nomination on the ground that Seth
Low was very popular in Brooklyn, and that in order to carry the borough and
city the Democrats should nominate a Brooklyn man rather than a member of
Tammany. See New York *Times,* September 18, 1903, and Brooklyn, *Eagle,* May
24, 1904.

[24] Seth Low was mayor 1901-03 and running for re-election on the Republican
ticket in 1903.

[25] The Democratic nomination of Grout and Fornes, in addition to being a
triumph for Murphy over the Republicans, was also part of Murphy's campaign
against McLaughlin. McLaughlin had expected to obtain these nominations for
Brooklyn men, but as a result of Murphy's maneuver, Brooklyn ended up without a single candidate on the city-wide ticket. McLaughlin bolted the ticket
and was soon supplanted by Patrick McCarren as the leader of the Brooklyn
Democracy.

as my campaign manager. Delany was the head of the Knights of Columbus in the state, a very powerful Roman Catholic society. Murphy rightly believed that having Delany as my manager would swing to my support many Catholic votes.

The press was almost solidly against me. In fact, the only newspaper that supported me was the *Daily News*, owned by Ben Wood, the brother of Fernando Wood, one of the former mayors, and Colonel Bill Brown.[26] There was a general disposition to misquote me and not to print my speeches as I delivered them. Accordingly, so as to avoid misquotation, we determined that it would be wise for me to read my speeches on the stump. This resulted in a great amount of additional work. Every night when my speaking was finished I returned to my headquarters and dictated my speeches for the next evening. These were then edited and handed to me ready for delivery the following night. Delany, who greatly fancied himself as a writer of the English language, did most of the editing and never could resist the temptation of interpolating his favorite expressions in my speeches. The phrase he liked most was "seemingly not unmindful," another was "the peaceful arts of life." I don't think that during the campaign I ever read one of my edited speeches that I did not find these two phrases staring me in the face.

The press had been so unwilling to print my "stuff" that before I delivered my last speech we sent an advance copy to all the morning papers for publication as a paid advertisement, and even the *Times* refused to accept it. Afterwards, however, the owner of the *Times* assured me that the speech had been refused through error.

Seth Low was entirely devoid of any sense of humor. Had he been a man of extraordinary ability, he might have overcome this terrible handicap, but unfortunately for him he was a dull, obstinate man with an excellent opinion of himself. He never could see a joke, especially at his own expense. I was chatting with him one evening at a White House reception

26 McClellan is somewhat confused, for Benjamin Wood had died in 1900, three years before McClellan's first mayoralty campaign. Frank A. Munsey bought the paper from Wood's widow in 1901 and soon forced out William L. Brown, a minority stockholder and the former managing editor. The *News* almost invariably supported Tammany. As McClellan subsequently indicates, he also received Hearst's support.

when we were joined by Arthur W. Dunn, who was the head Associated Press man at the Capitol. He greeted us and then said to Low, "I was just saying to some of the fellows, 'Look at McClellan talking to his predecessor.'" Low looked at him for a moment, scowled, turned his back on us and without saying a word walked away.

One of the first acts of the Low administration was the creation of the Art Commission charged with the duty of passing on the architectural merit of all buildings the city proposed to erect and on all objects of art the city proposed to acquire. This power is purely advisory, for even if the commission condemns the plan for a proposed building, the city may nevertheless go on with the work. . . . The Van Wyck administration had a favorite firm of architects who . . . were the object of the most violent attacks of the so-called "reformers" of the period, and especially of Low. One of the buildings that they had designed was not finished until after Low came into office. Low did all in his power to put obstacles in the way of its completion, and the Art Commission valiantly seconded the efforts of the mayor. The last project submitted by the architects to the commission was for a frieze sculptured in the round running around all four façades of the building. The Art Commission rejected the entire project. "There is not a single figure that is not a monstrosity," said the commission. "They are all out of scale, badly modeled, without the slightest suggestion of art or good taste to redeem them," and the mayor enthusiastically applauded the findings of the commission. Then, the architects replied that the figures for the front had been copied bodily from the figures of the Parthenon, while those on two sides were copied from Donatello and Michelangelo and in the fourth façade from the work of Bernini and his school. As the architects were not required under their contract to produce a sculptured frieze they accepted the ruling of the commission amid the uproarious delight of the public and the press, but I don't think that Seth Low ever saw the joke.

Cabot Lodge told me that after Low's father died he met the then mayor and offered appropriate condolence. "Yes," replied Low, "it was very sad. I was eating my breakfast when the nurse came into the dining room and told me that Father had passed away. I remember that I had buckwheat cakes for breakfast that morning. I finished my cakes and folding my napkin, I went upstairs to Father." "Just think of it," added Lodge, " 'I finished my cakes and folding my napkin I went upstairs to Father.' My God!"

When Low was finishing his term as mayor of Brooklyn he gave Columbia University, of which he was an alumnus, a million dollars for the University Library. This act of generosity is supposed to have so warmed the hearts of the trustees that on President [Frederick A. P.] Barnard's death [in 1889] they elected Low president of the university, an act that they very soon bitterly repented.[27] It was an open secret that all the Columbia influence was employed to secure for Low the Fusion nomination for mayor against Shepard, and that when he was elected Columbia heaved a sigh of immense relief.

Low made a respectable, honest, industrious, and incompetent mayor. With all his good intentions he never won the public who by the end of his term was thoroughly tired of him.

He was a poor candidate and made a campaign against me of vilification and abuse for which he should have been ashamed. His supporters, taking their cue from him, said things about me that were, to say the least, quite beyond the ordinary rules of decency, even in a desperate political fight. An organization of Low's women supporters flooded the city with leaflets on which were printed, "A vote for Low is a vote for the home, a vote for McClellan is a vote for the brothel. A vote for Low is a vote for woman's honor, a vote for Mc-Clellan is a vote for woman's shame." Many of the members of this organization knew me personally, some of them had called themselves my friends.

I used to be a good campaigner and when in active politics I had the ability of predicting results very accurately. I realized that I could win if I fought hard enough, but that the result was entirely in my hands [and] that I must speak as much as possible, and convince the voters of my honesty and good faith. It was before the day of the radio, and having practically no

27 The information in this sentence is not correct. Seth Low, who was an exceedingly generous alumnus of Columbia, did not give it a million dollars for a library before he became its president. What he did do was to give the university—that is, pay for—a new library after he had become president of the institution.

newspaper support . . . I could reach the public [only] . . . by my own word of mouth. As the campaign progressed, I spoke oftener and oftener, and during the last week averaged ten speeches a day, making altogether over a hundred and fifty.

I used a little open motor car for campaigning. It was in the early days of the motor, and this served to advertise me. I made speeches not only in English, but in French, German, and Italian. Whenever I spoke in a locality where there were foreign-born voters, I had someone of the race to which the foreign voters belonged planted in the audience. When I reached the end of my prepared speech, my planted foreigner would rise up and in his native language cry out, "Speak to us in our own language." Whereupon I would modestly shake my head and draw back. My planted foreigner's cry would be taken up by his compatriots, and I would then, after proper hesitation, burst forth into an apparently extemporaneous, but really carefully prepared, speech in the language requested. Strangely enough, Low's managers never "caught on" to the trick, and I worked it successfully throughout the campaign, sometimes speaking in all my four languages during the same evening.

I had on my staff at headquarters a very delightful and brilliant young Virginian, named James Lindsey Gordon, who was a real orator. I was very fond of him and sincerely mourned his premature death. Gordon went to my meetings ahead of me and roused the enthusiasm of my audiences so as to have them in the proper frame of mind to receive me. I, of course, never heard any of his speeches but the last words, which I always heard on my entrance to the hall, and they invariably ran somewhat as follows: "Fellow citizens, here he comes. Rise and greet him, for upon his breast I pin the white flower of a blameless life." By the time the campaign was over I must have been decorated with an entire garden of white flowers. I certainly should have been, had dear old Lindsey had his way.

One of Low's greatest assets, according to the newspapers, was his police commissioner, General Francis Vinton Greene, a retired officer of the regular army. During the last fortnight of the campaign the Low press and campaigners and Low himself incessantly asked me the question: "If elected are you going to retain General Greene?" It was an embarrassing question, for while there was no apparent reason why Greene should not be retained, I did not propose to hamper my administration with one of Low's ardent friends between whom and me no love was lost. Luck was with me, for about a week before election I was told that General Greene, while a resident of Philadelphia before he had moved to New York, had been mixed up in a very unsavory encounter with the courts. I at once sent one of my men to Philadelphia to examine the court records. It developed that Greene had been president of a corporation that had gone into bankruptcy, and that the court had in an opinion very seriously reflected upon his conduct. From the stump I announced that I should the next night inform the public what I should do with General Greene if I were elected. Accordingly, the next evening, to a packed house, I read what the Pennsylvania court had said about the general, and added, "It is needless, I trust, for me to say that no man with such a record will be a member of my administration. If and when I take office I find that General Greene has not resigned, my first official act will be to remove him." Some of the Low newspapers ignored my speech entirely; a few printed it on an inside page. From that time on, however, there was no further mention of the general, who resigned before I took office and retired into well-deserved obscurity.

During the last fortnight of the campaign the pace I set myself was terrific. I reached my headquarters at nine o'clock, and spent the day receiving delegations, giving out interviews, shaking hands and "jollying" the hundreds of callers who came to see what manner of man the candidate might be. Between twelve and one o'clock I visited the docks, markets, and factories and spoke to the workers during their dinner hour. At seven o'clock I went home (we were at the Murray Hill Hotel), took a bath, had something to eat, and at eight o'clock started out with Delany on my evening's speaking tour. This usually ended at about eleven, with an impassioned oration by Delany which was so fulsome in its praise of the candidate as to almost make me, hardened campaigner that I was, blush with shame. Then back to headquarters where I dictated my speeches for the next day and then to bed. I lost twenty pounds in weight between my nomination and election.

I closed my campaign at Durland's Riding Academy on the

Saturday night before election to an enormous crowd that cheered me for twenty minutes. In those days it was not considered good policy to have meetings on Sunday, and it was rightly assumed that by Monday no votes could be influenced as by that time the voters had made up their minds.

Two days before election, too late to be of any use, Hearst declared for me in a very halfhearted fashion.[28] On election night his reporter at my headquarters and a youth on my staff faked a statement from me, signed with my rubber stamp, giving Hearst the entire credit for my election. I at once wrote to Hearst that the statement which he had printed on the front page of the *American* was a fake. He never answered my letter, and I was told, was very angry with me for writing it. I could not, however, allow myself to be put on record as considering myself under such deep obligations to him.

I went to bed the night before election perfectly sure that I had won, and the returns bore me out, for my majority over Low was more than 42,000.

Low's supporters took their defeat with very bad grace, the newspapers deploring my election as a return to "all the infamies of the Van Wyck administration." The most fantastic newspaper story printed was one that appeared in the London *Times* from its New York correspondent, George W. Smalley, who said that all the gamblers and brothel keepers in the city had gathered in front of my headquarters to acclaim my victory and that they had been addressed by "the unspeakable Bourke Cockran," who had congratulated them on the return of "the wide open town." The story was a complete fiction. The very decent people who filled the square in front of the Bartoldi Hotel were neither gamblers nor brothel keepers, and they were not addressed by Bourke Cockran, whom I had not seen during the campaign, he having never forgiven me for taking his seat in Congress away from him nine years before. I was urged to sue the *Times* for libel, but of course did not. One of the rules of the game in politics in this country is that a public man must accept newspaper abuse with a smile and not retaliate, for nothing is ever gained by declaring a feud with the press.

Two of the telegrams of congratulations which I received

[28] McClellan is mistaken, for the Hearst papers supported him much earlier in the campaign than he indicates.

especially pleased me, for they were both from Republican friends. Senator [Joseph B.] Foraker, of Ohio, said, "If it had to be a Democrat, I am so glad that it was you," while James G. Blaine's charming and brilliant daughter Mrs. Blaine Beale said, "I am ashamed to be so glad." . . .

The day after I was elected mayor we went back to Washington for the rest I so greatly needed and to prepare for the extra session that the President had called for the enactment of a Cuban Reciprocity Bill. I spent most of my time studying the New York city charter, that very complicated and involved document, that was workable provided that those called upon to administer it were thoroughly familiar with it. Before I finished with it I knew it from one end to the other. William M. Ivins [29] once paid me the compliment of saying, "The two men who know most about the charter are myself and George B. McClellan."

John Delany as my successful campaign manager was, under custom, entitled to any reasonable reward he might ask. He asked me to appoint him corporation counsel. Delany joined me in Washington for the purpose of discussing my cabinet slate and of acting as my coach in my study of the charter, for his previous service as an assistant corporation counsel had made him an excellent charter lawyer.

Murphy had determined to fill my seat in the House with Bourke Cockran, who through his church influence had made his peace with Tammany Hall. Cockran was very anxious to get back to Washington and was extremely annoyed that I refused to resign at once so that he might forthwith be elected.

When Congress met Long re-introduced the Reciprocity Bill of the Fifty-seventh Congress, which we had no difficulty in reporting to the House. We determined that Long should open the debate and that I should close it as my last official act in Congress. The President's reaction to my support of the administration was to say the least peculiar. He said to Long, "What does McClellan want from me?" Long answered that he supposed that I was actuated by a sense of duty in bolting my party leaders. "Nonsense," said the President, "you may

[29] Ivins was the Republican candidate for mayor in 1905 in the election in which McClellan was re-elected for a second term.

be sure that he wants something. No man ever bolts his party without a price." And that was all the thanks I ever received from Roosevelt for taking my political life in my hands in his support. If I do say so myself, I think that I did well in closing the debate on the Cuban Reciprocity Bill.[30] I certainly received the hearty and unanimous applause of both sides of the House. When the bill went to the Senate, I was glad that I had done my duty and done it with success.

As the end of the session and the first of January drew near, I consulted Asher Hinds, our parliamentary expert, as to the form of my resignation. He suggested that, as Mayors Smith Ely and Hewitt [31] had resigned from the House to take the mayoralty, I could not do better than to copy exactly their form of resignation, which I did.

The last day of the extra session came and with it my last day of service in the House. During the morning, John Dalzell, who was acting speaker, called me to the chair. It was the only time between the passing of the Fifty-second Congress and the election of Champ Clark to the speakership that a Democrat presided over the House. When I left the chair, the House rose and cheered me. And so I left Congress.

As I was going down the steps in front of the Capitol for the last time, Uncle Joe Cannon joined me. He put his arms around me and hugged me and said, "Dear old George, goodby and God bless you," and I am not ashamed to say that I very nearly cried.

One of the greatest drawbacks to "arriving" young in politics is the near certainty of outliving one's contemporaries. I was only twenty-nine when, as its "baby," I entered the House of Representatives. All my friends were necessarily older than I was; many were old enough for me to have been their son. Because of the rapidity with which our people tire of their public men, seeking constantly new voices and new faces, my friends began to retire from the House and from politics (usually, be it said, against their wills) before I had been there very long. By the time I left there had been a drastic change

[30] McClellan won considerable favorable attention for his tariff stand during his last years in Congress. For example, see Brooklyn *Eagle*, December 7, 1902.

[31] Smith Ely, Jr. was mayor of New York from 1877 to 1878. Abram S. Hewitt held the same office from 1887 to 1888.

in the personnel of both branches of Congress, largely due to the campaign of 1896.

I have never entered the Capitol since resigning from the House. I have not had the heart to do so, for I should see too many ghosts. Of all the friends whom I knew and loved, all are gone, most of them are dead, none of them is still in public life. My years in the House, the House that I served so long and loved so well, lie behind me with my youth, never forgotten and always regretted. . . .

Chapter VIII

Always an Organization Man

When I became mayor of New York I was very much in the position of a medieval podesta called from outside to the chief magistracy of an Italian city with which he was utterly unfamiliar.

When I first went to Congress I had been a sachem of the Tammany Society or Columbian Order, the putative benevolent and democratic institution founded in 1789 as a protest against the supposedly aristocratic tendencies of the Society of Cincinnati and the owner of the building which it rents for one dollar a year to the strictly political organization of Tammany Hall. I had also been chairman of the Committee of Resolutions of the political organization, which made me ex officio a member of the Executive Committee. With the help of state Senator Thomas F. Grady and District Attorney John R. Fellows,[1] I ground out platforms for the local conventions and must have "pointed with pride" and "viewed with alarm" many dozens of times.

After I went on Ways and Means I found that my work in Washington kept me so constantly there that it was impossible to attend to the work of the Committee on Resolutions and the Executive Committee of the Tammany Society in New York without neglecting my congressional duties. I therefore resigned both positions and only went to New York for consultations with Croker and during the political campaigns, when my activities were necessarily confined almost entirely

[1] Fellows, Tammany politician and officeholder, was assistant district attorney (1869-73, 1881-87), district attorney (1889-90, 1895-96), and a member of the House of Representatives (1891-95).

180

to my own congressional district. While I continued to have a speaking acquaintance with the district leaders I lost touch with the rank and file, and generally with local politics.

I have always been an organization man and have always believed in political organization. That the wrong men only too often control our local politics is due to the fact that the right men refuse to do their duty. If those who spasmodically take part in so-called reform or fusion movements would join the organizations of the parties to which they profess to owe allegiance and would devote the time they spend in their clubs to the practice of the profession of politics (in other words were they public-spirited enough to act more and talk less), they could acquire control of the machinery of politics and bring forth works meet for repentance.

The vast majority of men and women are honest, decent, and God-fearing and would rather follow the political leadership of men and women like themselves than of those who are not. But honest men and women who aspire to leadership must have the active and vigorous support of other honest men and women or they will find themselves cast in the glorious but ineffective role of voices crying in the wilderness.

I have always believed that in a democracy when a man is elected to executive office by the votes of one or other of the great parties, he owes it to those who have chosen him to surround himself as far as possible by officials of his own political faith. All things being equal the applicant for an office who belongs to the party of the appointing power should be preferred to the applicant who does not.

I was determined to appoint none but Democrats to office, and as Murphy was the official head of the party in the city I turned, of course, to him for consultation in the selection of my cabinet. I believed Murphy to be absolutely honest. I had great respect for his judgment and felt perfectly sure that he would not "let me down." My disillusionment came later. . . .

During my service as mayor the salary of the office was $15,-000 out of which the incumbent paid all his expenses including his automobile and his telephone. The only perquisite was a pair of lamps placed in front of his home, which became his property at the close of his term. My lamps now stand in front of our house in Washington.

Had we not had some means of our own, it would have been
quite impossible for us to have lived and entertained even
approximately as the mayor and his wife should. The mayor
should be given a house and a salary large enough for him to
entertain on behalf of the city, just as the governor entertains
on behalf of the state. It is undignified and rather pathetic that
the city's entertaining, which should be done by the mayor,
should be in the hands of a ridiculous and incompetent committee acting on his behalf, or of certain notoriously rich people
who arrogate to themselves quasi-official functions and by so
doing give the impression that they are the real rulers of New
York. My wife and I entertained to the best of our ability,
the only case of a mayor and his wife trying to do their social
duty since the days of Mayor and Mrs. Hewitt.[2]

The question of finding a house which we could afford to
rent was a serious one. We were lucky enough to get No. 10
Washington Square, North, a large, old-fashioned house with
few modern conveniences but nevertheless comfortable and
well adapted for our purposes, and we paid for it $3,600 a
year. . . .

The day after I resigned from the House I went directly to
10 Washington Square to prepare to take over the mayoralty.

Soon after I arrived I received a hurry call from Murphy
asking me to meet him at once uptown. On my arrival I found
not only Murphy but also two justices of the Supreme Court.
Murphy opened the conversation by saying, "We want you to
appoint Blank" (this was not his name) "to be head of one of
the departments." Now Blank was a district leader who had
the general reputation of being about as crooked as possible.
The justices then proceeded to tell me what an extraordinarily
fine fellow Blank was, and how admirably fitted for the office
he sought. Murphy joined in, and among them they described
him as a sort of superman. When they were through, I said,
"I shall not appoint your man to any office in my gift, for he is
a crook and you men know it." They all three expressed themselves as being greatly shocked by what I had said. I then
turned to one of the justices and said to him, "Judge, will you
give me your word of honor that you think Blank an honest

2 Hewitt was mayor from 1887 to 1888.

man?" He replied, "Of course, I will. He is absolutely honest."
I then turned to the other justice and asked him the same
question to which he replied, "George, I don't think that is a
fair question, but as you insist, frankly, I cannot give you my
word of honor that I think Blank is an honest man." Then I
said, "That settles it, Blank will not be appointed" and left
the room.

I had already selected John Delany as corporation counsel. . . .
On the recommendation of Edward G. Riggs, of the *Sun*, I
secured as mayor's secretary, John H. O'Brien,[3] one of the
most brilliant of the younger *Sun* men. I had determined to
fill the commissionerships of police, street cleaning, and health,
and the presidency of the Tax Board with my own appointees.
For the other offices I accepted the candidates of the organization. Murphy's candidates, while almost all district leaders,
seemed to be a very decent lot. Of his non-district leader candidates, [John J.] Pallas for the presidency of the Park Board
[was] the head of the American Federation of Labor in the
state; [T. C. F.] Crain for Tenement House Department was a
vestryman of Trinity Church; and George E. Best for Bridges
and Tunnels was a reputable member of the civil service. The
district leaders whom he presented were as far as I knew perfectly respectable. I had no reason to object to the organization
slate.[4]

On the other hand Murphy raised serious objections to all
my personal appointees with the exception of Frank O'Donnel
for president of the Tax Board, who was as much a friend of
his as he was of mine. O'Donnel had been my neighbor when
we lived in Seventeenth Street, and I had always found him
an honest and able man. He had risen to the management of
one of the large mortgage companies and had a thorough knowledge of tax matters.

Bishop Potter had most enthusiastically recommended for the
presidency of the Board of Health, Dr. Thomas Darlington,

[3] O'Brien's job in the McClellan administration was the first of many political
appointments. After long service in the machine, he was elected mayor in 1932
to fill out the remaining year of James J. Walker's term. He ran for re-election
in 1933 on the Tammany ticket, but was defeated by Fiorello La Guardia.
[4] McClellan did not exaggerate Murphy's influence. Crain, for example, received his appointment after he had written to Murphy specifically requesting
it. (T. C. F. Crain to Charles F. Murphy, December 10, 1903, McClellan MSS.)

brother of the Episcopal Bishop of Pennsylvania, and on Bishop Potter's recommendation I appointed him.[5] Some years later I was sitting next to the bishop at a public dinner when Dr. Darlington came up and spoke to us. When Darlington left the bishop said to me, "Dear Mayor, who is our friend?" "The health commissioner," I replied. "And who may he be?" asked the bishop. "You ought to know," I answered, "for I appointed him at your request." "Indeed," said the bishop and changed the subject. He had evidently recommended Darlington without any personal knowledge, at the request of his fellow bishop.

In those days the street cleaning commissionership was the target of more criticism than almost any other office in the city government. Major John M. Woodbury had done extremely well under Low, and when his retention was personally urged by [William M.] Laffan, owner of the *Sun,* and by J. P. Morgan, I determined to retain him.[6]

The police commissionership was the most difficult office that I had to fill. I was unwilling to appoint a politician, or a member of the uniformed force, after Van Wyck's disastrous experience with Big Bill Devery. I first offered the post to my old friend Major General Samuel S. Sumner,[7] who had recently retired from the army, but the general declined. . . . As the first of January approached I was still without my man, when Murphy said to me, "If you don't find a commissioner pretty soon I shall have to take the job myself." As Murphy seemed to be in earnest, I made up my mind that I must at once find a commissioner or be faced with the necessity of personally

5 Darlington was one of the few original appointees to retain his office throughout McClellan's two terms. At the end of McClellan's second term, the New York *Evening Post* (December 31, 1909) wrote: "It is generally agreed that his [Darlington's] has been an exceptionally able and satisfactory administration of his department."

6 As a Republican holdover from the Low administration, Woodbury was intensely disliked by the Democratic politicians. McClellan, however, stood by him until 1906, when the two men had an acrimonious disagreement and Woodbury resigned. In 1904, when Tammany tried to force Woodbury from office, McClellan said: "Not while I am here will any attempt to force the Commissioner out succeed. I look upon Commissioner Woodbury as one of the best officers of the administration, and so long as I am Mayor the only way he will leave the service will be by resigning, and I am sure he has no intention of resigning." (New York *Sun,* June 27, 1904.)

7 Sumner was the son of General Edwin V. Sumner, who commanded the 2nd Corps of the Army of the Potomac under McClellan's father at Antietam.

turning Murphy down at the very beginning of my administration with the inevitable break that would ensue.

I had known William McAdoo [8] when he had been Assistant Secretary of Navy under Cleveland and liked him. Before serving in the Navy Department he had served two terms in the House from New Jersey. He was a practicing lawyer in New York and was not an active politician. On his record he seemed to have the makings of a good police commissioner, and with the awful prospect of Murphy as an alternative, I offered the place to McAdoo, who accepted.

Before my election Hugh McLaughlin, the Brooklyn boss, had died and had been succeeded by Patrick H. McCarren, an exceedingly able state senator. Murphy and he disliked each other intensely. Murphy thought him a crook, a sentiment which, with perhaps better reason, McCarren heartily reciprocated. McCarren was a self-educated man, who spoke correct English, made an admirable speech, and was a first-rate debater. He had read widely and was a very agreeable companion. We soon formed a political friendship which he never betrayed. He stood by me through thick and thin, gave me good advice, and never sulked if I refused to appoint the man he recommended for office, but always submitted other candidates until a satisfactory one was produced.

I found that Murphy wanted me to "starve out" McCarren by giving him no patronage, which I declined to do. The best man whom McCarren gave me, one of the best men whom I had under me, was M. J. Kennedy, park commissioner for Brooklyn. He was an honest and able Scot, who really loved his job. Under him Prospect Park became one of the most beautiful parks in the world, and the Vale of Kashmir which he created was during the azalea season as lovely a spot as I have ever seen. When I left office, I learned to my great regret that Kennedy had been bitterly disappointed at my failure to make him police commissioner at the close of my administration. He had been too modest to ask me to appoint him, and I had never supposed that he would accept the office. I should

8 William McAdoo should not be confused with William Gibbs McAdoo, who served as Wilson's Secretary of the Treasury. William McAdoo, in addition to his position in the McClellan administration, had been a member of the House of Representatives (1883-91) and Assistant Secretary of Navy (1893-97).

certainly have given it to him had I for a moment thought that he would accept.

Almost immediately after my election the newspapers that had most violently opposed me began to wave olive branches, and the reason for this was perfectly plain. Under the statute the mayor designates the newspapers that print the city advertisements. I do not know what the city's printing bill amounts to now, but in my time it ran to nearly $600,000 a year. The city advertisements must be printed in all the Brooklyn newspapers, but in Manhattan the mayor must designate three papers printed in English of which not more than two may belong to any one party, one paper printed in German, one in Italian, one in French, and one in Yiddish. It was a scandalous state of affairs, and I tried three times to have the law repealed so that the city's printing bill might be kept within bounds. Each time my bill was introduced the newspapers enthusiastically applauded my effort and then used pressure at Albany to prevent the bill being reported out of committee. I think that all this explains the olive branches.

One afternoon before I took office, I was arranging my books in the library of our Washington Square house when Harry McDona was ushered in. I had known McDona quite well before I went to Washington. He was a very charming, good-looking fellow with a curious inability to approach a subject directly and a habit of speaking in hyperboles and metaphors. Some years previously he had left the district attorney's office, where he was a $7,500 assistant, to work for Thomas F. Ryan.[9]

I climbed down from the ladder on which I was working in my shirt sleeves, shook hands with him, and having apologized, climbed up on my ladder again and for about half an hour we discussed with some animation the weather, the stock market, and the latest theatrical success. After a while McDona introduced the subject of the New York press and from that turned to the New York *World* and its owner, Joseph Pulitzer. For the life of me I could not understand what he was driving at. Presently it developed that, while Pulitzer had bitterly opposed

9 Ryan was a financier and promoter who made a fortune in New York City street railway franchises. When he died in 1928, his estate was estimated at more than $200,000,000. He joined Tammany Hall when he was a young man, and during the first decade of this century he played a prominent part in the national councils of the Democratic party.

me, he really held me in the most profound esteem. When about an hour had passed I came down from my ladder, put on my coat, asked McDona, who had been walking around the room, to sit down, and, sitting facing him, said, "Harry, you didn't come here to tell me of Pulitzer's secret love for me. What is it all about and what is it that you want?" For another half hour McDona talked of the excessive taxes that Pulitzer was paying on the World Building, and said that he had been sent by Pulitzer to say that he would very much like to support my administration. A great light dawned on me and I turned to McDona and said, "I gather that what you are driving at is this: Pulitzer offers me his support in return for a reduction of his taxes on the World Building to a figure that is satisfactory to him. Am I right?" McDona replied, "George, you have put the matter very crudely, but quite correctly." I stood up and said, "Harry, I am ashamed of you. What Pulitzer is offering me is a corrupt bargain, his support in return for a dishonest reduction of his taxes." McDona seemed greatly hurt. "George," he said, "I am surprised that you take the proposition in this spirit. I thought that you were more a man of the world." I bowed him out and never saw him again. I realized, however, that I had won the uncompromising enmity of Pulitzer at the very beginning of my administration.

My relations with Laffan, the owner of the *Sun*, went through three phases: when I had his enthusiastic support, when I had his equally enthusiastic enmity, and when I had his neutrality. Of the three I greatly preferred the last. He was so emotional and so extreme that, in supporting me, he overdid matters, and sometimes by his excessive praise made me ridiculous. His enmity was equally excessive and, while very unpleasant, overshot the mark and did not do much harm.

Louis Wiley, the very able business manager of the *Times*,[10] came to me and with perfect correctness asked for the continuance of the *Times* designation. He offered no terms and made no promises. I redesignated the *Times,* and received its loyal and friendly support as long as I was mayor and have ever since been treated by the *Times* with great friendliness.

[10] Although Wiley joined the *Times* in 1896, he did not become the paper's business manager until 1906.

My relations with the *Evening Post,* were to say the least, cool. Villard, its then proprietor,[11] is, I think, the most solemn individual I have ever known. He possesses a tenacity of purpose that would be admirable were it not only too often employed in the furtherance of his personal animosities, and a love of all lost causes, that makes him bitterly regret that as the result of an election someone must necessarily win. For him I was anathema, for I think that he was sincerely convinced that I could do nothing right. If I accomplished anything which had been previously advocated by his paper, he remained silent, if I did anything of which he disapproved he abused me with unrestrained enthusiasm.

At one period he began a crusade against me because of the condition of the street pavements in the Borough of Manhattan. I called the attention of his City Hall reporter to the fact that under the charter the street pavements were under the exclusive jurisdiction of the borough presidents. The next day he printed an editorial demanding that I at once remove the borough president from office. I marked the section of the charter which vests the removal of the borough presidents exclusively in the governor of the state and asked the *Post*'s City Hall man to show it to Villard. The only result was a violent editorial abusing me for not using my influence with the governor (which of course was nil, for the governor was a Republican) to have him remove the borough president.

When [Alton V.] Parker was running for President [in 1904 on the Democratic ticket], Villard supported him, presumably on the theory that anyone was better than Roosevelt, and that the Democratic ticket had not any chance of success. One day I received a subscription list, which was headed somewhat as follows: "As the *Evening Post* is being put to great expense in supporting Judge Parker, its editor believes that it is only fair that Democrats should financially help him in his efforts." The list was signed by a number of my subordinates with the amounts that they had paid to the *Post* opposite their names. The *Evening Post* messenger who obviously had called on me without Villard's knowledge was evidently ignorant of the provision of the Corrupt Practices Act, which forbids the

11 Oswald Garrison Villard was manager and owner of the *Post* from 1897 to 1918.

solicitation of campaign subscriptions from public officials. When I invited his attention to the terms of the act he immediately returned the subscriptions. For once, at least, I had scored on Villard, but I am sorry to say that he never saw the joke.

Curiously enough in my old age, now that the tumult and the shouting have died, I find myself reading Villard's weekly article with great and sometimes even sympathetic interest. How times have changed!

I never had a good press, for with the exception of the *Times,* whose owner and managers were personally my friends, none of them forgave me for having been elected.[12] What support I received from the others was purely perfunctory.

My relations with the City Hall reporters were exceedingly pleasant and friendly, as they always have been with newspapermen. Every year I had the pleasure of having them dine with me at my house, and I always dined with them. I received the evening-paper men in the morning and the morning-paper men just before leaving my office in the afternoon, and talked with them perfectly freely and frankly, always adding to what I might say, "This is for publication," or "This is in confidence." During my six years as mayor my confidence was never violated but twice, each time by a reporter of the *Post,* who was not the regular City Hall man.

One of the few disagreeable incidents that I ever had with a newspaperman was with a fellow alumnus of Princeton named Louis Lang, of the class of 1881 and of the New York *American.* One morning he came to see me and after "passing the time of day" said, "Mr. Mayor, Mr. Hearst wants to know if you have a corrupt motive in advocating the Remsen Gas Bill?"[13] To which I replied, "Louis, you know better than to ask me a question like that. Get out of my office and don't come back." The next day the *American* carried a "scare headline" across its front page: "Mayor does not deny that he has a corrupt motive in supporting the Remsen Gas Bill," which of course was literally, if not actually, true.

---

[12] McClellan fails to mention that, until his break with Murphy following the election of 1905, he was consistently supported by the pro-Tammany New York *Daily News.*

[13] For a discussion of the Remsen Gas Bill, see Chapter IX, 211-213.

Another disagreeable incident was connected with the City Hall reporter of one of the great dailies who was a good-looking and pleasant young fellow. One morning before the beginning of my second term he called and said, "Mr. Mayor, I have been a very good friend of yours and I think it's time that you reciprocated. I want you to appoint me to a tax commissionership. I might as well put my cards on the table at the start and say that if you don't you will be very sorry, for I shall never let up on you." I was very much surprised and distressed, for I had liked him. I told him that as he had threatened me I could, of course, have nothing further to do with him and should report the matter to his employer. This I forthwith did, only to be told by the latter that he could not possibly relieve the man from duty at the City Hall much less discharge him as "such action would be interpreted by others as being dictated by the mayor."

It was some time after I took office before my office staff was running smoothly. John H. O'Brien was an ideal mayor's secretary. He was a good executive, wrote really excellent English, was good-looking with good manners, and was a perfect and successful buffer between the mayor and the public. I appointed as clerk in charge of the records a nice-looking young graduate of Manhattan College recommended by Murphy. It was not long, however, before O'Brien discovered that so as to save himself trouble, he was filing the records by the simple process of throwing them into the wastebasket.

Thomas Hassett,[14] who had been with me as stenographer during my campaign, I made chief clerk. He could not have been better, and when on the creation of the Board of Water Supply, I had him appointed secretary to the board, he thoroughly deserved his promotion. When Hassett was promoted I put in his place a very efficient man named Dan Riorden.[15] Some years later I discovered that he had been in the habit of reporting to Murphy every evening all that had happened in the mayor's office during the day. I charged him with his dis-

[14] Hassett was appointed secretary of the Board of Water Supply in December, 1905. At the time the New York *Tribune* (December 17, 1905) commended him for his "intelligence" and stated that he was an anti-Murphy appointment.

[15] James A. (not Dan) Riorden, who had been on McClellan's staff since 1904, succeeded Hassett.

loyalty, he broke down, cried, and confessed. Whereupon I removed him.[16]

The question of my personal legal adviser at first gave me a great deal of trouble. A friend of mine asked me to appoint a young cousin of his of whom he spoke in the highest terms. I had a talk with him and he seemed qualified for the job, so I appointed him. He proved, however, so incompetent and so peculiar in his actions that I was obliged to get rid of him, and I subsequently heard that he had been in an insane asylum and that his family was at a loss to know what to do with him.

I finally appointed as my legal adviser Franklyn Chase Hoyt, grandson of Chief Justice Chase. He filled the position perfectly. A gentleman to his finger tips, a first-rate lawyer, who improved as he went on, hard working, patient, courteous, and absolutely loyal. I became very fond of him, and when I made him a judge of Special Sessions I parted from him with the greatest regret. Afterwards he went far, and as chief judge of the Children's Court made for himself a world-wide reputation. I am very proud that it was my good fortune to give him his start in life.[17] Hoyt was succeeded by William B. Crowell, an excellent lawyer and hard-working man who served the city and his chief with loyalty and devotion.

Later I created another secretaryship, as I found that the work was more than could be handled by one man alone. In all, I never had more than thirty-five men in my office, and it was run under John O'Brien, and afterwards by his brother Frank, smoothly and well. Every letter received was answered the day of receipt; no citizen was turned away without an interview with either the mayor or one of his secretaries. I doubt if the office has ever been better run than it was in my time.

When the first of January, 1904, arrived I reached the City Hall at eleven o'clock, as I was to take office at noon. I found Mayor Low waiting for me in his inside office. We had a very pleasant chat on generalities. Out of space he said to be, "Mr. Mayor, take my advice and always have a private secretary.

16 McClellan is mistaken, for Riorden served until the end of McClellan's second term.

17 Actually, Low gave Hoyt "his start" by appointing him assistant corporation counsel in 1902. Hoyt was the founder, as well as judge, of the Children's Court.

There is nothing that so adds to one's comfort and nothing that is so absolutely necessary. I have always had one and could not do without him." I have often thought of what Low said and wished that I were rich enough to have followed his advice. . . .

As the clock struck twelve Low and I walked together into the mayor's reception room, which was packed with a crowd of deserving Democrats all bubbling over with enthusiasm in the hope of favors yet to come. Low made a few perfunctory remarks, and then I made a very short inaugural address and afterwards shook hands with all and sundry for about an hour, Low meanwhile slipping out the side door into private life. . . . After the handshaking was over I returned to the inner office, summoned the press, and announced my cabinet, after which I swore them in, and sent them on their way rejoicing to take over their departments. . . .

I very soon fell into a regular routine in my office work. I left my house every morning at a quarter to nine and walked downtown, usually alone, although sometimes my neighbor and friend, Frank Witherbee, joined me. It became a terrible grind and I tried to vary my walks as much as possible. I reached the City Hall at about a quarter past nine and found the office in full swing. I first looked over my engagement book that had been written up by O'Brien, read such letters as required my personal attention, and then began the day's work.

As the mayor was a member of almost every city board it was a physical impossibility for him to attend all of their meetings. I always attended the meetings of the Board of Estimate, the Sinking Fund Commission, and the Armory Board, and very often those of the Art Commission. As far as I legally could I deputized the president of the Board of Aldermen to understudy me at the others, and gave him the entire control over delinquent city marshals and pawnbrokers.

When I took office the mayor was required personally to sign every bond issued by the city. This was a very severe task that often meant hours of work and not infrequently gave me writer's cramp. As soon as the legislature met, I had a bill enacted permitting me to designate an employee in my office to do the work.

As far as possible I saw my heads of departments in the morn-

Mayor McClellan in 1905

Mayor George B. McClellan voting at the
election of November 3, 1903

Colonel George B. McClellan
Aide to Governor David B. Hill

Mayor McClellan starting the first subway train

The opening of the New York subway, October 27, 1904

Charles F. Murphy

Reading the Civil Service law prohibiting assessments for
political purposes (Mayor McClellan, left foreground)

President Roosevelt and Mayor McClellan at the unveiling of the General Slocum statue, May 30, 1905

Mayor McClellan in his office, January 21, 1908

George Brinton McClellan in later life, from a
portrait by Charles C. Curran, in the possession
of the Art Commission of the City of New York

ing, receiving members of the public, who had business with me or who thought that they had, in the afternoon. I found that the usual downtown lunch hour between one and two was the most convenient for important men to come to the City Hall. I therefore lunched, when I could lunch at all, at noon and usually took to lunch with me some member of my cabinet with whom I had business to discuss. The Hardware Lunch Club, which was directly across Broadway from the City Hall, had very courteously elected me a member, ahead of the waiting list, and reserved for me a table in a quiet corner where the members with great tact left me undisturbed. I never lunched anywhere but there.

The ordinary run of citizens were gathered in the reception room where I went at intervals, shook hands with them, and listened to their requests and complaints. Those who had really important business I saw in my private office. I sometimes talked with as many as a hundred people during the day. As every one of them wished to commit me in favor of whatever he had come to see me about, I was necessarily constantly on the defensive, and the strain was very great. I soon learned that for a public official one of the most dangerous words in the English language is yes, one of the most useful is no. When I realized that a proposition submitted to me was either impossible or inexpedient, I unqualifiedly said no. When I was favorably disposed to it, I reserved my decision, subject to further investigation. I have often been most favorably impressed by a proposition submitted to me which on further study proved to have a catch in it. When yes has once been said, it is impossible to change to no without resulting complications and ill feeling. On the other hand a no once said can be changed to yes if necessary without inconvenience.

Some of the requests that were made to me as mayor were to put it mildly extraordinary.

John R. Claflin,[18] the drygoods merchant who lived not far from us, came to see me with the proposition that I should fence in Washington Square, keep it locked, and give keys only to residents on the north, east, and west sides. He said that

---

[18] The H. B. Claflin Company, of which John R. Claflin was president from 1890 to 1914, was the largest wholesale dry goods firm in the world. Claflin also controlled several large department stores in New York.

his children played in the square, and his wife and he did not like to have them run the risk of catching diseases from the sittees on the park benches. "Why," I asked, "would you limit the keys of the park to the residents of the north, east, and west sides?" He answered with perfect seriousness, "Because, Mr. Mayor, the people who live on the south side are very common," and he was a hard-headed businessman who had worked his way up from the bottom of the ladder.

A very rich man named [Albert R.] Shattuck, [a real estate dealer], who also lived on Washington Square and subsequently acquired fame by being locked in his own wine-cellar with the members of his household by two criminally-minded French men servants, worked out a very original plan. He, like a good many others in their day, always drove himself downtown to his office. As traffic increased the daily drive became ever less agreeable. Shattuck proposed that the city should open a new street from Eighth Street to Wall, and that this new street should be reserved exclusively as he explained "for gentlemen driving their own traps." He had taken his project so seriously that he had had the route of the proposed street surveyed and submitted working drawings.

I sometimes received as many as twenty delegations during a working day, sometimes friendly, sometimes quite the reverse, who had to be soothed, flattered, and put in a good humor in my speeches to them.

When the day's work was done, usually about six o'clock, I walked home, generally with one of my subordinates, and arrived just in time to dress for dinner. We restricted ourselves to accepting three dinner invitations a week, and besides I was obliged to go to a vast number of very tiresome public dinners.

There is one good that prohibition accomplished: it largely did away with public dinners. When I was mayor, the people of New York were "public-dinner minded," and gave them on all possible occasions. The mayor was invited to every one, and as I was supposed to make a rather good speech, the pressure on me to attend them was very great. I was always seated on the right of the chairman who usually, not being used to public speaking, was in a blue funk at the thought of standing on his feet and so was rarely a cheerful companion. On the other side of me was probably someone who was equally nervous. The dinner was generally bad, and the audience by the time the speeches began, while enthusiastic, was not in a condition to appreciate the fine points of what I had to say. I always spoke for the press and, as the radio did not exist, used the public dinners I attended as a means of getting before the public matters in which I was interested.

I very soon found to my great satisfaction that I had executive ability,[19] which is nothing but the ability to make the other fellow do your work for you. I have an excellent memory, which stood me in good stead, and I was able to keep in touch with the work of the departments and to carry in my head what they were doing. All this meant that by the end of the week I was very nearly "all in." My wife and I made up our minds that if I was to pull through my term, which was then two years, I must rest on Saturdays and Sundays, and that I could only get rest by going out of town.

We first rented a little cottage at Lakewood, that was run in connection with one of the hotels. When the hotel went out of business, we rented a cottage at Princeton and went there every Friday afternoon returning to town on Monday morning. In this way I was able to get two long walks every week, but what was of even greater importance, for three nights a week I was completely disassociated from the mayoralty. Thanks to these weekly rests I ended six grinding years of office almost as fit as I began. . . .

The Christmas before I took office I was inundated with presents from pseudo-admirers who presumably had axes to grind. One rather prominent lawyer sent me five hundred fifty-cent cigars and four cases of champagne. I received enough champagne and cigars to have kept me supplied for several years had I retained them. I, of course, returned all of these presents with a polite note saying that I was obliged to make it my rule to accept no present during my term of office. The only exceptions I made were to accept a bullfinch named Willy,

[19] McClellan's estimate of his own executive ability is substantiated by Lawson Purdy, whom McClellan made president of the Department of Taxes and Assessments in 1906. See Lawson Purdy, "Reminiscences," 8-10. On the other hand, the New York *World* (December 31, 1909) wrote that McClellan "did not inherit the administrative genius of his distinguished father," and the New York *Times* (December 31, 1909) stated that he was "only a commonplace administrator."

from Eugene Franer, the German barber at the Waldorf, who lived in my own election district and who was an old friend, an Irish terrier puppy named Tom from Tom Hassett, and a Scotty puppy named Jan Ben in honor of his doner John Bensel.[20] . . .

I found that it had been the custom of my predecessors to accept free tickets and boxes at the theatres and at the horse show. This custom I discontinued. . . . The only courtesy of the kind that I ever accepted was a permit from Mr. [Alexander J.] Cassatt, president of the Pennsylvania Railroad, allowing Tom to travel with us in the cars of the company.

I neither accepted nor asked favors, nor did I grant them. Years later my chamberlain, James J. Martin, said to Thomas F. Ryan, "Why have you always been down on McClellan? He has always given you a square deal, hasn't he?" "That's just it," replied Ryan, "he has given me a square deal and nothing more."

After my election as mayor, Murphy and his Wall Street backers, including Thomas F. Ryan and the Standard Oil crowd, thought they saw in me a presidential possibility, their plan being to first make me governor and from Albany work for the presidential nomination. As events proved, it was a fantastic scheme, for to insure their continued support would have meant my complete subservience to their wishes, which was of course impossible, as I happened to value my self-respect. Later the same people, having washed their hands of me, supported Oscar Underwood,[21] with the result that is well known.

I was perfectly willing to "go along with them" as far and as long as I conscientiously could, for while the prospect of landing me in the presidency was very slight, there was always a gambler's chance of success. It was determined to start the ball rolling by giving me a victory dinner to be presided over by Bourke Cockran and addressed by Richard Olney, who had been Cleveland's [Attorney General and] Secretary of State and was supposed to be very friendly to me. I took no part in the

[20] Bensel, a close friend of Murphy, served as commissioner of docks and ferries while McClellan was mayor.

[21] Underwood's campaign for the Democratic nomination for President in 1912 was financed in large part by Ryan. Tammany, on the other hand, supported Champ Clark.

arrangements for the dinner or I should certainly have objected to having Cockran speak, for he loved me not at all.

I never understood what happened, but the dinner was not the expected success as the start of my "boom." Cockran made an excellent speech, as a speech, but was very careful not to refer to me either directly or indirectly, while Olney not only did not refer to me but devoted his speech to nominating Grover Cleveland for the presidency. I was presented with a gold medal, the only positive result I obtained from the dinner. I afterwards heard that Olney was down on me for having consented to run on the Tammany ticket.[22] Such being the case he should not have come to the dinner, and certainly not have "queered" it.

While I was mayor there was, from time to time, a certain amount of discussion as to whether my foreign birth did not make me ineligible for the presidency. Those who held that it did had evidently not read the Constitution which provided that the President shall be a natural born and not a native born citizen. While I am not a native born citizen, there is of course no question but that, my parents being citizens, I am as much natural born as though my birthplace had been in the United States.

Mr. Justice [David J.] Brewer, who was born of United States parents in Syria, once told me that when he was being discussed as a presidential candidate he had canvassed his colleagues of the Supreme Court who were unanimously of the opinion that he was eligible, especially as he was covered by the statutory definition of a natural born citizen.

The New York *Tribune* once remarked sardonically in an editorial, "If the question of his eligibility were all that stood between McClellan and the presidency he would have no cause to worry." Actually I was never mentioned in but two national conventions: New Jersey was for me for Vice-President in 1900, and Ohio was for me for President in 1904.

It was not long before I realized that my cabinet left much to be desired. Of the men recommended by Murphy with the

22 In October, 1903, Olney had refused to campaign for McClellan for mayor on the ground that he did not wish to alienate the "considerable body of staunch Democrats who mean to support Mr. Low." (Richard Olney to H. St. George Tucker, October 15, 1903, McClellan MSS.)

exception of Hayes [23] and Featherson,[24] who were honest and efficient, none was better than a painful mediocrity. More than that, I found that all were going to the boss for orders and regarded him as their chief, and the mayor as only a necessary inconvenience.

I reasoned with Murphy on the subject, who explained that he had been giving his nominees orders so as to relieve me of unnecessary worry. I begged him to allow me to be the judge of the matter and to refrain from going behind my back in the effort to direct the policy of my heads of departments. He promised to comply with my request, but continued to issue his orders, so secretly, however, that it was some time before I found out that he had broken his word.

That the government of the city of New York functions smoothly and, take it all in all, very well, despite district leader commissioners and deputy commissioners under Tammany, and under incompetent theorists under "reform," is because each department has a permanent official, who is usually called the chief engineer, who really runs it. These men are able and efficient, are well paid and deserve every cent that they receive. What the city would do without them is difficult to imagine. . . .

[23] Nicholas J. Hayes was a Tammany district leader and commissioner of the Fire Department during McClellan's first term.

[24] Maurice Featherson was a Tammany district leader and dock commissioner during McClellan's first term.

Chapter IX

My Real Troubles Began

It took me more than a year to learn my job thoroughly. When I had mastered it, I was familiar with the work of all the departments and was able to gauge accurately the worth of the different department heads. My conclusion was that, with the exception of Delany, O'Donnel, Hayes, Featherson, Kennedy, Darlington, and Woodbury, the department heads knew little of their work and that the departments were really running themselves under my direction.

During my first term Delany was of great help to me. His advice was sound and he supported me loyally in my differences with the organization. Woodbury was very temperamental, and inclined to certain eccentricities which were finally his undoing. At first, however, he ran his department well, and because of his intimacy with Laffan and J. P. Morgan was enthusiastically supported by the press. Hayes and Featherson had easy departments to run and ran them beyond criticism. O'Donnel during my first administration gave me no cause for complaint, and Kennedy, as I have already said, was one of the best.

I found in the Health Department two civil servants who were quite remarkable in their efficiency. Dr. Herman Biggs was the technical head and Dr. Walter Bensel was the sanitary superintendent. The latter was one of the best executives that it has ever been my good fortune to work with.

McAdoo as police commissioner was a failure. He had no control over the force, which was really run by the inspectors. It was only by supreme good luck that there were no scandals. The New York police is as fine a body of men as exists anywhere. It contains crooks, as does every force in the world, but

I think that it is no exaggeration to say that ninety-five per cent of the men are honest. . . .

It is not so surprising to me that so many policemen fall from grace as it is that so many remain honest. In a great city the policeman is constantly subject to temptation. Money is actually forced on him, by gamblers, liquor dealers, and prostitutes, and even the traffic cop must have a very stern sense of duty to refuse the Christmas presents that are offered him by rich and generous passers of his station.

Every police scandal that breaks in New York is exploited to the limit by the press, which is very prone to compare our force with the Metropolitan Police Force of London to the great disadvantage of our own. When there is a scandal involving the London police, the British press minimizes it. The last two London police scandals, which were very serious, were investigated by a commission appointed by the Home Secretary from within the force, and this extraordinary procedure failed utterly to appeal to the somewhat eccentric sense of British humor.

When in London in 1906, I had an interview with Sir Charles Henry, then chief commissioner of the Metropolitan Police. I asked him how he handled solicitation by streetwalkers. He replied, "There is no solicitation, for it is illegal." To one who had walked down Piccadilly after dark his statement was rather a surprise. I then asked him how he handled gambling hells. He answered, "We have no gambling hells." "But there must be gambling in London," I objected. "Oh yes," he said, "of course there is gambling, but under the Licensed Clubs Act it is all in the clubs"; and with a smile he added, "One can join a club for one evening on the payment of as little as ten shillings. If a neighbor complains that a disorderly house is being maintained, that is, a house where there is much noise, or if we have evidence from within that a common gambling establishment is being maintained, then we make a raid. But the evidence must be very convincing to warrant our breaking in." I did not find Sir Charles very illuminating. . . .

Despite his shortcomings, McAdoo deserves credit for having enthusiastically carried out three reforms I proposed for the police. We put them in new and smart uniforms, substituting the blouse worn by the brigadier generals of the United States

Army for the frock coats the men had previously worn, and the army cap for the former unsightly and uncomfortable helmet. He weeded out the elderly, physically incompetent, walrus-moustached, enormously fat "flatties" who had made our force a joke and enlisted in their place young and active lads, many of them from the country. But best of all he introduced traffic regulation.

Very soon after taking office I sent Police Captain John J. O'Connor [1] abroad to study the traffic regulations of the principal European cities. On his return I had the commissioner place him in command of the traffic squad which was organized for the first time. O'Connor was a remarkably intelligent man, to whom is entirely due the inauguration of traffic regulations in New York. We worked out the system, and he put it into effect. Others have claimed the glory of being the "father of traffic regulation" in our city, but to O'Connor, and to O'Connor alone, belongs the credit. He died not long afterwards, too soon to have reached the rank in the department to which his honesty and ability as a policeman entitled him. For the first time the mounted squad appeared on the streets and it at once caught the public's fancy. It was a well-drilled and fine squadron of cavalry, and from its very novelty commanded instant respect in its very arduous task of making the public understand the new regulations.

The difficulties in installing the system were very great. It must be remembered that when O'Connor took hold, traffic had never been controlled. The driver of every truck, trolley car, horse-drawn vehicle, and motor was an absolute law to himself and moved through the streets as best he could, relying on his nerve, his agility, and his bullying to get through. During the rush hours it usually required forty-five minutes for a Broadway trolley car to make the journey from Forty-second Street to Wall, while a traffic tangle often took half an hour to straighten out. It took time and patience to teach drivers that the new regulations were to their advantage, for at first they violently and profanely objected to being held up by the traffic cops.

In Brooklyn that strange and eccentric person Justice Gaynor

---

[1] The only O'Connor listed in the *City Directory* as a police captain during McClellan's administration is John W. O'Connor.

of the Supreme Court, who succeeded me as mayor, did all in his power to prevent my putting the traffic regulations into force. He enjoined me permanently on the ground that any regulation of traffic was a curtailment of the constitutional liberty of the individual. It required nearly a year to win a victory over Gaynor in the Court of Appeals, which meant a year's unnecessary delay in straightening out traffic in Brooklyn.

In Manhattan I had great difficulty in persuading the magistrates to punish violators of the regulations, and Murphy, inspired by the truck drivers' union, was outraged at the thought that men should be fined for refusal to obey the orders of the traffic cop. I summoned the entire board of magistrates to my office and talked to them straight from the shoulder, ending by telling them that failure to back me up would be considered a bar to the re-appointment of any whose term of office might expire while I was mayor. Whatever may have been their motive they amended their ways, and thereafter I had no cause for complaint. [Herbert H.] Vreeland, the superintendent of the Broadway Street Railway Company, agreed to discharge any of his motormen against whom there was a complaint by a traffic cop. This helped enormously, for on Broadway, which was our greatest problem, the trolley cars set the pace for the other vehicles. By the end of my first term O'Connor had accomplished his task, and the traffic regulations were being smoothly enforced.

The three most serious police questions with which I had to deal were liquor, prostitution, and gambling. Soon after taking office I sent for Fitz Lengerke, the president of the Retail Liquor Dealers' Association,[2] and said to him, "It is generally understood that liquor dealers are obliged to pay the police for alleged protection." "Yes," he answered, "that is true." "I want you to help me stop it," I said. "Will you agree to refuse protection money? If you will, I will see that you come to no harm." He promptly agreed and went on his way. Some months later he returned and told me with great satisfaction that no more protection money was being paid. I was, of course,

---

[2] There is no record of either Lengerke or the Retail Liquor Dealers' Association. McClellan may have been referring to Fritz Lindinger, who was president of the Wine, Liquor and Beer Dealers' Association.

"Say, Honestly, Tell Me Is the Lid On?"

——*The New York Globe, March 3, 1904*

delighted. "How have you done it?" I asked. To which he replied, "We done it this way; we don't pay no more protection money. When Christmas comes, we just send the captains a good big Christmas present."

I was discouraged but resolved to make another effort, so I sent for McAdoo and told him that I had reason to believe that the liquor dealers were paying for protection by giving the captains Christmas presents, presumably of a size fixed by the latter, and that I wanted the custom stopped. The next morning O'Brien came to me and announced that the police commissioner and all the police inspectors wanted to see me. He then ushered in McAdoo, followed by everyone of the inspectors in full uniform. The commissioner then lined them up in a row and beginning at the left said to the senior inspector, "Inspector, on your word of honor do you know of any case of the payment, directly or indirectly to a policeman, of protection money by a liquor dealer?" To which the inspector solemnly replied, "On my word of honor I know of no such case." He then put the same question to the next inspector and so on down the line. When the last inspector had answered he turned to me and said, "Mr. Mayor, these are all honorable men, and they have assured you on their honor that they know of no protection money being paid. Are you satisfied?" "Yes," I answered, "I am satisfied that if the inspectors have told the truth they know very little of what is going on in their districts. Good day," and I sent them out.

The law forbidding the sale of liquor on Sunday was almost impossible of enforcement. During a strike in the Street Cleaning Department the men became very restive. As I did not want any disorder, I instructed the police commissioner to see to it that when Sunday came the strikers were prevented having access to the barrooms in the neighborhood of the department stables and headquarters, which meant practically the entire water front. He called out the whole force for riot duty, stationed two men at the door of each barroom, and gave the city what I imagine was the nearest approach to a dry Sunday it ever had under the old law.

In London the barrooms are open after one o'clock on Sunday. We should have been very wise to have followed the

English example, which we have now done, thanks to Commissioner Mulrooney.[3]

In the old days there were far too many barrooms in the city and the fault lay almost entirely with the brewers. Anyone who wished to go into the retail liquor business went to any one of the many brewers and was advanced the money necessary for his purpose on his written agreement to sell only that particular brewer's beer. The brewer took a chattle mortgage on the liquor dealer's possessions and thenceforth owned him body and soul. The brewers were utterly unreasonable, fighting every effort to reduce the number of saloons, so that the city was covered with them, some city blocks having as many as a dozen. It was largely due to the grasping, ignorant selfishness of the brewers that prohibition carried the state of New York.

I evolved a plan which I think, if adopted, might have greatly improved conditions. I proposed that the number of saloons should be limited to one to so many thousand of population; that the licenses for these saloons should be put up at auction once a year and sold to the highest bidders; that the licensee should be held responsible for the orderly conduct of the saloon; that if a man were arrested as drunk and disorderly in a saloon the license should be suspended for a certain time, and on, say, the third offense the license should be revoked. It would, in this way, be altogether to the advantage of the licensee to see to it that no drunkenness occurred in his saloon, and as the licenses would be very expensive the little "holes in the wall," which always gave the police the most trouble, would disappear. I submitted my plan to Murphy in the hope that he might be willing to back it. He, however, would have none of it, on the ground that neither the brewers nor the liquor dealers would consent to it.

The question of prostitution was also very difficult to handle. Dr. Parkhurst, in his spectacular and sensational campaign during the Van Wyck administration, had succeeded in scattering prostitution all over the city. Under the notorious Captain Alec Williams, almost all the prostitutes in New York had been

[3] Edward P. Mulrooney joined the police force in 1896 when he was twenty-one. He worked up through the ranks, and in 1930 he became commissioner of police. In 1934, he resigned as commissioner to become head of the State Alcoholic Beverage Control Board. Although named police commissioner by Mayor James J. Walker, he was not affiliated with Tammany Hall.

segregated in what he had named the "Tenderloin," a section running roughly from Fourteenth Street to Forty-second, and west of Sixth Avenue. I found a shocking condition, which had grown up under Low. There were brothels all over the town and streetwalkers were everywhere, especially on Fifth Avenue. I instructed the police commissioner to quietly and gradually round the brothels up west of Sixth Avenue, and at all cost to clear Fifth Avenue of streetwalkers. Within a year Fifth Avenue was, at night, as safe for a woman walking alone as was main street in a country town. In this way the policing of prostitution became much simplified.

Gambling was another problem almost impossible to solve. The gambling hell is, to my mind, the most serious menace to the youth of our community. I thoroughly agree with Jerome [4] in his statement that there is no honest professional gambler. The best that we could do was to keep them on the move, and to make life just as hard for them as possible. It was a great satisfaction to me that I was able to co-operate with Jerome in driving out of business that unmitigated scoundrel Canfield,[5] who had been permitted to run openly and unhindered next door to Delmonico's restaurant. Canfield's favorite method of drumming up new business was to get some poor but socially smart young man into his debt, take his notes, then offer to return the notes provided the victim induced some other young man, not necessarily smart, but necessarily rich, to come to the hell. Canfield then proceeded to trim him. . . .

[In addition to the departments, there were several other branches of the city government with which I had to maintain almost daily contacts. Of these none was more important than

---

4 William Travers Jerome was a courageous and colorful public prosecutor. Beginning his political career as a Tammany Democrat, he was appointed assistant district attorney in 1888. He broke with the organization in 1890, served on the staff of the Lexow Committee in 1894, was a justice of the Court of Special Sessions (1895-1901), was elected district attorney on the Republican ticket in 1901, and in 1905 was re-elected without any party backing. He retired in 1909 and did not again hold public office.

5 Richard A. Canfield, in addition to operating gambling houses for the rich in Saratoga and New York City, was a successful Wall Street operator, art connoisseur, and glassware manufacturer. Although Jerome raided Canfield's gambling establishment in Low's administration, it was not until 1904 that Canfield was convicted, and he was then fined only $1,000.

the Board of Estimate.] As the functions of the Board of Aldermen were extremely limited, the important and actual legislative body under the charter of the greater city was the Board
of Estimate and Apportionment. This consisted then as it
does now of the mayor, the comptroller, the president of the
Board of Aldermen, and the five borough presidents. Of these
the first three had three votes each, the presidents of Manhattan and Brooklyn two votes each, and the presidents of Queens
and Richmond one vote each, or fifteen votes in all. For ordinary business a majority vote was sufficient but for many
purposes including public improvements a two-thirds vote was
required. It will thus be seen that a combination of the
borough presidents could not vote down the three city officials,
while any two of the latter could block all public improvements.
Though the mayor had an absolute veto over expenditures
voted by the board, and what practically amounted to an
absolute veto over public improvements by the requirement of
the law that to become effective the map for such improvements
had to be signed by him, it was almost unheard of for the mayor
to exercise his veto power, the existence of which was not
generally realized. I determined to hold the veto power in
reserve and if possible to control the board without its use.

Of my two running mates at the election, Grout, the comptroller, was an able, honest, and ambitious man who had
dominated the board under Low. Fornes, the president of the
Board of Aldermen, was a kindly old German, perfectly honest
but equally incompetent. Of the five borough presidents,
[John F.] Ahearn of Manhattan was a near-illiterate, completely
under Murphy's thumb. Martin Littleton of Brooklyn was a
brilliant speaker with no great executive ability and with a
fiery temper. "Curly Joe" Cassidy of Queens was a very clever
crook who subsequently was sent to Sing Sing for graft in
office.[6] George Cromwell of Richmond was the only Republican
on the board. He was an honest and an able official.

Murphy gave me an excellent piece of advice when he said,
"If you don't boss Grout at the very beginning, he will boss
you." I had it out with Grout at the first meeting of the board

---

6 "Graft in office" is not quite accurate, for Cassidy, the Democratic boss of
Queens, was convicted in 1914 for having sold a nomination to the state Supreme
Court in 1911.

and successfully "bossed" him. After that I had no trouble with him, and we worked together in perfect harmony. As the borough presidents apparently could only think in terms of their own boroughs, in city matters they generally followed my lead, as did Fornes. In other words I was able to control the board without very much difficulty.

The chief engineer of the board, Nelson A. Lewis, was a first-rate official with a first-rate staff. He was a holdover from Low, and I had him converted into the classified service so as to make him immune from political influence. Hague, the secretary,[7] was competent, but as the years passed, fell more and more under Murphy's influence.

Before each meeting of the board I went over the calendar that had been prepared by Hague. I then went over it again with Lewis, when we usually radically revised it. No item went on that I had not approved in advance. There were often loud protests from the borough presidents and from Grout, but they generally ended by making the best of what they could not alter. In my time the budget was prepared in the comptroller's office, for there was no director of the budget, as now. I then redrafted it with the help of Lewis and his staff, after which it was submitted to the board. I always assumed full responsibility for it, and it passed subtantially as I had submitted it.

It may appear from all this that I was exceedingly dictatorial and arbitrary. I was, for I had to be, in self-defense. The charter intended to concentrate all responsibility on the shoulders of the mayor, and to carry that responsibility, which was heartbreaking, the mayor had to have great power. I not only used every power granted me in the charter but appropriated every last bit of power that I could seize by inference. It is the only way that a mayor can hope to avoid certain failure.

The first serious difference that I had with a department head was at the very beginning of my term. The New York Public Library, which was under construction, was surrounded by a high board fence. One morning New York awoke to find the fence covered with advertising signs which had been painted

---

[7] McClellan is somewhat confused, for the secretary's name was Joseph Haag (not Hague), and he did not become secretary of the board until 1906. During McClellan's first term the secretary was James W. Stevenson.

during the night and extended around the entire block. Without a single exception the newspapers denounced me as a vandal and very properly demanded that the signs should be painted out. I was as much outraged by the matter as were the newspapers.

The construction of the library was under the jurisdiction of John J. Pallas, the president of the Park Board, for whom I immediately sent. Pallas was the typical labor walking delegate, with whom I had had some experience when I was in Congress. When I was running for re-election in 1900, I was informed that the American Federation of Labor had blacklisted me. Fortunately "Big 6," the typographical union, bolted the blacklist and supported me, so that the blacklisting did me very little harm. After election I made inquiries as to the cause of the blacklisting and found that Pallas, then general secretary of the Federation, was responsible. It seems that during the previous session he had called on me and had been told that I was not on the floor of the House, which I probably was not, as I never received his card. He then went to the gallery and to his surprise and wrath saw me walking across the floor. Turning to his companion, Amos Cummings, who was my informant, he said, "I'll learn the aristocratic pup manners. I'll have him blacklisted when he runs next fall." And he did.

When Pallas reached my office, I proceeded to reduce the proud labor leader to a condition of pulp. He pleaded that he had allowed the signs to be painted much against his will under the direct orders of "The Commissioner," which was the title by which Murphy was known to the faithful.[8] He acknowledged that without consulting me he had granted the concession for a year without compensation to the city, to Harry Hart, one of the district leaders.[9] I then got in touch with Murphy who told me that he had given Hart the concession in lieu of an office, and that it would net Hart about $50,000 a year. I told Murphy that unless Hart voluntarily

[8] Murphy was called "Commissioner" because he served as dock commissioner during Van Wyck's administration.

[9] At the time the New York *Tribune* (March 5, 1904) wrote: "The contract given to Harry C. Hart . . . was without the knowledge of the Mayor, but Charles F. Murphy knew all about it. Mr. Murphy has told Mr. Pallas that the storm will blow over in a few days and said, 'Don't get nervous.' As is already well known, Harry C. Hart is the Tammany leader of the XXXth District."

yielded his concession I should have the signs removed anyhow and let him sue the city. After a great deal of grumbling and considerable ill temper, Murphy finally consented to make Hart yield gracefully and the signs were painted out.

The next departmental trouble that arose was with the Civil Service Commission. I found that its members never by any chance visited their office; they even had the payroll sent to their private offices for their signatures. After warning the members to attend to their duty, and finding my warning disregarded, I removed the entire board. Again to Murphy's intense indignation.

During my six years as mayor the state government was always solidly Republican, governor and both branches of the legislature, all of whom, with the exception of [Frank W.] Higgins, were constantly employed in trying to "put the mayor in a hole." Of the four governors who were at Albany while I was mayor (Odell, Higgins, Hughes and White [10]) Higgins in his relations with the city was the least partisan, the fairest, and the easiest to get on with. He had been chairman of the Senate Committee on Cities for a number of years, knew the requirements of New York, and loyally stood with me in trying to prevent steals and strike legislation.

The mayor has a suspensory veto on all state legislative bills involving the city, a veto which becomes absolute on bills which come to him after final adjournment of the legislature. During the legislative session it was therefore necessary to kill bad bills before they reached me, to avoid the possibility of their being passed over my veto. The Tammany delegation was a feeble reed to lean on in the cause of righteousness, although an assemblyman watched legislation for me at first with more or less efficiency. I could not, however, rely on his judgment. I therefore sent John B. McGoldrick,[11] an assistant

[10] McClellan is mistaken, for although Benjamin B. Odell, Frank W. Higgins, and Charles Evans Hughes were governors while he was mayor, Horace White was not. In 1910, the year after McClellan had left office, Hughes resigned as governor to become a Supreme Court Justice and was succeeded by White, the lieutenant governor. Odell served as governor from 1901 to 1904, Higgins from 1905 to 1906, and Hughes from 1907 to 1910.

[11] McClellan is referring to Edward J. (not John B.) McGoldrick. McClellan appointed McGoldrick, who got his start in politics as private secretary to Lieutenant Governor William F. Sheehan, assistant corporation counsel in 1907. McGoldrick retained this position under successive mayors until 1920, when he

corporation counsel, now a Supreme Court justice, to Albany as the city's watchdog. He did his work admirably and kept me informed as to what was going on in the capital. Higgins and also John Raines, the Republican Senate leader, were of great use, and helped me time and again to prevent committees reporting out bills designed to raid the city treasury or to put me in a hole.

Soon after I took office an assemblyman named [Jacob D.] Remsen introduced a bill to permit the New York Consolidated Gas Company to remove its manufacturing plant from near the Riverside Drive in Manhattan to Astoria in Queens Borough. This removal was a convenience and an economy for the gas company, but it was a necessity for the city, one of whose most attractive sections had been made almost uninhabitable by smoke and gas fumes.

Hearst, who after his two days' halfhearted support at the close of the campaign, had turned against me the day after I took office, promptly began a crusade against the Remsen Gas Bill on the ground that, as a corporation wanted it, it must necessarily be bad. The New York *World* joined him, and the rest of the press remained neutral. I favored the bill from the start, for it was greatly in the interests of the city, and I should have gladly paid any reasonable price to have got rid of the gasworks. The bill passed the legislature and came before me for the public hearing required by law. Before the hearing began Thomas F. Ryan came to see me and told me that Odell, the governor, had asked him to tell me that he, Odell, gave me his word that if I signed the bill he would also do so. This relieved my mind, for as there had been so much newspaper criticism of the bill, I did not enjoy the prospect of signing it only to have it vetoed by Odell.

In due course I signed the bill and sent it forward to the governor, who promptly vetoed it with a "ringing" message denouncing me as a servant of the gas company for having signed it.[12] After we had both left office, I met Odell who said

---

became a justice on the state Supreme Court. Throughout all of this period McGoldrick continued to serve as the legislative representative of the city administration in Albany.

[12] Hearst's New York *Journal* (July 25, 1904) wrote: "Mayor McClellan, instead of defending the people of New York City who elected him against the thieving Gas Trust, actually signed the bill that put the people at the mercy of

to me, "George, did anyone ever insinuate to you that if you signed the Remsen Gas Bill, I would also do so?" I answered, "Ben, no one ever made any such insinuation to me. But Tom Ryan came to me and told me that you had asked him to come to me with your promise that you would sign it if I did." Odell said nothing, but turned and walked away. It was a dirty trick to play me, especially as in Congress we had been great friends.

After the defeat of the Remsen Gas Bill I tried to get rid of the gasworks by agreement with the company, and finally succeeded in doing so, after Hearst had delayed the improvement for years in the courts. Meanwhile he greatly enjoyed himself by always referring to me as "The Gas Man."

It was in connection with the Remsen Gas Bill that I had my first disillusionment about Murphy. Murphy was always accompanied by one of his two inseparable pals, Phil Donohue and J. Sergeant Cram. The first time I ever met the former, by way of making conversation I asked, "How has business been this bright healthy winter?" He answered, "Business has been rotten, for the winter has been too damned healthy." In surprise I inquired, "What is your business?" to which he replied, "I'm an undertaker." [13] According to legend Cram had endeared himself to Murphy by teaching the latter to eat peas with a fork.[14] Be this as it may, his influence with the boss was otherwise anything but educational.

---

the trust. It was necessary for the people who elected the mayor and counted on him to protect their home rule rights to go to the Republican Governor—Odell—and get him to veto the Corrupt bill. . . . We feel sorry for this young man. . . . The machine was too much for him."

McClellan's reasons for approving this bill are stated in a memorandum that he sent to the governor when he returned the measure with his signature. See letter press memorandum, dated April 27, 1904, in McClellan Scrapbook, 1904-1905, New York Historical Society.

13 Philip F. Donohue and Murphy had grown up together in the same neighborhood and had been schoolmates. When Murphy became head of Tammany in 1902, he made Donohue treasurer of Tammany Hall, a position which he held until his death in 1937. He left the undertaking business in 1908 to open an advertising agency, and he served as commissioner of water supply from 1922 to 1934.

14 Cram and Murphy first became friendly when they both served as dock commissioners under Van Wyck. Cram was a Harvard graduate, and his name was listed in the Social Register. Most of the braves were appalled at Murphy's choice of Cram as a friend, and in 1903 William S. Devery told a group of his adherents: "Since he [Murphy] has gotten in with J. Sergeant Cram he has got into a habit of tucking up his trousers at the bottom and wearing glasses, and

Walking downtown one morning shortly after I had signed the Remsen Gas Bill, I was joined by Cram. He opened the conversation by saying, "Charley was very much relieved when you signed the Remsen Gas Bill." I asked, "Why was he so much interested? I know that some of his friends were anxious to have me sign the bill, but why his personal interest?" "Why, don't you know?" Cram replied, "Harry Rogers [15] (of the Standard Oil Company) agreed to carry Charley's stocks for him if Charley got you to sign the bill." "Let's get this straight," I said. "Am I to understand that Rogers agreed to pull Murphy out of a hole in Wall Street in return for my signature on that bill? In other words, do I understand that Murphy delivered me behind my back?" "Mr. Mayor," he said, "you are very simple. Of course Charley delivered you. You don't suppose that he would have taken any interest in the bill unless he had got something out of it." Shortly afterwards I learned that Oakley, commissioner of water supply, gas and electricity, had been negotiating without my knowledge with the gas company for the removal of its plant to Astoria. I found that as usual he had been obeying Murphy's orders, and [I] took the negotiations out of his hands and placed them in the hands of Lewis, chief engineer of the Board of Estimate.

One day Murphy called me up and told me that Bourke Cockran was anxious to have a talk with me and that they would call to see me that evening, if convenient. I agreed, and told John Delany that I wanted him present as a witness. Murphy arrived accompanied by Cockran and Cram. Cockran at once plunged into an oration on the beauties of New York as a cosmopolitan city. After a while I asked him to get down to brass tacks and tell me what he was driving at. And he proceeded to "demand on behalf of the millions of our cosmopolitan citizens," that I throw the town wide open. I asked him if that included prostitution, liquor, and gambling, and he replied that it did. I then told Cockran exactly what I thought of him, and I told him so as to leave no manner of

instead of being a respectable gas house gentleman he goes on Fifth Avenue. If he don't look out one lamp will fall out and he will have only one just like Cram, an' he will say: 'How do, chappie,' an' when a decent fellow will ask him for a job he will reply: 'I cawn't do it.'" (New York *Times*, October 24, 1903.)

15 Henry Huttleston Rogers was a pioneer in the oil refining business, an early associate of Rockefeller, and one of the leading officials of Standard Oil.

doubt in his mind that my opinion was anything but complimentary. When I had finished what I had to say, Cockran rose
and said, "I see that there is no use in arguing with a narrow-
minded puritan." As he went out, I did not offer to shake hands
with him.

As the days passed it became ever more evident to me that
Murphy and I could not work together much longer and that
the break would come at any moment.

As I was going into the Board of Estimate room one morning, Ahearn, the president of the Borough of Manhattan,
joined me and in the course of polite conversation said, "I'm
still holding up them permits," (pronounced in the best Tammany circles with the accent on the last syllable). I inquired
what permits he was holding up and why; whereupon he said,
"Charley told me not to give the Pennsylvania people their
permits to dig the foundations of their new station unless they
gave the contract to his brother Johnny. You know that Johnny
Murphy and Jim Gaffney" [16] (Murphy's alderman) "have
organized a contracting company with Charley as silent partner." This was all news, and very interesting news, to me. I
asked Ahearn to come to my office after the meeting, when
I said to him, "Mr. President, do you realize that what you are
doing is nothing short of the worst kind of a 'hold up'? If you
don't issue those permits this afternoon, I shall go before the
grand jury tomorrow and have you indicted." Ahearn was
surprised and hurt. "You can't mean that," he said. "Them's
Charley's orders." "You go to the Commissioner," I answered,
"and tell him what I have told you. I mean every word that
I have said." The permits were issued that afternoon.

Some weeks later the contract was awarded to Murphy and
Gaffney. I asked [Alexander J.] Cassatt, the president of the
Pennsylvania Railroad, why he had done so and he replied that
he recognized that he was being "held up," but had he not
given the contract to Murphy he would have been subjected
to endless delay and trouble. Later he told me that Murphy
and Gaffney were utterly incompetent. He had been obliged

[16] James E. Gaffney, an alderman, was a partner of John Murphy. In 1904,
a suit was brought against Gaffney for having an interest in a concern doing
business with the city while he held a city office, but the suit was dismissed. See
New York *Tribune*, February 17, 1904.

to put one of his engineers in charge of the work to save the contractors from bankruptcy and the Pennsylvania from the resulting delay.

When the time arrived for closing the tax lists, I told O'Donnel, the president of the Tax Board, that I wanted him to hurry his work. He told me that he could not close the lists for another week, because Murphy had directed him to send the tax books to his house so that he could go over them to make such reductions as he, Murphy, might desire. I was really very much shocked by what O'Donnel had told me, for I had thought him a perfectly upright man. I think that he was personally honest, but completely under Murphy's influence. Needless to say, the tax lists were closed the next day without having been taken to Murphy's house.

After this last experience of Murphy's methods my relations with him became extremely formal. I had lost all confidence in him and distrusted almost every department head whom I had appointed on his recommendation. I was obliged to be constantly on my guard against Murphy's acquisitive tendencies, for I never knew when or where he might display them. Murphy was never discouraged and showed a persistence worthy of a better cause, which he kept up to the very end of my administration. When I was on my vacation in the Adirondacks in 1909, Edward Cahill,[17] an old political friend of mine, who was a building contractor, suddenly appeared and told me that the aldermen had drafted a new building code which they proposed to pass in my absence and that [Patrick] McGowan, [president of the Board of Aldermen and] the acting mayor, had agreed to sign. He had a copy of the code with him, and it beggared description. Among its worst features was a provision requiring all woodwork in all buildings to be fireproofed by a process of which a small company in which Murphy was interested held the monopoly. I telephoned to New York and found that the code had been passed at a special meeting that morning and that the public hearing before the mayor, required by law, was to be held the next day, July 22, 1909. By driving fifteen miles I was able to catch a train that

---

[17] Cahill, like McClellan, was closely associated with Croker, and for a time he and the boss were co-owners of a restaurant at Broadway and Forty-second Street.

landed me in New York just in time to reach the City Hall as McGowan was taking the chair to begin the hearing. I shall never forget McGowan's face as I entered the room. He turned a pasty white and as I took the chair muttered, "By butting in you've done me out of the mayoralty," for Murphy had made the old man believe that he would nominate him in return for his signature of the proposed code.

Murphy sent Sheriff [Nicholas J.] Hays to beg me to sign the code. I told Hays that I should do Murphy a greater favor than by signing it, that I should veto it, thus keeping Murphy out of the legal and political trouble that would inevitably follow the code as he had caused it to be passed by the aldermen. Hays went over the code with me and agreed that it was very rotten. Hays told me afterwards that he had repeated to Murphy what I had said, and that Murphy had remarked, "McClellan thinks he's funny, doesn't he?"

[The most important achievement of my first administration was the inauguration of a project for increasing the city's water supply.] Early in his administration, at the instigation of Robert Grier Monroe, his commissioner of water supply, Mayor Low had appointed a commission of three distinguished engineers, with Professor [William H.] Burr of Columbia University as chairman, to study the question of additional water supply for the city, and just before he left office the commission had submitted a monumental report. The city was greatly in need of more water and of a modern sewage system, each requiring the expenditure of over $150,000,000. The borrowing capacity of the city did not permit the simultaneous undertaking of both projects. As the spadework for an additional water supply had already been completed in the Burr report, I determined to go on with it, leaving the question of a new sewage system for later. I, however, appointed a commission of engineers to study the sewage question. . . .

With the exception of the New York *Times,* I found the press of the city unconvinced of the necessity of increasing the water supply.[18] In fact the New York *World* fought me bitterly, step

18 In a speech in 1917 at the ceremonies on the completion of the Catskill project, McClellan stated: "The amount of mud which was thrown at me for having inaugurated this work was almost enough to have built the great Ashokan Dam." (Memorandum entitled, "October 12th, 1917 George McClellan said," McClellan MSS.)

by step, from start to finish. My friend, Adrian H. Joline,[19] told me that he had crossed the ocean with Joseph Pulitzer and had asked him why he so violently opposed me, to which Pulitzer had replied, "I helped to make McClellan; now I am going to smash him": a truly valid reason for trying to deprive New York of the additional water she so greatly needed. He assigned one of his most brilliant young men, William McMurtrie Speer, to hound me and all my works, and he did so very ably and very viciously.[20]

The chief engineer of the Croton Aqueduct Board was J. Waldo Smith,[21] one of the leading water supply engineers of the country. I said to him that I should appoint him in charge of the construction of the new work when and if it should be authorized. He, Professor Burr, Delany and I constituted my war board for the realization of the project.

The Burr report had submitted two alternative plans. One provided for the taking of water from the Hudson River from a point above Poughkeepsie, the water to be filtered and then pumped down to the city; the other provided for the taking of the water of the Ashokan River, which entered the Hudson near Kingston, by gravity through an aqueduct a hundred miles long to New York. Both projects would cost approximately the same, about $156,000,000. As the water of the Ashokan was very soft and very clear and required neither filtering nor pumping, and as the water of the Hudson has always been suspect in the popular mind and would require the maintenance of an expensive pumping plant, always liable to get out of order, I decided in favor of Ashokan.

The question of the source of our supply having been determined, we proceeded to draft our bill. The actual work of drafting was done by [Theodore] Connoly and [George L.] Sterling, the two wheel horses of the corporation counsel's

---

[19] Joline was a prominent New York lawyer and a director of several banks, insurance firms, and railroads.

[20] Speer, one of the most famous political reporters of his generation, was so successful in his role as a watchdog over the Catskill project that Mayor Gaynor subsequently appointed him special counsel in the condemnation proceedings for the Ashokan Dam lands. It was estimated that as special counsel he saved the city $1,000,000. See New York *Times*, April 3, 1923.

[21] Jonas Waldo Smith constructed and managed water systems in many parts of the United States before being appointed by McClellan. He was chief engineer of the city's Board of Water Supply from 1905 to 1922.

office. The bill was then introduced in the Assembly and my real troubles began. While Murphy did not dare openly to oppose the bill he gave me absolutely no help in the legislature, and I was obliged to make my fight without any political support. The *Times* backed me enthusiastically and loyally, the *World* and the *Evening Post* opposed me bitterly, while the other papers, suspecting that my motives were political and selfish, at first viewed the plan with suspicion, and only came to my help after its success was assured. There was great opposition in all the counties in which we proposed to build the reservoirs and the aqueduct, not only from the villages and towns involved but also from the railways and innumerable individuals who thought that their personal interests would be affected. After agreeing to amendments to satisfy the various objections, I still had to overcome the argument that had been advanced that I proposed to appoint at the head of the commission three of my personal friends and thus build up a McClellan political machine.

I therefore determined to have it out with the legislature in person and asked the privilege of appearing before a joint meeting of both houses. I appeared before the Senate and Assembly and spoke for nearly two hours. In conclusion I said, "If you will enact this bill I give you my word of honor that I shall ask the New York Chamber of Commerce, the New York Board of Fire Underwriters and the Brooklyn Manufacturers Association each to submit to me a list of three names and that from each of these lists I shall appoint a commissioner. Further, I shall fill any vacancies that may occur in the board during my tenure of the mayoralty in the same way." The legislature was convinced and the bill became a law.

I at once applied to the three organizations I had named for lists of candidates, which they forthwith submitted, and sorry lists they were. All three of these organizations were apparently actuated by a desire to unload on the city their associates who were in need of work either because of the salary, which was $12,000 a year, or because of the advertisement involved. I made the best selections I could from the material submitted and appointed as president of the board J. Edward Simmons, an old gentleman who had been president of the Chamber of Commerce but had long since outlived his usefulness, another old gentleman named Charles A. Shaw from the Fire Underwriters, who was a Civil War veteran, and Charles N. Chadwick from the Brooklyn Manufacturers Association, who, I afterwards heard, was on the verge of bankruptcy when I named him.

When I swore in the new board I told them that I wished them to appoint J. Waldo Smith as their chief engineer and to give him an absolutely free hand; I also told them to appoint as their secretary my chief clerk, Thomas Hassett. I knew that with Smith in charge the work would be well and honestly done and that with Hassett as secretary the executive offices of the commission would be admirably managed. Thanks to Smith the work was completed within the estimates and without a single scandal, despite Pulitzer's mad desire to besmirch it. It is an interesting fact that my successor, Gaynor, remade the board with three Tammany politicians without a word of protest from the press. Later Murphy's friend, Phil Donohue, the retired undertaker, was made a member of the board.

The act required the city to police the line of the aqueduct with its own police force. Accordingly under those two very efficient ex-army officers (captains, as they were then, colonels as the Great War made them), Rhinelander Waldo and Douglas McKay, there was organized a mounted force of 150 men, an almost perfect example of what such a force should be. The force was eventually absorbed into the New York Police Department, but it was the model on which was constructed the New York State constabulary.

When the aqueduct was completed with much ceremony, Gaynor did not invite me to attend. At the final opening of the whole project, however, Mayor Mitchel [22] very courteously asked me to deliver the principal address. . . .

I kept in constant touch with the work as it progressed, and left it with every contract awarded, all the necessary land acquired, and the work of construction three-quarters completed.

There is an unwritten law which governs the appointment of condemnation commissioners by the courts under which the justice making the appointments receives one and the city two of the commissioners. I tried to make an arrangement with the

---

[22] John Purroy Mitchel was mayor from 1913 to 1917. For McClellan's estimate of Mitchel, see below.

court by which all condemnation work should be done by two commissioners, ... [each to] receive an annual salary of $10,000. The court absolutely declined the arrangement, for the patronage was too attractive. Had the court consented, many hundred thousands of dollars would have been saved.

The triangulation tower on the dam was set aside by the engineers as a sort of monument to me. On it they placed an inscription stating that the project was conceived and begun in my administration. Since I left office the tower has served many purposes. Very soon afterwards Commissioner Chadwick caused his name with those of his colleagues and of the mayor to be added to mine. Subsequently Mayor Mitchel's name was also added. Quite lately the tower has been turned into a monument to Waldo Smith, the chief engineer, and the other names have disappeared. I wonder what further career of usefulness lies before it.

Chapter X

I Did Not Like Being Mayor

As MY first term drew to its close [in 1905], the intimation was conveyed to me that if I would quietly withdraw as a candidate for renomination Murphy would be very glad to send me back to the House of Representatives. I should have liked nothing better, for I did not like being mayor and missed my work in Washington very much. I had, however, made up my mind that I must seek another term in which to vindicate myself in the eyes of the people. I had thoroughly learned my job and believed that with efficient heads of departments I could give a good administration. I knew that I was legally responsible for much that had gone on under me of which neither I nor the public approved, and I had no desire to retire from the mayoralty with the reputation of having been nothing but another Tammany mayor. I therefore announced that I would seek renomination and re-election.

The prospect of another term was especially unpleasant, as the legislature had lengthened it from two to four years. It had originally been four years, had for some unexplained reason been reduced to two years, and then restored to its previous length.

Hearst had announced that he would run as the candidate of the Independence League, a party that he had himself organized, and Murphy was faced with a very disagreeable alternative. He was obliged either to refuse me a renomination, with the possibility of my running as an independent candidate, which would have meant the certain election of Hearst, or renominate me, whom he now thoroughly disliked and distrusted, with the certainty of having for the next four years a city administration in which the possibilities of making money would be reduced to its lowest terms.

Very grudgingly and much against his will he kept hands off and allowed the convention to renominate me. As McCarren was ready to make the fight of his life in my behalf on the floor of the convention if Murphy opposed me, I think that the latter chose the least of two evils.

I went before the convention in person and said to the delegates, "I wish it to be clearly understood that if I am re-elected, membership in my first administration will not of itself entitle any man to membership in my second. Under this condition, and this condition only, I will accept your nomination." Not in the least understanding what it was all about, the delegates cheered me wildly and unanimously renominated me. Murphy, while understanding perfectly what I meant, did not take my statement seriously but, nevertheless, from that moment lost all interest in my campaign.

McCarren had forced Murphy to consent to the nomination for comptroller of Herman Metz, a very able and honest man, who made an excellent official.[1] For president of the Board of Aldermen Murphy nominated Patrick McGowan, a decent old Irishman, not very bright but honest and hardworking. The *Sun* had great fun with him for having stated to the press that he was "a manufacturer of fancy ladies' underwear." The *Sun* was unkind enough to suggest that if his customers were "fancy ladies" he ought not to boast of it.

For presidents of the boroughs, Murphy renominated Ahearn, McCarren nominated Bird S. Coler, Queens nominated [Joseph] Bermel, and Bronx and Richmond renominated Haffen and Cromwell respectively.

Jerome was a candidate for renomination as district attorney, as were Justices [George L.] Ingraham and [Henry A.] Gildersleeve for the Supreme Court. I found that Murphy proposed to accept none of the three. I urged him to nominate all three, but this he absolutely refused to do. I finally told him that if he turned down the judges I should refuse to support his

---

1 McClellan's favorable estimate of Metz may be due in part to the fact that the comptroller was Patrick McCarren's political lieutenant, and as such he sided with McClellan rather than Murphy in the ensuing fight between the mayor and the boss.

candidates. He then said, "You can have either the judges or
Jerome, but not both." As Jerome was not an organization man
and the judges were organization men, and as, moreover, the
turning down of the judges would have certainly meant the
defeat of the ticket, I opted for the judges, who were renominated. For district attorney Murphy nominated James W.
Osborn, who had been an assistant district attorney and was
the son-in-law of Judge Gus Van Wyck.[2] He was an able man
who should have made a good candidate but had fallen into
bad habits and made such injudicious speeches as to almost
wreck the ticket.

When the ticket had been put in the field Murphy retired
to Delmonico's, where he had his headquarters, and left the
candidates on the city ticket to shift for themselves. It was
evident that if I was to be re-elected I must depend entirely on
myself, as far at least as all the boroughs were concerned, with
the exception of Brooklyn, where McCarren handled the fight
aggressively and well. Delany had been promised by Murphy
a nomination for the Supreme Court and held me personally
responsible for his failure to get it, because of my insistence on
the renomination of Justices Ingraham and Gildersleeve. He
turned against me and was not only of no use to me during the
campaign but never again showed me the slightest friendliness.

I put my secretary John H. O'Brien in charge of my fight,
including the raising of campaign funds. He did his work
admirably. Voluntary contributions came in in sufficient
amounts to permit us to pay the expenses of my headquarters
as well as printing, halls for meetings, music, and so forth.

Some time after my re-election I met John W. Gates, the
Wall Street plunger, whom I knew slightly. "Did you ever get
that contribution I sent you for your campaign?" he asked.
"No," I answered. "Had I received it, I should certainly have
thanked you for it." "That's what I thought. I gave ——"
(naming one of Murphy's jackals) "$10,000 in bills to give to
you, telling him that it was for your personal use. I thought

[2] Augustus Van Wyck of Brooklyn was Mayor Robert Van Wyck's brother.
He was a member of the McLaughlin machine and McLaughlin's personal legal
adviser. In 1898, when he was serving as a justice on the state Supreme Court,
he was nominated for governor by the Democrats and was defeated by Theodore
Roosevelt in the ensuing election.

—— was a friend of yours, but he evidently either pocketed it or turned it over to Murphy."

After election Mr. Adolph Pagenstecker [3] sent me $10,000 by a Tammany lawyer whom he occasionally employed. I told the messenger to express my gratitude to Mr. Pagenstecker for his generosity and to take back to him the money as I had enough to meet all my expenses. Years later I learned that Mr. Pagenstecker had never received his money nor heard from me. I never knew if the messenger had pocketed the money or turned it over to the boss.

In my fight for re-election I very soon found that Hearst was a far stronger candidate than anyone had supposed that he would be and showed his great ability in making a very effective campaign. He had unlimited money, was a good campaigner, and of course had his newspapers behind him. On the other hand, every other newspaper supported me, with the exception of the *Tribune* which supported the Republican candidate William M. Ivins, who was running almost openly in Hearst's interests.

Realizing Hearst's strength I had hoped that the Republican convention would endorse me, but Hearst's influence with the Republican bosses was so great that my hope came to nothing. There was no possibility of electing their ticket, and its nomination could have no other result or purpose than to help Hearst. Probably ninety per cent of those who voted for Ivins would have voted for me in preference to Hearst; a vote for Ivins was, therefore, nearly half a vote for Hearst. That Ivins was running in Hearst's interest was evident from his speeches, in every one of which he denounced me, treated Hearst with marked consideration, and urged his hearers, if they were unwilling to vote for him, to vote for Hearst in preference to "the wicked McClellan." Ivins polled more than 40,000 votes. Had he not been in the field my race would have been easy and my victory overwhelming.

Hearst appealed to the passions of prejudice and discontent. He promised anything and everything, pledged himself to the municipal ownership of public utilities, and showed very

[3] McClellan is presumably referring to Albrecht Pagenstecker, who was the head of a large paper manufacturing concern.

CAN THEY OVERTHROW HIM?

—*The Brooklyn Eagle, October 18, 1905*

plainly that, at heart at least, he was a socialist.[4] His strength
was chiefly among what has since become known as the white-
collar proletariat, the clerks, small employees, and small
shopkeepers. The so-called intelligentsia was solidly with me,
as were the vast majority of the manual workers. The Catholic
Church that has always been the bulwark of sane, moderate
conservatism supported me quietly, unofficially, and most
effectively.

My task was far from easy. I not only had my work as mayor,
including the making of the budget, but I had on my hands
the hardest campaign that I had ever fought. Without Murphy
to rely on, I was obliged, with O'Brien's very efficient help, to
map the strategy and carry the speaking of the campaign entirely on my own shoulders.

I stayed at the City Hall until four o'clock in the afternoon
when I went to my headquarters at the Bartoldi Hotel, to remain until seven when I went home for an hour and then
started out on my speaking tour. During the last fortnight of
the campaign I averaged ten speeches a night, winding up with
fourteen on the Saturday before election. I spoke nearly two
hundred times in all. It was impossible for me to prepare my
speeches in advance, so I spoke extemporaneously. Hearst
inaugurated the custom in New York of planting hecklers at
my meetings, and I enjoyed it, for it gave me the opportunity
of scoring on them and of raising a laugh at their expense. . . .

Hearst charged me with almost every crime in the calendar
and showed himself to possess a vast vocabulary of abuse. On
the other hand I never alluded to him, either directly or indirectly, and confined myself to a defense of my administration.

Osborn, the candidate for district attorney in New York

---

[4] A contemporary has written of the campaign: "Mr. Hearst gave to the campaign all that it exhibited of any interest, as Mr. McClellan pursued a normal
course and as it was assumed from the beginning of the campaign that Mr.
Ivins had no chance to win. . . . The Hearst campaign was something in the
nature of a crusade. His meetings were characterized with a fervor usually
lacking in political audiences. There is no doubt that many who voted for Mr.
Hearst felt that he was trying to do something for the so-called 'common man,'
in whom the old parties seemed to have little real interest. From information I
gathered after the election, I am satisfied that there were a good many Republicans who would have voted for Mr. McClellan if they had had any idea Mr.
Hearst would poll the large vote he received." (Prendergast, "Reminiscences,"
222-223.)

County, was a very sore trial to me, for he attacked Jerome so outrageously that finally I was obliged to interfere. I arrived one night at a meeting where Osborn was in the midst of an attack on Jerome that was positively indecent. When I rose to speak, I repudiated all that Osborn had said and spoke up for Jerome as a man and as an official. This did not serve to endear me to either Osborn or Murphy.

On election night the returns, as they began to come in, were far from satisfactory. An apparent plurality of over 9,000 early in the evening rapidly dwindled to 3,500 where it remained until all the votes had been counted.

Hardly had the polls been closed when Hearst raised the cry of fraud which he continued to utter for two years and eight months. After midnight on election night I was told that McAdoo, the police commissioner, had allowed Hearst's manager to remove some of the ballot boxes from the custody of the police and to store them in a private warehouse that he had hired. Repeated telephone calls developed the extraordinary fact that McAdoo had gone home to bed "with a bad cold." I put O'Brien in charge, who rescued the ballot boxes and restored them to the police. They had, however, been in the care of Hearst's people, unprotected by the police for over three hours, hardly a pleasant thought for me.

I was declared elected by 3,600, and at once Hearst announced that he would begin proceedings for a recount, and until the matter was finally settled invariably referred to me in his newspapers as "The Fraud Mayor." I had no objection whatever to a recount under existing law, but that was by no means what Hearst desired or required. A bill had been introduced in the legislature which permitted him to go before any justice of the Supreme Court of the state, and demand a recount, whereupon the justice was required to appoint tellers to make the recount, and the findings of these tellers were to be conclusive. At the previous election the Independence League, Hearst's party, and Tammany Hall had divided the nominations for eight new Supreme Court justices who had been elected. The Independence League had four justices whom it presumably controlled. The result of the recount bill would have been that Hearst's counsel, Austin G. Fox,[5] might

[5] Fox fought Tammany on many fronts during his lifetime. He was the spe-

have gone before one of these justices who would have appointed tellers who would have counted the vote as directed, and a change of 1,900 votes would have unseated me. The result of the recount would have been a farce. I was anxious to have a recount even under the proposed law, but my counsel absolutely vetoed my desire.

I fought the recount bill to the Court of Appeals which declared it unconstitutional on fourteen counts. Chief Judge [John C.] Gray, [associate judge of Court of Appeals], who wrote the decision of the unanimous court said, "If necessary many more unconstitutionalities might be pointed out, but fourteen are sufficient." It is an interesting fact that Governor Hughes, now Chief Justice of the United States, signed the bill.[6]

With the recount bill out of the way Hearst's lawyers turned to the existing law for redress, and timed their actions so that the case would be tried before Justice McLean,[7] one of Murphy's friends who was coming up for re-election the next autumn. Here again the cards were obviously stacked against me. That such was Murphy's belief was evident from an incident which occurred about that time. I was informed that two of the largest steamship companies that were applicants for some of the new Chelsea piers were approached on behalf of Murphy with a proposition that in return for a lump sum paid to him he would guarantee them leases at satisfactory terms. I sent for Edward J. Berwind and Vernon Brown,[8] the

---

cial district attorney prosecuting police officials after the Lexow investigation from 1894 to 1896, candidate of the Citizens' Union for district attorney in 1897, and counsel for the defense in the Tammany-inspired impeachment trial of Governor William Sulzer in 1913.

6 McClellan's view of the recount bill is substantiated by the New York *Times* (December 31, 1909), which wrote: "He [McClellan] vetoed the Recount bill, which the Legislature never ought to have passed, the passage of which the Governor never ought to have recommended. There was no occasion for a recount, although it is possible that, instead of opposing in the courts the attempt to question his title, it would have been a better policy for the Mayor to assent at once, embarrassing his opponents by granting everything they demanded."

7 Before becoming a justice of the state Supreme Court in 1896, Charles F. McLean had served in various Tammany administrations as police commissioner, park commissioner, and health commissioner. Although he denied purchasing his judgeship, when asked if he was opposed to judges making "contributions" in return for their nominations, he replied: "I would not say that I have a belief on that one way or another." (*Mazet Investigation*, 3597.)

8 Berwind and Brown were New York businessmen with a wide range of in-

representatives of the lines, and was told by Berwind that the story was perfectly true, but that if I ever used it he would deny it. He said that he asked Murphy's messenger, "How can Murphy deliver McClellan?" To which the messenger replied: "He don't propose to, but in a month McClellan will be out, and Murphy thinks that he will be able to fool Hearst." I asked Berwind what he had answered, and he replied, "answered nothing, kicked the fellow out of my office." Brown at first denied the story, but when I told him of Berwind's statement, he acknowledged its truth.

The prospect of having the case tried before McLean was, to say the least, not encouraging. When my cause looked almost hopeless, the situation was entirely changed by the unexpected action of the Appellate Division of the Supreme Court. Entirely unsolicited by me or by anyone in my behalf, the court took the recount case away from McLean and brought a Republican justice of the Supreme Court [9] from upstate New York to try it. The case was tried impartially and well; 650,000 ballots were recounted with the result that I gained 200 votes.[10] It was a remarkable tribute to the honesty and accuracy of the much abused election officials.

Jerome had urged me to sue Hearst for libel if he continued to call me "The Fraud Mayor" after the verdict. Hearst was, however, too canny. The day after I was at last finally established in office, June 30, 1908, he dropped the libelous adjective and ever after, when he referred to me at all, called me "The Mayor." . . .

The litigation over the recount occupied two years, and I

---

terests in a great variety of businesses. Berwind in 1905, for example, was a director of twenty different corporations.

[9] The judge was John S. Lambert, a state Supreme Court justice for the eighth judicial district.

[10] At the time McClellan wrote: "My final plurality for the office of Mayor in the election of 1905 has been fixed at 2,971 in the *quo warranto* proceeding before Justice Lambert in the Supreme Court. My official plurality as declared by the Board of County Canvassers in December, 1905, was 3,474. The contestant has gained, therefore, in this action, . . . the sum of 503 votes, due solely, as I am advised, to legal decisions on certain disputed ballots. In fact, my total vote is shown to have been 228,665, instead of 228,434 as declared by the official count, thus proving that I have actually gained in gross votes, not lost, through the recount." (Memorandum entitled "Statement by the Mayor" and dated June 30, 1908, in Mayors' Papers, New York City Municipal Archives.)

spent over $40,000 to defend my title to office.[11] Most of this money was subscribed by friends, and was paid back under an enabling act passed by the legislature. What it cost Hearst I have no idea, but it must have been a very large sum. . . .

Hearst was a hard-hitting, two-fisted fighter, who never pulled his punches, gave quarter, or asked for it. I had known him when we served together in the House of Representatives and liked him. Years after the recount fight had been forgotten we met one day at the Union Club. We shook hands and lunched together. We saw each other several times afterwards, and I am glad to remember that we buried the hatchet and forgot our past differences. . . .

Election being over and the budget for 1906 being out of the way, I turned to the serious problem of my cabinet for the next four years. As I have always considered myself an organization man, I was perfectly willing to recognize Murphy as the head of the Democratic organization in New York County, and to appoint the men he favored, on condition that the men he favored were fit.

With McCarren I never had any trouble. When he recommended a man whom I felt that I could not appoint, he would at once withdraw his name and submit another, and if necessary a succession of names until at last some deserving Democrat was found whom I could accept. More than this, when I had determined on the appointment of someone in whom he had no interest, he was always ready to make the best of a situation which did not appeal to him and endorse my man. In this way he not only saved his face but secured the good will of the official whose appointment he had not sought.

Murphy was made of different stuff from McCarren. He was very masterful and lacked McCarren's tact, pliability, and good sense. He had never believed that I had meant what I had said to the convention, so he was horrified when I told him I had determined to make a clean sweep of all my department heads, with the exception of Delany, Darlington, Woodbury, and Kennedy, but that I was willing to accept his recommendations if his men were fit for office. Several days later he sent me word

11 According to the city's auditor of accounts, the cost of McClellan's recount fight was $83,576.44. (Joseph L. Hance to Herman A. Metz, June 4, 1909. McClellan MSS.)

that he would come to my house that evening, and in due course he arrived. He had evidently been drinking and was in the condition that is known colloquially as "fighting full." He sat down and pulling a list from his pocket began by saying, "What about Delany?" I told him that, as I had already stated, I should keep him. He continued, "I don't care a damn about Delany, I want you to appoint Cram." I answered that Cram was absolutely unthinkable for corporation counsel.

There is no office in the city government more important for the honest administration of public affairs than that of corporation counsel, and Murphy thoroughly appreciated the value that it would have for him could he control it. Not satisfied with submitting Cram's name for the place at the beginning of my second administration, he took the opportunity of Delany's resignation to approach me once more. William F. Sheehan [12] came to see me on Murphy's behalf and told me that Murphy had authorized him to say that in return for the appointment of Cram, he, Murphy, would be willing to "forgive and forget." When I declined the offer, Sheehan said, "I said to Murphy that there wasn't a chance of your listening to the proposition, for I knew you to be 'money honest.' " To which Murphy replied, "Yes, he is money honest, damn him." It is interesting to note that Murphy and Cram quarrelled beyond hope of repair, when the former refused to send the latter to the United States Senate in 1911.

When I announced to Murphy that I should not keep Oakley as commissioner of water supply, gas and electricity, he said that as Oakley had tuberculosis and was unable to do any work it would be an outrage to deprive him of his job. I said that I was sorry but that Oakley was incompetent, even when present for duty, and that he had gone behind my back more than once in reversing my policy in reference to the light and power

[12] Sheehan, a prominent figure in the state and city Democratic organizations, was the younger brother of John C. Sheehan. He was the lieutenant governor during David B. Hill's last term (1888-91) and afterwards practiced law in New York City in partnership with Alton B. Parker. It was Sheehan who indirectly and inadvertently helped Franklin D. Roosevelt first attract attention to himself as a politician. In 1911, Sheehan sought election to the United States Senate from the state legislature. Roosevelt, who was serving his first term in the state Senate, led a band of insurgent Democrats who opposed and eventually blocked Sheehan's election on the ground that he was a representative of Tammany Hall.

companies.[13] Murphy then said, "Will you appoint Bill Dalton?"[14] I answered, "You can't possibly mean him. He was the man around whom the entire Ramapo scandal centered. I certainly won't appoint him. Give me another candidate." "I got no other candidate," said Murphy. "All right," I answered, "who's your next candidate?" "Will you appoint Tom McAvoy[15] police commissioner?" "Certainly not," I answered, "I allowed McAvoy to retire from his inspectorship to avoid trial under charges." Murphy, thereupon, made his usual reply, "I got no other candidate." For the other offices he demanded the retention of the incumbents, and as I declined to comply added in each case, "I got no other candidate." In conclusion

13 "When disclosures were made late in the first term of the Mayor about the contracts which Commissioner John T. Oakley had made for public lighting, there was a great outcry. The public was sensitive on the subject of the lighting monopoly in the city. The contracts were so manifestly in the interests of the corporation and against good business sense from a city taxpayer's standpoint that the criticism extended even to Commissioner Oakley's friends. Even Tammany district leaders urged the Mayor to remove Oakley from office. The election was coming on, and such action, they said, would tend to check criticism. But Mayor McClellan took a different attitude. 'I will not remove Oakley,' he said. 'He is part of my administration, and shall serve to the end of his term. I knew nothing of these contracts when they were made, but I am in a measure responsible, because I am supposed to know. I will not plead the baby act.' So Oakley remained all through the campaign of 1905." (New York *Herald*, September 2, 1906.)

When the lighting contracts were made public, the secretary of the City Club of New York in a letter to McClellan protested that the negotiations had been conducted in secret, that there had been no competitive bidding, and that as a result of the contracts New York would pay $140 per lamp while the average paid by sixty-eight other American cities was $88.60. (Lawrence Veiller to McClellan, December 8, 1904, McClellan Scrapbooks, 1904-1905, New York Historical Society.)

14 William F. Dalton, a Tammany district leader and former butcher and carpenter, became involved in the Ramapo water scandal in his official capacity as commissioner of water supply during the Van Wyck administration. His testimony before the Mazet Committee revealed that he had no qualifications for his job but that he was not necessarily corrupt. When asked about his "knowledge or ability in the matter of engineering and water supply," he replied: " 'Well, so far as engineering, yes, sir; I owned an engine for some years. . . . It was small, about eight horsepower.' " (*Mazet Investigation*, 2682-2683, 2769-2792.)

15 Thomas F. McAvoy joined the police force in 1870 and by the early nineties had risen to the rank of inspector. In 1894, the Lexow Committee's investigation of the Police Department revealed many irregularities in his official conduct, and as a result of these revelations he was forced to retire on half pay in 1895. He then entered politics and became the Tammany leader of the Twenty-third Assembly District. He served as deputy police commissioner during McClellan's first administration.

OUT DOORS.

The Sleeping Outdoor Fad Has Reached Political Circles.

—*The New York Herald, January 22, 1906*

Murphy said, "That's my slate, take it or leave it. I got no other candidates." He then tried to rise from his chair and found that his legs had gone back on him. I was obliged to help him up and support him to his cab where I delivered him to the care of the faithful Phil Donohue, who was waiting for him.

Thinking that Murphy might prove more reasonable when he had sobered up, I waited a few days and then sent word to him by Hayes, my fire commissioner who had been elected sheriff, to inquire whether his slate stood unchanged. When Hayes reported that Murphy had no candidates to propose, other than those whom he had already submitted, I realized that the final break had come.[16]

The finding of the right men for the heads of departments proved to be an extremely difficult task. Most of the men whom I wanted were unwilling to make the sacrifice of accepting $7,500 salaries to serve the city. For the minor jobs the bright young men whom I tried to interest were equally unresponsive. Boys just out of college were perfectly willing to head departments or become magistrates, but usually scorned the small offices for which they were fit. It was a nearly heartbreaking work to form my cabinet, but I was finally successful in collecting a very excellent group of men.

The police commissionership gave me a great deal of trouble. I finally appointed General Theodore A. Bingham, who had been retired from the army after the loss of a leg in an accident.[17] I had known him in Washington as a man of great ability. He was honest and very energetic, but as I discovered to my cost, with no tact, a violent temper, and not the least idea of either subordination or loyalty to his chief.[18] He had

16 At this point McClellan abruptly breaks off his account of his relations with Murphy, despite the fact that the "break" to which he refers proved to be the turning point of his political career. For an account of the subsequent relations between the mayor and the boss, see the Introduction, 26-27, 28.

17 "For Police Commissioner he [McClellan] has selected an army officer not a Democrat, not even a resident of New York City. In making General Theodore A. Bingham head of the police he has indicated his determination to use the police force as an instrument, not for party reward, but for public service." (*Outlook*, 82 [January 6, 1906], 1.)

18 Despite McClellan's statement, Bingham showed great loyalty to his chief. On the other hand, he never hesitated to tell the mayor how the government should be run. For example, see Theodore A. Bingham to McClellan, September 28, 1906, McClellan MSS.

been in charge of public buildings and grounds at Washington, and as such in those days was a sort of chief of the protocol at the White House. Later, after I had dismissed him, Roosevelt said to me, "You stood Bingham much longer than I thought you could. I had to get rid of him, for it became a question whether he should run the government or I. One of us had to go. As I had taken an oath of office to the people to run the government for them and Bingham had not, I fired Bingham."

Dr. Charles Parkhurst, who had always abused me and continued to do so until I left politics, came to see me with a delegation of his admirers. He said to me, "We are not satisfied with the way that McAdoo is running the Police Department, and demand that you do not retain him." I replied much to the good doctor's surprise, "I quite agree with you. McAdoo has been a failure, and I shall not retain him. If you gentlemen will submit the name of a candidate for the office who is qualified for the job I shall be very glad to appoint him." Thereupon Parkhurst replied, "It is not our duty to find you officials. Our duty is to see that they do their work after you have found them." Several days later Parkhurst sent me word that he would like to have a secret meeting with me at some place, other than the City Hall or my own house. I replied that I would be glad to see him at the City Hall and nowhere else, [and] that if I could afford to have it known that I had met him, he could certainly afford to have it known that he had met me. I never heard from him again, until he preferred charges against me to the governor for non-enforcement of the liquor laws, charges which, to his credit, the governor ignored.

McAdoo had become more and more incompetent as the months had passed. I had given him a free hand in the selection of his deputies, and his choice had been anything but happy. The force was not as efficient as it should have been, and discipline was slack. His action on election night in letting Hearst's agent take possession of the ballot boxes was alone enough to warrant his removal, and his conduct the day after election thoroughly disgusted me with him.

Hearst had, among other charges against me, stated in season and out of season, that I was "The Hireling of Great Britain" —exactly in what respect he never explained, except that, when in Congress I had repeatedly dined at the British embassy, a charge which, incidentally, was quite true. About ten days before election I received word that the British North Atlantic Squadron, under the command of Prince Louis of Battenberg, was to arrive in New York the Saturday before election. I saw in the visit at that time not only the possibility of grave disorder but also an excellent campaign argument for Hearst. I at once called up Sir Mortimer Durand, the British ambassador, whom I had known in Washington, and explained the situation to him. He was not a very bright man, and it was difficult to make him see the point. At length he seemed to understand and said that he would arrange matters. The next day he telephoned that he had arranged to have Prince Louis's visit postponed until the day after election. I begged him to postpone it still longer but he said that that was impossible as Prince Louis had gone out to sea and could not be reached.

I sent for McAdoo and told him to make the arrangements for Prince Louis's call on me and for my return call on the day after election, and then added that I should want him to go with me. McAdoo, although an Episcopalian, was a very enthusiastic Fenian and had once been head of the Clan na Gael. For this reason I thought that it would be advisable to have him with me in case of any Irish demonstration. McAdoo at once began to make excuses: he was not very well, he had a great deal of work to do, he had a number of engagements and so forth. I told him that he must break all his engagements and come with me.

On the appointed day Prince Louis arrived, under a perfect bombardment of abuse from the Hearst papers. He paid his official call on me, and in the afternoon McAdoo and I returned it. On our return we landed at Twenty-third Street and found an enormous crowd awaiting us, a crowd that had been drummed up by the Hearst papers and was very antagonistic to me. As we got into the open police car McAdoo put his hand in his hip pocket and drew out a revolver. "What are you doing with that?" I asked. "Put it down at once." I finally took it away from him and dropped it on the floor of the car. The crowd was very large, and the police had some difficulty in forcing a way through for us. Finally we were completely halted, and the mob began to climb up onto our running boards, shaking their fists and saying things that were not at all polite. I turned and said to McAdoo, "This is getting lively," and there was McAdoo trying to leave the car. I said to him, "Sit down at once and behave yourself."

Poor McAdoo meant well but he was no man to command the police. During December he came to me and told me that he had heard a rumor that I did not intend to keep him. He said that he had been appointed under the charter for a term of four years and that I could not remove him. I invited his attention to the wording of the charter which gave him a four-year term "unless sooner removed." He demanded to know if I intended to retain him and if not, why not. I told him that he had not made good and that if he did not resign December thirty-first, I should remove him. In due time he resigned.[19]

Thomas F. Ryan strongly urged me to appoint former Superintendent of Police Thomas F. Byrnes.[20] When I objected that Byrnes had an exceedingly bad reputation for honesty and that every newspaper in town would be against him, Ryan replied, "Byrnes has made over a million dollars, all he can possibly need. He wants to leave a good name behind him for his children's sake. If you appoint him, I am perfectly sure that he will prove, not only honest, but exceedingly efficient." Ryan may have been right, but I did not care to take the chance. Byrnes had the experience and ability to have made an admirable commissioner; unfortunately, his reputation was against him.

I called on Cardinal Farley[21] and consulted him in reference to the three appointments in which he would presumably have been most interested, Charities, Corrections, and Tenement House. I asked him if he had any candidates to propose or any suggestion to make. He replied, "I have no candidate for any of these offices and only one suggestion to offer: that is, that in making these appointments you do not name Catholics. I

19 The correspondence between McClellan and McAdoo during the latter's last days in office is reprinted in the New York *Tribune*, December 31, 1905.

20 Byrnes, who joined the police force in 1863, subsequently won a nation-wide reputation for his work as a detective and his handling of the city's detective force. In 1895, he was made chief of police but within a month he retired because of the shake-up in the force resulting from the revelations before the Lexow Committee. He admitted that he made $350,000 in the stock market from tips that he received from Jay Gould and other large speculators.

21 When McClellan called on Farley, the latter was Archbishop of New York. He did not become a cardinal until 1911.

should much prefer that you should appoint fair-minded Protestants. All that the Church wants is a square deal from these three commissioners, that we shall always receive from fair-minded Protestants; on the other hand, Catholics of the kind you should appoint, and of course, would appoint will lean over backwards in their effort to avoid the appearance of favoring their own church, and the church will suffer as the consequence." A very broad-minded, liberal, fine old man was the Cardinal.

I was immensely pleased to learn that the fairness of my administration to the Catholic Church had been appreciated, when one of the leading Jesuit universities, Fordham, made me an L.L.D., despite the fact that I was a Protestant. While I felt much honored by the action of Princeton and Union in giving me an L.L.D., I was profoundly touched by the distinction I received from the Jesuits.

I appointed as commissioner of charities, Robert W. Hebberd, who was the secretary of the State Board of Charities, and a Protestant. He performed the duties of his very difficult office without a word of adverse criticism from any source.[22] At the head of Corrections I put John J. Barry, who made as great a success as did Hebbard.[23] The Tenement House Department under Crain had been constantly under fire and needed a complete reorganization. I sent for the heads of the four leading charitable societies, Fulton Cutting of the Society for the Improvement of the Condition of the Poor, Robert deForest of the Charity Organization Society, Nathan Bijur of the United Hebrew Charities, and Thomas Mulry of the St. Vincent de Paul. I then asked these four gentlemen to agree on a candidate for the office, and left them to discuss the matter. After about an hour they reported in favor of Edmond J. But-

[22] At the end of McClellan's second administration, the New York *Evening Post* (December 31, 1909) wrote: "Robert W. Hebberd . . . has . . . by sheer industry, devotion, and absolute rectitude, given an administration of his department which has satisfied the most critical, and pleased everywhere the charitable and philanthropic workers who know the city's institutions from the inside."

[23] The impression given by McClellan at this point is not altogether accurate, for Barry served as commissioner of corrections for less than a year. Francis J. Lantry, who had been commissioner of corrections during McClellan's first term and was one of the few Tammany district leaders to support the mayor rather than Murphy, was reappointed at the beginning of the second term. In October, 1906, Lantry was succeeded by John V. Coggey, who held the position until January 1, 1909, when he, in turn, was succeeded by Barry.

ler, the secretary of the St. Vincent de Paul, whom I sent for
and swore in. Butler reorganized his department from top to
bottom and left it in a very high state of efficiency.[24]

DeForest's attitude in reference to the Tenement House
Department was very peculiar. He had been commissioned
under Low, and when I first took office I inquired if he would
care to continue under me, and received a negative answer.
At a meeting in celebration of the fiftieth anniversary of the
founding of the Charity Organization Society, Münsterberg,[25]
the German authority on organized charity, in a speech said
that he had only just heard that a corrupt Tammany mayor had
removed his friend deForest from office. DeForest had deliber-
ately misstated the facts to Münsterberg, for what purpose I
cannot imagine.

Some time after Butler's appointment deForest said to me,
"I don't know why you ever appointed that utter incompetent,
Butler, to office." I replied, "He is a most excellent official,
and moreover you recommended him for appointment."
Whereupon deForest said, "Oh, you know that one must make
recommendations like that, that one doesn't mean." I always
found deForest unreliable. He became a sort of first citizen,
accepting any appointment he was offered on any committee or
board and never pretending to do any work or even attend
meetings. He was chairman of the Art Commission for many
years and a very poor one.

I promoted John H. O'Brien, my secretary, to fire commissioner, filling his place with his exceedingly able and tactful
brother Frank, now the brilliant editor of the New York *Sun,*
and promoted John Bensel, chief engineer of the Department
of Docks, to be commissioner. As commissioner of water supply,
gas and electricity I appointed William B. Ellison, a prominent
lawyer, who had been strongly recommended to me, and as
commissioner of bridges I appointed James W. Stevenson, who
had been a very able deputy comptroller under Grout.

I entirely reorganized the Department of Taxes, putting
Lawson W. Purdy, a well-known tax expert, at the head [26] and

24 According to Lawson Purdy, Butler was "a straight-laced gentleman . . . ,
who rigidly enforced the law." (Purdy, "Reminiscences," 36.)

25 McClellan is presumably referring to Hugo Münsterberg, a German-born
psychologist, who was a professor of psychology at Harvard from 1892 to 1916.

26 McClellan at this point gives a somewhat inaccurate impression of his

giving him as colleagues, among others, [Charles] Abram Putzel, a very able lawyer, and my old friend Hugh Hastings, who had been state historian after his retirement from newspaper work.

Delany had never recovered from his failure to obtain a Supreme Court nomination and sulked like a five-year-old child. While I was in Europe during the summer of 1906, he so mismanaged the city's part in Hearst's recount suit against me as not only greatly to imperil my case but very strongly to suggest that he was not playing fairly with his chief. When I returned, I had a very unsatisfactory talk with him at the end of which he resigned.[27] I accepted his resignation with much regret, for he had, during my first two years of office, served the city and me well, and I had grown fond of him. I suspected that Murphy had "got at" him, a suspicion that was later confirmed by Murphy's putting him on the Supreme Court bench. Years later I met him and, offering him my hand, I said, "John, I am very glad that you are on the bench." He told a friend of mine that I had greatly surprised him, for he did not think that I would ever speak to him again.

I put Ellison in Delany's place, transferred John O'Brien from Fire to Water Supply, Gas and Electricity, and put Lantry in O'Brien's place.[28] Ellison at first did extremely well and

policy, for he did not reorganize the Board of Taxes and Assessments until some time after the start of his second term. Frank O'Donnel had served as president of the board during McClellan's first term, and in December, 1905, McClellan reappointed him for a second term. At the time the New York *Tribune* (December 31, 1905) stated that O'Donnel was closely allied with Murphy. McClellan soon realized that O'Donnel was giving his allegiance to Murphy rather than the mayor, and in 1906 he supplanted O'Donnel with Purdy.

27 "The Mayor's first corporation counsel was John J. Delany. Mr. Delany served until October 8, 1906, and then resigned. . . . It was generally understood that Mr. McClellan did not consider that the corporation counsel was sufficiently in sympathy with him to be continued in office." (New York *Evening Mail,* December 30, 1909.)

28 The shifts described by McClellan in this sentence represent a much more complicated maneuver than is indicated. John O'Brien was McClellan's closest political adviser during the second administration, and his official position did not necessarily reflect his importance to the mayor. Francis J. Lantry was a district leader who had deserted Murphy for McClellan after the election of 1905. At the outset of his second administration, McClellan rewarded Lantry by making him commissioner of corrections and in 1906 named him as successor to O'Brien in the Fire Department. To succeed Lantry as commissioner of corrections, McClellan named John V. Coggey, a former Murphy man, who agreed to stand by the mayor in his fight against the organization. In sum, all these

then, without warning, and for no apparent reason, fell into bad habits. It was really a tragedy for he was a very able man with brilliant political prospects as well as having an assured position at the bar. There was nothing for me to do but very regretfully to ask for his resignation.[29]

I was at a loss to know whom to put in Ellison's place, for the three or four prominent lawyers to whom I offered it all declined, when William F. Sheehan, the former lieutenant governor, came to me and said that Francis K. Pendleton would like the appointment. Pendleton was the son of George Pendleton who had been my father's running mate when the latter had been candidate for the presidency. He was a well-known lawyer of ability and high standing, and a personal friend. I sent for him, offered him the place, he accepted, and I swore him in. He made an excellent corporation counsel and thoroughly deserved his subsequent promotion to the Supreme Court bench.

Woodbury, as street cleaning commissioner, gave me a great deal of trouble. He had no tact, especially in dealing with politicians, and kept me in constant hot water. One day McCarren came to me and said that the superintendent of street cleaning in Brooklyn, who was a Republican, was openly forcing the men under him to work for the local Republican candidate. I sent for Woodbury and told him that he must order the Brooklyn superintendent to stop his political activities. Woodbury flatly refused to issue the order, and said that he would not interfere with the political activities of his subordinates. He then left my office and during the afternoon sent me his resignation, which I accepted, for I made it a rule never to refuse a resignation.[30] John Bensel told me the next

changes represented an attempt on McClellan's part to strengthen his administration in its fight against Murphy.

29 "To fill Mr. Delany's place, Mayor McClellan named William B. Ellison, at that time his water commissioner. . . . Mr. Ellison at once became the confidant of Mr. McClellan, and the Mayor came to rely greatly on his judgment. The Corporation Counsel worked to bring about peace between Tammany and the Mayor and was actually accomplishing this when he spoiled the truce by talking too much about the matter, the Mayor claiming that he had been misrepresented by Mr. Ellison in his public statements. The result was that on July 8, 1907, the Mayor removed Mr. Ellison." (New York *Evening Mail*, December 30, 1909.)

30 In his letter of resignation Woodbury stated that he was resigning because McClellan was "insistent upon the injection of politics into my department."

day that Woodbury had gone to him and had said that he had had too many cocktails and had made a fool of himself, and asked Bensel's advice as to what he should do. Bensel told him to go back to the mayor's office and apologize and to agree to issue the order that I had required. Unfortunately for Woodbury he ran into his friend Laffan of the *Sun* before he had had time to reach City Hall. Laffan said to him, "Send in your resignation, McClellan will not dare to accept it, and you will then have him on the hip." Woodbury followed Laffan's advice rather than that of Bensel and was greatly surprised and disgusted when I called his bluff.

Laffan turned on me and abused me with great vigor. I stopped sending the *Sun* advertisements and let it be known that I should take away its designation unless it ceased attacking me. Riggs came to see me and we patched up a truce under the terms of which Laffan agreed to preserve towards my administration a position of neutrality in return for which I agreed not to disturb his designation, but not to give him any additional advertisements. The agreement worked satisfactorily, for Laffan's neutrality was far better from my point of view than his extremely fulsome praise.

I put Walter Bensel, the sanitary superintendent, in charge of the department as acting commissioner, and some weeks later appointed Captain [MacDonough] Craven, a retired naval officer, who was in command of the naval reserves of the state, but he failed to make good and I was obliged to get rid of him. In his place I appointed William Edwards, the Princeton football player, who had been deputy under Craven.[31] Edwards did his work well, and I had no reason to complain of him as an official.

During the second year of my first administration I had found myself in control of the Board of Education. In my time there were forty-five members of the board, all serving without

(John Woodbury to McClellan, October 11, 1906, Mayors' Papers, New York City Municipal Archives.) For Woodbury's effort to enlarge on this charge and McClellan's denial of it, see New York *World* to McClellan, October 13, 1906; McClellan to New York *World*, October 13, 1906, McClellan MSS.

31 McClellan has confused the order of these appointments. Following Woodbury's resignation in October, 1906, McClellan appointed Craven commissioner of street cleaning. Craven held this job until July, 1907, when he was succeeded by Walter Bensel. Edwards, in turn succeeded Bensel, who finished out McClellan's second term as sanitary commissioner.

pay. I have always found that even the best of men are inclined to shirk the work of an unpaid office. It requires a very high sense of duty for a man to devote his time to a job for which he receives no compensation but honor. In a large board, especially when its members are unpaid, there are always a few conscientious men who do all the work, and so it was in the Board of Education.

As soon as I found that the majority of the board would accept my suggestions I requested them to elect as president Egerton L. Winthrop, Jr., who had married my sister-in-law and who had been my friend for many years. He was an able lawyer, a man of high standing in the community, and one of the most hard-working and conscientious men I have known. He served as president of the Board of Education longer than has any man in the history of the city and stands out as by far the best president the board has ever had.

During my first term I had appointed, as president of the Civil Service Commission, Frank L. Polk,[32] afterwards Undersecretary of State, under Woodrow Wilson, and had urged him to cover, under the civil service law, all offices in the city government except the heads, deputies, and secretaries of departments, and the purely confidential positions. It was a task that required much time and had to be done gradually. Polk was an excellent public official, who carried out his orders faithfully and well and besides he was a man of infinite tact and very great personal charm.

Toward the close of my administration the Civil Service Reform Association in its annual report said that in New York City civil service conditions were almost ideal, and then went on to make the following extraordinary statement, "This is entirely due to the courage of Mr. Polk who has made these reforms in the teeth of the Mayor's opposition.[33] It has not been due to McClellan, but despite him." Which was typical of the unfairness of the professional "reformer."

[32] McClellan is mistaken, for he appointed Polk, not in his first term, but in July, 1907, of his second term.

[33] At the conclusion of McClellan's second administration, the New York *Evening Post* (December 31, 1909) wrote: "In Mr. Frank Polk the city loses a head of the Civil Service Commission who has made a pleasing impression, worked intelligently and usefully, and grown steadily in the respect of those who have come into contact with him."

Chapter XI

Public Improvements

HAVING PREVIOUSLY taken the oath of office before my friend, Justice David Leventritt, of the New York Supreme Court, on January 1, 1906, I began my second term without the support of the Democratic organization, but with a cabinet that was efficient, that I trusted, and that had the confidence of the public and the approval of the press. . . .

I had four years before me in which to make good, and thanks to the experience of my first term I had not only learned my job but I had a very clear idea of exactly what I wanted to accomplish in the way of public improvements. Some of these were already under way, some were still on paper, while many were only nebulous.

Early in my administration I appointed Professor Edwin R. A. Seligman of Columbia University, and Edgar Levy, who had been a most excellent deputy comptroller, as a commission to report on the question of municipal taxation. As the result of their report, the municipal taxing system was greatly modified and simplified. Rebates for the prompt payment of taxes were done away with, uncollectable taxes were made good by budget provision, and the constitutional limit of indebtedness was altered so as to permit the non-inclusion of self-sustaining improvements. Under the personal advice of Professor Seligman I secured a constitutional amendment permitting the city to take by condemnation more property than it actually needs for the improvement involved. For example, if a new street is opened, under my amendment the city has the power to take the land on one or both sides which can be sold to the public profit. Unfortunately, the amendment did not become law until just before I left office. Had I been able to use it, my bill for public improvements would have been greatly reduced.

The first underground railway was opened by me during my first week of office.[1] I was very anxious to get the second route under way during my time, but the inertia of the Rapid Transit Commission was so great that I only succeeded in having the plans approved after nearly six years of hard work. The commission was outside of my jurisdiction in that I did not have the power of removal over its members, although I filled vacancies and was *ex officio* a member of the board. Low had made the original appointments, and they were a group of very worthy old gentlemen of large business experience but extreme old age, who nevertheless seldom died and never resigned. When a vacancy at last occurred I induced Lewis Cass Ledyard,[2] a very distinguished and able lawyer, to take it, but after a few months the limit of his public spirit was reached and he resigned. I replaced him with a nominee of McCarren's, who surprised me by beginning his service with a violent attack on me. He was an active man, but was only one among many slow coaches. I was unable to obtain legislation for the reorganization of the board, for as all the members but my appointee were Republicans, the Republican state government was unwilling to disturb existing conditions. It was not until the Republican organization was assured of the appointments that

[1] When the subway opened, McClellan served as engineer for the first train, which consisted of flatcars and whose passengers were city officials and well-to-do financiers. A contemporary newspaper reporter, recalling the trip, has written: "Mayor McClellan without any experience in operating a train, . . . ran the train from City Hall at good speed up to 14th Street. From 14th Street he speeded up so that the train was running from about 40 to 45 miles an hour. You had to hold on to your hat on that first ride through the subway. . . . From 14th Street up to 42nd Street Mayor McClellan had gotten the hang of the speed and was pleased with his job. He slowed the train to stops at stations but he got the feel of the power which would propel it. The Mayor felt he was an expert motorman in one day. He drove up to 42nd Street station at about a speed of 25 miles. From 42nd Street running north, he got up to a speed of from 40 to 45 miles an hour. . . . The train made 72nd Street in remarkable good time. The train went ripping by the stations . . . and on the open cut above the 116th Street station, the train was stopped and the two or three hundred Wall Street financiers got off and their picture was taken on that station. In that group there was represented an estimated wealth of well over a million dollars." (Hettrick, "Reminiscences," 112-113.)

[2] Ledyard was an exceedingly successful corporation lawyer and the personal counsel for J. Pierpont Morgan. In his obituary the New York *Times* (January 28, 1932) referred to him as "one of the great American lawyers of his time."

the Rapid Transit Commission was finally abolished, but that much needed event occurred long after I had passed from the scene. . . .

Having in mind a great deal of building, I took a leaf from the experience of European cities and created the office of city architect and appointed to the place Walter Cook, afterwards president of the American Institute of Architects. He was a good architect, and a very honest and able man, and saved the city many millions of dollars during the time he was in office. His salary was only $5,000 a year, and in return for it he supervised the plans for all public works, saw that they were carried out properly, and organized the competitions that I held for public buildings. It is a regrettable fact that my experience with some of the leading architectural firms was far from satisfactory. I had dealings with most of them, but found only too many of them anxious to take advantage of the city. Cook stood up for the interests of the city like a man and protected her from those who were rapaciously inclined.

The Queensboro Bridge had been begun under Low, and I am not responsible for the ugliness of that horror. When I decided to name it the Queensboro Bridge, every Irish society in the city protested on the ground that the name was pro-British and therefore an insult to the Irish race. It seems today almost unbelievable.

Low had retained a German engineer to design the Manhattan Bridge, and he proposed a suspension bridge of chains, which was of very doubtful engineering strength and was almost as hideous as the Queensboro Bridge. I got rid of Low's man and appointed a board of consultants. . . . The board reported in favor of a wire cable suspension bridge, and the present beautiful Manhattan Bridge was the result. It was begun under me and I opened it on the last day of my term. In addition to these two East River bridges, [James W.] Stevenson, my very efficient bridge commissioner, built twelve bridges of importance over the Harlem River, Newtown Creek, and Gowanus Canal.

The city had acquired a block of land at the Manhattan end of the Brooklyn Bridge for an underground terminal for the Long Island trains. It seemed to me that it was a great waste not to use the space above ground for some other purpose. We were paying a very large rental for office space, and I determined to build an office building for the city over the bridge terminal, thus saving the rental and not wasting the space we had already acquired. Under the charter the construction of buildings was under the borough president. As I did not dare to entrust the new office building to Ahearn and Murphy, I went to the legislature and against Murphy's bitter opposition had the direction of the building transferred from Ahearn to my commissioner of bridges.

I had Cook prepare the terms of the competition and invited six leading architectural firms in the city to compete. I brought them together in my office and said to them, "Gentlemen, I propose that you elect your own jury, that each of you shall receive $2,000 for the expenses of the competition except the winner who will of course receive the contract." Cass Gilbert [3] then inquired, "What assurance have we that we shall receive the $2,000? Has the money been appropriated?" I answered that it had not been appropriated, and that the competitors would have to take my word that I would secure the appropriation, and turning to Gilbert I said, "I trust, Mr. Gilbert, that my word will satisfy you?" To which Gilbert answered, "It certainly will not satisfy me." Upon which I said, "Then, Mr. Gilbert, I wish you a very good morning," and showed him to the door. The other competitors were less skeptical than Gilbert and were perfectly satisfied with my assurance. I left them, and they elected their jury which in due time selected the very beautiful and brilliant project of McKim, Mead and White. The office building was completed within the estimates, eight million dollars, the only case of which I know that a great public work has not largely exceeded the estimated cost. Incidentally, the new building saved the city $130,000 a year net in rentals for office space.

The foundation gave us a great deal of trouble, for except at one corner we could not find rock bottom, the rest of the site being a bottomless mass of mud and quicksand. I finally found a contractor named [John F.] O'Rourke, who undertook

[3] Gilbert was one of America's best known twentieth-century architects. His style, if not his personality, was conventional, and he designed many well-known public and commercial buildings, including the Supreme Court Building and the Woolworth Building.

to anchor the foundations on the rock corner and to float the other parts on a great number of concrete piles. It was the first time that this method of construction had been undertaken, a method that has been followed very frequently since.

I laid the cornerstone of the office building the day before I left the mayoralty. One of Gaynor's first official acts when he succeeded me was to order my name chiseled off the stone. He was greatly disgusted when informed that I had never placed my name on any cornerstone that I had laid, for I always limited the inscriptions to the date.

The transatlantic steamship companies told me that unless I could provide docks long enough for their large new vessels they would be obliged to leave New York. I applied to the War Department for permission to build docks long enough for the purpose and was promptly refused on the ground that any extension beyond the established pier line would be dangerous to navigation. I sent for Bensel, the dock commissioner, and asked him if under the circumstances it would not be possible to dig inland and in this way obtain the required length. Bensel, who was an excellent engineer with imagination, at once rose to the occasion and replied that it could be done.

My father in 1872, when chief engineer of the Department of Docks, had built the Battery sea wall and three stone docks immediately above, his intention being, had he remained in office, to extend the work to the north to include the Chelsea section. I had always had a sentimental desire to complete the work my father had begun, and the ultimatum of the steamship companies gave me the opportunity I needed. The eight Chelsea piers, 825 feet long with the plaza in the rear, were completed before I left office, as well as eight new recreation piers and a promenade on the roofs of the pier sheds from Cedar to Albany Streets. In addition we built eight piers from 1,200 to 1,800 feet long, between Twenty-eighth and Thirty-sixth streets, Brooklyn. We built in all thirty-five miles of new wharfage, including fifty-one new piers and thirty old ones extended.

I have always held that the growth of New York in population must depend upon two factors, an adequate water supply and adequate dock facilities. Having solved the first requirement for many years to come, I turned my attention to the second.

Jamaica Bay on the south shore of Long Island and within the city limits, with comparatively little dredging and the construction of a deep channel to the open sea, has enough shore line for the construction of as many long docks as could be built on the whole of Manhattan Island. Besides, there were many advantages. The docks could be built of any desired length without permission of the United States government, and steamers could reach blue water within twenty minutes of leaving their berths. I talked the matter over with representatives of the transatlantic companies, all of whom agreed that they would gladly move to Jamaica Bay when and if the improvement was completed.

The first necessary move in the work was the acquisition of options on the shore property, all of which was in private hands. I realized that these options must be secured without letting the owners know for what purpose they were intended if prices were to be kept within reason. Accordingly, I discussed the matter in confidence with the comptroller and the president of the Board of Aldermen, and we agreed to try to secure them informally without any action of the Board of Estimate, and we placed the work of buying the options in the hands of Douglas Robinson, a well-known real estate man, who was brother-in-law of Theodore Roosevelt. Unfortunately too many people knew our secret, someone had talked and Robinson found options on every piece of real estate adjoining Jamaica Bay had been secured by a little syndicate of Democratic politicians, friends of Charley Murphy.

The syndicate thought that it had a stranglehold on the city, a stranglehold that I determined to break. I found that under an old law the city owned in fee simple the land abutting on Jamaica Bay between high and low water, which was a very wide strip. I therefore abandoned the old plans that had been drawn and moved the bulkhead line down to low water mark, which left in the possession of the city sufficient land not only for a wide marginal street but also for deep warehouses in the rear. The syndicate was left literally high and dry with options on land far inland from the marginal street.

The drafting of the new plans, as well as securing the initial

appropriation from Congress for the construction of the
channel, took so much time that I left office with the physical
work of construction not yet begun. My successor, following a
consistent policy of reversing everything that I had undertaken,
promptly abandoned the work which has never been resumed.
Sooner or later, however, Jamaica Bay must be developed if
the city's dock facilities are to be materially increased. . . .

The New York Central had two major projects in mind
that required the consent and co-operation of the city, the
construction of the new Grand Central Terminal and the
elimination of the tracks on Eleventh Avenue.

Before giving my consent to the plans for the new terminal
I insisted that the company should carry Park Avenue by a
viaduct around the new station. It was an expensive undertaking to which the New York Central people strongly objected.
As I flatly refused to approve their plans without the viaduct,
they finally agreed. When the viaduct was completed, after I
had left office, the Tammany borough president of the day
placed a large bronze tablet on the side of the structure proclaiming himself as its author.

The elimination of the tracks on Eleventh Avenue was a
project not only of great convenience to the railroad but of real
necessity to the city, for the street was rightly called "Death
Avenue" because of the great number of fatal accidents that
occurred from running freight trains through a street crowded
not only with traffic but also with the children from the near-by
tenement houses. The railroad offered to cover its tracks along
Riverside Drive and elevate them and depress them along
Eleventh Avenue at its own expense, provided the city would
recognize the legality of its franchise on the West Side of Manhattan, of which there had been some question. Under the
terms of the proposition Death Avenue would have been
entirely eliminated, Riverside Drive would have been parked
to the water's edge, and the unsightly tracks removed, all at
the expense of the road, in return for the recognition of a
franchise that might just possibly have been annulled but only
after long and costly litigation. There was no question in my
mind of the advantage to the city of the offer and I asked
Senator Martin Saxe,[4] a Republican from New York County,

[4] Although McClellan does not mention the fact, Saxe served in the first Mc-

to introduce the necessary bill. Saxe did so, and his committee had reported it out when the Hearst papers began violently to oppose it. They did so with such great effect that Saxe weakened and opposed his own bill which never came to a vote. It was a great public improvement, and the Hearst papers have much to answer for in defeating it. Lately the city has begun at its own expense to do the very work that I proposed to do without costing the city a penny.

With the Pennsylvania Railroad, after the death of Cassatt, my relations were by no means so pleasant. The new president was Samuel Rea,[5] an arbitrary and ill-mannered man, who sulked when he could not have his way. He required a franchise for the extension of the road under and across Manhattan and Brooklyn and into the Bronx and the construction of the Sunnyside Yards in Brooklyn. Without this franchise his new terminal at Seventh Avenue could not be operated, nor the bridge into the Bronx built.

At that time the franchise power was in the hands of the Board of Aldermen and the mayor. By using strongarm methods and a certain amount of tact, I had had no trouble in getting the board to do its duty. I used to have the franchises prepared by the engineers of the Board of Estimate, then send for the leader of the aldermen, who was Little Tim Sullivan, and say to him, "I shall sign this franchise just as it is. If you change a word, I shall veto it, and if I hear of any of you men trying to get any money for your votes I shall expose you." I don't know how honest I succeeded in keeping the board, but I certainly made it more difficult for them to graft.

Little Tim Sullivan was a member of what was known as the Sullivan Clan, which consisted of Big Tim, Little Tim, Florrie, and Christy. Little Tim was supposed to be "The Big Fellow's" nephew, the others his cousins. Actually Little Tim

Clellan administration despite his Republican affiliation. Appointed assistant corporation counsel by Low in 1902, he continued in the same office under McClellan until his election to the state Senate in 1904.

5 McClellan is mistaken, for Rea did not become president of the Pennsylvania until 1913. During the negotiations between Rea and the city for a franchise for the New York Connecting Railroad, Rea was a third vice-president of the Pennsylvania. McClellan kept a record of the negotiations which he describes below. See memoranda dated April 29, 1905, McClellan Scrapbooks, 1905, and December 22, 1906, McClellan Scrapbooks, 1906-1907, New York Historical Society.

was his cousin, the others no relations at all.[6] They ruled four
Assembly districts below Fourteenth Street, chiefly inhabited
by Sicilians, Neapolitans, and the lowest class of Yiddish Jews,
and held their power by the practical use of the principle of
dividere et imperare, setting the Sicilians against the Neapolitans and both against the Jews. Big and Little Tim were
corruptionists and grafters, frankly and unashamedly. Big
Tim [7] once expounded to me his ethical standards. "I don't
hold," said he, "for any man taking the stuff from them poor
women, but the liquor dealers and the gamblers ought to pay
and they do." Murphy once said to me, "The Big Fellow will
sometimes tell the truth, the Little Fellow never does. If it's
worth his while the Big Fellow will keep his word after he had
passed it, the Little Fellow just don't seem to be able to keep
his anyhow."

Without consulting me Rea went directly to the Board of
Aldermen for his franchise. The franchise he proposed was
utterly unacceptable to me, for it was altogether in the interests
of the railroad and not at all in those of the city. I never knew
what he proposed to do, but I rather thought that he intended
to pass his franchise through the aldermen and then try to bully
me into signing it. At any rate he struck a snag in the aldermen,
for I warned Little Tim that if he passed the franchise as
presented I should certainly veto it. Little Tim held the
franchise up perhaps because of my threat, perhaps because as
Rea insinuated, he wanted his price. Rea became very indig-
nant and very impatient, and went to Albany for relief.

I heard that he had arranged to have the legislature transfer
the franchise-granting power from the aldermen to the Board

6 McClellan is mistaken, for Florrie, as well as Little Tim, was Big Tim's
cousin.

7 During the first decade of the twentieth century Big Tim (Timothy D.)
Sullivan was the boss of the Bowery and one of the most powerful men in New
York City politics. In 1902 he could have become leader of Tammany, but he
refused the job and used his influence to make Murphy boss. He was part-
owner of a very successful vaudeville circuit, the head of a syndicate that controlled and exacted tribute from every prize fight in the city, and the head of
another syndicate that received regular payments from the city's gambling establishments. He served several terms in the state legislature and was responsible
for the Sullivan law making it a felony to carry concealed weapons. He had the
law passed so that armed repeaters could not invade the Bowery on election day.
It was then possible for his own followers to vote as often as he saw fit without
outside interference.

of Estimate, and one morning Edward F. Shepard as counsel for the Pennsylvania came to see me and told me that unless the aldermen passed the franchise as drawn, arrangements had been made to enact a law at Albany transferring the franchise power from the aldermen to the Board of Estimate and to pass the bill over my veto should I veto it. I said to him, "Mr. Shepard, do I understand that this is a threat?" "Yes, Mr. Mayor," he replied, "it is a threat. If the aldermen do not give us our franchise, their power will be taken away from them, and you will not be able to prevent it." I then said, "That being the case, Mr. Shepard, I wish you a very good morning," and showed him the door.

When I saw the newspapermen, I told them of my interview without mentioning Shepard's name. The papers were frankly skeptical and demanded that I name the man who had threatened me, for the Pennsylvania, for various reasons, had the friendship of almost all the New York newspapers. When I gave them Shepard's name, they were still skeptical until Shepard acknowledged the truth of my statement, after which they remained silent. The Pennsylvania had evidently made a deal with Murphy for the passage of its bill and for his support in the Board of Estimate. In due time the bill was passed, came to me, I vetoed it, and according to schedule it was passed over my veto.

By this time I had succeeded in arousing a good deal of public opinion in support of my position, and Murphy found it impossible to control any votes in the Board of Estimate except those of the presidents of Manhattan, Bronx and Queens, and with only four votes at his disposal he was helpless. I had the engineers of the board draw a franchise that gave the city a million dollars more than Rea had been willing to pay and safeguarded it in every particular. I had several interviews with Rea, in all of which I managed to keep my temper and in all of which he lost his, running up and down the room, swearing a good deal and denouncing me as pig-headed, a socialist, and almost everything else that he could think of. He finally said that under no circumstances could he or would he accept my franchise. "All right," I said, "take it or leave it." He expressed himself as being particularly outraged by a provision I had inserted in the proposed franchise forbidding the

Pennsylvania to place any advertisements on its right of way in or out of its cars. He said that that was an insult to the road which never under any circumstances allowed advertisements. I have since noticed that the road has greatly fallen from this state of grace.

Rea held out for nearly two months and then very grudgingly accepted the franchise I had proposed without dotting an "i" or crossing a "t." Subsequently Rea had what he considered his revenge. When the Pennsylvania Station was at last opened, he placed in its entrance a large bronze tablet on which were inscribed the names of all the city officials who had had to do with the granting of the franchise required for the work, with one exception and that was mine.

My relations with Cassatt were always pleasant, for he was a different type of man from Rea. The last time I had anything to do with him was in reference to the so-called McAdoo tunnel. William G. McAdoo, recently a senator and sometime Secretary of the Treasury,[8] was at that time a little-known promoter who had not yet acquired fame. He had secured a franchise for the construction of a railway from Newark to New York with two tunnels under the Hudson. He had not been able to sell it or to raise the money to begin work within the time named in his franchise and came to me for an extension. I consulted a number of men in high finance, all of whom advised me to refuse the extension on the ground that he could not possibly make good. I had made up my mind to refuse his extension when Cassatt came to see me. Cassatt told me that the completion of the McAdoo tunnels was essential as a part of his project to bring the tracks of the Pennsylvania into the city. He said, "If McAdoo falls down on the job, I give you my word that the Pennsylvania will see him through." I replied, "Mr. Cassatt, your word is good enough for me," and granted the extension. Cassatt kept his word, and the project was completed on time and established McAdoo as a very able and coming man. . . .

Early in my first administration the Baltimore and Ohio Railroad announced that in thirty days it would abandon its Staten Island ferry service. I found the city confronted with a

8 McAdoo was senator from California from 1933 to 1938 and Secretary of the Treasury under Wilson from 1913 to 1918.

very serious problem. Without the ferry service the Staten
Islanders could only have reached Manhattan via Elizabeth,
New Jersey, a three-hour journey. I have always held that
municipal operation of public utilities should be resorted to
only when private ownership fails to render satisfactory service.
The Staten Island ferry problem was a case in point, so much
against my will I concluded that I must face the necessity of
building and operating a municipal ferry, which, judging from
the experience of the Baltimore and Ohio, would be a financial
loss.

For the emergency we took over the rotten old boats of the
Baltimore and Ohio and used them until the five large and
excellent new boats, that we had contracted for, were ready.
We also built new terminals at the Battery and at Staten Island,
and under the very efficient management of Commissioner
Featherson had a new, comfortable, and fast service in operation
before the end of my first term. We were subsequently obliged
to take over the ferry to Thirty-ninth Street, Brooklyn, and
build three boats for the service.

We built a new police headquarters building and six precinct
station houses.

Under the excellent administration of the Park Department,
of which Henry Smith was president, with M. J. Kennedy and
Joseph I. Berry,[9] as his colleagues, 277 acres of new parks, and
98,600 feet of new parkway were acquired, two new wings
were added to the Metropolitan Museum and one new wing
to the Natural History Museum, the New York Public Library
was completed, and the Brooklyn Public Library begun.

We built six new armories, for the 22nd, 69th, 71st Regi-
ments, the 2nd Battery, Squadron C and the 2nd Naval Battalion, and rebuilt and enlarged six others.

Under Commissioner John H. O'Brien, the street gas lamps
were entirely replaced with electricity.

The many large fires in New York in November, 1903, just
before I took office, followed by disastrous fires in Baltimore
and Rochester, brought the city face to face with a situation
which had to be met without delay. In spite of the efficiency

---

[9] In addition to being president of the Department of Parks, Smith was commissioner of parks for Manhattan and Richmond. Kennedy was commissioner
for Brooklyn and Queens, and Berry was commissioner for the Bronx.

of our Fire Department, the constantly increasing number of large fires showed very cleary that we were running the constant risk of an uncontrollable conflagration that would be calamitous in its result. I determined that, regardless of cost, New York must be made as fireproof as possible. Accordingly, I at once took steps to install in the business districts the first high-pressure water service for fires in the world. Under this system both salt and fresh water could be pumped so that if anything happened to the fresh water supply the Atlantic Ocean could be drawn on as a reserve. The system could pump fifty million gallons in twenty-four hours at a pressure of 350 pounds per square inch, and could be concentrated within two minutes at any point in the high-pressure fire districts.

Thanks to Commissioner John H. O'Brien, the system was in working order within seventeen months from the time the contracts were let. We also built four new fireboats, nineteen new firehouses, rebuilt and modernized sixty-four old houses, and organized twenty-four new engine companies, twenty-four new hook and ladder companies, seven new hose companies, and increased the personnel forty per cent, entirely abolishing the volunteer system that I found existing in the outlying parts of the city. We also installed an entirely new fire alarm system, putting the wires underground. Without exaggeration it may be said that when I left office New York had the best fire protection of any city on earth. The immediate result . . . [was] a reduction of insurance premiums of over a million dollars a year.

It is almost unbelievable how we have advanced in thirty years, for during my administration the city bought its first motor fire engine as well as its first motor ambulance and its first official motor car, and licensed its first cab, a horse-drawn hansom, equipped with a taxi meter.

Under the charter, as it then was, the hospitals of the city were divided among three different departments, those for contagious diseases were under the Department of Health; Bellevue, Harlem, Fordham, and Gouverneur were under the Department of Bellevue and Allied Hospitals, while all the other hospitals in the city were under the Department of Charities. It was a wasteful and complicated system which I tried to remedy by legislation but without success.

As my predecessor had failed to make the necessary expenditures for the proper upkeep of the hospitals and for the improvement of the public health, it fell to me to do so. The cost was very large, but was fully justified by the results.

For Bellevue Hospital we built two new wings and a nurses' home and training school, for Harlem and Fordham hospitals entire new buildings and a new wing for Gouverneur. Under Commissioner Hebberd a survey of Blackwell's Island, for some unknown reason now called Welfare Island, was made, looking to the ultimate development of the island as a hospital park. This plan originating with Hebberd has been adopted by one of his successors as an invention of his own.

The City Hospital and the Metropolitan were greatly enlarged, the new Bradford Street Hospital in Brooklyn was built, while a new nurses' home was built at City Hospital as well as one at Kings County Hospital, and a new headquarters building in Brooklyn for the Health Department, and a new municipal lodging house with one thousand beds.

It has always seemed to me a crime against civilization that tuberculosis has not been abolished, as to do so is only a question of the expenditure of money. In view of the limited funds at my disposal I did what I could. Under the city charter, the Board of Health is given very great powers over the control of communicable diseases of which tuberculosis is one. Tuberculosis cases may be forcibly isolated so as to minimize the danger of their spreading infection. We built the Coney Island Hospital in Brooklyn for articular cases, and the Riverside Hospital on North Brothers Island with 200 beds and the Sea View Hospital on Staten Island with 1,500 beds for pulmonary cases. As an experiment we built at Otisville, not far from Tuxedo, a sanitorium with 250 beds, which we increased later to 1,000 beds, for primary cases. In three years we had only three deaths from tuberculosis and a record of eighty per cent of the cases completely averted and twenty per cent completely cured. In all we provided 6,000 beds for tuberculosis patients which was thirty-six per cent of the total of 16,500 beds in the entire United States.

Until my time the inspection of milk, that great carrier of tuberculosis, had been confined to the retailers in the city.

Under Dr. Bensel [10] the inspection was extended to the dairies which supplied the milk, making it possible to check infection at its source.

When in this country in 1908 Dr. Koch [11] was kind enough to tell me that he thought that more had been done in New York to check tuberculosis than in any city in the world. He had a very interesting theory about the origin of the evil eye, according to which its possessor has the unwished-for power of causing death of those with whom he associates. Koch thought that, undoubtedly, the possessors of the evil eye were typhoid carriers, whose very existence was unknown until Koch himself discovered them.

I came in contact with two cases of typhoid carriers. One was a prosperous dairy farmer in an upstate county, who as soon as he learned of his condition sold out and moved to a camp in the Adirondacks. The other was a domestic cook named Mary Mallon who had been spreading infection far and wide when she was discovered by Dr. George A. Soper and her case reported to the Board of Health. We made an agreement with her under which she consented to live at the expense of the city on Ward's Island and seemed thoroughly to enjoy her life of leisure. Unfortunately, as soon as my successor had heard of "Typhoid Mary," [12] as she was called, he was greatly outraged, denounced me for having illegally deprived her of her liberty and ordered her turned loose to spread infection wherever she went. The poor woman had been having a very happy life in the hospital and was there of her own free will. As soon, however, as Gaynor began to talk about her being a prisoner, she concluded that she was a martyr and went blithely out into the world to face the problem of earning a living. It was a brutal thing for Gaynor to have done. She was later returned to Ward's Island where she died quite recently.

10 Walter Bensel was the assistant sanitary superintendent for Manhattan and served for a few months in 1906 as commissioner of the Street Cleaning Department.

11 Robert Koch was a German bacteriologist, who in 1905 received the Nobel Prize for his work in developing tuberculin as a test for tuberculosis.

12 At the time that Soper, one of the country's leading sanitary engineers, discovered "Typhoid Mary," he was employed as the sanitary engineer of the city's Department of Health. He was also responsible for the plan used for ventilating the city's subways and the method adopted for the disposal of New York's garbage.

Another improvement of great importance to the public health was the elimination of the mosquito on Staten Island. This was entirely due to the admirable work of Dr. Alvah H. Doty, health officer of the Port. Dr. Doty convinced me that both the striped-legged, salt water breed of mosquito and the Anopheles, or malarial mosquito, can be abolished by draining marshes and stagnant pools. I gave him total appropriations of $42,000, and for this insignificant sum he completed his work. The mosquito ceased to breed on Staten Island. In 1905, the year when Doty began his work, ninety-one cases of malaria were reported on Staten Island, in 1906, sixty-eight cases were reported, in 1907, five, in 1908, three, and in 1909, after the work had been completed, none. Surely Dr. Doty deserved a better fate than to be removed from office by Governor Dix,[13] for no reason but that he was a Republican and that Charles F. Murphy wanted the place for one of his friends.

The net result of the admirable work of the Departments of Health, Charities, and Bellevue and Allied Hospitals, and Tenement House, under Doctors Darling, Biggs,[14] Bensel, Doty, and Branan,[15] and Commissioners Hebberd and Butler, was the reduction of the death rate in the city from 20.06 per thousand in the year I took office to 16.60 in 1908, which meant an actual saving of 15,302 lives during the latter year, and the lowest death rate at that time of any great city in the world but London.

I was anxious to reduce, as far as possible, the so-called part-time system that was in force in our public schools under which, in congested districts, the children received only half a day's schooling, spending the rest of the time on the streets. This necessitated an immense amount of schoolhouse building, for Low had been very niggardly in his policy of construction. The funds available did not permit me to go as far as I wanted, but, nevertheless, under the able management of Winthrop, [president of the board of education,] extraordinary progress was made: 190 new sites were acquired, 150 old buildings were

[13] John A. Dix, an upstate lumber and marble dealer, was governor from 1911 to 1912.

[14] Herman M. Biggs was general medical officer of the Department of Health.

[15] John W. Branan was president of Bellevue and Allied Hospitals.

enlarged and rebuilt, 110 new buildings constructed, including 11 new high schools, 272,000 new sittings were provided, reducing the number of part-time pupils from 76,000 to 54,000, while the part-time day was increased from 2½ hours to 3¾, the normal school day being 5 hours. Besides all this 5 new evening high schools and 20 new evening elementary schools were organized, as well as the first parental school, the first school for deaf mutes, and the first school for backward and defective children the department had ever had. Four new athletic fields were built, and with the co-operation of the Department of Health a special corps of nurses was appointed for the inspection and care of children at the schools and in their homes.

Early in my second term I appointed Mrs. Herbert D. Robbins and Miss Olivia Leventritt, daughter of Justice Leventritt, of Manhattan, and Mrs. Pratt, of Brooklyn, as school commissioners.[16] They were the first women ever appointed to important office in New York and thoroughly justified their appointments.

As the traffic congestion on Fifth Avenue was already becoming very difficult to handle, I determined on two experiments for its relief, with the idea that if they succeeded my successors could carry them to their logical conclusion. One was the widening of the roadway by the removal of illegal stoops and steps beyond the building line which would permit a material widening of the roadway without any serious narrowing of the sidewalk. I made the experiment by widening the Avenue from Twenty-third to Forty-second streets. Of course I was obliged to fight for it, not only in the courts against property owners affected, but also against Tammany Hall, for the borough president had been in the habit of exacting illegal fees for the maintenance of sidewalk encroachments. I finally won out, and the experimental widening was so successful that George McAnenny, subsequently borough president, continued the widening as far as Fifty-ninth Street and received a medal from his admirers for having conceived the whole scheme, which was of course nothing but the completion of what I had begun.

The other experiment that I was unable to put into effect

16 There is no record of McClellan having appointed a Mrs. Pratt to this position.

was the depression of Forty-second Street under Fifth Avenue.
I had the plan very carefully worked out by that very able
architect Thomas Hastings,[17] and had my project been put
through and proved a success, I had hoped my successors would
depress the cross streets wherever there was great congestion so
as to eliminate the necessity of holding up traffic at the most
congested points. Unfortunately I delayed the undertaking
until 1908 when Murphy had inspired McGowan, the president
of the Board of Aldermen, with the expectation that he would
succeed me as mayor. The Board of Estimate voted down my
proposition, only the comptroller and the president of Richmond voting with me. I asked McGowan why he had deserted
me and he told me that Murphy had made a personal appeal
to him on the ground that John D. Crimmins, a very rich
Tammany contractor and contributor, had large real estate
holdings on Forty-third and Forty-fourth streets which he
thought would be injured by a steady flow of traffic through
Forty-second Street. So for the sake of a Tammany contractor's
pocketbook a public improvement of the greatest importance
was killed.

Murphy also killed my project for a new penitentiary, to
house two thousand male and five hundred female prisoners,
on Rikers Island, which would have been a model of its kind,
and for which plans, and very beautiful plans they were, had
been drawn by Breck Trowbridge,[18] and for a Hudson-Fulton
memorial bridge at Spuyten Duyvil, for which plans had been
drawn by Whitney Warren.[19] I think that his action in these
two latter cases was inspired simply by a desire to be disagreeable to me.

[17] Hastings was one of the early advocates of city planning in the United
States, and in 1911 he prepared a city plan for Hartford, Connecticut. His buildings all reveal the classical influence. Examples of his work are the Frick house
in New York and the Memorial Amphitheatre in the National Cemetery in
Washington.

[18] S. Breck Parkman Trowbridge was a member of a New York architectural
firm that specialized in bank buildings. In New York the firm designed buildings for the Bankers' Trust Company, Chemical National Bank, and J. P. Morgan & Company.

[19] Warren was a well-known architect who designed the Grand Central Ter-
minal, the reconstruction of the Louvain Library in Belgium after the First
World War, and several New York hotels, including the Ritz, Biltmore, and
Commodore.

I appointed a commission with Whitney Warren as chairman to develop a plan for the future development of the city. It was the first planning commission ever appointed in this country and its report was a model of what such reports should be. Unfortunately, it has ever since been officially disregarded but many of the ideas advanced by the unofficial planning organization, that has for some time been in the limelight, have been taken bodily from the Warren report.

It was a great satisfaction to realize that my building program had been appreciated by those who understood, for the Society of Beaux Arts Graduates gave me its medal, and the American Institute of Architects elected me an honorary member.

During my second term I had a good deal of trouble with the lighting and power companies because of the excessive rates they charged the city. As they were powerful enough to block my efforts to obtain legislative relief at Albany, I determined to bring them to terms by what they were pleased to call "strong-arm" methods. I had the engineers of the Department of Water Supply, Gas and Electricity prepare a table of rates, fair to the city and the companies as well, and then submitted it to the latter, who indignantly refused to accept it. I then bought a site, not far from Bellevue Hospital, and upon it began the erection of a municipal power plant, large enough to supply the city's needs in lighting and power. As soon as the companies became convinced that I meant business, which I assuredly did, they surrendered, and accepted my terms. I never had any further trouble with them. On the site of the proposed power house we built a psychopathic observation hospital. In recently announcing the proposed construction of a municipal power plant, the New York City government has merely taken a leaf from the experience of my administration.

In these days of constantly increasing governmental expenditure in nation, state, and city, when it costs, to maintain the government of New York City, the almost unbelievable sum of more than six hundred and fifty million dollars annually, a fifth more than it cost to maintain the entire United States government before the Spanish War, it may be of some interest to note the cost of municipal government in my time.

The total budget for my first year of office, 1904, was $108,592,643.48; for my last year of office, in 1909, it was

$156,545,148.14, an increase of $47,952,504.66. Of this increase 38½ per cent was accounted for by "debt service," that is the interest and amortization of the city's debt, which had increased under me by approximately three hundred million dollars. 14½ per cent of the total increase went to the Board of Education, while the remaining 47 per cent of increase was distributed among the different departments, running from 4½ per cent each to the Police, Fire, Street Cleaning, and Charities for increased service, to .12 per cent for the mayor's office and .002 per cent to the examining Board of Plumbers.

With the exception of the item for debt service, the increase was almost entirely due to the necessity of maintaining the new plant and equipment which I had provided as absolutely essential to the needs of a rapidly growing community.

Increases in personnel included 1,500 new policemen, 1,300 new firemen, and some 300 new streetsweepers to clean a total of 1,250 miles of street which had risen from 971 miles in 1904, and the new teachers and caretakers to man some fifty million dollars of new schools built under me.

What salary increases my last budget contained were almost all due to mandatory legislation passed by the state legislature over my veto.

Chapter XII

Incidents That Are Amusing to Remember

While the unpleasant incidents that occurred during my six years at the City Hall were very many, there was also a goodly number that are pleasant, or at least amusing, to remember. None more so than the memorial meeting in honor of Augustus Saint-Gaudens [1] on February 29, 1908. The committee of his friends and fellow artists, who had the matter in charge under the chairmanship of the painter Will Low,[2] was kind enough to ask me to deliver the oration. I accepted with considerable hesitation, as I knew that my audience would consist almost entirely of artists and art critics, always inclined to be censorious of a layman. However, everything went off well and as the result of the meeting's success I made many artist friends whose friendships have endured.

At the opposite extremes of public monuments in New York stand Saint-Gaudens's Sherman and Vinnie Ream's [3] Samuel S. Cox.[4] With the exception of his Farragut in Madison Square the former is the greatest of Saint-Gaudens's statues. I had

[1] The outstanding American sculptor of his generation, Saint-Gaudens had died on August 3, 1907. His two most notable works are perhaps the Sherman statue in New York City and the figure marking the grave of Henry Adams's wife in Rock Creek Cemetery, Washington, D. C.

[2] Low was among the first American painters after the Civil War to reject native schools of painting for those of France. He did murals for many private and public buildings in the Northeast, but he is remembered today primarily as a teacher and publicist.

[3] Miss Ream, a native of Mississippi, was a sculptor of no apparent merit. When she was twenty-one, she attracted considerable attention by completing a statue of Lincoln for the rotunda of the Capitol.

[4] Cox was an Ohio and New York Democrat who served in the House almost continuously from 1857 to his death in 1889. He was called "Sunset" Cox because of his florid style of writing and speaking.

several requests from other cities for permission to copy it, but felt constrained to refuse them all. As all who have seen it know, the rugged old soldier sits his horse as one who really knew how to ride while a figure of Victory floats in front of him. There used to be a story of a Southerner who seeing it for the first time exclaimed, "Anyone would know that he was a damned Yankee, for he lets the lady walk while he rides."

The "Sunset" Cox statue had been given by the postal letter carriers of New York whose pay Cox had caused to be raised. It was and is probably one of the most atrocious horrors ever modelled and was placed at the junction of Fourth Avenue, the Bowery and Lafayette Street. In justice to the Art Commission it should be said that it was accepted by the city long before the commission was created. Cox clad in a tightly buttoned frock coat stands with his right arm raised aloft with his index finger extended in the attitude of one asking a hitch-hike from the passing traffic. His left arm, much shorter than his right, is pointed stiffly to the ground. The Art Commission, deploring the prominence of its position, did not care to offend the donors by moving it. Accordingly, I sent for the officers of the Letter Carriers' Association and suggested that as Cox had represented a part of the lower East Side the proper place for his monument was in his old district. They agreed with me and accordingly the statue was removed to where it now stands in Tomkins Square. The Art Commission was satisfied, and the letter carriers seemed very much pleased.

I had always been intrigued by the monument to General Worth [5] at the junction of Broadway and Fifth Avenue. No one seemed to know whether the general's body was buried underneath or not. There was nothing on the monument to show, and not even his daughter who was still living as a very old lady could enlighten me. Towards the close of my second term it became necessary temporarily to move the monument because of the new subway which was being built. We dug down underneath and found the general's coffin with a silver name-plate on its lid. As soon as the obelisk could be restored

[5] William J. Worth served in the War of 1812, was superintendent of the United States Military Academy, was second in command to Scott and Taylor in the Mexican War, and died in 1849 when he was in command of the Department of Texas. The monument to which McClellan refers was erected in 1857.

I had the coffin replaced, with appropriate ceremonies, under the direction of the Aztec Society of which the general had been a founder, and caused a bronze tablet to be affixed to the monument recording the fact that it marked the general's grave. . . .

Before I had taken office a certain Mrs. Angelina Crane had died leaving her residuary estate to the city for the purpose of building a fountain in her memory. Her niece contested the will, and finally before I left office the Court of Appeals handed down a decision in favor of the city. The total amount paid the city was slightly more than $62,000. I gave the contract for the work to Frederick MacMonnies [6] and left him a free hand in its execution. Together we selected as its site the park in front of the City Hall which was encumbered by a horrible fountain of the U. S. Grant period.

Like all artists MacMonnies took his time and the fountain was not finished until some ten years later during the administration of Mayor Hylan.[7] It proved to be a nude male figure symbolizing civic virtue. There was at once a storm of protest from certain prudish sources, and the New York *Sun* greatly enjoyed itself in making fun of MacMonnies, the contractor who had made the statue, and the statue itself, the "Tough Guy" as the *Sun* called it. Mayor Hylan was greatly disturbed and took very seriously the charge that he was responsible for an "act of civic indecency." The secretary of the Art Commission told me that one morning Hylan burst into his office and said, "Who ordered that lewd statue anyway?" The secretary replied, "Mayor McClellan was entirely responsible." Upon which kindhearted Hylan said, "Oh, my God, we must at all costs protect McClellan."

I gave Hylan his first public office. One day in 1906 he came to see me and called my attention to a law that I had never heard of, which had been enacted many years before, that made it mandatory for the mayor to appoint two additional magistrates in Brooklyn. He asked if I had any objection to his bringing mandamus proceedings against me to require me to

<hr/>

[6] MacMonnies was a well-known sculptor who studied under Saint-Gaudens. In addition to "Civic Virtue" mentioned below by McClellan, his work included statues of Theodore Roosevelt and General McClellan and the monument commemorating the Battle of Princeton.

[7] John F. Hylan, a Brooklyn Democrat, was a city magistrate, County Court judge, mayor (1918-25), and justice of the Children's Court (1925-36).

make the appointments. I told him to go ahead, and, after the mandamus was granted, I appointed him to one of the new vacancies and he made an excellent magistrate. He never forgot and was always grateful for what I had done for him.

One day after he became mayor I called on him to pay my respects as I have done to most of my successors. He asked me, "What can I do for you?" "Nothing," I answered, "I have only come to pay my respects." "But you must want something," he rejoined. "Tell me what it is." It took me fully ten minutes to convince him that apparently for the first time in his experience as mayor he had received a caller who had neither favor to ask nor axe to grind.

Curiously enough three of my successors received their political starts from me. Hylan as magistrate, Mitchel as commissioner of accounts, and O'Brien as one of our most useful assistant corporation counsels.

Mrs. Russell Sage very generously gave the city one of the finest collections of rhododendra in the world and selected as the site for its installation the eastern side of Central Park on Fifth Avenue. The old lady and I with much pomp planted the first bush. Unfortunately, the newspapers "played up" the little ceremony with the result that the next morning more than half the plants had been stolen.

Seth Low had a very similar experience in Brooklyn. When Fourth Avenue was completed with its stretch of parkway between the roadways he had the parking planted with shrubs and flowers and put up at frequent intervals signs reading, "These flowers are given into the keeping of the people." The next morning there was not a plant left, every bit of green along the whole length of Fourth Avenue had disappeared. The people had literally accepted the gift.

Russell Sage was notorious for his miserliness. At his death he left some fourteen million dollars without restriction to his wife, whom he had stinted beyond belief during their entire married life. She had been a schoolmate of my aunt's to whom she would confide her troubles when they occasionally met. The Sages lived in a gloomy house on Fifth Avenue which was a landmark from the fact that its shutters were always closed. Mrs. Sage was required to maintain it with two servants and was only allowed by her husband to buy one new dress a year.

Mr. Sage, or, as he liked to be called, The Honorable Russell Sage, for he had served a term in Congress, dressed like a tramp. He never kept carriages or horses and always lunched on a single apple, which he carried to his office in his pocket, until the Western Union of which he was a director began the practice of providing a daily free lunch for its executive board, after which he lunched copiously at the expense of the Western Union.

One day when I was covering railroads for the *Herald*, Eddy Riggs of the *Sun*, who was on fairly intimate terms with Sage, and I called on him. We found the old gentleman immensely amused by a letter which he had received and which he showed to us. It purported to come from a little girl in the Middle West, who said that she had lost one of her eyes, that her parents could not afford to buy her a substitute, and that, having heard of Mr. Sage's great generosity, she had written him in the hope that he would be so kind as to buy her one.

It was a pathetic little letter and when Sage said that he intended to throw it in the wastebasket, Riggs asked if he might have it. The next time I saw Riggs he told me that he had had the letter checked by the *Sun*'s man at the little girl's home, and that her story was perfectly true. Riggs asked me to go with him to see Sage, and I did. When Riggs told Sage that he had verified the little girl's story Sage seemed quite unimpressed. "Aren't you going to send her a glass eye?" asked Riggs. "Certainly not," replied Sage. "Do you take me for a sucker?" "Mr. Sage," said Riggs, "if that child doesn't get a glass eye, I shall publish the story in the *Sun*, and it won't make pretty reading for you." "But, Eddy," protested the old gentleman, "you can't be serious. You wouldn't force me to buy her a glass eye. It might be very expensive, it might cost four or five dollars." "The story is going to be printed anyway," said Riggs. "If you send the eye, I shall emphasize your generosity." "Yes," interrupted Sage, "and have every beggar in the United States appeal to me. I'll tell you what I'll do. If you say nothing about the matter in the *Sun*, I'll give you three dollars. If the eye comes to more than that you can pay the difference." "Oh, no," answered Riggs, "I'll do nothing of the kind. I have written a letter for you to sign authorizing the girl's parents to buy for her the very best glass eye obtainable and to send the bill to you."

The old man and Riggs argued for more than a half hour when finally the former threw up his hands and surrendered, saying as we left his office, "Eddy, you can have the satisfaction of knowing that you are the first man who ever sandbagged me into committing an extravagance." . . .

I was anxious to acquire Rockaway Beach for hospital purposes, but did not have the necessary funds for the purchase. Accordingly, I approached several multi-millionaires with the suggestion that they should buy the land and give it to the city. All but one of those I spoke to agreed to give half the purchase price, if the city would give the other half and I would agree to call the property after them. The one who refused even to listen to me was Andrew Carnegie. It seems that I had inadvertently aroused him as he had a horror of everything suggesting death and would never give a penny to a hospital or any purpose indirectly connected with one.

I remember hearing my father tell how at the beginning of the Civil War he had advised Lincoln as a war measure to place Tom Scott, president of the Pennsylvania Railroad, in general charge of railroad transportation. Lincoln had agreed, and Scott had accepted the office with the proviso that he should have as his principal assistant, his general superintendent, a young Scot named Andrew Carnegie. From that time on Carnegie's progress to fame and power was exceedingly rapid.

When I knew him he had practically retired and was enjoying his old age in the glory of past achievement and enormous wealth. It seemed to appeal to his sense of romance to visualize himself as a Scottish chieftain of the long ago and he referred to himself as "Chief" when speaking of his Scottish castle and liked to be addressed and spoken of as "the Laird." He entertained a great deal in his very large home in New York and frequently seated his dinner guests on one side of a long table, very like the seating arrangements of the apostles in the pictures of the "Cena" [Last Supper]. Going out to dinner the company was always proceeded by George, the Piper, who continued to skirl the pipes all through the meal.

No matter how much money he gave away he never forgot

his native canniness. When the Carnegie pension fund was endowed, he announced at the first meeting of the trustees that he would send the treasurer ten millions of Steel Trust first mortgage bonds. Whereupon the trustees adjourned for the summer. Time passed, and as the bonds did not arrive the treasurer became worried and called on Carnegie's man of business, who turned on him wrathfully and said, "You idiot, don't you know that the Laird is keeping the bonds until he has clipped the July coupons?"

Carnegie had three major passions: the building of libraries, the building of lakes, and the making of speeches.

In giving libraries he gave nothing but the building, the recipient being obliged to furnish the site, the equipment of the building, and its maintenance. My predecessor, Seth Low, had agreed to accept from Carnegie ten million dollars' worth of branch libraries under the New York Public Library. When I took office, I found that four million dollars' worth of branch libraries had been built, which had cost the city over fifteen millions in real estate, furnishing, and equipment as its share of the bargain. I told Carnegie that the city could not afford to accept any more of his gift, and he was very much annoyed, so much so that when I afterwards went to him about another matter, he said, "I shall not give another cent to the city until all of my ten million library gift has been accepted."

Woodrow Wilson told me the story of the acquisition of Lake Carnegie. Princeton greatly needed a new lecture hall, and Wilson invited Carnegie to lunch with him and afterwards walked around the campus telling how much the university needed new buildings. The Laird seemed unimpressed, in fact remained distinctly cold, until on the way back to Princeton Junction he asked in some excitement why the marshy stream known as Stony Brook that they were crossing had never been drained. Wilson replied that it was because of lack of funds, to which Carnegie almost dreamily answered, "What a site for a lake." Three days later Wilson received a letter from the Laird informing him that the Laird proposed to build and give to Princeton a lake on the site they had inspected, with the understanding that it should be called Loch Witherspoon in honor of Princeton's Declaration-of-Independence-signing president. Wilson swallowed his disappointment as best he could and wrote an appropriate letter of thanks for Loch Wither-spoon. Its receipt was almost immediately acknowledged by Carnegie in a letter beginning:

> "My dear President Wilson:
> I have received your letter in reference to Lake Carnegie,"
> etc. etc.

The lake thereupon became and remained "Lake Carnegie."

Carnegie greatly fancied himself as a speechmaker and never lost an opportunity to orate, which he did rather badly. At a dinner Carnegie gave to a Peace Congress held in New York, I was sitting beside Mr. Choate [8] when our host came up and, leaning across the narrow table, said, "I suppose everyone will expect me to make a speech. What do you fellows think I ought to do?" To which Mr. Choate who did not suffer Carnegie gladly said: "Those who know their Carnegie will, of course, expect him to speak. But for God's sake, spare us and don't." The Laird look startled, said nothing, and trotted off, but that night at least he made no speech.

The panic of 1907 brought me for the first time into close relations with J. P. Morgan, the elder. I had always known him, for my father had known his father, Junius S. Morgan, and my grandfather, when stationed as a young man on recruit-ing duty at Hartford, Connecticut, had known his grandfather.

During the summer of 1907 I was on my vacation in the Adirondacks when I received a telegram from the deputy and acting comptroller (the comptroller was in Europe) saying that an issue of fifteen million dollars of city bonds which he had advertised had failed to receive a single bid, and appealing to me for help. While technically it was none of my business, the Finance Department had a habit of appealing to me whenever it was in trouble. I cut short my vacation and returned to New York, where I found the entire Finance Department in a con-dition bordering on panic. I sent for the heads of the bank-ing houses that had taken our bonds in the past and was told by all of them that in the then panicky condition of business they would not touch a city bond under any circumstance. I

---

[8] Joseph H. Choate was a well-known New York lawyer, who played a promi-nent part in the destruction of the Tweed Ring and served as United States ambassador to Great Britain under McKinley.

really did not know which way to turn, when my bridge commissioner, Stevenson, who had made many friends in Wall Street when deputy comptroller, told me that he had heard in confidence that Mr. Morgan was expected home from Europe late that night. I directed Stevenson to see Pliny Fisk,[9] Morgan's bond man, and to ask him to meet Morgan on his arrival at Quarantine and to arrange for a meeting between Morgan and me for as early a date as possible. Late that night Fisk called me on the phone and told me that Morgan thought that it would be less conspicuous if we met at his office the next morning at half past eight.

When I presented myself at Morgan's office, I found him and the watchman in possession. Fisk had told him the details of the city's situation so we were able at once to get down to business. "How much do you want?" asked Morgan. I answered that I thought that twenty-five million dollars would answer for the present. "Offer forty million dollars in your advertisement," said Morgan. "But, my dear sir," I replied, "if we failed to get bids for fifteen million dollars how can we possibly hope to sell forty millions?" "Leave that to me," replied Morgan. "If you don't get any bids, I give you my word that I will give you my personal check for the whole amount." I expressed my sincere appreciation of his public spirit and then asked him what I should say if questioned by the press. He said, "Leave everything to me. Say nothing. Just get out your ad as soon as possible, and I will do the rest."

When the City Hall reporters asked me whether there was any truth in the rumor that Morgan had agreed to underwrite the next issue of city bonds, I replied that I had nothing to say. When he was asked the same question he replied, "I decline to deny or affirm the rumor." When the bids for the forty million dollar issue were opened, they were found to have been oversubscribed three times, the firm of J. P. Morgan and Company not bidding.

During the panic year of 1907 Morgan either took up himself or caused his subsidiary banks to take up over three hundred

9 Fisk was a prominent New York banker, who was head of the family firm of Harvey Fisk and Sons. In a single day's trading on the stock exchange in 1901 he made $800,000, and the Pujo investigation in 1913 revealed that his firm was closely linked to that of J. P. Morgan. When he died in 1939, he was penniless.

millions of the city's long and short term bonds, and by his individual support really saved the city from bankruptcy.

I thought that it would be a graceful gesture to give him the freedom of the city and consulted his son as to whether his father would like it. The younger Morgan told me that Mr. Morgan would be delighted. I sent a message to the aldermen urging them to confer the freedom on him, when Pulitzer began to froth at the mouth declaring that Mr. Morgan had been paid at usurious rates for all that he had done—which was, of course, untrue—and that it would be a scandal to officially thank him. The aldermen were terrified by the attitude of the *World* and could not be persuaded to act on my message. And so Mr. Morgan was never officially thanked by the city whose credit he had saved.

While the financial crisis lasted, frequent meetings were held in the Morgan library for the purpose of keeping in touch with what was being done to better conditions. The meetings were always attended by Mr. Morgan himself, his partner [George W.] Perkins, who acted as secretary of the meetings, his partner [Charles] Steele, who acted as telephone operator, James Stillman, president of the National City Bank, George Baker, president of the First National Bank, Lewis C. Ledyard, Morgan's lawyer and myself, representing the city, and usually four or five other bank presidents attended from time to time. The meetings were sometimes very stormy, for Mr. Morgan's ideas of the law were rather sketchy.[10] When he thought that anything should be done, he violently objected to legal limitations, and would stride up and down the room expressing his opinion of laws, lawyers, and lawmakers in anything but parliamentary language. Stillman was the only one who could calm him. He used to lead the enraged Morgan into a corner where he would

[10] Lawson Purdy, who attended one of these meetings in his capacity as president of the Department of Taxes and Assessments, has recalled that Morgan did not bother to consult the other bankers who were present and who were members of the syndicate buying the city's securities. Instead, "Morgan went over to his desk and wrote on a sheet of notepaper a contract saying that they would pay the city 70 million dollars on behalf of the syndicate upon the terms stated. He read the contract aloud and all assented. I was just a spectator, but it was all very interesting. Morgan had to lend the money to the city for fear the city would shop around the open market for it and further disturb the market." (Purdy, "Reminiscences," 17.)

whisper to him for several minutes after which Morgan would resume his seat, growling, "All right, have it your own way. But I still maintain that it is a damned silly law."

For all his forcefulness he was at heart an extremely kindly man. At one of the library meetings he showed me a letter that he had received from someone who said that if he wanted to gain the good will of Herman Metz, the comptroller, he should ask him to dinner, for Metz had social ambitions. Metz came later to the meeting and by mistake Morgan gave him the letter to read. Metz took it very well; he handed the letter back, laughed, and said, "I think that you have given me the wrong letter." Morgan was very much distressed and told me afterwards that he really did not know how to make amends to Metz for his mistake.

Morgan's methods were extremely direct, and he was always surprised if he did not get what he wanted on demand. He called me up one day and asked if the New York and Westchester Railroad had applied for a franchise. When I answered that it had, he said, "I want that franchise granted today." I explained that that was impossible, that the law required a public hearing, and that the proposed form of franchise that had been submitted was quite unsatisfactory to the city. He grunted and said, "Always the damned law. I think that you might oblige me." I found out afterwards that certain individuals interested in the franchise had, without Morgan's knowledge, made a deal with Murphy to have it put through exactly as drawn and to pass it over my veto. The press supported me valiantly in my fight so that, when finally granted, the franchise was perfectly satisfactory to the city but by no means satisfactory to its proponents.

On another occasion he called me on the telephone and said, "I want you to appoint Howard Townsend [11] commissioner of charities." I told him that Commissioner Hebberd was perfectly satisfactory to the public and to me and that I could not possibly remove him. To which he replied, "Damn Hebberd,

---

[11] Townsend was a New York lawyer who devoted a great deal of energy to improving standards of health. He led a campaign to have the state care for poor consumptives, was first president of the New York State Hospital for Consumptives, served as manager of St. Luke's Hospital (1896-1902), and was on the boards of several other New York hospitals.

I never heard of him, remove him and appoint Townsend." When I again declined, he grunted and rang off.

He was the president, and a very good president, of the Metropolitan Museum of Art and greatly fancied himself as an art critic. He bought largely and, when relying on expert advice, wisely. When he bought on his own, he was not always so successful. His nephew Junius once told me that he had estimated that his uncle had spent fifty million dollars on art objects of which he had probably been cheated to the extent of about half. Junius used to buy books for his uncle. He said that, if a dealer wanted to "get" the old man, it was only necessary to have the catalogue of the books to be sold written in script in a good round hand and then bound in vellum with a blue ribbon.

One morning in Rome, Mr. Morgan came to our hotel and sent up to my wife and me saying that he had something most interesting to show us. We went downstairs and found him in his car. "Jump in," he cried, "I have bought a picture that you must see." He drove us to a dealer's, and said that he wanted to see the picture that he had bought the day before. The dealer replied that the picture had already been packed for shipment to London. A photograph was produced, and the dealer said that it was Raphael's "Madonna of the Veil" which had been stolen from the Pilgrim Church at Loreto in the sixteenth century and that he had only recently acquired it. Mr. Morgan was very proud of his acquisition.

When I returned to our hotel, I consulted my Morelli [12] and found that before its abduction the "Madonna of the Veil" had been copied by Perino del Vaga and by Giulio Romano.[13] I then consulted my Berenson [14] and found that Giulio's copy was in the possession of one of the smaller galleries and that Perino's copy was in the possession of a private collector at Florence. When we reached Florence, I asked one of my dealer

---

[12] This is a reference to Giovanni Morelli, *Italian Painters; Critical Studies of Their Works* (London, 1892), 2 vols. Morelli was among the first art experts to use a technical examination of a picture rather than historical data as a means of determining who was the painter of the picture in question.

[13] Both Perino del Vaga and Giulio Pippi, known as Guilio Romano, were contemporaries, students, and imitators of Raphael.

[14] This could refer to any one of a number of works by Bernard Berenson, an American and one of the world's greatest authorities on Italian art.

friends if he knew that particular collection, to which he replied that the owner had died and that the collection had recently been sold.

I was afterwards told that when Mr. Morgan reached London he summoned Roger Fry,[15] who expertized for him, and displayed his newly acquired Raphael. Whereupon Fry broke to him the news that he had bought Perino del Vaga's copy. Fortunately for Mr. Morgan, the dealer took the picture back. Years later . . . [a friend in the Netherlands] told me that he had bought what might or might not be Raphael's lost "Madonna of the Veil," and so apparently after much wandering Perino del Vaga's copy has at last found a resting place at The Hague.

One afternoon Jacob H. Schiff, the banker, and his friend and lawyer, Louis Marshall, called on me and entered a complaint that the Metropolitan Museum of Art, of which Mr. Morgan was president, had no Jew on its Board of Trustees. Mr. Schiff said that he and Marshall had drawn a bill which they had every hope of inducing the legislature to pass, vesting the appointment of the trustees in the mayor, instead of by co-optation as it then was and now is, and requiring two of the board to be Jews. He wanted me to agree to sign the bill when it came to me. I told him that at first blush I was not inclined to sign the bill, but that I would not commit myself one way or the other until it came before me. As they were going out, Marshall lagged behind and said to me, "Of course, Mr. Mayor, it is understood that if the bill becomes a law you will appoint Mr. Schiff to one of the vacancies." I answered that I would make no pledges of any kind, whereupon he left my office and Schiff came back and said, "By the by, Mr. Mayor, of course it is understood that you will appoint Marshall to one of the vacancies." Whereupon I repeated what I had said to Marshall.

As soon as they had finally gone, I called up Mr. Morgan and told him of my interview and added, "The sooner you put a Jew on your board the better it will be." The next day he

15 An English art critic and artist and an authority on Italian Renaissance art, Fry was asked in 1905 by Morgan to serve as curator of paintings at the Metropolitan Museum of Art. Fry remained at the Metropolitan from 1905 to 1910, and during this period he accompanied Morgan on his buying trips to Europe.

called a meeting of his trustees, accepted the resignation of one of them and filled the vacancy with George Blumenthal,[16] who has since become the best president the Metropolitan Museum has ever had. . . .

My mayoralty covered the last part of Roosevelt's administration and the beginning of Taft's. Of Roosevelt I saw but little. When I was running for mayor, he, like one of his predecessors on the same spot, went out of his way in making a speech at Antietam battlefield to ignore my father, apparently on the assumption that it would hurt me. It had precisely the opposite effect, and his discourtesy to my father's memory made me votes. Recognizing his mistake, he determined to make amends and announced that he would deliver the principal address at the unveiling of my father's statue in Washington, May 2, 1907.

He had an arrangement with the press by which the latter agreed to print his speeches as given out by his secretary. He used to speak extemporaneously, his speech being taken down by his own stenographer, to be later revised, flimsied, and given out. When speaking he seldom completed a sentence, a paragraph, or a thought, and very often his spoken speech differed radically from that which was furnished to the newspapers.

At the unveiling of the McClellan statue he faced a large audience of veterans and began a very appropriate address. Suddenly he was seized by an inspiration. Turning around he faced my mother, who was sitting in the front row, and in his highest falsetto shouted at her, "Madame, you are a good woman." My mother, who was very deaf, thinking that the President had gone suddenly mad, threw up her hands and screamed. Roosevelt, nothing daunted, turned back to the veterans and said to them, "This lady has done her duty and borne children," and then launched into an impassioned oration against birth control, which was his fad of the moment. The

16 Blumenthal, a prominent financier and philanthropist, became a member of the board of the Metropolitan Museum of Art in 1909 and served until his death. He was made president of the board in 1934. At that time the board stated that he was "a distinguished amateur, notable as a collector of judgment, and as one foremost in the encouragement and promotion of the arts." He gave the museum $1,000,000 in 1928, and at various other times gave it valuable pictures from his own collection.

speech as given to the press contained not one word on birth control but was quite appropriate to the occasion.

Whenever he came to New York his brother-in-law, Douglas Robinson, preceded him and came to see me to ascertain what plans I had made for his protection. Robinson always insisted on having me show him on a map exactly what arrangements had been made for the guarding of the President's route from the ferry to his destination and for his protection during his stay. Roosevelt was brave himself, and obviously the over-emphasis on police protection did not originate with him.

The last time that he came to New York as President was to the unveiling of General Slocum's [17] statue at Brooklyn, where we both spoke. I asked my detective lieutenant, who constituted my only guard, to find out for me how many secret service men the President had brought with him. He reported that he had brought thirty-five, and they were literally falling over each other.

As we stood reviewing the parade, Roosevelt suddenly turned to me and said, "He is a damned liar." "Who is, Mr. President?" I inquired. To which he answered, "Your friend Alton B. Parker. I have wanted to say that to you for a year, and now I have said it, so there." During the previous campaign Parker had accused him of receiving large campaign contributions from the Steel Trust which Roosevelt had denied by calling Parker a liar.

When Grover Cleveland died, Roosevelt wired to Mrs. Cleveland, "Am greatly distressed to hear of your husband's death. Hope funeral will not be on Friday as I want to go to the Harvard-Yale boat race that day." The funeral was not on Friday, and he came. He was met at the station by Archy Russell [18] who was an old friend of his as well as a friend of the Clevelands. Russell, who was greatly distressed by Cleveland's death, was much shocked when the President jumping off the train punched him in the stomach and shouted, "How is my old college chum?"

[17] Henry W. Slocum was a Union general, lawyer, and Democratic politician and officeholder in Brooklyn.

[18] Archibald D. Russell was the senior partner in the real estate firm of Russell, Robinson & Roosevelt. Robinson was the Douglas Robinson mentioned above. The other member of the firm was Elliot Roosevelt, Theodore Roosevelt's brother.

Mrs. Cleveland had rather mistakenly refused to allow the press to come to the house. Roosevelt arrived with his usual escort of secret service men and newspapermen, all of whom, to Mrs. Cleveland's disgust, he introduced into the room where the services were to be held. I sat next to him and found him in uproariously good spirits. As Dr. Henry van Dyke began the service, Roosevelt began in a loud stage whisper to tell me how "they tried to make me take another nomination, but I wouldn't touch it." He kept his hat in front of his face as he talked and would from time to time lower it and at most inappropriate moments shout, "Amen," apparently under the impression that he was covering his conversation with me.

Taft I knew much better than I did Roosevelt and got on very well with him, for after his election I won his heart by a speech I made at a dinner that was given by the Ohio Society of New York, December 16, 1908. In later years, when he was Chief Justice, I saw a good deal of him.

It would be difficult to imagine two more dissimilar men than Wilson and Bryan—Wilson, cold, selfish, calculating and cynical, Bryan warmhearted, generous, and naïve. Their only resemblance lay in their gift of speech, and even in this they differed widely. Wilson had by hard work made himself a good speaker. His speeches were eloquent, polished and correct, models of diction and of form. Bryan, on the other hand, was a born orator. He had a message to deliver, and he gave it to the world with all his heart and soul, ignoring form and content in his impassioned effort to carry his audience with him. In his prime there was none like him. [He was] young and handsome with a marvellously beautiful voice [, and] his earnestness and his enthusiasm made of the mistaken cause of "free silver" a vital, burning issue.

I first met him in 1896 and saw him from time to time thereafter until his death. In 1900 when he came to New York he greatly embarrassed me by offering to speak in my district. He meant it most kindly, for it was the only time during the campaign that he spoke at a local meeting. As I had no large hall in the district I was obliged to hold the meeting in the open air, and I staged it on Second Avenue at the corner of Twentieth Street where it would excite as little comment as possible. As the free silver question was taboo in New York, I was on pins and needles for fear Bryan would discuss it. Fortunately, before he spoke he asked me what I wanted him to talk about. I suggested imperialism as a safe subject, and he discreetly stuck to that.

In 1906 Hearst paid his expenses for a journey around the world. Before he left India he sent word through a mutual acquaintance, a newspaperman named Harry Walker,[19] that he would like to see me and would meet me any place in Europe that I might name, as he had heard that I intended going abroad for six weeks. He further asked me to see Cleveland and find out, if possible, how the latter felt in reference to his nomination in 1908. I agreed to meet him in London and went to Princeton to see the ex-President. I told Cleveland of Bryan's message and of my proposed meeting with him. "Well," said Cleveland, "I don't feel as bitterly about Bryan as I used to. I don't think he is such a damned scoundrel as I once did. You can tell him that, if you like, in your own words."

What with a desperately fought campaign for re-election and the worry of Hearst's recount proceedings, I was very much in need of a rest, which I should have had great difficulty in obtaining in this country. My wife and I, therefore, decided that the wisest thing for us to do was to go abroad for six weeks.

The press conceded that I had earned a holiday, with the exception, of course, of Hearst's papers and the *Evening News*. The *Evening News* which had been a very profitable one-cent workman's paper under Ben Wood and Colonel Bill Brown had been bought and ruined by Frank Munsey who, while a successful publisher of cheap magazines, successively wrecked the *Evening News,* the New York *Press* and the New York *Sun.*[20] The *News* went through several hands and finally with Murphy's backing fell under the control of one of the boss's friends, who in the course of a few months gave it its *coup de grâce.*

Its last manager was a pleasant and persuasive little Irishman who used to wangle from me a considerable amount of advertising which probably kept the paper going. Just after I an-

19 Walker, a member of Tammany Hall, had served as secretary of the Aqueduct Commission under Van Wyck. He was Washington correspondent for the New York *Herald* when McClellan worked for the same paper.

20 McClellan is mistaken only in his details in his description of Munsey's methods, for when Munsey died in 1925 he still controlled the New York *Sun* and it was one of the three most successful papers in New York.

nounced that I was going abroad, the *News* published with scare headlines and a wealth of detail a story to the effect that my mind had gone and that my wife was taking me to England to shut me up in an insane asylum. The next day the nominal proprietor of the *News* called and explained that the story had been published under Murphy's orders, begged me not to mind, and trusted that it would not "disturb our pleasant relations." I assured him that I didn't mind in the slightest, but that he would get no more advertising and that I would probably sue him for libel, which I should certainly not have done, as I always followed the unwritten law of accepting newspaper abuse without protest. His reply was another scarehead story to the effect that I had tried to sandbag and "intimidate" him by depriving him of city advertising. As none of the other newspapers paid the slightest attention to the story, neither did I, and within a fortnight the *News* had ceased to exist.

We sailed on the *New York* of the old American Line. My wife went to Paris, and I to London to buy some clothes. . . . When I reached London, I found Bryan stopping at the Hotel Cecil in a very grand suite. As I entered his sitting room, he was dictating to Mrs. Bryan, whom he at once shooed out of the room. Having done so, he turned to me and eagerly inquired, "Did you see Cleveland, and what did he say about me?" I answered that I had seen Cleveland and that he seemed to be more sympathetically inclined to Bryan than I had ever known him to be. "Thank God for that," said the Commoner. "Do you think he will back me for the nomination?" While I expressed grave doubt as to that, I assured him that, nevertheless, Cleveland was much less bitter about him than formerly. "You will see him when you get back, won't you?" said Bryan. "I wish you would, and when you do tell him about this talk we have had." Bryan then jumped to his feet and resolving me into a sort of metaphorical national convention proceeded to try to stampede me. He paced the room for nearly an hour talking of national political issues with a reasonableness and a conservativeness worthy of Cleveland himself. His purpose evidently was to convince me that a new Bryan was before me, a Bryan whom all conservative Democrats could support, so that on my return home I might carry the news to Cleveland and in turn convince him. It was a truly oratorical "stunt" . . . to capture his audience even though it was an audience of only one. When he reached New York a fortnight later, he had forgotten his talk with, or rather at, me and gave out an interview quite as radical as anything he had ever written.

The last time I ever saw Bryan was shortly before his death [in 1925]. He arrived in New York one morning after an all-night journey from Wilmington where he had been lecturing. I sent up my card, and the colonel [21] received me in his bedroom. Physically he was a very different Bryan from the one I had first known so many years before. He had grown stout, nearly bald, with what hair he had left unshampooed and uncut, and no longer kept himself tidy and trim. I found him sitting on the edge of his bed in his shirt sleeves holding a collar. He jumped up as I entered, shook hands with great vigor, and seemed really glad to see me. "Glad to see you, Mac," he said, "excuse my appearance. Been travelling all night, felt rather dirty, thought to change my collar."

Alton B. Parker, for a man who had been through the mill of practical politics as chairman of the New York state committee and who had been the chief judge of the Court of Appeals, was the most guileless presidential candidate I have ever known. His nomination was made financially possible by the efforts of August Belmont, the banker, and brought about largely by David B. Hill. Bryan and his friends realized that nothing could stop Roosevelt's election and were perfectly willing to allow the conservative wing of the party to have the discredit of the inevitable defeat. It was a comparatively easy matter to obtain for Parker the nomination which was going abegging.

At the very outset of the campaign Parker showed great moral courage, for he sent a telegram to the convention saying that he would not run except on the understanding that he favored the maintenance of the single gold monetary standard. Despite his agreeable personality, his excellent speeches, and his transparent honesty he was doomed from the start. He was the only man in the United States who really believed that he would be elected. He told me that Senator DuBois of Idaho,

21 Although Bryan is frequently thought of as a pacifist, he, like Theodore Roosevelt, commanded a group of volunteers in the Spanish-American War. Unlike Roosevelt, Bryan never reached Cuba.

chairman of the National Committee,[22] had assured him that he would carry Pennsylvania, and he believed it. Six weeks before election day he sent for me and said, "Mr. Mayor, I want to tell you that you are just the sort of man whom I shall want in my cabinet. Just the kind upon whom I shall expect to rely when I am President, as I assuredly will be." I expressed my appreciation of the compliment he had paid me and hurried down to the City Hall to a meeting of the Board of Estimate. Grout, the comptroller, was very late. When he appeared, he apologized by saying, "I have been having an important conference with Judge Parker, and could not get away." I said to him, "If it is not indiscreet, Comptroller, may I ask if by any chance you are just the sort of man whom the judge wants in his cabinet?" Grout was much confused and rather annoyed and asked me if I had also seen the judge. I told him that I had and wondered how many hundreds of other deserving Democrats besides us two were just the sort of men whom he wanted in his cabinet. . . .

[22] Fred Thomas DuBois was not chairman of the National Committee in 1904. Although elected to Congress in 1901 as a silver Republican, he became a Democrat and took an active part in the campaign of 1904.

Chapter XIII

And So Ended My Mayoralty

FOR THE smooth working of the government it was absolutely necessary to have supporters at Albany, not only to get through the legislation that was required but to prevent "strikes" on the city treasury. On matters of legislation, as well as on questions of ethics, Murphy and I seldom if ever saw eye to eye. It was impossible to keep clear of politics if I were to accomplish results. There were those who urged me to rely on the force of public opinion in a righteous cause. Unfortunately, it is difficult, if not impossible, to arouse public opinion on any issue short of one involving a great question of public morals. Besides as I was always requiring legislation, often on very petty matters, I should have been obliged to spend my time in trying to interest the public in mere questions of routine administration.

As a nucleus I had the legislative support of Brooklyn and Richmond, and by the judicious use of patronage I usually secured enough Democratic and Republican votes to prevent the passage of offensive bills over my veto. At the beginning of 1906 Pulitzer, in a *World* editorial, called on me to fight for the leadership of the Democratic party in New York, as a duty I owed the people, only to turn against me when I began to fight.

There was another reason which impelled me to take an active part in politics. Murphy had decreed my political death. I realized that he would probably succeed in killing me, but before he accomplished his purpose I determined to go down fighting, and I don't think that anyone with the slightest sporting instinct will blame me for my decision.

284

Had McCarren lived, I should have had better than a sporting chance of landing the governorship,[1] which was the goal I set myself. In fact, I think that I should have won, despite Murphy, which would have put me in the running for the presidency in 1912.

McCarren died very unexpectedly in 1909, and on October twenty-six I marched in the funeral procession as chief mourner. Certainly no one in the church that day had greater reason to mourn a loyal friend than had I. The loss of McCarren left me entirely on my own, with my prospects of success reduced to the minimum. The Brooklyn organization chose as its new boss McCooey,[2] who was completely ruled by Murphy, which, of course, meant that I must rely for support entirely on the upstate Democrats.

When, during the summer of 1906, Murphy announced that he proposed to nominate Hearst for governor at the state convention in the following September, I made up my mind that I would do all in my power to stop him. Under the law as it then was, the state committee made up the temporary roll of the state convention, which in its turn appointed the Committee on Credentials, which reported back to the temporary organization on the question of contested seats, the report of the committee being accepted or rejected in whole or in part by the temporary organization, which thereafter became the permanent convention. It will thus be seen that the control of the convention depended entirely on the control of the state committee, which had it in its power, indirectly at least, to determine exactly who should sit as delegates in the permanent convention.

---

[1] A year before his death, McCarren had said: "I do not know whether he [McClellan] is a candidate for re-election in 1909, but I feel safe in saying that he is not lacking in any of the qualities essential to an ideal mayor." (Brooklyn *Eagle,* December 19, 1908.)

[2] A former shipyard worker, John H. McCooey held a succession of minor political jobs until 1904, when McClellan made him a member of the Municipal Civil Service Commission. In the same year McCooey resigned to become deputy collector of assessment in the Department of Finance, and in 1906 he was appointed clerk of the Kings County Surrogate's Court. He was boss of the Brooklyn Democratic machine from McCarren's death in 1909 until his own death in 1934. Reversing the Anti-Tammany policy of both McLaughlin and McCarren, he co-operated closely with both Murphy and the subsequent bosses of Tammany.

While Connors,[3] the chairman of the state committee, with
Erie County behind him, was working hand in hand with Murphy
in Hearst's behalf, the vast majority of the upstate committee-
men were opposed to Hearst. It needed only two votes from
New York County to produce an anti-Hearst majority in the
committee. These I found in Big Tim Sullivan and in another
committeeman who was my personal friend.[4] Big Tim had
frequently expressed to me his ill feeling to Hearst and to
Murphy and agreed to support my efforts to stop the former's
nomination. The morning before he left for Buffalo and the
convention he came to my house and renewed his offer of support, and as he was leaving said, "Mr. Mayor, if I am in the
meeting of the committee I swear to you, so help me God, I
shall stand behind you to the finish." I felt perfectly satisfied
that I had Sullivan. My other supporter, who owed his first
political office to me,[5] had given me his word that he would
vote in the committee as I directed.

When I reached Buffalo, I was confident that I controlled
a majority of the state committee, and that I should be able to
defeat Hearst's nomination. The first shock that I received was
when I learned that Sullivan had left an hour before my arrival, presumably for Niagara Falls, first giving his proxy to
Murphy. His subsequent excuse was that he had promised to
stand by me in the event that he was at the committee meeting, and that his promise did not include any undertaking to
attend the meeting, nor to refrain from giving Murphy his
proxy. I think that Big Tim was the slickest crook who ever
sold me out.[6] My personal friend gave his proxy to Murphy

3 William J. Connors of the Buffalo *Courier* dominated the upstate Democratic organization, and in return for the help he gave Murphy in securing the
gubernatorial nomination for Hearst he was made chairman of the state Democratic committee.

4 In his manuscript McClellan wrote in, and then crossed out, the name of
Francis Burton Harrison after the words, "my personal friend."

5 This is a reference to Harrison's nomination for Congress.

6 "Just before the New York City primaries [in 1906] there was great doubt
about what Timothy D. Sullivan would do. He controlled perhaps eight assembly districts out of the thirty-five. His strength, added to that of Mayor
McClellan, might control the Tammany delegation against Hearst. Sullivan had
promised to stand with the Mayor. Suddenly one morning in September the
American [Hearst's paper] appeared with an exposure of Sullivan as a keeper
of pool-rooms and a protector of gamblers. He was attacked and cartooned as

LOSING HIS HOLD ON TIGE.

—*The New York Evening Mail, March 21, 1907*

and then shut himself up in his room at the hotel and remained barricaded until after the committee had adjourned.

The loss of these two votes lost me the control of the committee. Murphy then proceeded to make up the temporary roll so as to give Hearst a majority by unseating enough anti-Hearst delegates and substituting in their places contesting delegations, which he controlled. I persuaded William Travers Jerome to allow his name to be used against Hearst, and his action in agreeing was very public spirited, for there was not the slightest possibility of his nomination. Hearst was nominated with Lewis S. Chanler as his running mate for lieutenant governor.[7]

On reaching New York I announced that I would not support Hearst and that I should support Hughes.[8] I organized an independent Democratic movement in Hughes's behalf and raised $75,000 for his cause. Hughes was elected by a comfortable majority.

The following autumn I determined to enter the primaries for the purpose of seeing what could be done against Murphy within the organization. I contested sixteen districts and carried twelve. Within a fortnight Murphy had taken nine of my leaders away from me. The case of one who had carried an upper West Side district was typical. He came to me and said, "Mr. Mayor, I will stay with you if you will appoint me park commissioner. The Commissioner (Murphy) has offered me a good job under Ahearn if I leave you, but I will stick for the park commissionership." I answered that I could not misuse my power of appointment in that way, and he promptly went over to Murphy.

---

the dirtiest 'crook' in the city. Then there was silence. Sullivan had been bludgeoned into supporting Murphy." (*Outlook*, 84 [October 20, 1906], 403.)

7 Although Hearst was defeated in the ensuing election by Charles Evans Hughes, Chanler was elected lieutenant governor. In 1908, Chanler was the Democratic candidate for governor and was defeated by Hughes.

8 McClellan is not altogether frank at this point. On the day that Hearst was nominated, McClellan said: "The Democratic State convention has nominated a ticket. I am a Democrat and of course I accept its action." (New York *Post*, September 27, 1906.) But on arriving in New York the next day, he changed his mind and stated: "As I said yesterday, I am a Democrat. . . . But as a Democrat and as Mayor of this town, I am unalterably opposed to Charles F. Murphy and to everything he stands for. I recognize the humiliation that I must endure, in common with other Democrats. Nevertheless, I will vote the ticket of my party in this State, but never for William R. Hearst. Him I will not vote for." (New York *Sun*, September 28, 1906.)

The truth of the matter is that the game of municipal politics is not one that a self-respecting man can play with success under present conditions. Until more of the right kind of men and women enter municipal politics, the better type of men, especially in the congested districts, will continue to have but little chance against more unscrupulous opponents.

Of the three leaders [9] who remained loyal to me Keenan was city chamberlain. He resigned his leadership and the Executive Committee filled his place with one of Murphy's supporters. Featherson declined any office.[10] Later, on Keenan's resignation,[11] I put James J. Martin [12] in his place as city chamberlain. As I had given up any hope of shaking Murphy's control of the Executive Committee I did not object to his resigning his leadership. Martin was one of the best officials who served under me and made of the chamberlainship, until then a sinecure, a very important position in the city government.

Before I left office, Conners came to me and said that he and I between us controlled the state committee and that, if I would support him in his chairmanship, he would support me for the governorship in 1912. I agreed and when I left for Europe at the end of my term, I left my cause in the hands of my friend John Bensel, with the belief that I had an excellent chance for the nomination. Before I sailed Murphy met me and proposed that I should throw Connors over and join him

[9] The three leaders to whom McClellan is referring were Francis J. Lantry, Patrick Keenan, and Maurice Featherson. Lantry served successively as commissioner of corrections and fire commissioner; Keenan, as McClellan states, was city chamberlain; and Featherson, as McClellan indicates below, held no job in the second administration.

[10] The relationship between the two men was somewhat more complicated than McClellan indicates. Featherson, who had originally been a protégé of Croker and had served in the state Senate for five years, was dock commissioner in McClellan's first administration. Because of a misunderstanding, he was not reappointed for the second term, but when McClellan found out that Featherson opposed Murphy, he offered the district leader a job as tax commissioner, which Featherson refused.

[11] McClellan is mistaken, for Keenan did not resign, but died.

[12] Martin was an old Tammany stalwart, who broke with the organization and Murphy when he was appointed by McClellan. He got his start in politics under Honest John Kelly, held several city jobs before being named police commissioner in 1889, was chairman of the Tammany Executive Committee (1892-98) and a Tammany district leader (1882-1907). His appointment by McClellan was generally interpreted as an anti-Murphy move. See New York *Herald*, July 14, 1907.

in supporting "some high class fellah like John A. Dix," of Kingston, for the place. I told him that I had agreed to stand by Connors and could under no circumstances break my word.

Just after reaching Buffalo for the convention of 1906, a rather pompous man of about forty came to see me with a letter of introduction from Alton B. Parker. The judge said that the bearer, John A. Dix, of Kingston, was the chairman of the Ulster County delegation and was also authorized to vote the delegates from Columbia County, or some sixteen more or less in all. The judge said that he had directed Dix to take his orders from me. Having read the letter, I said, "Mr. Dix, we have decided to support Jerome for the nomination for governor, so please vote your delegates for him." Dix enthusiastically agreed. When the roll was called he voted his sixteen delegates for John A. Dix for governor. It was his first appearance in the limelight; Murphy seemed much impressed by him. Why, did not appear, for Dix was a very dull man who always, in the words of politics, "put up a hell of a front." When Connors finally disappeared, Murphy put Dix in his place and the next year made him governor.

As governor, Dix was far from a success. He was utterly subservient to Murphy and only achieved fame by designing for himself as chief of the National Guard a uniform of much gorgeousness which he wore on state occasions until laughed out of it by a disrespectful press. During the close of his term I made the dedicatory speech at the unveiling of the Civil War monument at Albany. Dix was there, and before the ceremonies began said to me, "I don't know why Murphy went back on me and nominated Sulzer for governor. I have always done what Murphy wanted. He never gave me an order that I did not promptly and cheerfully obey." And Dix was governor of New York.

After leaving the governorship Dix, who was in the lumber business, went into bankruptcy. He died a few years later in the enjoyment of a $2,500 job that Woodrow Wilson had given him.

During my absence abroad Murphy began an attack on Connors who became demoralized and without in any way consulting me resigned his chairmanship, and Bensel had gone over to Murphy,[13] who nominated him for state engineer. When I returned I found that my house of cards had collapsed.

From the time that I had taken the mayoralty the borough presidents had caused me a great deal of anxiety. In my second term, with the exception of George Cromwell of Richmond, who was above criticism, all impressed me with being at least incompetent. I therefore determined to investigate their offices and, if the facts disclosed warranted that course, to prefer charges against them to the governor. The instrument of investigation that I selected was the office of the commissioners of accounts. My two commissioners, [John C.] Hertel and [George] Von Skal, were good accountants, but nothing more, and I needed someone who could make a real investigation. I sought a young, able, and ambitious man with his reputation to make and who was absolutely incorruptible. Ellison, then corporation counsel, suggested the name of John Purroy Mitchel, the nephew of Harry Purroy who had been county clerk when I had been president of the Board of Aldermen. I sent for Mitchel and at once liked him. I asked my two commissioners to resign, consoling them with condemnation commissionerships and appointed Mitchel to serve alone.

Mitchel began his investigation with the office of the president of the Bronx, Lewis Haffen, and soon developed a condition of affairs that warranted my directing him to prefer charges to the governor on my behalf. Manhattan followed with the same result. When Mitchel turned his attention to Queens, he unearthed a condition of corruption so scandalous that [Joseph] Bermel, the president, did not wait for the conclusion of the investigation but resigned and fled to Europe.

Charges were preferred against Haffen in the Bronx, Ahearn in Manhattan, and Coler in Brooklyn. Governor Hughes very promptly removed Haffen and Ahearn but never acted on the charges against Coler, who remained in office until the end of his term. As soon as the governor had removed Ahearn, Murphy caused the aldermen from Manhattan to re-elect him.

---

13 Bensel's defection should not have come as a complete surprise to McClellan. When Bensel was named commissioner of docks and ferries at the beginning of McClellan's second administration, the New York *Tribune* (December 31, 1905) stated that he had been closely associated with Murphy in the past and would remain so in the future.

I brought *quo warranto* proceedings, and the Court of Appeals held that he was ineligible for re-election.

Mitchel did his work extremely well, for he had all the elements that go to make a good prosecutor. He would have made an excellent district attorney, far better than he made mayor. His point of view was entirely that of a prosecutor, for he lacked fairness and could not see both sides of a question.

There was a citizens' organization called the Bureau of Municipal Research of which an able and agreeable young man, named Henry Bruère,[14] was the head. Its purpose was the uncovering of graft in the city government. I could have made of it a very disagreeable enemy but preferred to keep its good will and use it to help Mitchel in his work. One day Bruère came to me and said that he strongly suspected that one of the city departments [15] was honeycombed with graft and that he would like to investigate it. I told him to go ahead, that the books of the department and the staff of the commissioner of accounts were at his service. Some months later Bruère and Mitchel came to me and announced that the investigation of the department was completed. Mitchel said, "Mr. Mayor, we have very bad news for you." I was terribly shocked. "What's wrong?" I asked. "That's just the trouble," replied Mitchel. "There's nothing wrong."

That was Mitchel's weakness, as it is the weakness of most so-called reformers. He was always looking for corruption, always suspecting officials of being grafters.[16] Later in life he modified his point of view, but he never quite lived down his suspicion of his fellow men. . . .

During my day, and I doubt if conditions have changed very much since, New York possessed an enormous number of citizens' organizations. Some of these were purely local in their

[14] Bruère, a former social worker, was a founder of the Bureau of Municipal Research. McClellan made him a member of a subcommittee in 1908, and he was city chamberlain from 1914 to 1916.

[15] The department in question was the Department of Water Supply, Gas and Electricity.

[16] "John Purroy Mitchel . . . was empowered to go into any office in the name of efficiency and he was supposed to do this without publicity. Mitchel, however, got into things rather rashly and stirred up quite a bit of trouble. McClellan used to call him 'John Torquemada Mitchel.' McClellan never knew when Mitchel would turn over another stone with a lot of bugs under it." (Purdy, "Reminiscences," 23.)

purposes and were called Taxpayers Alliances, Protective Associations and the like, and existed to get from the city government every possible improvement and favor for their immediate locality. The most successful of these was the Flatbush organization that, under the extremely efficient management of its secretary, so constantly bombarded the administration that sooner or later it usually obtained what it wanted. There were many trade and business associations like the Merchants Association of Brooklyn, the Board of Trade and Transportation, and the Underwriters' Association, which in season and out of season clamored for favors in behalf of their members.

Besides these various organizations that knew exactly what they wanted, there were a great number of so-called reform associations. A few of these, like that of which Henry Bruère was the head, served a useful purpose, but most of them had only a hazy notion of what they were after and were absolutely unmitigated nuisances. Most of them were organized in very much the same way. Some enterprising young man who needed a job interested a few men and women with money to work in some cause that he had devised. An association was organized, money was subscribed, and the young man elected secretary with an adequate salary. The "cause" was then exploited as loudly and as widely as the secretary's push and lungs permitted. After a while the subscribers lost interest, the "cause" languished, and the association died. The secretary disappeared for a time only to reappear pushing a new "cause" with the same vigor as before.

There were societies whose purpose was to obtain increased salaries for the schoolteachers and for the employees in the Health Department, for the planting of kitchen gardens in vacant lots, and for the distribution of flowering plants in the windows of tenement houses. This latter soon died when it was pointed out to its secretary that his very laudable purpose was in violation of the fire law. Another society, of which a very charming and good-looking lady was the head, required its members to walk the streets noting in memorandum books, provided for the purpose, the location of all ash cans they saw which had not been emptied by ten o'clock in the morning. Every Monday this lady insisted on seeing me personally and submitting to me her report for the week. Fortunately for my peace of mind this society only lived through one winter.

Every public hearing that I held was attended by the representatives of some of these various societies, and the secretaries of taxpayers' associations, citizens' alliances, and reform organizations always insisted on being heard. Then there were stray citizens who represented no one in particular except themselves who demanded speech on nearly everything that came before me. Dudley Field Malone [17] began his brilliant oratorical career by bringing me a letter from the Cardinal who said that his "young friend" who had just left college wanted practice in public speaking and would I recognize him as often as possible at public hearings. I gladly complied with His Eminence's request, for Malone spoke very well and furnished a pleasant interlude to the dreary flood of oratory I was obliged to endure.

Another inveterate speaker at public hearings who was the antithesis of Malone was Redfield,[18] afterwards, for some unknown reason, Secretary of Commerce under Wilson. He never missed a hearing and never failed to subtract from the sum of human knowledge. If, for any reason, he did not have an opportunity to speak, he would come to me afterwards and ask me to tell the reporters that he had been present. One day I was obliged to call him to order, whereupon he said, "I shall never appear before you again." I thanked him warmly, and to my great happiness he kept his word.

The presence of self-advertisers at public hearings so greatly hampered the work of those who were there seriously to discuss the merits or demerits of the questions at issue, besides wasting my valuable time, that I was obliged to curb and limit their ardor. With one accord they protested that I was depriving them of the right of free speech, but as I had the enthusiastic support of the unfortunate reporters who, like myself, were

[17] Malone was made a city attorney by McClellan in 1909. In subsequent years he served as collector of the Port of New York under Wilson, was associated with Clarence Darrow for the defense in the evolution trial in Dayton, Tennessee, and was an outspoken advocate of both women's suffrage and the repeal of the prohibition amendment.

[18] In addition to serving as Wilson's Secretary of Commerce (1913-1919), William C. Redfield was commissioner of public works of the Borough of Brooklyn (1902-03) and a member of Congress (1911-13).

obliged to listen to them, they received very little sympathy from the press.

During the winter of 1908 the legislature sent to New York a joint committee to investigate my administration.[19] Before I went on the stand the counsel of the committee came to my office and told me not to worry as the committee would not ask me trick questions. I thanked him and went on the stand. I soon found that no member of the committee had the slightest knowledge of the charter and that counsel had little more knowledge of it than had the committee. As soon as I had developed this fact I turned to the chairman and said, "As you gentlemen don't seem to know very much of the government of the city, it may be well for me to tell you something about it." I then lectured them for the rest of the day on the charter and on the history of my administration, all of which I had at my finger tips. I was never recalled and the committee turned its attention to the presidents of the boroughs. The committee never made a report.[20] It was created for partisan purposes but I successfully spiked its guns. . . .

Commissioner Bingham gave me more trouble than any man who served under me. He was utterly tactless and arrogant. Without the slightest conception of loyalty to me, he played for his own hand all the time. I found out later that he had ambitions to be nominated for mayor on the Republican ticket, which accounted for many of his apparent eccentricities. He assumed that every Democrat was a crook,[21] and that every Republican a saint, which made a difficult situation for his Democratic chief. He was always getting himself and incidentally me into hot water, and I spent much time that might have been more profitably employed in getting him out again. I gave him a perfectly free hand, not only in the appointment

[19] The committee examined the way in which the various city departments spent the money entrusted to them.

[20] McClellan is mistaken, for the committee did make a report, and his testimony before it can be found in the report. See *Report of the Joint Committee of the Senate and Assembly of the State of New York Appointed to Investigate the Finances of the City of New York. March 1, 1909* (Albany, 1909), 1855-1914.

[21] Bingham's assumption may not have been altogether untenable, for on one occasion he wrote McClellan: "I hardly dare breathe it, but we have had several applications in person and by letters from people who apply direct to learn 'whom to pay.' It would be funny if it were not so serious." (Theodore Bingham to McClellan, November 29, 1908, McClellan MSS.)

of his deputies, but also in the promotion of the members of the uniformed force, and stood behind him loyally to the end. He had the press with him in the beginning, for he was "good copy," as is always any official who bangs his desk and swears a great deal, until the public tires of him. This the public did when Bingham made the utterly ridiculous and unsupported charge that three-quarters of all the convicted criminals in New York were Jews. The storm of indignation that followed this outburst of injustice resulted in a widespread demand for his removal on the ground that no one who was so reckless in his statements was fit to command the police. I should have been well advised had I removed him then. Instead, I stood by him, after I had induced him to issue a complete retraction and apology, which I followed by the public expression of my sincere regret that so erroneous and cruel a charge should have been made by anyone under me.

I had hoped that I could complete my term without changing police commissioners. Six months before leaving office, however, events occurred that disappointed me. In June, 1909, I received a letter from Judge Gaynor, who afterwards succeeded me as mayor, in which he told me that the police were "framing" a boy, named George B. Duffy,[22] who drove the milk wagon that served the judge's home. I referred the letter to the Police Department and received a reply which, while denouncing the boy as a degenerate and a burglar, at the same time reflected severely on Judge Gaynor's moral character.

The reply was so unsatisfactory and Judge Gaynor's letter so specific that I determined to investigate the matter, acting in my capacity as magistrate, a procedure which had not been followed for many years. My investigation not only proved the boy's entire innocence of the police charges, but also, that to protect certain members of the force who had begun the "frame up," witnesses had been suborned and when subpoenaed by me, spirited out of the state, and that members of the

[22] Gaynor's complaint was that Duffy had been arrested on several occasions by the police, but had never been convicted. The police, moreover, had photographed him and taken his measurements. Gaynor maintained that, as Duffy was innocent, both his picture and measurements should be removed from the police files. See *Outlook*, 92 (July 10, 1909), 574; McClellan to William J. Gaynor, June 2, 1909, McClellan Scrapbooks, 1909, New York Historical Society.

uniformed force, even of high rank, had not hesitated to do everything in their power to defeat the ends of justice.

The investigation very seriously implicated an inspector and a captain of police, as well as one of the deputy commissioners and the commissioner's own secretary. While I did not have sufficient evidence to ensure the success of a criminal prosecution, it was obvious that the men implicated were unfit to hold their jobs. I ordered the commissioner to remove the deputy and his secretary, to reduce the inspector to the rank of captain, and to banish the latter and the captain involved to the back of the beyond.

Commissioner Bingham was apparently unaware of what had been going on in his own office and was unwilling to believe any ill of either his deputy or his secretary, who were his intimate friends. As he flatly refused to obey my order, there was nothing for me to do but to remove him from office for insubordination, and I removed him.[23] He afterwards published a series of abusive articles about me, predicated on notes that he had made of confidential conversations we had held, articles which I am sure he must have subsequently regretted.[24]

I appointed [William F.] Baker,[25] the first deputy commissioner, in Bingham's place, and promoted [Frederick H.] Bugher to be first deputy, as Arthur Woods, the second

23 For McClellan's reasons for Bingham's dismissal, see McClellan to the police commissioner, McClellan Scrapbooks, 1909, New York Historical Society.

At the end of McClellan's administration, the *Times* (December 31, 1909) stated that he was "criticized more severely for the removal of Commissioner Bingham than for any other act of his Administration." At the time of the dismissal, newspapers of almost every shade of political opinion interpreted it as a surrender by McClellan to Tammany. See July 2, 1909, issues of the New York *American, Evening Post, Sun, Tribune,* and *World.* The charge, however, was groundless, and some months later the *World* (December 31, 1909) wrote that the Police Department was in better condition after Bingham's dismissal than before it.

24 The articles by Bingham to which McClellan is referring are: "New York Police in Politics," *Century,* 78 (September, 1909), 725-728; "General Bingham's Revelations," *Outlook,* 92 (August 28, 1909), 959-960; "Why I was Removed," *Van Norden's Magazine,* VI (October, 1909), 19-28.

25 "Into General Bingham's place the Mayor has put a Mr. Baker, formerly a Deputy Commissioner, . . . a man of no force or initiative. . . . He is now dutifully doing what the Mayor has bidden him to do. The fact is that Mayor McClellan himself is virtually Police Commissioner, and the man who is nominally at the head of the police is his clerk." (*Outlook,* 92 [July 17, 1909], 617-618.)

deputy,[26] to whom I first offered the promotion preferred to resign. For the rest of my term of office the Police Department ran smoothly and well and gave me less trouble than it had at any time that I was mayor.

The case of Judge Gaynor's protégé has made me often wonder how many innocent people are "framed" by the police. I had a very interesting proof of the efficiency of the police "system" when one day Inspector [Thomas J.] Kelly told me that the private telephone wire between my office and that of the police commissioner was being "tapped" and that he had recently learned it had been tapped ever since I had had it installed. He offered to bring me a transcript of any conversation I might have with the commissioner within ten minutes of its conclusion, and forthwith did so. I sent for the telephone people and submitted the case to them, whereupon they installed another private wire, but whether it was tap-proof or not, I had no way of knowing.

The origin of the so-called "third degree" in the administration of criminal justice may be traced directly to the late Superintendent Thomas J. Byrnes when he was inspector in charge of the Detective Bureau of the New York Police Department. He was a very large and powerful brute of a man who had earned in his youth the reputation of being one of the best "scrappers" on the force. His methods were exceedingly direct and ruthless. It must be remembered that under the New York law a suspect may after arrest be kept at police headquarters for forty-eight hours before arraignment. It is perfectly true that he has the right immediately to demand counsel, but if, as is usually the case, he is a member of the underworld, or a friendless and homeless mendicant, he is either unaware of his right or it is calmly ignored by the police. In other words, for two days he lies incommunicado, at the mercy of headquarters. Byrnes usually kept his victim in the "cells" for twenty-four hours, with nothing to read and very little to eat. He was then brought before the inspector whom he found writing at his desk. After keeping him waiting until he became intensely nervous Byrnes would rise, walk up to him, and knock him down. He would then be lifted to his feet and Byrnes would

---

[26] McClellan is mistaken, for at the time Woods was fourth deputy commissioner, and Bugher was second deputy commissioner.

again knock him down. This process would be repeated until the prisoner had become thoroughly demoralized when Byrnes would charge him with having committed the crime for which he had been arrested. If the prisoner confessed well and good; if not, the knocking down would begin again until the prisoner either confessed or was carried unconscious back to the cells. . . .

During my last six months as mayor I was practically my own police commissioner, running the department through Commissioner Baker and Inspector Kelly as my two assistants.

Except the mayoralty there is no more difficult public office in the United States to fill satisfactorily than that of police commissioner of New York. As commissioner the average outsider finds it almost impossible to know what is going on about him and under him, while the army officer is almost incapable of success because of his professional training and point of view. He is inclined to sacrifice the essentials of police work for the non-essentials. . . .

The Hudson-Fulton celebration was held in the autumn of 1909. The legislature created a commission to be appointed half by the governor and half by the mayor. Governor White appointed General Stewart L. Woodford as chairman, and I appointed Herman Ridder, chairman of the executive committee. Woodford was a fussy old gentleman who had been our minister to Spain at the outbreak of the war in 1898. He was quite incompetent, but as Ridder, the owner of the *Staats-Zeitung,* was an extremely able man and the executive committee did all the work, the celebration was a tremendous success. It was held in September and was really my farewell to public life. On September 28, I marched at the head of the procession from 112th Street to Washington Square and received an ovation all along the route. The people knew that they were saying goodby to me, and they said it with so hearty a good will as to almost make me wish that the end had not come. It was a good example of the mutability of the New York public. Only a year before I had been mobbed and stoned while driving through the lower East Side, a Hearst stronghold. In a year the same people who had hissed me gathered to cheer. The people did their best to show me that they were with me, and it was really a splendid goodby.

Will the time ever come when the mayoralty of New York

is a steppingstone to other offices? Thus far it has proved the graveyard of political ambitions.[27] Of the mayors who have been elected, since the office became elective in 1834, only one has gone further, John T. Hoffman,[28] whom Tweed made governor in return for faithful service to the ring. All the rest of us have entered the office with the conviction that we would prove exceptions to the rule, and none of us ever has.

The mayor stands constantly in the spotlight at the front and center of the stage. He has absolutely no privacy, his every act being public property, almost before he performs it. Under the most favorable circumstances, our people soon tire of an elected public official. Our mayors are so constantly discussed, so constantly in the public eye that they very soon outlive their popularity. Besides, a mayor, be he ever so amiable, is bound to make many enemies. If he has a strict sense of the obligations of his office the number of the enemies he makes becomes enormous. If he is inclined to be complaisant and to play the demagogue, he disgusts the decent people of the community. If, on the other hand, he plays the game as it should be played, he antagonizes the countless hordes of those to whom he has said no.

The power of the mayor is so great and his responsibility for all that goes on in the city so well known that he is held accountable by everyone who has suffered disappointment in dealing with the city government. When one realizes that this includes not only every disappointed office seeker, but also every disappointed contractor, every householder who wants something done or not done, every businessman, big or little, who asks some favor, it is really remarkable that four mayors of greater New York, McClellan, Hylan, Walker, and La Guardia, should have been re-elected to a second term.

During my last year in office, I was approached by several

27 "Mayor McClellan writes that he retires to private life at peace with all the world. We fear that all the world will say that this is because no one thinks him important enough to fight. . . . The great moral of it is the fatal blight which Tammany puts upon the fairest fruit. It is an old saying that the New York Mayoralty is the graveyard of political reputations. It cannot fail to be so when the Mayor chooses the Tammany boss as grave-digger, and assists at his own interment." (New York *Evening Post*, December 31, 1909.)

28 Hoffman was elected governor in 1868. His victory was achieved by Tammany casting more fraudulent votes than have been cast in any other election in the state's or city's history.

men acting for Murphy with the suggestion that an arrangement might be made with the boss, whereby he would be willing to nominate me for a third term. I knew that no such arrangement could be made except at the cost of my self-respect, and, therefore, declined to discuss the matter. Even had there been a certainty of another renomination, I should have refused it, for I had given the city my best for six years and I had had enough of the mayoralty. I felt that I could retire from office with the satisfaction of having run for office eight times and of having never been defeated.

So that there might be no mistake in the matter I announced early under no circumstances would I be a candidate again. Murphy nominated Judge Gaynor as the Tammany candidate while a fusion ticket was put in the field with Hearst at the head and J. P. Mitchel for president of the Board of Aldermen and Prendergast,[29] a Brooklyn Republican, for comptroller. With the exception of Hearst the entire fusion ticket was elected.

Gaynor was a most peculiar and eccentric man, who had the knack of writing rather clever and very insulting letters, with which he terrorized his correspondents, for he always gave his letters to the press and the press will always print anything insulting from or to a public official on the ground that it is news.

One night, during the campaign, Gaynor stated in a speech that R. Fulton Cutting [30] and I had entered into a corrupt bargain under which in return for Cutting's support, during my second campaign for mayor, I had bought for the city certain dock property in South Brooklyn owned by him, for which I had paid him three times its assessed value. Thinking that he had been misinformed I sent Crowell to see him to explain the facts, and to request him to withdraw his charges. The

29 William A. Prendergast, at the time of his nomination for comptroller, was the register of Kings County. He served as comptroller from 1910 to 1917.

30 Cutting, who is mentioned by McClellan in Chapter X as the head of the Society for Improving the Condition of the Poor, was a financier, civic reformer, and philanthropist. He was the founder and first chairman of the Citizens' Union and was the principal sponsor of Seth Low's candidacy for mayor in 1901. According to Lawson Purdy, who knew Cutting well, "Cutting led the Citizens' Union to back McClellan for a second term and this ended the political efficiency of the Citizens' Union." (Purdy, "Reminiscences," 46-47.)

facts were that I had bought for the city the property in question from Mrs. Bayard Cutting, Fulton Cutting's sister-in-law, at much less than its assessed value as she wanted the money for reinvestment. The city bought a great bargain, and Fulton Cutting had nothing to do with the transaction.

I waited two days, and as Gaynor did not retract I wrote him stating the facts and suggesting that he publicly withdraw his charges. As he still remained silent, I again wrote him and told him that if he did not withdraw and apologize during the speech he was to make that night I should explain the facts and denounce him as a liar from the platform of the Republican candidate, besides suing him for libel and going before the grand jury in the effort to have him indicted for criminal libel. That night Gaynor at the beginning of his speech said, "I want to withdraw my charges against Mayor McClellan, in reference to the South Brooklyn dock matter. His conduct throughout was that of a perfectly honest man, there was absolutely nothing even questionable in anything he did in the proceedings, and I hereby apologize to him for anything I may have said to the contrary, and deeply regret that I said it. As to R. Fulton Cutting, however, I withdraw nothing, and repeat with even greater emphasis every word I said about him." It was difficult to see how Cutting could have been guilty of corruption and not I, but Gaynor had saved himself from a libel suit which was all he cared about. I begged Cutting to sue him for libel, but Cutting preferred to let the matter drop.

I doubt if Gaynor was ever quite normal, certainly not after he was shot at the base of his brain by a lunatic. I was told by an employee of the Harriman Night and Day Bank that about two o'clock one morning a bearded face appeared at his window, and the owner asked him to cash a check for ten dollars. The employee recognized the mayor and cashed the check. Whereupon the mayor, evidently intending to return the courtesy, said, "Wouldn't you like to feel the bullet in my throat? If you will stick your finger into my mouth you will be able to do so." He seemed rather hurt when my informant politely declined to accept his offer.

I was told that during the last months of his life Gaynor was in the habit of appearing at the City Hall at all hours of the night, routing out the night watchman, and sitting for hours in his office with his eyes fixed on vacancy.

The day he took office he said to me that he wanted to speak to me and drawing me aside said, "If there is any favor that you care to ask of me, provided it is a small favor, a really small favor, I will grant it. For example, I will keep in office any minor official, not more than one, whom you may designate." I told him that I had absolutely no favor to ask of him. Within a week he had removed every personal friend whom I had appointed to office, who was removable.

When he died [in 1913], Seth Low and I, as the two surviving ex-mayors, were invited to march at the head of the funeral procession as chief mourners. The services were held at Trinity Church, although Gaynor was apparently an agnostic, having in early life been a member of the Catholic order of Christian Brothers and having apostatized, he never adhered to any other church. As we marched down Broadway, Low asked me if I had liked Gaynor and on my answering that I had not, said that he had had "no use for him." He then asked me if I thought Gaynor honest, and on my replying that I did not know him well enough to say, continued, "I am perfectly sure that he was not honest. Yes, perfectly sure." He failed to explain whether he meant "money honest" or morally honest, and I trust that he meant the latter.

It was to this equivocal person that I turned over the city government on January 1, 1910. I made him a little speech welcoming him to office and wishing him success, to which he replied, utterly ignoring me and my administration.

Frank Polk was there waiting for me, and together we went to the Lafayette-Brevoort Hotel for lunch. No one else offered to go with me, except my office staff; no one else was at the City Hall to say goodby. I was a dead cock in the pit and no longer of any public interest.

And so ended my mayoralty. I had given to the office all that I had to give, mentally and physically, and for it I had sacrificed any political future I might have had. Thanks to the ability and the devotion of the men who had served under me, my administration was a success, and I am not praising myself, but only doing them simple justice when I say that New York has never had a better. When I think that had I not been mayor I should, in all probability, have spent my life in the House of Representatives, I am consoled by the thought that, thanks to the help of those who worked with me, I was able to leave the city which I served with all my heart and soul a little better than I found her.

Chapter XIV

A Very Pleasant Resting Place

We sailed for Europe, on the *Adriatic* on January 10th, 1910. The Frank Polks, the John P. Mitchels, Dr. Branan, Tom Hassett, and Swann [1] saw us off. The only official notice taken of my departure was by two of the Staten Island ferryboats that I had built, both of which dipped their colors and blew whistles as we passed them.

We returned the following autumn to spend the winter in a little house in Princeton on a street that I had induced the Borough Council to name Cleveland Lane. It was a house that Richard Stockton [2] had built according to our plans three years before and that we rented from him as annual tenants.

I opened a law office in New York in company with Eugene Lamb Richards [3] and Philip J. McCook, . . . a Supreme Court justice [from 1920 to 1943]. I soon found, however, that the law was not for me. I had never really practiced but, nevertheless, knew almost as much of municipal law as there was to know. Under ordinary circumstances I should have been able to build up a good practice in representing clients who had litigation with the city. Unfortunately for my hopes Murphy decreed that I was to be blacklisted by his judges, and no one dared to retain me to appear before them. Besides this, Richards told me one day that his association with me was

---

[1] Benjamin Swann was a clerk in the mayor's office throughout McClellan's two terms.

[2] Stockton was a former diplomat who was a New York stockbroker when McClellan knew him at Princeton. He had homes in both New York City and Princeton.

[3] Richards, a Democrat, had been one of McClellan's attorneys in the recount fight against Hearst.

305

hurting him politically with Murphy. Inasmuch as I had given Richards the most important case he had ever had in retaining him to defend me in the recount suit, and afterwards made him Democratic leader of Richmond County, inasmuch, in other words, as he owed any political standing that he had entirely to me, I thought that he might have spared me the remark.

I took his hint and did not renew my lease when it expired. After a year's trial I concluded that there was no use of trying to drum up a practice. The future for useful work seemed very dark. I was at the top of my form, only forty-five years old, in perfect health and with unbounded energy, and yet I could find nothing to do. No one offered me a job and I did not know where to turn. When I had reached a point of real discouragement my old friend James J. Martin, who had been my chamberlain, came to the rescue.

Grover Cleveland had held the Stafford Little Lectureship of Public Affairs at Princeton, which had been founded for him by his admirer Stafford Little, for many years clerk of the New Jersey Court of Errors and Appeal. On Mr. Cleveland's death the Princeton trustees had appointed me to the vacancy. The salary was only $700 and the work required was only two lectures a year; nevertheless, it gave me an official standing in the university. During my last two years as mayor I had lectured at Princeton with considerable success and had greatly enjoyed doing so.

Martin asked me if I would care to accept a professorship at Princeton if one were endowed for me. I told him that I would like nothing better, as, regardless of salary, I was most anxious to have some active work. Whereupon the loyal fellow started out singlehanded to raise the endowment, and before the year was out had collected $52,000. He told me afterwards the story of his adventures, and some of them were very amusing. They convinced me of the truth of the old saying that "gratitude is a lively expression of the hope of favors yet to come." On the other hand, men whom I did not know and who were under no possible obligation to me subscribed generously.

Before beginning the collection of the endowment, Mar-

tin had had an understanding with Woodrow Wilson and
Moses Taylor Pyne [4] of the Princeton trustees, the heads of
the two rival factions in the board,[5] that the money would be
accepted and that I would be appointed to fill the chair. On
Wilson's resignation Martin had a satisfactory interview with
Dean Fine,[6] the acting president. After the money had been
collected and paid in, Dean Fine reversed himself and denied
that he had ever agreed to my appointment. Martin told Fine
what his opinion was of a man who would repudiate a formal
agreement, and Fine at length compromised and permitted my
election as a "university lecturer." Hibben [7] went to Wilson
and asked him to bring Fine into line with the agreement that
Wilson had made with Martin when he, Wilson, had been
president of Princeton. Wilson replied that he had no influence
over Fine.

The next year, 1911, after Hibben had become president,[8]
I was elected professor of economic history on the endowment
that Martin had raised and began twenty very happy years of
work with the undergraduates. I can never be grateful enough
to Martin for what he did. I was very much down on my luck,

[4] Pyne was a lawyer and director of various corporations. He became a
Princeton trustee in 1885 and remained on the board until his death in 1921.

[5] Pyne and Wilson were old and close friends when the latter became president of Princeton in 1902. They remained so until 1907, when Wilson began
to push his plan for the abolition of the undergraduate clubs and the construction of "quadrangles" for housing the students. Pyne opposed Wilson's program
and became his leading opponent on the Board of Trustees. The rift between
the two men was further widened in the dispute over the new Graduate College.
Wilson wanted the Graduate College located in the midst of the university and
did not want it controlled by Dean Andrew West. Pyne sided with West, who
wanted the Graduate College located on a near-by golf course. Wilson was re-
soundingly defeated on both the quadrangle and Graduate College proposals.
See Arthur S. Link, *Wilson: The Road to the White House* (Princeton, 1947),
45-91.

[6] Richard B. Fine joined the Princeton Department of Mathematics in 1885,
was made dean of the faculty by Wilson in 1903, was among Wilson's supporters
among the faculty in the bitter fights that raged at Princeton, and became dean
of the scientific departments in 1909. During the period referred to by McClellan, John A. Stewart, the senior member of the Board of Trustees, was nominally
the acting president of the university, but Fine was acting president in everything but name.

[7] A former minister, John G. Hibben joined the Princeton faculty as an instructor in logic in 1891, was made professor in 1907, and succeeded Wilson as
president of the university in 1912.

[8] McClellan is confused in his chronology, for Hibben became president of
Princeton in 1912.

and thanks to him I found myself in congenial surroundings with useful and congenial work to do.

Before the great war Princeton was a far more agreeable place of residence than afterwards. In our visits there we had kept very free from "entangling alliances" and had friends both among Wilson's supporters and his enemies, the latter of whom were in a large majority in the faculty. Dean West [9] was in his prime, a very charming, brilliant, and able man, a delightful friend, but a ruthless enemy. The van Dyke brothers, Henry and Paul,[10] were at their best, the Clevelands, the Junius Morgans,[11] the Marquands,[12] and the Pynes, kept hospitable and agreeable open house. Among my colleagues in the faculty Thompson,[13] Phillips,[14] and McClure [15] had been undergraduates with me, while Veblen, Abbott, Foster, Kennedy, Prentice, Vreeland, Philip Brown, Priest, and Myers [16] were very agreeable friends, and although younger than I, were near enough my age to furnish me equal opponents at tennis of which I played a great deal.

As soon as we returned to Princeton in the autumn of 1910 we began our house on Battle Road, into which we moved on October 30, 1911, and in which we lived very happily for thirteen years.

Spending the weekends at Princeton, I became intimate with Grover Cleveland and fell into the habit of going to see him

[9] Andrew F. West was a professor of Latin at Princeton and the dean of the university's Graduate School (which did not open until 1913) from 1901 to 1928. When Wilson was president of Princeton, West was his leading opponent on the faculty.

[10] Henry van Dyke was professor of English literature at Princeton from 1900 to 1923, and Paul van Dyke was professor of modern history from 1898 to 1928.

[11] Morgan was the son of J. P. Morgan's sister Sarah. Like his illustrious uncle, he was a banker and a collector of rare books and manuscripts.

[12] Allan Marquand had been a member of the Princeton Archeology Department since 1881.

[13] Henry D. Thompson was professor of mathematics at Princeton.

[14] Alexander H. Phillips was a professor of mineralogy at Princeton.

[15] Charles F. W. McClure was a professor of zoology at Princeton.

[16] The first names and departments of the faculty members mentioned by McClellan follow: Oswald Veblen, Mathematics; Frank F. Abbott, Latin; William Foster, Chemistry; Charles W. Kennedy, English; William K. Prentice, Greek; William U. Vreeland, Romance Languages; Philip M. Brown, International Law; George M. Priest, German; William S. Myers, History and Politics. All these men were at Princeton before the First World War.

every Sunday. Old age sat very gracefully on him, and he became mellowed and softened, very different from the Cleveland
whom I had known years before at Washington. He liked me
and liked to have me with him, I think, because I spoke his
language.

The autumn before we took our cottage we went to Princeton
for a ball game, and dined that night with Paul van Dyke.
Besides our host and ourselves there were only the Clevelands
and Henry van Dyke, Paul's brother. After dinner as we four
men were smoking in the dining room Cleveland told us a
quite banal anecdote, the point of which was that someone had
asked him to do something and that he had refused. Whereupon Henry van Dyke exclaimed, "How like you, Mr. President. How courageous, how splendid!" Paul joined in and
said, "It was magnificent of you, Mr. President. It was heroic
and superb!" Cleveland stood it as long as he could and, when
he could stand it no longer, with great emphasis said, "Oh,
rats!"

Princeton put Cleveland on a pedestal, bowed down, and
worshipped him. He seemed to like it up to a certain point,
after which it bored him, and he was glad to see me and talk
of old friends and old times. One Sunday he said, "I had the
time of my life yesterday. There was a gang of wops out in
the street laying a gas main. They had an Irish foreman whom
I spoke to and found quite a politician. We talked for over
an hour and I hope he comes back again."

When the recount bill was pending at Albany my counsel
thought that it would be wise to have a number of letters from
reputable and prominent men to be read at the hearing before
the acting mayor against the approval of the bill. Alton Parker
suggested that Cleveland be asked to write a letter to be used
for this purpose and saw him about the matter. Cleveland
readily agreed and sent me a very friendly letter arguing
against the recount bill. As I was returning from Princeton
the following Monday I found him on the train. He asked me
if I had received his letter and then said, "Of course, Mac, that
letter is not for publication nor must you show it to anyone."
Exactly what purpose he thought he was accomplishing by
writing the letter I do not know.

On his seventieth birthday I greatly pleased him by sending

a message to the Board of Aldermen on the subject requesting them to call the square at the entrance of the Manhattan Bridge "Cleveland Square," which they promptly did, only to change the name, after I had gone, to Kenmare Square in honor of Little Tim Sullivan's birthplace. Cleveland asked me to give him the original copy of my message, under the impression that I wrote my public papers with my own hand as he had always written his, instead of dictating them. I carefully copied it in my own writing and gave it to him. He had it framed and hung it in his library. It was I think the only official notice of his seventieth birthday taken anywhere in the United States.

The last time that Mr. Cleveland ever spoke in public was at the commencement of the Albany Law School in the spring of 1906. Some time before, he asked me if I would see David B. Hill and try to arrange to have the latter meet him at Albany. "It may be the last chance I shall ever have of seeing him," he said, "and before I die I should like to shake hands with him and make up." Very soon afterwards I saw Hill and told him what Cleveland desired. "No," said Hill, "I won't see him. I don't want ever to see him again, and I won't meet him." Old age sat more gracefully on Cleveland than it did on Hill.

Before he was attacked by his fatal illness he urged me to make up, at least on the surface, with Charley Murphy, who had been striving for some sort of a rapprochement with me. He insisted that with the presidential campaign only two years off there should be at least apparent harmony in New York; that without it, the state would unquestionably go Republican; and that if I did not meet Murphy halfway, I should be responsible. I saw the force of his argument, and much as I disliked to do so I asked Murphy to lunch on March 25, 1908, at the Hardware Club and agreed to fill the existing vacancy in the dock commissionership by the appointment of the chief engineer,[17] at Murphy's "request," and to appoint my friend Nick Hayes fire commissioner, also "at Murphy's request." The rapprochement did not fool anyone, least of all Murphy, but at least I kept my record straight and satisfied Cleveland.

Cleveland's reminiscences were sometimes very interesting.

[17] This is a reference to Allen A. Spooner, who actually was the assistant engineer before his promotion.

To my great regret he demolished the legend that when he had refused to grant a request made to him by Timothy J. Campbell, a notorious Democratic New York congressman, on the ground that it was unconstitutional, Tim had replied, "Ah, Mr. President, what is the Constitution between friends?" He told me the story was absolutely apocryphal.

He minimized the story that when Daniel F. Manning, the chairman of the National Committee during his first campaign for the presidency, had asked him what should be done in reference to the Maria Halpin incident,[18] he had looked Manning sternly in the eye and said, "Tell the truth." He said, "They made a lot of fuss over a very ordinary incident. When Dan asked me what we had better do, I said, 'Oh, hell, Dan, I suppose we had better tell the truth.' Of course, there was nothing else to do. I don't know why people seemed to think that I would tell him to do anything else." I always thought the offhand way that the old man described the most courageous act of his life was very fine.

As he lay adying, just before he lost consciousness for the last time, he said to Mrs. Cleveland, "Frank tell Mac—" but he never told her what to tell me. They were the last words he ever spoke.

At his funeral, as a pallbearer, I marched at the head of the procession from the house to the grave. I took a shovel and threw into the grave the first spadefuls of earth, then handed it to Paul van Dyke, the pallbearer next in line. The grave was filled by his pallbearers, all his dear friends.

I organized a memorial meeting for Cleveland at Carnegie Hall for March 18, 1909, and asked Francis L. Stetson, who had been his law partner, to act as chairman of the committee of arrangements and Murray Butler as chairman of the executive committee. We decided to have the speeches delivered by Taft, the President of the United States, Hughes, the governor, Wilson, the president of Princeton, and myself, as presiding officer and mayor. Stetson went to Princeton to ask Mrs. Cleve-

---

[18] Maria Halpin, a widow, was the mother of a child whose father, she said, was Cleveland. When the report that Cleveland was the father of an illegitimate child began to circulate in the presidential campaign of 1884, he readily conceded that he had had relations with Maria Halpin and that he had assumed financial responsibility for the child. He always maintained, however, that he was not sure that he was the child's father.

land if the arrangements were satisfactory. He returned very crestfallen and reported that Mrs. Cleveland had said that if either Butler or Wilson had anything to do with the meeting neither she nor her children would attend. As both Butler and Wilson had accepted, the situation was extremely awkward. Both, however, were very decent and when told of Mrs. Cleveland's position at once declared themselves out of the picture.

I never knew what Mrs. Cleveland's opposition to Butler was based on. The reason for her enmity to Wilson was however perfectly plain, for her husband and Wilson never liked or trusted each other. Their difference arose from the fight that had been going on for years in the Princeton Board of Trustees, which was sharply divided into two factions, Wilson's supporters and opponents. When Cleveland had first gone to Princeton, he became intimate with the dean of the Graduate College, Andrew Fleming West, Wilson's most bitter enemy, who secured Cleveland's election to the Board of Trustees. The difference was first emphasized in the selection of a site for the new building for the Graduate College. The difference was intensified over Wilson's proposal to inaugurate what was called the "quad system" to divide the university into little colleges somewhat on the system existing at Oxford and Cambridge, a system now in force at Harvard and Yale.[19] The trustees and the faculty made of a matter of administration a great question of morals, and lifelong friendships were broken. To an outsider the whole question seemed merely one of expediency, but Princeton, having lost its sense of values, took it most seriously.

Cleveland told me that a trustee meeting was called for the same day that there was to be an important meeting of the trustees of the New York Life Insurance Company, of which he was one. He called up Wilson and asked him if the question of the site of the new Graduate College building would be brought up at the Princeton trustees meeting, for if so he would attend and not go to New York. Wilson replied that

[19] McClellan has the order of these disputes reversed, for the fight over the "quad system" preceded that over the location of the Graduate College. McClellan, however, does not exaggerate the bitterness engendered by these disputes, although it is probably more correct to attribute the injection of questions of morality to Wilson rather than to the trustees and faculty.

nothing would be done at the meeting in reference to the Graduate College site. Cleveland, not trusting Wilson over-much, asked him to give his word, which Wilson solemnly did. Cleveland went to New York, relying on Wilson's assurance. At the meeting Wilson found that there was a majority of his supporters present, called up the Graduate College site matter and passed it according to his wish. When Cleveland returned and found what had happened, he told Wilson, in no uncertain terms, exactly what he thought of him.

I once asked Wilson for his version of the story. He tapped his forehead with his finger and said, "Poor old Cleveland, poor old man." My impression is that Cleveland's version was correct.

Cleveland never forgave Wilson for having deceived him and never had anything more to do with him. Mrs. Cleveland's objection to having Wilson speak at her husband's memorial meeting was quite understandable.

I never knew Wilson before he became president of Princeton. He had been a favorite of his predecessor, Dr. Patton,[20] who missed his vocation in not entering civil politics instead of becoming a very able church and college politician. Dr. Patton was no executive, although a brilliant man and scholar, and the university went steadily downhill under his management.[21] The trustees determined that his usefulness had ceased, and C. C. Cuyler,[22] one of their number who told me the story, was delegated to invite the president to resign. At first Patton declined the invitation, but when he found the trustees meant business, he agreed to go quietly on certain conditions, which included full salary for life for himself. The conditions having been accepted, the trustees set to work to find a new president. The leading candidates were Professors West and William M. Sloane of the faculty and Dr. Henry

[20] Francis L. Patton, after fifteen years as a pastor, lecturer, and writer for religious journals, joined the faculty of the Princeton Theological Seminary. He was president of Princeton University (1888-1902) and president of Princeton Theological Seminary (1902-13).

[21] For a much more favorable view of Patton as an administrator, see George McL. Harper, "Francis Landley Patton," *Dictionary of American Biography,* XIV (New York, 1934), 315.

[22] Cornelius C. Cuyler was a New York City banker, who was a partner of Junius S. Morgan and a director of several financial institutions.

van Dyke, then pastor of the Presbyterian "Brick Church" in New York.[23]

It was the intention of the trustees to take their time and not make a selection until the end of the year. But they reckoned without their Patton. At the next meeting of the board, without the slightest warning, Patton who was in the chair offered his resignation to take effect at the end of the academic year, declared it accepted, then nominated Woodrow Wilson as his successor, and declared him elected.[24] Before the trustees had recovered from their surprise Patton had sent for Wilson, who was waiting outside, informed him of his election, and received his acceptance. It was a very sharp trick, but the trustees had no business to be caught napping.

Professor Sloane was so much disappointed by his defeat that he soon afterwards accepted a call from Columbia and resigned from Princeton.[25] West on the other hand stayed on and declared a blood feud against Wilson which he waged with only indifferent success [26] until his enemy resigned the presidency of the university.

Wilson was the most self-assured, the most egotistical, and the vainest man I ever knew, and I saw more or less of him while I was mayor. He once said to me, "I am so sorry for those who disagree with me." When I asked why, he replied, "Because I know that they are wrong." In some ways he had a good sense of humor, in others, none at all. He told a funny story well, was a good mimic, but bitterly resented any joke at his own expense. When he was running for governor of New Jersey, the New York *Sun* published one of its delightfully amusing editorials about him, evidently written by that greatest of editorial writers, Edward P. Mitchell.[27] There was nothing

23 McClellan is mistaken in both instances. When Wilson succeeded Patton as president of Princeton, Sloane was a member of the faculty of Columbia University and van Dyke at the time had left the Brick Presbyterian Church and was a member of the Princeton faculty.

24 Although McClellan's account of Patton's resignation is not the official version, it is in general correct. See Link, *Wilson*, 37.

25 Sloane went from Princeton to Columbia in 1896, or six years before Wilson became president of Princeton.

26 This is not altogether accurate, for West defeated Wilson on both the location of the Graduate School and the point that West should control the Graduate School before Wilson resigned. Both were major victories for West.

27 "Edward P. Mitchell, petulant editor of the New York *Sun*, had been the chief antagonist of Wilson's new progressive course since the spring of 1911. He

in the editorial to which anyone with the slightest sense of humor could object. The day it appeared I was going to New York and joined Wilson on the train. I sat down beside him and found him in a towering rage. "Have you seen this outrageous editorial in the *Sun?*" he asked. "It is written by that unspeakable ingrate Jimmy Fadden (the pen name of Edward W. Townsend) [28] who owes his prominence entirely to me." I told him that the editorial bore all the marks of Mr. Mitchell, and then asked him what he had done to bring Townsend into prominence, he having been one of the best known professional humorists in the country for a generation. He answered, "Townsend has been nominated for Congress and would have no chance of election were he not running on the same ticket with me. He thinks that he can safely attack me, but I shall destroy him." Despite Wilson's threat to destroy Townsend, the latter was elected in a normally Republican district and re-elected for a second term.

I could not convince the irate candidate that the editorial was the work of Mitchell and not Townsend. I asked him how he could possibly stand the rough and tumble of political life, if he took a very kindly editorial so much to heart. He said, "I will be fighting my enemies in the open in politics. Since I have been president of Princeton I have been fighting concealed enemies who have masqueraded as my friends."

Wilson could be a most delightful companion, for he possessed the French art of the raconteur to perfection, but if he did not like his audience or think it could be of use to him, which for him was the same thing, he did not take the trouble to be agreeable.

He unquestionably assumed the presidency of Princeton as a steppingstone to the presidency of the United States, and is the only man in history who carried to success a carefully planned and very long campaign from obscurity to the highest office in the land. The first intimation that I had that he had great ambitions was shortly after his health broke down in

was, after all, the spokesman par excellence of the Wall Street, big business, Old Guard Republican line, and that was reason enough for his opposition to the candidate he had once ardently supported." (Link, *Wilson*, 348.)

[28] Townsend, who joined the staff of the *Sun* in 1892, wrote humorous pieces for that paper in what he called a "Bowery dialect." Defeated for Congress in 1908, he was elected in 1910 and 1912.

1908. I wrote him to say goodby as he was sailing for England to recuperate and said in my letter that I regretted that the Democrats had not nominated him for the presidency instead of Bryan. I wrote this simply by way of blague, but Wilson took it seriously and thanked me warmly for my support. Junius Morgan met him that summer in England and told me that Wilson had surprised him by asking if he thought a university president would be justified in resigning to accept a senatorship or governorship. Junius replied that he did not think so, to which Wilson replied, "Suppose that he were offered the nomination for President?" Junius said to me, "George, I really believe that Woodrow has hopes of a presidential nomination."

Not long afterwards St. Clair McKelway, the editor of the Brooklyn *Eagle,* told me that he had had a very peculiar experience with Wilson. He said, "I was writing an editorial trying to prove that the Democrats need not necessarily nominate Bryan. I gave a long list of Democrats of presidential standing, and as Princeton had given me an honorary degree the year before I thought it only polite to include Wilson's name. By the next mail I received a letter from Wilson thanking me for my support for his presidential ambitions and asking me not to go further in the matter before he had had an opportunity to confer with me. Do you know, McClellan, that I think the damned fool thinks that he has a chance for the nomination?"

Wilson thought that I was a coming man in politics and believed that I controlled the New York state committee, which, at the time, I did. He went out of his way to be friendly, had the trustees give me an honorary LL.D. in 1905, came to see me frequently when I was weekending in Princeton, and was as agreeable as possible.

Ex-Senator Jim Smith,[29] of New Jersey, was the man who really brought about Wilson's nomination. Smith, whom I had known in Washington, told me the story. The senator's two boys were undergraduates at Princeton. One day the eldest, who was home for Sunday, told his father that Wilson had sent

---

[29] James Smith, Jr., served in the Senate from 1893 to 1899 and was the most powerful Democratic boss in New Jersey. He was president of a trust company, head of several manufacturing concerns, and a newspaper publisher.

for him and asked him to invite the senator to call the next
time he was in Princeton. The senator, fearing that one of his
boys was in trouble, went to see Wilson the next weekend.
Wilson began the conversation by announcing, "Senator, I
want to be president." Smith, not understanding what Wilson
meant, replied, "But you are already president." "I don't mean
president of Princeton," answered Wilson, "I mean President
of the United States." Naturally Smith was astounded. When
he found that Wilson was in earnest, he said, "This is rather a
surprise. I am a member of the Executive Committee of the
National Committee. It has its next meeting in Chicago next
month, and I will talk over your suggestion with the members."
When he did so, the members of the committee were very much
amused and said, "Why don't you try him out first, run him for
governor or senator and see if he makes a good candidate. If
he does, then come back and talk to us, but don't spring an
utterly unknown man and expect us to take him seriously."

When Smith next saw Wilson he asked him if he would care
to run for governor as a "try out." Wilson replied that if a
try out were necessary he would be willing to run for senator.
Smith broke the news to Wilson that he himself proposed to
try to get back to the Senate and that it was the governorship
or nothing. Wilson reluctantly agreed, and Smith proceeded
with his arrangements to force Wilson's nomination.

After Wilson had been nominated I received a message from
him asking me to come to see him. I had no sooner arrived
. . . than Wilson said to me, "McClellan, I am in a hole, and
I want your advice as to how to get out. Oswald Villard of
the *Post* has agreed to support me if I give him my word that
I have made no deal with Jim Smith. I need the *Post*'s support,
in fact, I must have it. What am I to do?" I answered, "Give
him your word that you have made no deal with Smith. Why
not?" "The trouble is," said Wilson, "that I have made a deal
with Smith. I have promised him to give him a clear field for
the Senate. If I tell that to Villard, I shall lose his support. If
I give Villard my word that I have made no deal with Smith,
Smith may hear of it and I shall lose him. What shall I do?"
I answered, "Of course, there is only one thing for you to do.
You have made a perfectly proper arrangement with Smith,

which you must stick to at all costs to yourself, even if it costs you Villard's support. You can't possibly think for a moment of breaking your word." Wilson looked glum and said, "I am very much disappointed, for I thought that you would help me to get out of the hole I am in. I must, at all costs, have the support of the *Evening Post.*" I was not only surprised but thoroughly disgusted by Wilson's attitude, and as I rose to go I said, "I will give you one piece of advice at any rate. If you determine to sell out Smith, kill him, for if you don't, he will certainly kill you." "Don't worry about that," answered the candidate. "If I sell out Smith, as you express it, I shall certainly kill him."

I assume that Wilson gave Villard the required assurance, for the *Evening Post* swung into line in his support. As soon as Wilson was elected he began the process of killing Smith who had not only nominated him but had loyally supported him and raised $80,000 for his campaign.

This was before the day of the election of senators by popular vote. There was in New Jersey at the time a so-called preferential primary law, which permitted voters, if they saw fit, to express their preference on election day in favor of any one they chose for the office of United States senator. This was in no way legally binding on members of the legislature and had become an absolutely dead letter, no senatorial candidate ever bothering his head about it. At the election at which Wilson was elected governor, some few thousand voters expressed their preference for the election to the Senate of a certain South Jersey politician known as "Farmer Martine."[30] No one else was voted for in the primary,[31] although some hundreds of thousands of votes were cast for the general ticket. . . . After election Wilson announced that as Martine was the unanimous choice of the preferential primary, it was the duty of the legislature to elect him. By the use of his power as governor, Wilson persuaded a majority of the legislature to vote for

[30] James E. Martine came from Plainfield, from which it is possible to see New York City, rather than from South Jersey. He was something of a joke in New Jersey politics, for he repeatedly ran for office and was repeatedly defeated. He was, however, the leading Bryan Democrat in the state. He received more than 48,000 votes in the preferential primary.

[31] Actually, there was another candidate who received more than 15,000 votes.

Martine.[32] Smith retired into private life, heartbroken, bank-
rupt, and ill, and soon after died. Wilson had in one respect
at least kept his word—he had killed Smith.

The last time that I ever saw Senator Smith was at a funeral
where I sat directly behind him. Just as the services began,
he turned around and in a loud whisper said, "Why did no
one tell me that Wilson was a liar? I found out that he was,
but I found out too late."

George Harvey told me of his experiences with Wilson.
Harvey was the editor and putative owner of *Harper's Weekly.*
He had been one of the original Wilson men for whom he had
great admiration and had used his paper to the limit in support
of his candidate. After Wilson became governor, Harvey was
sent for and the governor said to him, "Colonel, I think that
the support of *Harper's Weekly* is hurting me more than it is
helping me. I think that you had better not be quite so enthusiastic." [33] "Wilson never expressed the slightest gratitude,"
said Harvey, "for my support nor for the $75,000 that I had
raised for his campaign for governor. I said to him, you need
not worry, I shall never support you again. And I never have."
As long as Wilson lived, Harvey never ceased to attack him,
and while he did not succeed in hurting Wilson politically he
undoubtedly caused him many a disagreeable hour.

Wilson used the so-called "quad fight" at Princeton with
great skill for purposes of self-advertisement. He made a
regular crusade against the upper class clubs, claiming that they
were undemocratic.[34] In a sense, of course, they are, but my
experience has been that, while in some cases boys who ought
to "make clubs" fail to do so, very little hardship actually results. He claimed that if the university should be divided up
into a number of units of say two hundred each, the members
of each unit living in the same dormitory and eating in the

[32] In fairness to Wilson, it should be mentioned that he was under constant
pressure from his party's Progressive wing to support Martine.

[33] The conference in question took place at the Manhattan Club, and Harvey
was not "sent for" by Wilson. Harvey rather than Wilson brought up the matter. When Harvey asked Wilson if his support was hurting Wilson's candidacy,
Wilson reluctantly replied that he thought it was.

[34] Although it is widely believed that Wilson fought the quad fight on the
issue of democracy, Link demonstrates that others raised the issue and Wilson
refused to attack the clubs on the basis of their alleged lack of democracy.
(Link, *Wilson,* 50-51.)

same room, democracy would triumph, for in some unexplained way the members of each unit would be made to chum
together and not divide up into groups. In other words, by a
stroke of the pen he proposed to transform human nature. It
served his political purposes extremely well, and before long
newspapers that had not the slightest idea what it was all about
were proclaiming that Wilson was the only college president
with an accurate conception of college democracy. Wilson
toured the country making speeches wherever two or three
alumni could be found and thanks to very efficient press-agent-
ing achieved a reputation as an ideal democrat.

Under the leadership of West, the faculty was almost unanimously against him, as was a majority of the trustees. It
is probable that Wilson would have been very much disappointed had his trustees agreed with him, for in that event
he would have been obliged to raise the money to put the
quad system into effect and to prove that it was all that he
claimed.

I once said to him that he seemed to have both the faculty
and the trustees against him. To which he replied, "What do
I care for either? I am speaking to a larger audience over their
heads. I am appealing to the alumni, and even more than that
I am appealing to the public at large." At any rate the "quad
fight" made him a national character, a knight errant, roaming
the country fighting the battle of democracy.

While insisting that he proudly ignored the opponents to
his policy as being beneath contempt, he actually took their
opposition very much to heart and treated it as a personal
matter. Those who did not blindly follow him he denounced
in conversation as either crooks or "miserable creatures," a
favorite expression of his, and broke off all relations with them.

John Grier Hibben, who afterwards succeeded him in the
presidency of the university, had been a lifelong and intimate
friend, so much so that for years it had been the Wilsons'
custom to take midday dinner every Sunday with the Hibbens.
One weekend Hibben telephoned me that he was anxious to
see me about a very important matter, and when we met it
developed that Wilson intended to appoint a committee to
settle the question of the site of the new building for the
Graduate College, a matter in which he was deeply interested

and which he had in some mysterious way tied up to the quad system as being a sort of minor work of democracy. The committee was to consist of Deans West and Fine and Hibben. Wilson had told him that he was absolutely free to vote according to his convictions in favor of any site he might deem best. I told Hibben under no circumstances to serve on the committee. Hibben, who was very simple-minded and straightforward, replied, "You don't suppose that Woodrow would tell me to vote according to my convictions and not mean it, do you?" I said that I supposed exactly that and added that Wilson would not appoint the committee unless he desired the moral support of its vote in behalf of the plan he was on record as favoring. "If you favor Wilson's site go on the committee and vote for it," I said, "but if you don't favor it or if you are undecided don't go on. If you vote against Wilson's site, he will never forgive you." Hibben insisted that he had an open mind on the question and absolutely trusted Wilson's good faith. He went on the committee, voted against Wilson's site, and Wilson never spoke to him again.

While Wilson was running for the presidency, I was walking with Dr. and Mrs. Hibben when we met the candidate. Hibben and I took off our hats, and Mrs. Hibben bowed. Wilson took off his hat and turning to me said, "How do you do, McClellan," and cut the Hibbens dead. When Wilson came to Princeton for the thirty-fifth reunion of his class, he refused to meet Hibben and ignored the card that Hibben left on him.

Wilson was in the habit of saying, "I never can remember small matters of detail." I had an excellent proof of this. He wrote me asking me to appoint as police magistrate a friend of his, formerly of Baltimore, whom he said he had known most favorably as a fellow of Johns Hopkins. As the young man, who had a pleasant personality, seemed to fill the requirements, I appointed him. Not long afterwards he was charged with selling decisions. I sent for him and told him that unless he at once resigned I should seek his removal by the Appellate Division, whereupon he sent me his resignation. The newspapers severely criticized me for having made the appointment and demanded to know on whose recommendation I had made it. I told them that it had been made at the request and on the recommendation of President Wilson of Princeton University, who made a statement to the effect that he had never heard of the man and knew nothing of the matter. Fortunately I had Wilson's letter, which I gave to the press. I presume that he regarded the incident as a small matter of detail, which he was justified in forgetting.

Wilson was very thrifty. Soon after he became governor of New Jersey he appealed to the legislature for an allowance for the support of a motor car. The legislature granted him $3,000 a year for the purpose, which he drew and never kept a car. He had the salary of the governor raised from $5,000 to $10,000 annually, and induced the legislature to enact a law pensioning the widows of ex-governors at the rate of $1,500 a year.

The trustees of the Carnegie pension fund for college professors consists of various college presidents who, despite the near collapse of the fund, have kept unchanged the rule that grants ex-presidents full pay for life. One of the committee told me that when Wilson became governor he applied to the trustees for his pension and felt very much outraged when they refused his application, telling him that he might renew it when he found himself out of a job.[35]

Before Wilson went to his inauguration as President, ex-Senator George Gray [a Democrat] of Delaware, then a judge of the United States Circuit Court, came to Princeton to stop with us. He expressed a desire to pay his respects to the President-elect. I arranged an interview, and we went to the cottage where the Wilsons had lived during his governorship. Wilson we found in very good spirits. He told us what exercises he took before going to bed every night, assured us that his stomach muscles were as "hard as iron," and then out of space said, "I have made it a rule that no one who asks me for an office will get it, and that anyone who asks for an office for a friend will *ipso facto* disqualify that friend for holding any office under me." He then bowed us out. As we walked away Judge Gray was very silent. Suddenly he turned to me and said, "McClellan, do you suppose that the fellow thought that I was after a job?" "It looks very much that way," I answered. "Well, I'll be damned," said the judge.

[35] The story of Wilson's application was first made public by the New York *Evening Sun* on December 5, 1911, in an effort to undermine his campaign for the Democratic nomination for President.

Before Wilson was nominated for the presidency but after he had become an avowed candidate, Mrs. Archibald Alexander and Mrs. J. B. Harriman, whom Mrs. Wilson once described to us as "the only two society ladies we know intimately," determined to help Wilson's boom by giving him a dinner. They hired the gymnasium at the Colony Club for the purpose and invited every Democrat they knew and his wife. They invited well, but scarcely wisely. Mrs. Harriman began the proceedings by making a nominating speech in Wilson's behalf. After Wilson had replied indirectly accepting the nomination, a succession of guests were called upon to speak. First Jacob Schiff [a prominent New York banker] . . . proclaimed himself a Republican and therefore opposed each and every Democratic candidate. Next Arthur Brisbane [36] . . . made an impassioned appeal for the nomination of Hearst. Then John H. Finley,[37] who hadn't spoken to Wilson in ten years, told us what a fine fellow he considered the Wilson "I used to know." Afterwards came Jimmy Gerard,[38] who ignored Wilson and made a high protection tariff speech. Then I closed the evening. I was the only man who spoke who was on fairly friendly terms with the evening's guest.

When the Wilsons left Princeton for Washington, my wife and I saw them off at the station. I never saw him again. I had retired from politics and so was of no further use to him.

During the time that he was president of Princeton, the university was really managed by Dean Fine, for Wilson was too busy with his greater ambitions to attend to his legitimate work. Fine was the most loyal and devoted friend whom Wilson had and actually sacrificed his university future by his loyalty to his chief. When Wilson went to the White House, it was generally expected that he would give Fine a job commensurate with his ability and that would take him away from Princeton, where life under Hibben and West had become extremely unpleasant for him. Wilson offered Fine the em-

---

[36] After working for the New York *Evening Sun* and the New York *World*, Brisbane joined the New York *Evening Journal* in 1897 and became famous as an editorial writer for the chain of Hearst papers.

[37] At the time of this speech, Finley was president of the College of the City of New York. He had been a professor of politics at Princeton from 1899 to 1903.

[38] A justice of the Supreme Court of New York from 1908 to 1913, Gerard was appointed ambassador to Germany by Wilson in 1913.

bassy at Berlin. Fine did not have a cent and the rent of a suitable embassy building cost more than the ambassador's salary. When I met Fine the following autumn, I asked him why he had not accepted. He replied, "He offered me Berlin because he knew I hadn't a cent and couldn't possibly accept it, damn him!"

While the national convention was in session at Baltimore, Wilson lost courage and sent McCombs,[39] who was in charge of his fight, a telegram directing the latter to withdraw his name. McCombs put the telegram in his pocket and paid no further attention to it, thus ensuring Wilson's nomination. Until his health failed, McCombs was chairman of the National Committee and ran the presidential campaign. In reward for his services Wilson offered him the embassy to France, and McCombs, like Fine, did not have a cent to his name. It cannot be said that Wilson was overgrateful.

We found Princeton much excited on the question of who was to be Wilson's successor as president of the university. When Wilson had been elected governor of New Jersey, he had tried to induce the trustees to give him a three years' leave of absence, so that if the governorship led to nothing else in politics he would still have Princeton to fall back on. The trustees flatly refused his request and began the task of finding a new president. They appointed a committee of three of their number consisting of Cleveland Dodge,[40] Moses Taylor Pyne, and John Cadwalader,[41] as chairman.

"Moe" Pyne was one of those whom Wilson heartily disliked and referred to most unjustly as "that wretched creature Pyne." Dodge and Pyne had been in college together and had been lifelong friends only to break finally over Wilson. They were by far the most generous friends of the university among the trustees, vying with each other at the end of each year as to which one should pay the annual deficit.

39 William F. McCombs, a former student of Wilson at Princeton and a New York lawyer, played a key part in originating and furthering Wilson's first campaign for President.

40 Dodge was an official of Phelps Dodge & Company, a leading copper concern, and the director of several banks.

41 Cadwalader, who served as Assistant Secretary of State under Hamilton Fish, was described by the New York *Times* (March 12, 1914) as "one of the most prominent members of the bar in this state."

John Cadwalader was a well-known New York lawyer, who had once been an Assistant Secretary of State. In New York he was known as "Slick Old John." In Princeton he had an entirely factitious reputation and was always referred to with great solemnity as "The Honorable John Cadwalader." The trustees in their innocence expected "Old John" to decide with great wisdom between Dodge and Pyne and with his casting vote submit to the board a candidate for president on whom all could unite. But they did not know Slick Old John who was not to be caught so easily.

At the first meeting of the committee Dodge proposed Dean Fine for president. Pyne voted no, and then both turned expectantly to Cadwalader to await his decision. Cadwalader waited a moment and then in his high nasal voice said, "Gentlemen, as I conceive it, the duty of the chairman of a committee is not to vote until his committee has made its decision. When you two agree on a candidate, I shall vote, but not before." It was certainly a very novel conception of a chairman's duty, but it relieved Cadwalader of any responsibility and of the necessity of taking sides. He lived up to his reputation for "slickness."

Then followed months of deadlock between Dodge and Pyne. First and last over a hundred names were proposed, including my own, and failed for want of a majority. By the close of 1911 the deadlock began to be ridiculous, for it was obvious that the committee could never reach an agreement. In the Board of Trustees Dean Fine undoubtedly had more supporters than anyone else but by no means a majority, while a majority were undoubtedly bitterly opposed to him. On the other hand, Professor Hibben was the least disliked of anyone who had been seriously talked of. At the April meeting in 1911, Dr. [John] De Witt of the [Princeton] Theological Seminary, who was a trustee and a warm friend of Hibben, found to his surprise and satisfaction that a number of Wilson's most influential friends were absent, while his opponents were almost all present. He moved to discharge the Cadwalader committee, and on his motion being agreed to, nominated Hibben for the presidency. Hibben received almost a majority, whereupon enough of those who had voted "no" changed their votes just to elect him.

Hibben's election caused intense ill feeling among the trustees. Dodge immediately resigned and never gave another cent to the university, while the other Wilsonians shook their heads, said unkind things about the new president, but stayed on the board.

Hibben took office under extremely difficult circumstances. He had been elected by what Wilson's friends did not hesitate to call sharp practice, and was not only faced by an extremely hostile group among the trustees, but by a large, discontented, and bitter minority in the faculty. That he succeeded in harmonizing the trustees and in uniting the faculty in his support was due entirely to his fairness and kindliness. Hibben was neither a great nor a strong man; in fact, in many respects he was lamentably weak, but he was essentially a just man with a very kind heart. A stronger man might have failed where he succeeded, and if he was no executive, at least he did not interfere with those whom the trustees placed in office under him to run the university for him. He usually followed the line of least resistance, and, fortunately for Princeton, at the outset of his administration the easiest course was the best. He was urged to proscribe his enemies, and to request the resignations from the faculty of Fine, Capps,[42] and Elliott, Wilson's brother-in-law. Hibben declined. It was the easiest thing to do, but also it was the wisest. Before many years had passed the rift had been healed, and while his former opponents may not have greatly admired him, they certainly no longer disliked him, for knowing him at all well, it was impossible not to like him.

Hibben would have made a first-rate headmaster of a boys' school. He had great sympathy with and understanding of the undergraduates, with whom he was deservedly popular, and encouraged them to bring their troubles directly to him. The result was that most of his time was spent in adjusting petty matters that should have been the task of one of the deans, instead of in the larger work of the university. If half a dozen members of the faculty sought audience with him on important questions, and a freshman appeared, who desired to readjust his course of study, instead of having his secretary send the freshman to the dean charged with the matter, he would re-

---

[42] Edward Capps was professor of classics, and Edward Elliott was professor of politics.

ceive the freshman ahead of the professors and personally adjust his difficulties. As Hibben would have himself expressed it, his conduct was "lovely" but most destructive of good order and efficiency.

Just after he took office I suggested to him that my friend, Nelson A. Lewis, the chief engineer of the Board of Estimate of New York, would be willing, if asked, to go to Princeton and make a survey of the business arrangements of the university for the purpose of showing what economies could be effected and what reorganizations should be undertaken, and that Mr. Lewis would make no charge for his services. It was an offer that any wise man would have jumped at, but Hibben declined on the ground that he had no reason to suppose that conditions in Princeton were not all that they should be. He never screwed up his courage to the point of discharging a superfluous or incompetent employee. When any of them failed to function he secured from the trustees the appointment of another official to do the work of the failure. The cost of the management of the business and physical part of the university grew under Hibben to vast proportions and could easily have been cut in half. That the university functioned at all was due almost entirely to the ability and energy of Dean Eisenhart [43] who, during the Hibben administration, strove valiantly to manage its affairs, despite the grave handicap of the constant interference and meddling of the president in petty and unessential things. Hibben even kept in his own hands the assignment of branch line telephones to the preceptorial rooms of the professors, and also the distribution among the members of the faculty of the keys to the private toilet rooms in Nassau Hall.

Mrs. Hibben watched over her husband with the utmost care and did her best to save him from worry. In doing this she failed to realize that she reduced to its minimum what little work he was capable of doing. The day after I had submitted to him Nelson Lewis's offer I met her on the campus . . . [and] she said to me, "Mr. McClellan, I don't think it is at all lovely of you to worry Jack as you have. You ought not

[43] A mathematician who joined the Princeton faculty in 1896, Luther P. Eisenhart was dean of the faculty (1925-33) and dean of the Graduate College (1933-45).

to have told him about that Mr. Lewis, for he has worried about it very much. I wish that you would leave him alone and not bother him with business matters." "All right, Mrs. Hibben," I answered, "I shall never trouble him again about business," and I never did.

The Hibbens, for she was far more president than he, played favorites to the limit and seemed to be under the impression that the university was an eleemosynary institution for the benefit of their friends. While he treated all with fairness, it was those who paid their court to Mrs. Hibben who received the favors.

By the time that Hibben had been in office five years the bitterness in the faculty had largely disappeared, thanks to his kindliness and good will. If he had then retired, he would have gone down in Princeton history as one who had deserved well of the university. Unfortunately for his own sake and for that of Princeton he stayed on, and stayed too long. It is very seldom that a man has the good sense to know when the time for his retirement has arrived. Poor Hibben was not such a man. There is nothing more pathetic than the man who has overstayed his time.

I was greatly disappointed to find that university life was exceedingly narrow and exceedingly petty. I had expected to find it quite the contrary and had looked forward with great pleasure to an interchange of thought with my colleagues and to agreeable companionship. When two or three members of the faculty are gathered together, the subject of their conversation is almost invariably small gossip and even smaller scandal, the chances of the football team, the inadequacy of their salaries, the rumor that Professor X is flirting with Professor Z's wife, and so on and so on. . . .

The members of the Department of Economics and Social Institutions, to which I belonged, resented my appearance among them as the intrusion of an outsider, or as they preferred to express it of one "not a scholar." If they were scholars, God save the mark! I tried my best to be friendly, but never was accepted as one of them. My class of seniors was the largest elective in college, usually running to about 250. During my twenty years' service the senior class elected me "the most popular professor," and my course "the most popular course,"

sixteen times. The undergraduates added a verse in my honor
to the faculty song which ran as follows:

> Here's to the man of great renown,
> The former Mayor of New York Town,
> George McClellan tried and true,
> We wish there were more in the world like you.

All this did not tend to help my standing with my departmental
colleagues, who did not hesitate to proclaim that I was popular
because my course was a "snap."

One year, when I was in Europe, without saying anything
to me, my colleagues quietly dropped my course from the department, so that it did not count in making up the required
number of departmental courses. When I returned in the
autumn, I only found out about my colleagues' action by accident. I appealed to Hibben, who could not summon the
courage to straighten the matter out and seemed to think that
he had done all required of him by assuring me that Professor
[Frank H.] Dixon, the department head, had told him that no
discourtesy to me was intended. Despite the grossly dis-
courteous conduct of my colleagues I continued to lecture as
a sort of outsider, my classes being larger than ever and my
boys continuing to elect me "most popular professor."

The salaries of college professors are so pitifully small that
it requires a real call for the work for a boy of the right sort
to be willing to devote his life to teaching, unless he has independent means. The result is that the vast majority of college
professors are men who have never had ambition and have
taken up teaching as a means of livelihood and not because
they have been attracted by the work. There are comparatively
few college professors who ought to be teaching boys and very
few who would not jump at the opportunity of leaving their
chairs if offered better salaries outside. While there are glorious
exceptions, most college professors are mediocre men who have
not made good and would have been failures in any other walk
of life. One professor who had been an undergraduate with
me said to me rather pathetically, "I don't see how you, who
have been out in the world, can be willing to shut yourself
up in a college faculty."

My relations with my boys were most pleasant. I have always

been able to get on well with men younger than myself, as in youth I was able to make friends with men much my senior. The boys liked me almost as much as I liked them. I used to have as many as possible to lunch on Sunday, and they reciprocated by making me an honorary member of most of their clubs. I taught a very live subject, for as no one interfered with me, especially after the department had put me out, I lectured on whatever I wanted to talk about. During my first years at Princeton I lectured on the economic history of Europe, but after the war I entirely altered my course and talked on the political conditions of the European nations. It was one of the very few "live" courses given, and for that reason and my ability to interest young men, I not only had large classes but usually had twenty or thirty outsiders who came to hear me.

The best thing that Wilson accomplished while president of the university was the creation of the preceptorial system, which unfortunately even before he left had been allowed to go to pieces. In theory the system is admirable, but to be successful it is almost prohibitively expensive. Theoretically the professor in charge of a course lectures twice a week. For a third period the men who elect him divide into groups of not more than six, meet in conference with a preceptor, and discuss with him the lectures and the collateral reading of the course. Custom decrees that a college instructor ought not to be required to teach more than fifteen hours a week, and he certainly cannot be at his best if he teaches more. Wilson recruited from all over the country a force of fifty preceptors, the number never exceeding a hundred, although to properly precept the undergraduates would have required a force of over four hundred. The result was that the system broke down. The only department in which it continued to function effectively was English, which for some reason had enough preceptors to do the work. In the Department of Economics there were altogether five preceptors, although in my course alone to have properly precepted the class would have required sixteen besides myself. Actually I never had more than two and usually only one part-time instructor. The consequence was that in most departments preceptorial sections numbered from twenty to twenty-five, and the work of the preceptors consisted of nothing more than either quizzes or lectures of their own. Despite all this, the catalogue continued to boast that Princeton was the only university in the country having a preceptorial system, and I really think that President Hibben believed that this was true, so little did he know of what was going on in the university. During the twenty years that I lectured at Princeton neither the president nor any member of the Board of Trustees ever came to hear me, with the solitary exception of James W. Alexander,[44] who took his duties as a trustee more seriously than did any of his colleagues.

Society in Princeton when we first lived there was not at all unlike that in Mrs. Gaskell's *Cranford.* The Clevelands were the center of attraction, and Mrs. Cleveland with her good looks, charm, and pleasing hospitality was the focal point around which it revolved. The place was very small and very narrow, and those who lived there resented any divergence from type. Newcomers not connected with the college were viewed with grave suspicion and had to produce good reasons for their presence to be even tolerated. I suppose that all college communities are bigoted, but Columbia, Harvard, and Yale have the advantage of being in cities that serve to a certain extent as broadening influences. Princeton, on the other hand, is in the country and has absolutely no outside influence to mitigate its parochialism. It is a pleasant place to visit for weekends, but as a place of steady residence before very long it begins to pall. We kept a small apartment in New York for some years and went there nearly every week to keep dinner engagements. This made Princeton a very pleasant resting place, for we did not see too much of it.

I taught only one term a year, and at the close of my work in February we always went abroad to remain until the following October, spending most of our time in Paris, Italy, and Germany. First and last we have been a great deal in Europe and thus far I have crossed the ocean fifty-five times. . . .

---

[44] Alexander was a New York lawyer and president of the Equitable Life Insurance Company until 1905, when he retired.

Chapter XV

Our War Hysteria Had Begun

At the end of July, 1914, we were at San Martino de Castrozza [a hospice and resort] in [southern] Tyrol, where I had done some climbing and where our friend, John C. van Dyke,[1] had joined us. On the first of August we went by motor diligence to Karer See [a resort in southern Tyrol]. There had been rumors of possible war, but we had seen only local papers that did not mention the subject. Where we stopped for lunch there was a man posting a proclamation, around which a village crowd rapidly gathered. The proclamation was addressed to tourists and stated that the rumors of possible war were unfounded, that Austria was at peace and intended to remain so, and that tourists had no reason to worry but might freely continue their travels. We found Karer See crowded and settled down for a fortnight's stay.

On the third of August we walked to one of the D. O. Alpen Verein huts. I walked ahead to order our lunch and passed on the way a lad who was running as though the devil were after him. When I reached the hut, I found a young woman, evidently the caretaker, sitting on a stool with her head in her hands and sobbing as though her heart would break. At first she paid no attention to me, so I went up to her and putting my hand on her shoulder said, "Fräulein, what's the matter?" She pulled herself together with an effort and answered, "Ach! Herr Gott! They have taken my man from me and they are going to kill him." The order for

---

1 Van Dyke was a professor of the history of art at Rutgers University and the author of several books on the history and appreciation of art.

mobilization had been issued. It was my first glimpse of the "romance of war."

We had left the hotel in the morning crowded; at five o'clock in the afternoon, on our return, we found it empty. Not only had every guest but ourselves gone, and every employee under sixty years of age, but every horse, every cow, every goat had been commandeered. The director told us that he was closing the hotel as soon as possible and that he could only keep us for one night longer. As to how we should get down to Bozen [a town in southern Tyrol] all that he could suggest was that we should walk and have our luggage accompany us on a hand cart propelled by a venerable peasant past the military age.

The next morning as I was shaving in my window I saw drawing up in front of the hotel a landau driven by an old fellow who had evidently had a little too much to drink and was singing at the top of his lungs. I rushed downstairs in my pajamas and asked him how much he wanted to take us to Bozen. With a crafty grin he replied, "Not one penny less than the tariff." Where he had been I don't know, but he had not heard of the mobilization. I promptly clinched the bargain under the Austrian custom by giving him ten per cent of the price and went upstairs to warn my wife and her maid and van Dyke to be ready as soon as possible. Within an hour we were off.

All the way to Bozen we found desolation. The men had all gone, the cattle had been taken, and the women were everywhere crying their eyes out. And they cried with good reason. The men of Tyrol belonged to the 12th Corps, the best in the Austrian service. It was at once thrown into the front line and very few Tyrolers ever came back.

On our way down we discussed the question of where we should go and evolved the bright idea that most tourists would undoubtedly go into Switzerland and to France, and that few would go to Italy, and therefore opted for Italy. It was a very bright idea and would have been successful if some twenty-five thousand other Americans had not had exactly the same thought. When we reached Bozen we found that a train would leave for Milan that afternoon with the intention, but by no means the certainty, of reaching there some time that night.

Meanwhile, as our cash supply was low, van Dyke and I

thought it would be wise to draw some money. At the bank
we received our first hint of the inconveniences of war, for we
were faced with a sign informing us that no drafts or checks
would be cashed. We boarded the train early and were all of
us lucky enough to obtain seats, although the aisles were packed
with people standing. In my compartment, besides myself,
there were an Italian girl, going home to Turin, a German
professor of advanced age, two Frenchmen, getting out of the
enemy's country, and a man of unknown nationality who
seemed unable to speak any known language. As none of my
fellow travellers could speak a second language, I acted as
interpreter, translating from the language spoken into the
other two languages of the carriage. It was rather slow work,
but it helped to kill time. The Italian girl told us that while
she was waiting on the platform at Bozen a trainful of Italian
Bersaglieri had gone through bound for the Austrian front
and that she had spoken to her cousin who was a captain in
the regiment. She was evidently convinced of the truth of her
statement, while of course no Italian troops had passed through.
Later when reputable witnesses reported that they had seen
Russian troops passing through Britain I could understand
that they might really have thought that they had seen them.

Our train crawled at about ten miles an hour, so that when
we reached Riva [a town in northeastern Italy] after dark we
detrained and went to the only hotel that was open. We found
it being run by the *portière*, an old man, wearing a *Landsturm*
brassard and his idiot grandson, obviously unfit for military
service. We reached Milan for lunch, after which van Dyke
and I, being by this time quite penniless, went to the Banca
Commerciale to draw some money. We found a line of compatriots extending from the door of the bank clear across the
square in front; there must have been over a hundred people
bound on the same mission as ourselves. After waiting in line
for over two hours we were told that the bank would not pay
more than £10 on any one letter of credit and that there was no
use in returning for more the next day or on any following
day, for they would not give it.

Van Dyke and I next visited the Banca di Sconto where we
were refused any money as soon as it appeared that we had
already drawn £ at the Banca Commerciale. I saw the manager

with whom I pleaded so successfully in my best Italian that he gave us another £10. We now had enough for our immediate needs.

At the consulate there was an excited horde of our compatriots, the men cursing, the women crying, and the consul quite demoralized and helpless. I found Murray Butler and Frederick W. Vanderbilt,[2] and we organized an American committee for the purpose of seeing what we could do in the way of getting home. Butler was, with good reason, immensely proud of his extraordinary achievement in having brought his family from Lausanne to Milan with only ten francs in cash. He had made his way down by introducing himself as the president of Columbia and had everywhere been passed on his I.O.U.'s and been treated with extreme courtesy.

Taking a leaf out of his book I went to the Italian Steamship Line and found Vanderbilt's courier there, who introduced me and persuaded them to give me a cabin on a ship sailing from Genoa. At the only meeting that our committee held it was decided that the best thing for all Americans to do was to go to Genoa as soon as possible. Meanwhile, Butler told me that his pull at the steamship office had failed him, and I took him there and, explaining that I was a friend of Vanderbilt's courier, induced them to book him. The president of Columbia and the ex-mayor of New York meant nothing, but the name of Vanderbilt's courier was an open sesame.

On reaching Genoa the sailing of our ship was cancelled and we were in a quandary. The consul at Genoa was a retired dentist who had received his job for faithful services to the Democratic party in his home town. He may have been a good dentist and doubtless was a good Democrat, but he was a very poor consul, from whom no help could be expected. A committee was formed having as its chairman R. A. C. Smith,[3] the shipping man, with Vanderbilt and Butler as members. They hired from the shipping company a 12,000-ton vessel of sorts that had been in the South American trade and had no difficulty in selling every berth. The company was very thrifty.

---

[2] Vanderbilt was the grandson of Cornelius Vanderbilt, the founder of the family fortune. He worked for a time for the New York Central, which had been founded by his grandfather, and was a director of several corporations.

[3] Smith was an officer and director of a sugar company, a coal company, and several public utilities, but he was not involved in the shipping business.

No sooner had a price been agreed upon than it announced that it would be necessary to return via Palermo to deliver freight. To obviate the Palermo call the price was raised. When everything appeared satisfactory, the company announced that the ship would, of course, be obliged to make four stops on the North African coast to pick up freight. To obviate this the price was again raised. Finally, when everything was settled, the cost of the ship was so high that we paid $1,200 for a two-bunk room in what had been the second cabin, with a bunk in the former steerage for my wife's maid. Had I not been due at Princeton for the opening of college, we should, of course, have waited until things had settled down. Almost all of our fellow passengers were also due home at the earliest moment and had to take what they could find.

The ship given us was the *Principe di Udine,* and while seaworthy was not much more and left much to be desired in the way of cleanliness. She was overrun with rats whose capture furnished a simple indoor sport for those sportingly inclined. . . . As I learned that she would not hoist her ensign until the morning of sailing we went to Portofino . . . [a town on the Gulf of Genoa] to await the day of departure. The heat was intense, but at Portofino, the most beautiful spot on the Riviera, there was always a breeze, and the hotel was excellent. While our fellow passengers sweltered at Genoa, we were comfortable. Every morning I focused the hotel telescope on our ship as she lay in dock and finally saw her ensign. We were driven in on the hotel bus with what luggage we had and boarded the ship an hour before she sailed.

Van Dyke had left us at Milan and had gone home via London, and chose the more comfortable route. Our large luggage had been sent from Italy direct to Hamburg as we had engaged our cabins to return to the United States on the *Vaterland* on her second voyage out. We had only the clothes that we had taken to the Alps. The American Express undertook to rescue our luggage from Germany, and a month after our arrival home it reached us unopened and unhurt.

At Genoa I succeeded in getting another £10 on my letter of credit so that with strict economy we were able to pay our way, arriving on the steamer with exactly ten lire in my pocket. The Italian hotelkeepers in Milan and Genoa were extremely decent to American travellers. Bartolini, the proprietor of the Hotel Europa, where we have been going for many years, was especially kind. He told me afterwards that of all the Americans to whom he had given credit, and they numbered over a hundred, only one welshed, the rest paying by check or draft after they reached home.

None of us had the cash with which to finance the chartering of the *Principe di Udine,* and Vanderbilt acted as the guarantor for the whole amount. It took nearly a week to prepare the vessel for sea, but finally we set sail. We were terribly crowded and frightfully uncomfortable. Fortunately the food was good and the weather perfect, and everyone determined to make the best of things. I doubt if a ship's company of any other people but Americans could have been as good-natured and as cheerful as were we. The passengers organized a committee on entertainment, and we had concerts and lectures. Murray Butler spoke, and I lectured on political conditions in Italy and afterwards published my lecture in *Scribner's Magazine.*

At Gibraltar we were stopped and looked over and hardly had we reached the Atlantic when a war vessel bore down on us. The cry was raised that she was German, and although we were at peace with Germany our passengers became very much excited, several women dropping to their knees and loudly praying for deliverance from the Hun. When she proved to be British, there was great relief. We reached New York after a twelve days' voyage and were much disappointed to find that ours was by no means the first ship to arrive after the declaration of war. As soon as we had been cleared by the customs, we went to Princeton and found that Princeton had gone quite mad with war fever.

The very clever French propaganda was nowhere more effective than among college professors. They are a simple, guileless race, utterly without worldly experience and ready to accept anything they read in the newspapers as the truth. They accepted as gospel the obvious propaganda that was printed and believed every story of German atrocities. With a few square yards of red ribbon, France made millions of American supporters.

When Dr. Dernburg [4] came to this country at the beginning of the war, a Princeton undergraduate organization asked him to speak. Its president came to me and told me that they were in serious trouble as none of the authorities were willing to have anything to do with him. I said, "I shall be very glad to have him stop with me. He is a cabinet minister of a country with which we are at peace, and Princeton ought not to be rude to him." He stopped with us and we gave him a dinner before he spoke.

We invited the Hibbens and received a note from her saying that her husband and she could, "of course, not meet any German," and this was nearly three years before we entered the war!

My wife and I kept our heads and declined to be stampeded. We supported a nurse in the French service but, nevertheless, lived up to the President's proclamation of neutrality to the very best of our ability. We became members of the executive committee of the local Red Cross but were soon forced to resign. At one of its first meetings a resolution was proposed that any money or supplies delivered to the chapter would be sent as requested by the donor to France, Britain, or Belgium. I moved to amend to add Germany. My amendment was voted down, only my wife, Forrestal,[5] the undergraduate representative, and one other voting with me. I inquired of the chairman if it was the purpose of the Red Cross only to serve the Allies and she informed me that it was, whereupon, I wired to the national secretary, for a ruling on the matter, but the secretary replied that each chapter might make its own rules on the subject. Forrestal, my wife, and I thereupon resigned, and the undergraduates were never again represented on the committee.

Early in 1915 my mother died at Nice, France, where she had been spending the winter to be near my sister and the latter's husband, Paul Desprez, who had recently retired from the French diplomatic service as Minister of the First Class. My mother, who was nearly eighty when she died, had spent

4 Bernhard Dernburg, a German financier and statesman who served as Colonial Secretary from 1906 to 1910, was a German propagandist in the United States from 1914 to 1915.

5 This is presumably the same James Forrestal who served as Secretary of the Navy and Secretary of Defense during the nineteen-forties, for he was a Princeton undergraduate from 1912 to 1915.

most of her time abroad after my father's death in 1885. We buried her beside my father in the cemetery at Trenton, New Jersey.

Shortly afterwards we sailed for Europe, going direct to Naples on a very uncomfortable little French ship, which was the only vessel available, by the southern route.

Italy was still neutral, but we found the people much stirred up by the propaganda of the "Interventionists" on the one hand and the "Neutralists" on the other. Most of the hotels were closed and tourists were almost non-existent. By May, Italy had joined the Allies and the Great War was in full swing on the western front. . . .

As we did not know when we might have another opportunity, we determined to make a flying visit to our beloved Venice to see her under war conditions. . . . Venice was one of the saddest places I have ever seen. The people realized that the city was bound to suffer greatly from the war, and even during our three days' stay we were bombed three times by Austrian planes. No lights were permitted, and sentries posted on the roofs of houses were under orders to fire at any light that was shown, which they did with right good will. Venice was like a stage set for an elaborate production with no actors and the lights turned off.

From Venice we returned to Florence and from there went to Paris. The treatment of the foreigner in France was very different from what it was in Italy. The assumption of all French officials was that every stranger was a possible spy and was treated accordingly. . . . From Paris we went to St. Moritz, where at the Palace Hotel there were only twenty guests. There were only seventy guests in the entire Engadine. Climbing over the mountains I was able to see a good deal of the marvellous system of military roads and defenses that the Swiss had constructed almost overnight, with which to protect their neutrality. I was very favorably impressed with the Swiss Army and only wish that we might copy its organization. With a population of less than three and a half millions they mobilized over 300,000 men. The officers and non-coms were kept constantly under arms, the men were released on pass for every other month so as to attend to their work in civil life. In twenty-four hours the full strength of the army was available.

The men were neither smart nor picturesque, but they were hard as nails and very efficient.

It was a great strain on the resources of the Republic, but had they not kept armed to the teeth, either the Central Powers or the Allies would undoubtedly have crossed the Swiss frontier. In addition to the cost of maintaining the army on a war footing, Switzerland spent vast sums in caring for the great number of badly wounded prisoners of both sides, who, under a convention of the combatants, were turned over to her care. The part Switzerland played in the Great War has never been appreciated at its true value.

From St. Moritz I wrote to our ambassador at Berlin, James W. Gerard, asking him if we could visit Germany with comfort. He answered advising us under no circumstances to cross the border. I then wrote to our consul general at Munich, T. St.-John Gaffney,[6] who replied urging us to come. From St. Moritz we went to Bern to make the necessary arrangements for crossing the frontier. Bern was a great international spy center, very much as Basle had been during the Napoleonic wars. Almost every other man or woman whom one met was connected with one or other of the multitudinous espionage or counter-espionage services, and every foreigner in the city was an object of suspicion to the authorities.

Our minister at Bern was a worthy old soul named Pleasant A. Stovall,[7] who, it soon developed, while undoubtedly a most deserving Democrat, knew very little about his job. He could give me absolutely no information as to what was necessary in the way of permits to enter Germany and turned me over to his stenographer. She, poor girl, had excellent intentions but knew as little as her chief, and finally advised me to call on the German minister, which I did. I found him a very pleasant young man, who in less than a day had received the required permits from Berlin. I lost no time in wiring to Gaffney that we were about to start and telling him the train we were taking. When we reached Lindow we found that Gaffney had smoothed

6 Thomas St. John Gaffney, who had been born and educated in Ireland, was an enthusiastic supporter of Irish independence. He served as consul general at Dresden (1905-13) and at Munich (1913-15).

7 Stovall, a former newspaper editor and publisher and member of the Georgia House of Representatives, was envoy extraordinary and minister plenipotentiary to Switzerland (1913-20).

our journey to such an extent that we were met by an official in a frock coat, bowler hat, and green gloves, who passed us through the customs and ushered us into a reserved carriage on the train. At Munich Gaffney met us at the station and took us to the Hotel Continental where a suite had been reserved for us at a price at about half the peace level.

The affairs of the British were in the hands of our representative, and our consul general at Munich had quasi-diplomatic functions, and was acting for Britain as much as for us. When I called at the consulate . . . the morning after our arrival, Gaffney introduced to me a tall, handsome, bearded Englishman, as I supposed, but whose name I did not catch. Presently I learned that my bearded Englishman was Sir Roger Casement,[8] the Irish patriot, who had come to Germany from the United States after a most sensational journey for the purpose of enlisting an Irish Legion among the British prisoners to fight in the German Army, and that Gaffney had allowed him to make his headquarters at the United States consulate.

While we were in Munich we saw Casement several times, for everywhere that Gaffney took us he went along. He was a very charming and agreeable man, an enthusiast and an idealist, who had no other thought in life but the freedom of his country. He said that Ireland could never be freed except through the shedding of the blood of her sons, and that his greatest ambition was that he might be permitted to die for her. His efforts to raise an Irish Legion were a dismal failure for, with the exception of a mere handful, the Irish prisoners were true to their salt and refused to listen to him.

Finally the German government began to be bored by him and even to doubt his good faith and determined to get rid of him. They agreed to an almost insane plan that he submitted to them. Accompanied by two Irish prison sergeants, Casement was landed from a German submarine on the south coast of Ireland, Casement believing that if he appeared among them the Irish people would proclaim the Irish Republic. The two

---

8 Casement was an Irish rebel, who was a member of the British consular service from 1895 to 1913 and was knighted in 1911. Following the outbreak of the First World War he went to Germany to gain help in the fight for Irish independence. Following his return to Ireland in a German submarine, he was arrested and taken to London where he was tried, convicted of high treason, and hanged.

sergeants left Casement sitting on the shore while they went to the nearest village to announce his arrival. Meanwhile, a coast guard found him and asked for his papers. As Casement had none, the coast guard took him to the nearest police station where he was recognized and sent to London for trial and execution as a traitor.

Of the two sergeants, one turned King's evidence and the other made his escape to the United States. After we had entered the war a lawyer, who had been one of Casement's counsel at his trial, wrote to me and asked if I could not find a place in my outfit for "a most excellent ex-British Sergeant Major, named Robert Montieth." I recognized the name as that of Casement's sergeant who had escaped and, thinking that the lawyer's friend might be he, answered that I had no place for him. What became of him I do not know.

Not long after our visit to Germany, Wilson removed Gaffney at the request of Great Britain.[9] The newspapers said that the cause of his removal had been a lunch that he had given us "at which Casement had been present and at which toasts were drunk damning the British cause." I at once wrote to the President telling him that no toasts of any kind had been drunk at the lunch nor, so far as I knew, had any sentiments been expressed inimical to Great Britain. Wilson replied very coldly, "Mr. Gaffney was removed for causes in no way connected with the lunch to which you refer."

Gaffney had been in the service for many years, and, until the war came, had done his work without criticism. Had Wilson transferred him to South America, he would have met the demands of Great Britain and not unduly punished a faithful public servant.

From Munich we went to Berlin where Gaffney had engaged rooms for us at the Hotel Esplanade and arranged an interview for me with [Alfred] Zimmermann, the Foreign Minister. The next day I called on Zimmermann and found him very polite and agreeable. He asked me if there was anything particular that I cared to see, and when I told him that I wanted to visit

[9] Actually Gaffney was permitted to resign. There were, however, ample grounds for his removal, for he was decidedly pro-German and was in direct contact with Casement. At the time of his resignation he announced that he planned to return to the United States to lecture on behalf of Germany. See New York *Times*, September 30, 1915.

a prison camp, he offered to send me the next morning. He then asked if there were anything else. I replied that I supposed that it would be impossible for my wife and me to visit Belgium. When he inquired, "Why impossible?" I answered, "To be perfectly frank, your Excellency, because according to rumor there may be war between your country and mine." "Make no mistake," he replied, "there will be no war at any time between your country and mine. Of course, you can go to Belgium. Let me know when you are ready to leave Berlin, and I will arrange everything for you."

The morning after my interview with Zimmermann a card was brought to me bearing the name of Dr. Roediger,[10] of the Foreign Office. I went downstairs and looked everywhere for a man who might be a doctor. The only man I saw in the lobby was a good-looking young fellow, dressed like an Englishman, with a single glass in his eye. I sought in vain for my doctor, when presently the man with the eyeglass came up to me and in the most perfect Oxford English asked if I were Professor McClellan. When I told him that I was, he said that he was Dr. Roediger. It seems that he had been a Rhodes Scholar at Oxford and had been at Rugby before. He began by apologizing for not being at the front and explained that he had been wounded and invalided out of the service.

He then asked me where I wanted to go, and when I said that I should like to see French prisoners, gave me the choice of three camps. I selected Müchberg, without knowing anything about it. There was no opportunity for him to telephone, so we arrived unannounced. I talked freely with the prisoners, especially with a professor of philosophy at the University of Caen, and found them fairly well satisfied with their treatment. Their only complaint was that there were Russians in the same camp who were extremely dirty and hard to get on with. We lunched on the prisoners' food, which, while very simple, was perfectly eatable. Later in the war the food became worse and more meager, but Germany was on the verge of starvation and the prisoners were fed as well as most of the non-combatants in the country.

We visited some of the hospitals under the guidance of a

10 This presumably was Dr. Max Roediger, who before the war had been a professor of German literature and history at the University of Berlin.

nice young man named Hahn, whom Zimmermann had assigned to us as our guide, counselor, and friend, and went wherever we desired.

The atrocity stories we heard in Berlin reminded me very much of those circulated by the Allies, except that in the Berlin version the perpetrators were Frenchmen, Belgians, and Russians, instead of Germans. I was given a large book, which reminded me of Foxe's *Book of Martyrs*. It contained some hundreds of hair-raising stories of the fiendishness of the Allies, quite as circumstantial and probably quite as untrue as those described in the Bryce Report.

We were accompanied to Belgium by a young German-American, assigned to us by Zimmermann, who had been an engineer in the employ of General Electric at Schenectady. Our way was made extremely smooth and when we reached Brussels we were permitted to go where, and when, we pleased entirely unaccompanied. We found conditions at Brussels much better than in Germany. There was plenty of food, the restaurants were crowded with natives, and everything was as in time of peace. We visited Louvain by ourselves and in the company of a young Belgian priest, whom we picked up on the street, saw the scenes of the various "atrocities." The cathedral was not in ruins as had been reported, and the town hall, reported destroyed, was unharmed except that a statue of St. George had been decapitated. The Allies had published a photograph showing the town hall in ruins. It was a clever piece of photography, but it was an absolute fake.

From Brussels we went to Antwerp, which was a dead city but had not suffered greatly from bombardment. The thrifty citizens had carefully glassed in every unexploded shell that had struck their houses and on returning after the war we found the unexploded shells still under glass. From Antwerp we went to Holland and sailed for home from Rotterdam on the S. S. *Rotterdam*.

I had written a series of letters to the New York *Times* of my experiences during the summer. On my return they were republished in book form under the title of *The Heel of War*. In the book I merely told of what I had seen without comment, under the naïve impression that a plain statement of facts by a neutral observer would be welcomed by the public.

The book was received with a perfect storm of abuse. I was called a German secret service agent, charged with being in the employ of Germany, and an enemy of my country. My statements were called lies and I myself a liar. For example, I stated that the Belgium government had issued three separate official versions of what the Germans had done in Louvain. I quoted the three versions and gave my authority for the quotations. I pointed out that, as the three versions were mutually contradictory, it was only fair to assume that two of them were incorrect. For this I was called "pro-German" and a liar. Our war hysteria had begun and the Allied propaganda was hard at work.

Toward the close of my mayoralty the Metropolitan Museum of Art, in co-operation with the German Emperor, organized a loan exhibition of German pictures, which was opened by a concert and reception at which the German ambassador, Count von Bernstorff, Mr. Morgan, who was president of the museum, and I stood in line and shook hands with the museum's guests. Bernstorff devoted himself to the task with great earnestness but much gloom. He soon tired and kept muttering to himself in a stage whisper, "Ach Gott, Ach Gott!" Finally, he turned to me and inquired, quite audibly, "Did you ever in your life see a more common, ill-dressed lot of women?" To which I replied, "I am sorry that your Excellency finds them so, for they are almost all German-Americans." Upon which, he once more muttered, "Ach Gott!" and thereafter remained silent. And it was this tactless, ill-mannered person, who was charged with the management of his country's affairs at the most critical moment in its history.

At Princeton, as the result of my book, we were practically sent to Coventry, and an effort was made to have me put out of the faculty. And this was two years before we entered the war. Truly the way of one who tries to keep his head in wartime is hard!

I did not hear the last of my book until the war was over. During the summer of 1918, just before I went overseas, an explosion occurred at Frankford Arsenal causing a considerable loss of life. A boy who had been carrying a tray of fulminate of mercury caps had tripped and fallen, and the caps had at once detonated and caused a tableful of fulminate to follow suit. To my great surprise General Crozier [11] sent me two letters he had received, one from a Fifth Avenue jeweler, the other from George Haven Putnam, a New York publisher, charging me with having brought about the explosion, in the interest of Germany, while in command of the arsenal. In addition, Putnam charged that my father-in-law, August Heckscher, who by the way was not my father-in-law but only a distant cousin of my wife, was a notorious "pro-German" and that I had aided and abetted him in his activities. General Crozier inclosed his reply to the two letters and asked from me the usual official answer.

I wrote a general denial, that I had never been in command at Frankford, that I had not been near the place for over a year, that the Board of Inquiry had determined that the explosion had been purely accidental in its origin, and finally that I was not the son-in-law of August Heckscher, with whom I had only the slightest acquaintance.

James Speyer, the banker, organized a committee to raise money for German widows and orphans, and asked me to take the chairmanship, which I did. This did not tend to endear me to the hysterical war people, but we did good work and raised a very considerable amount. A great many sent us large sums with the request that their names should not be published as they frankly said they were afraid of the resultant publicity. It was for the same reason very difficult to get the right kind of people to serve on the committee. It was a revelation to me of the moral cowardice of most respectable men and women. . . .

We spent the summer of 1916 at Mount Desert and returned to Princeton in the autumn firmly believing that the United States would remain neutral, as Wilson made his campaign for re-election on the platform, "He kept us out of war." The war spirit was confined almost entirely to the East and among college professors and the "smart" people in the great cities. It required a long time to develop it among the farmers and the plain people. I supported Wilson and made several speeches during the campaign, although not as many as I had in 1912. During his first campaign I had stumped for him in New York, New Jersey, and Connecticut and did so with far more en-

---

[11] William Crozier was chief of ordnance, U. S. Army, from 1901 to December, 1917.

thusiasm than I should have had, but for an interview with Hibben. He sent for me and asked me if the rumor was true that I was to take the stump for the Democratic candidate. When I replied that it was quite true, he said, "Your friends think that you are making a great mistake, and I do not wish you to do so." "Am I to assume, Mr. President," I answered, "that this is an order, that, as president of Princeton, you forbid me to speak for Wilson? If it is an order, I shall resign from the faculty and publicly announce the reason for my resignation." Greatly excited he replied, "Oh, no, this is not an order. It is merely the expression of my wish." "Very well then," I said, "I shall go on the stump. I did not particularly want to do so, but your statement has turned what was a hateful *corvée* into a great pleasure, and I shall now speak with right good will."

On election night 1916 I went at eleven o'clock to national headquarters at the Hotel Manhattan to see if I could get any news more cheering than that of the newspapers. I found everything shut up. McAdoo, who was in charge, had given up the fight and gone to bed, as had Wilson and his family. As I was leaving the hotel I ran into Henry Morgenthau, whom I had known when I was mayor and he was a practicing lawyer. He was now ambassador to Turkey and one of Wilson's closest friends. I asked him if there was any hope and he replied that, while McAdoo had given up the fight, he believed that everything pointed to Wilson's re-election. He was the only prominent Democrat who had not abandoned hope, and he was the only one who was right.

As soon as Wilson had been re-elected, less and less was heard of the cry, "He kept us out of war." The President became much more firm in his dealings with Germany, and the drift towards war became more marked every day. The logical and proper moment to have given Bernstorff his passports was after the sinking of the *Lusitania*. Wilson allowed that opportunity to pass and broke off relations in February with much less forcible reasons.

When Bernstorff had been sent home it was obvious to all that war was inevitable. . . .

Chapter XVI

MY BIT

[EVEN BEFORE the United States had broken relations with Germany I had] made up my mind that, as I had no sons [and] because of my name, I must be ready when war came to do my bit. I was fifty-one years old, past the military age, and except for five years in the National Guard in my youth, I had had no military experience. I wrote to Elliot Wadsworth, head of the Red Cross at Washington,[1] and asked him for a job. He replied that as I was a resident of New York he could give me nothing, which of course was inexact, and referred me to Mrs. [William K.] Draper, head of the Red Cross in New York. I then wrote to her and received a letter by return mail telling me that she had no work for me to do and referring me to Elliot Wadsworth. The Red Cross evidently did not want me. I then wrote to United States Senators James W. Wadsworth and James A. O'Gorman from New York and asked them if they would help me to get a staff commission as I was too old for the line. Wadsworth praised my patriotism and regretted that it was impossible to help me. . . .

O'Gorman, on the other hand, was too willing to help. He asked me in which staff department I wanted a commission, and when I said that I should like a commission in the Adjutant General's Department but that I was six years past the maximum age, replied, "Just leave that to me, and I will arrange the matter." I left it to him, only to receive a letter from him two days before we declared war telling me that I was six years beyond the maximum age, a fact that I already knew. I

---

[1] Actually Wadsworth was vice-chairman of the Central Committee of the American National Red Cross.

realized that if I was to get a commission, I must rely entirely
on my own efforts and went to Washington to make personal
application. I called on my old friend General Crozier, the
chief of ordnance, on April sixth and was with him when
Colonel C. C. Williams [2] came in and announced that war had
been declared. General Crozier said, "Of course, I will give
you a commission," and forthwith proceeded to do so. Before
I left Washington the matter had been arranged, and on April
16, 1917, I was commissioned major, receiving the second
commission in the Ordnance Department, General Drain [3] receiving the first. Had it not been for the time I wasted waiting
for O'Gorman's help I should have received the first. As it
was, I was the first Princeton graduate and the first member
of the Princeton faculty to be commissioned. I returned to
Princeton to await the call to active duty and to learn my job
as well as I could from books. . . .

At the end of April I received my orders to report at the
Frankford Arsenal, at Bridesberg, one of the many suburban
slums of Philadelphia, on May fifth, and accordingly did so.
The commanding officer, or in the army slang, the C.O., was
Colonel George Montgomery,[4] an exceedingly capable, but
peppery little Ulsterman, who was most unpopular in the
service but with whom I got on perfectly. I was assigned to the
office of the very efficient principal assistant, Colonel Bricker,[5]

[2] Charles C. Williams, a regular army officer in the Ordnance Department,
was chief ordnance officer, A.E.F. in France, from 1917 to 1918 and became
chief ordnance officer, U. S. Army, in 1918.

[3] James A. Drain, a Washington, D. C. lawyer, served as an ordnance officer
for the 1st Division, A.E.F. in France.

[4] Montgomery was born in Ireland, was graduated from the United States
Military Academy, transferred from ordnance to artillery in 1894, and at the
outbreak of the war had risen to the rank of lieutenant colonel.

In the journal of his wartime experiences abroad McClellan describes Montgomery as "a man without tact, but great ability and punch. Very unpopular
and therefore not used as he should be." (George B. McClellan, "1918 Journal
of the Great Adventure of George B. McClellan, a Lt. Col. of the Ordnance
Dept. . . , U. S. A. in the A.E.F.," 19a. This journal is in the McClellan MSS,
Library of Congress.)

[5] Edwin D. Bricker, a graduate of the United States Military Academy, trans-
ferred from infantry to ordnance in 1901, rose to the rank of colonel, and was
chief ordnance purchasing officer, A.E.F. In his diary McClellan describes
Bricker as "a rather solemn man of 44." (George B. McClellan, "My War Diary,"
May 15, 1917. McClellan's war diary, covering the period from February 3 to
August 8, 1917, is in the McClellan MSS, Library of Congress.)

to learn my job. For some weeks I was the only reserve officer on duty at the post, and as all hands were most kind and helpful I very soon mastered the mysteries of "paper work" and the routine of an army post. I commuted from Princeton, leaving there at seven in the morning and returning in time for eight o'clock dinner. I lunched at the unmarried officers' mess until the arrival of some sixty young reserve officers of whom I was put in charge, and on Bricker's transfer I was made principal assistant.[6]

We had with us a company of Pennsylvania National Guard assigned to guard Delaware River bridge, and as two of its privates were rated as cooks, I assigned them to cook for the reserve officers' mess. As in happier times one of these cooks had been a telegraph linesman and the other a keeper in an insane asylum, their cooking left something to be desired; in fact, the only dish that they knew was canned pork and beans, which after a time became rather monotonous.

I was given as my assistant a very good-looking and agreeable young regular, Captain Freeman Bowley,[7] whom, I am sorry to say, I have never seen since the peace came. My work was very interesting, and I enjoyed it very much.

First and last during my two years' service I saw a great deal of regular officers and was intimately associated with them during most of the time. The ordnance officers and the engineers were excellent; in fact, I met very few regulars who were not up to their jobs.

The curse of the army was red tape, making officers unwilling to assume responsibility and experts in the art of "passing the buck." There was and, I assume, still is far too much "paper work." Every smallest transaction was recorded in triplicate on its proper form, and the number of forms was endless. One copy was retained by the maker, another filed in the post archives, and the third sent to headquarters. For the transfer

6 " 'Principal Assistant' . . . means that I am the C.O.'s right-hand man, a sort of combination of assistant general manager of a factory and a glorified private secretary." (McClellan, "My War Diary," June 9, 1917.)

7 Bowley was graduated from the United States Military Academy in 1911 as a second lieutenant in the field artillery. When he and McClellan were together at the Frankford Arsenal, the latter wrote: "I have taken a great fancy to him, for he is straightforward, naïve, and he is a gentleman." (McClellan, "My War Diary," May 25, 1917.)

of property a copy followed the article transferred with endorsements made by each office through which it went.

One of my earliest experiences was in reference to an automatic pistol. During the Mexico expedition a National Guard officer had had issued to him an automatic. Being a very conscientious person, when he was demobilized at the end of the trouble, he turned it in to his regimental quartermaster, who forwarded it to the Q. M. General at Washington, who sent it back to the regimental Q. M. informing him that the Q. M. G. had no jurisdiction over it. The regimental Q. M. then sent it to the chief of ordnance, who sent it to Frankford Arsenal to be returned to the National Guard officer to be started properly on its journey. But meanwhile he had died. His executor who was also conscientious started it off again, this time to army headquarters in Philadelphia, which indignantly sent it to the Q. M. G. and so on and so on until it reached me with twenty-three endorsements. I was very anxious to put it in stock and let the matter drop, but the C.O., who was the proud author of a book of forms, would not hear of such an unethical proceeding, and I endorsed it back to the chief of ordnance. Shortly afterwards I left Frankford, and I do not know whatever became of the automatic. In all probability it is still wandering hopelessly from headquarters to headquarters seeking a final resting place.

The amount of time wasted on paper work was inconceivable. When I was ordnance officer at the Port of Embarkation at Hoboken, I sent to Washington every day eighteen separate reports. When Washington wanted information on any subject, we were obliged to forward an additional report, as they always pleaded that they did not have time to wade through the eighteen that they had already received. We finally worked out a plan by which we covered the ground of the eighteen reports in three. That remarkably able chief of ordnance, General C. C. Williams, at once agreed to the change, and eight enlisted clerks who had been wasting their time on the eighteen reports were released for other and necessary work.

At the outbreak of the war the chief of ordnance was General William Crozier. He had been in office for nearly twenty years, having been promoted from captain to brigadier general over the heads of most of the corps, and had thoroughly justified his selection. The Ordnance Department was the elite of the army. Under General Crozier's reorganization the corps was recruited by competitive examination from the first lieutenants of all the other branches of the service who, while on duty with the corps, received the rank, pay, and allowances of one grade above their regular rank. Thus, a lieutenant became a captain, a captain a major, a major a lieutenant colonel, and a lieutenant colonel a colonel. The result was that the ordnance officers were the very pick of the army, and, realizing that fact, were thoroughly disliked by all the rest, especially by the general staff, which, being recruited largely by pull, lost no opportunity "to put the ordnance in its place." At the close of the war, with the exception of those who had served on General Pershing's staff and the general officers, no ordnance officer received the D. S. M. We had our own board to recommend officers for the D. S. M., and the entire list was ignored, thus putting us in our place with a vengeance.

General Crozier had done his best to get appropriations from Congress, but his best had been in vain. Nevertheless, with the small sums at his disposal he had accomplished excellent results in preparing the country for war. He had gone on the assumption that the Ordnance Department should be ready for the mobilization of 400,000 men, and by 1917 we were ready to equip that number. When the first draft was ordered and the equipment proved to be insufficient, Congress and the press demanded a victim, and General Crozier was ready at hand.

Joe Cannon raised a laugh and started the attack on the general by saying, in a speech, that the reason that the ordnance officers wore spurs was to prevent their feet from slipping off their desks as they slept on their useless jobs. During the preparedness parade in Washington the ordnance section was hissed by the crowd, so far had the attack progressed. General Crozier had a list of senators and representatives who had asked impossible favors, and their letters making the requests, including several from Joe Cannon. He steadfastly refused to publish the list, although had he done so it would unquestionably have helped his cause. In the same way he flatly refused to defend himself from the thoroughly unjust attacks of his former friends in Congress. General Crozier argued that his record spoke for itself. So it did to those who were ordnance officers, but unfortunately for him his critics were civilians. . . .

General Crozier was relieved by his principal assistant General Wheeler,[8] as acting chief of ordnance, who only lasted a few months. He was a man of limited vision who surrounded himself with so-called experts from the Taylor Efficiency Company,[9] who seemed to think that the chief function of the army was to save the pennies and the war would win itself. General Clarence C. Williams, chief of ordnance with the A.E.F., was called home as chief, while Wheeler was sent to replace him overseas.

General Williams was, with the exception of Thomas F. Gilroy, the ablest executive with whom it has ever been my good fortune to come in contact. He went overseas with General Pershing at the outbreak of the war and was soon after made chief of ordnance with the A.E.F. He had nearly a year of intensive training in France under war conditions and learned all that there was to be learned from the French and from the British. When he assumed command at Washington, he was forty-nine years old, at the top of his form, a man of tremendous energy and great ability. No better appointment could possibly have been made. He had a supreme contempt for red tape and for the vaporing of the so-called efficiency experts. He realized that the war must be won at all costs and that the purpose of the army was to win the war and not to save the pennies. He selected his subordinates with great care and having once chosen them backed them to the limit. He demanded results from them and left them absolutely free as to how these results were obtained. During 1918 one of the efficiency experts, who under the orders of the commanding general at the Port of Embarkation had been inspecting my command, went to General Williams and told him that I was

[8] Charles B. Wheeler, a graduate of the United States Military Academy, transferred from artillery to ordnance in 1890, was appointed chief of ordnance in December, 1917, and became chief ordnance officer, A.E.F., in April, 1918.

McClellan thought Wheeler "a sad failure everywhere; a man without punch who gave himself body and soul to a group of theatrical civilians." (McClellan, "The Great Adventure," 19a.)

[9] This is a reference to the theories introduced and popularized by Frederick W. Taylor, who made a career out of developing plans for increasing industrial efficiency. His ideas can be found in his book, *The Principles of Scientific Management* (New York, 1911).

not living up to efficiency rules. The general asked him if I was "delivering the goods." On the expert regretfully acknowledging that I was, he said, "If McClellan is delivering the goods I don't give a damn how he is doing it. Don't bother me with your foolishness."

It was an honor and a pleasure to serve under him, and he had the loyalty and the respect and the love of his entire command. General Williams was a great executive who did as much, if not more, than any single individual to win the war.

At the beginning of August [1917], I was told by my C.O. [at Frankford] that the chief at Washington had decided to send me overseas as ordnance officer at the principal Port of Debarkation at St. Nazaire. As a preliminary I was ordered to Rock Island Arsenal for two weeks' training for my new job. . . .

When I reached Rock Island, I reported to the C.O. who was Colonel George Burr,[10] one of the kindliest and most delightful men, as well as one of the best soldiers, with whom I served during the war. The garrison at Rock Island was a happy family, every member of which was devoted to the colonel and equally devoted to his charming wife. The two weeks I served there were among the pleasantest of my war experiences. I was given the run of the establishment and under the guidance of the civilian foremen did my best to qualify for work overseas. I found myself a very popular person among the workmen as the son of my father, not because he had been the general commanding the army, but because he had been the inventor of the McClellan saddle, the only invention by an army officer which is known by its inventor's name and not by a number. The foreman of one department would pass me on to the next, introducing me as the "son of the McClellan saddle."

At the end of a fortnight I went to Washington to get my final instructions before sailing for France. Waiting in the outer office for General Crozier to receive me, I chatted with

10 Burr, a graduate of the United States Military Academy, transferred from artillery to ordnance and achieved the rank of colonel in 1916. From 1911 to 1918, he was chief ordnance officer of the Central Department at Rock Island Arsenal.

A year after McClellan had served at Rock Island he again met Burr abroad and described him as "a pleasant fellow of no great ability or punch." (McClellan, "The Great Adventure," 19a.)

his principal assistant, General Babbitt.[11] Babbitt said, "I don't envy you your new job." I answered that I thought St. Nazaire would be a very interesting job, to which he replied, "St. Nazaire nothing. You are going to Hoboken." The news was far from agreeable. From service with the A.E.F., to serve at the most unlovely town in the United States was a comedown. When I saw General Crozier, he told me that I was to take the place of the regular who had been at the Port of Embarkation at Hoboken, and organize the Ordnance Office there as the regular had failed to make good.

On my arrival at Hoboken I reported to General Shanks,[12] the commanding general. He was an elderly, fussy, and typical line regular, greatly devoted to paper work and routine. . . . I asked the general if he had any specific instructions to give me, to which he replied, "Yes, for God's sake, don't bother me." During my service under him he only called his staff together twice: once to urge us to subscribe to the Liberty Loan and the other time to complain that our men were not saluting smartly enough to please him. From the general I went to the Ordnance Office and took over. The office consisted of a balcony on the second floor of the residence of the dock superintendent of the North German Lloyd S. S. Line, whose piers we had commandeered and used as headquarters. . . .

As we began to ship munitions overseas, my outfit rapidly increased in size . . . [until it] consisted of some twenty-five officers and three hundred men. . . . By the spring of 1918 I had the most efficient group of men with whom it has ever been my privilege to work. During the war my outfit shipped overseas sixty per cent of all the munitions sent to the A.E.F. without the loss of a single life or a dollar's worth of property. Besides my headquarters at New York, where I removed from Hoboken early in the war, I had under my charge a pier in the North River in New York and ordnance establishments at South Brooklyn, Elizabeth Port [in] New Jersey, Camp Mills

11 Edwin B. Babbitt, a graduate of the United States Military Academy, transferred from artillery to ordnance, and at the outbreak of the First World War held the rank of lieutenant colonel.

12 David C. Shanks, a graduate of the United States Military Academy, was appointed to the rank of brigadier general in 1917 and served as commander of the Port of Embarkation, Hoboken, from April, 1917, to September, 1918.

on Long Island, Camp Merritt in New Jersey; and we built
and organized the arsenal at Metuchen, New Jersey. . . .

It was a real and great pleasure to command my outfit at
the Port of Embarkation. I had what to all intents was an
independent command. While headquarters at Hoboken
hampered me to a certain extent, Washington stood behind
me so that I was able to do my work very much as I pleased. . . .

During the summer of 1918 General Williams told me that
he wanted me to go overseas to have some experience of actual
conditions at the front and to work out for us a plan for the
handling of munitions overseas, based on a study of the systems
in force in the French and British armies. He told me that I
could take one of my officers with me, and I selected Kennedy,[13]
who at that time expected to apply for a commission in the
regulars after the war, but later changed his mind and remained
at Princeton. . . .

We sailed on the transport *Orduna* on September eighth, . . .
debarked at Liverpool,[14] and at once entrained for Southampton, which we reached after a ten-hour journey. . . . We stayed
at Southampton for two days. . . . On the afternoon of the
second day we marched to the docks and went on board the
. . . *Harvard,* which, with her sister the *Yale,* was used to carry
troops from Southampton to Le Havre. . . . We officers had
bunks without mattresses or blankets, but the men slept on the
deck crowded together like sardines.

The management of the ports of debarkation in France
varied very much. I was sent to inspect the ordnance establishments at all of them and know whereof I speak. None was
better than Le Havre. When we reported at H. Q. we were
turned over to a sergeant who routed us to our destinations,
bought our tickets, cared for our luggage, and had our places
reserved for us on the train. He said to us, "If you want a
bang-up meal, go to the Hotel du Casino; if you want a cheaper
meal, here is a list of restaurants that will do you pretty well."

13 Charles W. Kennedy, an assistant professor of English at Princeton before
the First World War, served as a captain in the Ordnance Department during
the war.
14 "[When we landed at Liverpool,] a few people (very few) on the passing
ferryboats waved their hats at us, but altho' we were 28,000 on the different ships,
our dear English cousins did not seem to give a hang whether we had come to
save them or not." (McClellan, "The Great Adventure," 7-8.)

We went to the Casino and had the first "bang-up meal" since we had left the United States. . . .

[We went from Le Havre to Paris, and after a brief stay there we proceeded to] Tours, which was the H. Q. of all the supply services. I found the Ordnance Department seething with politics. The officers were sharply divided into factions, the supporters and opponents of General Wheeler, the latter being in a very large majority.[15] On reporting to Wheeler I was turned over to Colonel Shinkel,[16] one of the most competent officers I met overseas. He was chief supply officer and at once annexed me as an inspector. He first sent me to inspect the ordnance establishments in and around Bordeaux and St. Nazaire, at La Rochelle and at Brest. We went to Bordeaux by rail and made the rest of our journey by motor. . . .

On my return to Tours from Brest I asked Colonel Shinkel to send me to the front to do the job for which I had been sent overseas. He agreed, and Kennedy and I set out for Chaumont. There I reported to Colonel O'Hern,[17] the chief ordnance officer at G. H. Q. and with him toured the front.

O'Hern was a sentimental Irishman who had discovered Jeanne d'Arc, and had all the enthusiasm of a discoverer for his find. We set out early one morning for the firing line and as we motored the colonel told me the story of his heroine under the impression that I had never heard of her. When we reached Domremy, we stopped so that he might worship at her shrine. We then resumed our journey, and the colonel resumed his

[15] "When Gen'l Williams came over, he seems to have organized a fairly efficient department. . . . Gen'l Williams surrounded himself with his friends, most of whom seem to have been good men. When Williams and Wheeler changed places, Wheeler brought over . . . a number of his pets from Washington. . . . Wheeler with great thoroughness bounced all of Williams' men and put in his own. . . . The results were disastrous. Much talk, much reorganization, little accomplishment." (McClellan, "The Great Adventure," 91a-91b.)

[16] Edward M. Shinkel, a graduate of the United States Military Academy, served in the Ordnance Department throughout his military career.

After meeting Shinkel, McClellan wrote in his journal: "Forceful, with lots of punch. I took a great fancy to him." (McClellan, "The Great Adventure," 20a.)

[17] Edward P. O'Hern, a graduate of the United States Military Academy, transferred from artillery to ordnance and held the rank of major at the outbreak of the First World War. McClellan thought O'Hern "sound, efficient and had good reputation at home, but not liked by the . . . crowd [at Tours] and canned—sent to relieve a 1st Lieut. at Brest." (McClellan, "The Great Adventure," 20a.)

story. Towards afternoon we reached the front and got out to send the car back to cover, the colonel still talking eloquently about the Maid. Suddenly the Germans got the range of a battery of field artillery that was very near us, and a shell exploded within a few yards of where we were standing. Being the first time that I had been under fire, I jumped. The colonel turned to me with a very pained expression on his face and said, "If I am boring you, say so, and I will stop talking." I assured him that I was greatly enjoying his discourse, and he promptly resumed it. Another shell dropped, this time a little nearer, and again I jumped. "I am sure that I am boring you," said the colonel. Again I reassured him, and again he resumed his story. The shells now began to drop with much frequency, and I had to explain that this being my first time under fire I was a little nervous. "Oh," said the colonel, "is that all? It is getting rather hot, so perhaps we had better get into a dugout until it slackens." There was one not far off, and we crawled in. It was already packed with men who were rejoining their units, and they were a typical cross section of our army.

As the colonel interrupted his story, I was able to talk to the men. I asked each in turn what he had been doing before the war came. Three had just left college, one was a dental student, two were farmers, one a prize fighter, two truckmen, four day laborers in cities, and one grinned when I questioned him and said, "I guess I better not say what I was doing when the war came." . . .

We spent that night at Bar le Duc, . . . [where] I left O'Hern and hunted up young Bowley who was in command of an ammunition dump. With him I visited Verdun and the country thereabouts. To Verdun we travelled over "La Voie Sacrée," the Sacred Way, which was kept open from Bar le Duc to Verdun throughout the war. It was very broad, and one side was constantly under repair while the other was in use. It was protected by camouflage screens throughout its length, but, nevertheless, it was extraordinary that the enemy never destroyed it. As the rail was out of commission, La Voie Sacrée was the only means of communication between Verdun and the base of supplies, and had it been broken up Verdun would have been cut off.

On the way we stopped at the emplacement of two 15-inch

naval guns on their railway mounts. They were manned by crews of bluejackets and we were shown over them by a pink-cheeked young ensign who was in charge. He said to me, "I am so sorry that you shouldn't see the guns in action. Last Sunday we got the range of a village behind the German lines and scored some bully hits. We have heard that we smashed a movie theatre and killed a couple of hundred women and children. I tell you, sir, that was good practice." The war had made him a little machine, thinking only of the record of the guns in scoring hits, and boasting of the non-combatants who had been killed.

At Verdun we went into the underground citadel, which was a miniature city of great extent. The surrounding villages had been wiped out of existence, and the countryside was a lake of mud, for it rained incessantly while I was at the front. On the site of what had once been a popular summer resort I saw a German boot lying on the ground. Without thinking I gave it a pull and out came the owner who, poor fellow, had been dead for many weeks. From there we went to Montfaucon where I called on General Duncan,[18] the C.O., of the sector. . . .

From the front we took the train to Marseilles, for Shinkel wanted me to inspect the ordnance establishments in the south of France. We broke our journey of necessity at Dijon. There I ran into a good-looking young captain who had been shell-shocked and had been evacuated from the hospital before he had been cured and was on his way to join his unit. I asked him his name, and he was obliged to refer to his orders before he could answer me. His memory was almost gone, and it was a shame to have turned him loose in such condition. If he did not lose his papers, he probably found his outfit; without them he would have been hopelessly lost.

After leaving Dijon, we found on the train Captain Dicky Stockton [19] of Princeton. He had been badly wounded at the base of his skull and was on his way to the rest camp at Nice.

18 George B. Duncan, a graduate of the United States Military Academy, fought in the Spanish-American War, served with the A.E.F. from June, 1917, to May, 1919, and emerged from the First World War as a major general.

19 Richard Stockton, the son of the Richard Stockton from whom the Mc-Clellans had once rented a house in Princeton, entered the regular army after graduating from Bordentown Military Academy and was on active duty in both World Wars.

He had been evacuated before cure and hardly knew where he was going or why. I annexed him and kept him with me until I returned to Tours.

Shortly before my arrival at Marseilles Lieutenant Colonel Watson [20] had been sent there to take over the outfit. He was the Democratic candidate for United States Senate in West Virginia, who had been sent overseas to acquire a war record for political effect. When his Democratic opponent went overseas, the Republican candidate was obliged to follow suit and not long afterwards [he] appeared at Paris.

From Marseilles we went to Toulon where I selected a pier for the Ordnance. After which I inspected Aigue Morte and then returned to Tours via Bourges. The C.O. at Marseilles was a disagreeable old regular who at first refused to give me a car with which to make my inspection, and it required the persuasion of the would-be senator from West Virginia to soften his heart. He absolutely declined to give me a car to take me back to Tours. Fortunately I heard that a convoy of new cars was to start for Bourges that afternoon, and I wished myself and Kennedy on the young officer in charge. I certainly paid my way, for the lad spoke no French and had just landed, as had all of his enlisted men. We stopped the first night at Avignon, in what was then one of the most delightful hotels in France, the Europa. The dear old lady who owned it was the only hotelkeeper I found in the country who was not a highway robber. . . .

When we reached Tours I gave my report to Shinkel who pleased me by telling me that it was the first constructive report that he had read since coming overseas.

From Tours we went to Paris for the last time. . . . Paris was full of our officers, many of whom were drunk and many of whom were accompanied by *marraines* whom they had apparently picked up on the streets. The last night in Paris I took Kennedy to dine at Voisin's, which was as good as in peacetime and where, of course, there was no music. Kennedy said to me, "Colonel, do you notice anything peculiar about this res-

---

[20] Clarence W. Watson, an official of several coal mining concerns, was a United States senator from West Virginia from 1911 to 1913 and was defeated for the Senate in 1918 by Davis Elkins, his Republican opponent. He was a lieutenant colonel in the Ordnance Department, U.S.A., from March, 1918, to January, 1919.

taurant?" I answered that I did not except that there were hardly any United States officers there but ourselves. He continued, "This is the first restaurant we have been in in Paris where there have not been United States officers the worse for wear and in company of streetwalkers," and it was so.

From Paris we went to Le Havre where I reported to the British C.O. and spent two very interesting days studying their methods of handling munitions. The British were handling nearly twice as great an amount as were we and were doing it with about half the number of officers and a third the number of enlisted men. Their men were working about eight hours a day and were required to play cricket, football, or some other game for two hours, seemed well and happy and full of "pep." They had, of course, had four years' experience, and in time we might have done as well, but I doubt it. I left Le Havre full of admiration for the quiet and efficient way with which the British were doing their job.

From Le Havre Kennedy and I crossed over to Southampton on a British officers' transport and landed early on the morning of November eleventh. There had been rumors that peace was in sight but we in the service knew nothing definite about the matter. As our train neared London, we began to see women and old men leaning out of the windows of the houses we passed, waving and shouting. By the time we reached Charing Cross we realized that peace had come. As there were neither cabs nor porters at the station, we footed it to the Savoy Hotel carrying our portmanteaus. From there we went to H. Q. to report and found H. Q. deserted. We finally discovered an old caretaker asleep in the cellar whom we roused and learned from him [that] as soon as the news of the Armistice had been received the entire force, officers and men, had left to celebrate. From there we walked back in the direction of the Savoy and as we passed Westminster Abbey went in. A verger met us and said that the Dean was about to hold an informal *Te Deum* for the peace. He escorted us to the choir where, as the only American officers present, we assisted at the most impressive service in which I have ever taken part. I would rather have thanked God for the peace in Westminster Abbey than in any other spot on earth.

London gave itself up to rejoicing in a typically British way.

The streets were packed for three days which had been proclaimed holidays. While there was a good deal of drunkenness, there was very little disorder. The crowds moved slowly through the streets cheering and singing, but not very much. They seemed almost dazed and took their pleasure very solemnly. The only disorder I heard of was the burning of a captured gun at the base of the Nelson Monument and, incidentally, the serious injury of the monument itself by a party of young enthusiasts. Until the three days were over no business was done, not even at our H. Q. When the life of the city was resumed, I made application for transportation home.

I found food conditions much worse in England than in France. In France there was no lack of anything at a stiff price, greatly exaggerated for us Americans. In England everything was rationed strictly, and there was little to be had. The French complained of their hard life; in England much worse conditions were accepted in the best possible spirit.

As there was no news of our transport, Kennedy and I went to Oxford where I had never been. There we were treated most politely and were made free of the place. After we had been in England a week, we were told that we were to sail from Liverpool on the *Lapland,* a Red Star ship taken over by the White Star Line. We went to Liverpool, where we waited two days for our ship in that most dreary of all cities. The only rooms that we could get were in a third-class hotel, and we found little to do after we had gazed at the outside of Mr. Gladstone's very unattractive birthplace.

We sailed November twenty-second and landed in New York December fourth. On the ship were some three hundred young aviation officers, most of whom had been badly wounded, many of them burned, and six of them were blind. Our ship was not a regular transport but carried a number of civilian passengers to whom the thrifty White Star had given the good rooms. As they were sure of our money, we were given what was left.

I was the senior officer on board and presided at tea every afternoon. I got to know a great many of the aviators very well and heard some very pathetic stories. One day the six blind lads and half a dozen others who had been badly smashed came to me and asked my opinion as to whether it would be possible for them to get an order "putting them out of the way." Every one of them wanted to die, and they were perfectly serious in their proposition. Poor boys, they had very little left to live for.

When we reached New York, a policeman came to me and said, " 'Colonel' Wanamaker [21] would be glad to see you in the cabin." Rod Wanamaker, who had been at Princeton with me, was a colonel on the governor's staff, Home Guard, and chairman of a ridiculous reception committee that Mayor Hylan had organized. I told the policeman that if Mr. Wanamaker wished to see me I was at his service, but that as I was busy getting my officers off the ship I could not go to him. I then marched my officers to the dock, lined them up, and dismissed them. . . .

[Right after the Armistice] there began a regular stampede of reserve officers to return to civil life. Most of mine obtained their discharges early, and I was left with . . . [a few regular army men] and half a dozen youngsters who stuck to the outfit to the end. I discharged the enlisted men gradually, not giving any discharge unless the man had a job in view. . . . From having had an entire floor in a large office building, we rapidly shrank to two rooms, where with [a] captain . . . and three lieutenants I carried on.

General Burr called me up one day and asked me if I cared to serve as chairman of a claims commission in Washington. I told him that I had done my job and wanted to be demobilized as soon as the work in New York was finished. Had I accepted the assignment, I should have got my star, for the man who was appointed was made a brigadier general. . . . [During my final days in the service] I was left with [only one] lieutenant. . . . On April 17, 1919, he received his discharge, and the next day, April eighteenth, I received mine, exactly two years and two days after I had been commissioned.

That morning I had discharged my orderly. After I returned from Hoboken with my discharge in my pocket he and I closed the office. "Does the colonel mind," he said to me, "if I take the sign on the door with me?" I gave it to him and locked the door. I shook hands with him and wished him luck and he started for Central America and I went back to Princeton. . . .

21 (Lewis) Rodman Wanamaker was the son of the merchant, John Wanamaker, and the head of the firm founded by his father.

Chapter XVII

At Long Last I Had Become a Statesman

SOME TIME before I was demobilized Tom Foley, who was a Tammany district leader whose friendship I had won by supporting him when he ran for sheriff while I was mayor, came to me and told me that he thought that Murphy would send me back to Congress. Foley controlled Manhattan Island below Fourteenth Street and was very close to the boss. I accepted Foley's statement at its face value, but, in looking back, I doubt if Murphy ever seriously intended to give me a nomination. Two or three times I apparently came within measurable distance of being nominated, but at the critical moment something always turned up to stop me. Foley's intentions were of the best, and I think that he sincerely wanted to see me back in Congress, but curiously enough, like most of the district leaders, he was afraid of Murphy and did not dare to force the latter to nominate me, which he very easily could have done. Jimmy Martin used to say to me that Murphy hated me with such bitterness that he would never allow me to hold public office again if he could avoid doing so, and I think that Martin was right. At least I had the satisfaction of knowing that Murphy never realized how much I wanted to go back.

In 1932, Senator Wagner[1] told me that Curry, Murphy's successor,[2] was anxious to send me to the House. The senator

[1] Robert F. Wagner was one of the most illustrious products of Boss Murphy's Tammany Hall. After practicing law in New York City, he served in the state Assembly (1905-08) and the state Senate (1909-18), was a justice of the Supreme Court of New York (1919-26), and was a United States senator (1927-49).

[2] McClellan is mistaken, for John F. Curry succeeded George W. Olvany rather than Murphy. Curry obtained his first political job in 1897 when he went to work in the comptroller's office, and he remained on the public payroll until

asked me to leave the matter entirely in his hands and that he would attend to it. . . . A few months later I wrote to him asking what developments there were in the matter. He did not answer my letter, nor have I heard from him since.

When I think of the men who comprise the New York delegation and the way in which they are obliged to take the boss's orders without question, voting like rubber stamps, I am quite content not to be in the House. Membership from New York is a very different affair from what it was in my day, and I realize that were I to go back it would only be for one term, as I should find it utterly impossible to play the game of "follow the leader." . . .

In 1920 I made a few speeches for [James M.] Cox and in 1924 stumped the city for John W. Davis. In the latter year I was asked to close the campaign in Brooklyn at the Academy of Music. The morning of the meeting I stopped at the office of the speakers' committee to learn the arrangements for the evening. The secretary who was in charge said, "I'm glad that you dropped in, for Judge Olvany" [3] (the then boss of Tammany Hall) "thinks he has got Jimmy Walker" (then a state Senator) "for tonight, and, of course, if Jimmy speaks, they won't want you." "Then that lets me out," I said. "Yes," he answered, "I guess that lets you out." I turned from his desk and went down the steps, realizing that at long last I had become a statesman, according to Tom Reed's definition, for I was a dead politician. None could have been deader.

When I was teaching at Princeton, many of my boys asked my advice about entering politics. I used to answer them somewhat as follows:

"If you are willing to make of politics your profession, if, in other words, you have for it a flair and ambition and are willing to prepare for it as earnestly as you would for the law,

---

1929 when he became head of Tammany Hall. In 1934, he was voted out of the leadership.

[3] George W. Olvany, a Tammany stalwart, obtained his first public job in 1900 as a law clerk in the office of the city's corporation counsel. He was subsequently an alderman, deputy fire commissioner, counsel to the sheriff of New York County, and judge of the Court of General Sessions. During Murphy's last years, he was the boss's right-hand man, and when Murphy died in 1924, Olvany succeeded him as leader of Tammany. Olvany resigned in 1929 and was succeeded by Curry.

medicine or teaching, if you are willing to begin at the bottom and work your way up, and work hard and all the time, if you are willing to face the fact there is no 'honest money' to be made in politics, that, with very few exceptions, salaries are barely sufficient for a decent living, and sometimes not even that, and that unless you have some means of your own you must be content to live modestly, then by all means enter politics.

"You must realize that the great offices to be filled are few and far between and that the chances are overwhelmingly against your ever filling one. You must understand that never having reached high office, or having attained one with every prospect of going higher and you do not do so, may be because of no fault of your own.

"Always remember that in other professions success or failure depends almost entirely on the ability of the individual. The scholar working in his study, the lawyer in the courtroom, the clergyman in his pulpit, or the surgeon in the amphitheatre knows that ultimate professional success or failure depends upon him and upon him alone and that in the long run if he possesses the necessary qualifications he is bound to succeed. On the other hand, the politician knows that, be he ever so able or honest, success depends far more on extraneous circumstances, over which he has no control, than upon himself.

"It may be that deservedly or undeservedly the public tires of him, it may be that the cause he advocates ceases to be popular and that he is unwilling to barter self-respect for votes even though no question of deep principle may be involved. Most certainly sooner or later to everyone who holds high office 'comes the moment to decide in the strife of truth with falsehood for the good or evil side,' in which event no honest man can hesitate in his choice, although he knows that political oblivion will follow.

"Besides, there is the factor that is usually called luck, that intangible something that without any apparent reason brings success or failure.

"If you are willing to face the prospect of almost certain disappointment at the end of a life given to the public service and to accept it philosophically and cheerfully as a necessary part of the game, then by all means make of politics your profession.

"I can assure you that a politician's life is never dull, that it is intensely interesting and always stimulating. The excitement and downright pleasure of a political campaign are very great, and the satisfaction that comes from a hard and cleanly fought victory is more intense than any that I know.

"When it is all over, no matter what the disappointment at the end, you will have the satisfaction, and it is very great, of knowing that you have done your best, that you may truthfully say, 'I have fought a good fight, I have finished my course, I have kept the faith.' "

I had always had a horror of men who outstayed their usefulness in their jobs and did not have the sense to go "when the going was good." I had seen so many men in the Princeton faculty hang on when they should have retired that I made up my mind that I would retire as soon as I reached retiring age. Accordingly in 1930 I told President Hibben that I should retire at the end of the year. I was at the top of my form, my classes were the largest in the university, and for sixteen times [the students] had voted me the most popular professor. It was the ideal moment to go.

Hibben expressed conventional sorrow at my departure. I said to him: "I suppose that my pension will be paid me." "No," he replied, "as you have only taught one term a year, under the new Carnegie rule you are not entitled to any pension"; and so after twenty-three years at Princeton, during twenty of which I was a full professor, I found myself not only out and unpensioned, but with the endowment of my chair, which had been raised by my friends for me, quietly deflected from its purpose by the authorities and turned into the general fund of the university. I protested with great vigor to Hibben, who, of course, did nothing. He did, however, offer me the Vanuxon Lectureship for the following year, which I formally accepted only to be told by him the next week that he had had no authority to make the offer.

When I was in the House, Sam McCall constantly urged me to write a book, on the ground that, if the book was a success, it would help me politically. Accordingly, I set to work and produced my *Oligarchy of Venice,* which made no claim to originality, met the want for a short history of Venice, and had a good sale. As it was published in 1904, just after I became mayor, most of the reviews, which were very kindly, expressed surprise that a Tammany mayor was capable of writing the English language.

It was nearly a quarter of a century before I again had leisure to turn my hand to bookmaking. I had published *The Heel of War* in 1916, but that was merely a reprint of letters to the New York *Times* that I had written from Germany at war. My wife and I cared so much for Venice that I had always felt I should like to express my gratitude by contributing something original, no matter how modest, to the record of her history. One of its most interesting phases was the fall of the Republic at the word of Napoleon. On this phase I found that there existed only some three or four monographs in Italian or French, all very sketchy and in only one instance based on the archives of the Republic. Not only was there no monograph in English, but those who had written of the period in more extensive histories had shown a lamentable ignorance of the subject.

Accordingly, I determined to write a monograph on *Venice and Bonaparte* based on the Venetian archives and devoted three springs to working in the Venetian archives, chiefly at the Frari, and never enjoyed anything more. The superintendent of the Frari and all his assistants were most friendly and courteous and exceedingly helpful. Unfortunately, for lack of money, of the nearly one million portfolios of documents which the Frari contains, only about a hundred thousand have been very inadequately catalogued. Of the thousand or more portfolios covering the short-lived democracy there is no catalogue whatever. The superintendent assigned to me an employee to climb ladders and pull down portfolios and allowed me to roam freely all over the vast building. I was able to dig up a great deal of hitherto unpublished information about the last years of Venice. There is unquestionably an enormous amount of unknown history awaiting the explorer at the Frari. . . .

I offered my book to Scribner's who replied that it did not interest them. I then took up the matter of its publication with the Princeton University authorities, who decreed it worthy of publication by the university and at the university expense and ordered its publication. Shortly afterwards the director of the Princeton University Press told me that, as there was no money with which to meet the cost of publication, unless I "put up," the book would remain a university publication but without being published. As this was before the depression, I "put up." The copyright was retained by the university on the ground that the book was a university publication. When *Venice and Bonaparte* appeared, it received some very flattering criticism, especially in England.

The director of the Princeton University Press, apparently believing that the trustees had not played cricket in the matter of my book, asked me if I cared to write a short history of modern Italy, this time entirely at the expense of the Press, I to receive thirty cents a copy. I promptly agreed, and my *Modern Italy* was published with, I take it, very fair success, for I am still receiving royalties. The English reviewers were again most complimentary, as were the Italian and some of the American. The London *Times Literary Supplement,* as before, gave me a two-column review. . . . A copy of my book [was sent] to Mussolini, who . . . [stated] that he had found it interesting, fair, and "most objective" and proceeded to make me a Commander of the Order of the Crown of Italy, to be followed on my seventy-second birthday by promotion to the rank of "Grand Officer" of the same order.

I remember when I was a boy hearing that delightful man Arthur Gilman,[4] whose books have been all too soon forgotten, tell of an experience he had had at the country house of his fellow publisher, the third John Murray.[5] As Gilman was waiting in the drawing room for his host before dinner, he idly turned the leaves of a Bible which, to his great surprise, he found on one of the tables. On the flyleaf was written "To John Murray from his friend Byron." Much intrigued, he sought further for information. The book opened almost of itself at the eighteenth chapter of the Gospel according to St. John, the fortieth verse of which reads, "Now Barabbas

---

[4] Arthur Gilman was the author of a great number of popular histories dealing with a wide variety of nations and periods.

[5] John Murray, III, like his father and grandfather before him, was a leading British publisher. His firm published the books of many outstanding British authors including Charles Darwin and George Grote.

was a robber." Byron had with great care run his pencil through the word "robber" and had inserted in the margin the word "publisher."

I said goodby to my boys at Princeton with great regret when I spoke to them for the last time, the last time I was ever destined to speak to a Princeton audience. We had sold our house in Princeton and built a house in Washington, from which I "commuted" during my last two years as professor.

We had spent the happiest years of our lives in Washington when I was in the House of Representatives and had always hoped that some day we might return, if not to the House, at least to the city we liked best of all. . . . The Washington to which we returned was in many respects a very different city from that which we had left so many years before. It still had the charm of the old place, but the faces had changed, and far too many of the old friends had gone, never to return. . . . Fortunately we still have the faculty of making friends, and we have made many in the new Washington, friends in Congress, among the officials, among the diplomats, and among the civilians. . . .

I soon found a great deal to do in Washington, for there is plenty of useful work for the otherwise unemployed. I am not idle and am finding the end of the grand tour as interesting and as happy as was its beginning. Not long ago someone wrote me and asked the question, "When is old, old?" To which I answered: "As long as the heart stays young, old is never old."

And so with hearts still young, my wife and I are watching the years pass, happy with each other, happy that we have our friends, happy that old is never old.

INDEX